Brokers of Public Trust

Brokers of Public Trust

Notaries in Early Modern Rome

∽

LAURIE NUSSDORFER

The Johns Hopkins University Press
Baltimore

This publication was supported in part by a grant from The Colonel Return Jonathan Meigs First (1740–1823) Fund, which was created with the funds left by Dorothy Mix Meigs and Fielding Pope Meigs, Jr., of Rosemont, Pennsylvania, in memory of that soldier of the revolution, whose home was in Middletown, Connecticut, from 1740 to 1787.

The Johns Hopkins University Press
2715 North Charles Street
Baltimore, Maryland 21218-4363
www.press.jhu.edu

Library of Congress Cataloging-in-Publication Data
Nussdorfer, Laurie.
Brokers of trust : notaries in early modern Rome / Laurie Nussdorfer.
p. cm.
Includes bibliographical references and index.
ISBN-13: 978-0-8018-9204-2 (hardcover : alk. paper)
ISBN-10: 0-8018-9204-X (hardcover : alk. paper)
1. Notaries—Italy—Rome—History—1420–1798. 2. Recording and registration—Italy—Rome—History—1420–1798. 3. Legal documents—Italy—Rome—History—1420–1798. I. Title.
KKH9857.36.N87 2009
347.45'632016—dc22   2008050545

A catalog record for this book is available from the British Library.

Special discounts are available for bulk purchases of this book.
For more information, please contact Special Sales at 410-516-6936 or
specialsales@press.jhu.edu.

To Natalie Zemon Davis
dolcissima maestra

CONTENTS

It seemed like a simple question, "Why did people go to notaries?" Answering it has taken me on a journey with countless twists and turns, and whatever answers I can now give to the question are owed to the aid of many scholars and friends in the United States and Italy. It is a pleasure to be able to thank them at last. I want also to express my appreciation for the support of the American Philosophical Society, the National Endowment for the Humanities Summer Seminar, and Wesleyan University for four project grants. I am indebted to the rare-book librarians of the Lillian Goldman Library at Yale Law School, Harvey Hull and Mike Widener, who supplied a most pleasant work setting, as well as the staffs of the rare-book collections at the law libraries of Harvard University, the Library of Congress, and the University of Pennsylvania.

Although I did not know it at the time, this book had its inception twenty years ago in a pertinent conference comment from John Martin and a brilliant Wesleyan undergraduate history thesis by Daniel Rosenberg. It began its winding course at an NEH Summer Seminar at the Newberry Library directed by Armando Petrucci and Franca Nardella in 1993. Among those who have given me invaluable assistance at numerous points along the way I would especially like to acknowledge the efforts of John Pinto, Irene Fosi, Orsola Gori, and Nicholas Adams. I am grateful to Thomas Kuehn and Simona Feci for answering questions over many years and also for having kindly read drafts of chapter 1. In the course of my research I have benefited from the expertise of many scholars and friends, and I would like to thank them all, especially Renata Ago, James Amelang, Stefano Andretta, Daniel Brownstein, Eleonora Canepari, Elizabeth S. and Thomas V. Cohen, Sherrill Cohen, Lucilla Cola, Michele Di Sivo, Bruce W. Frier, Anthony Grafton, Julie Hardwick, Isa Lori Sanfilippo, John Marino, Donna Merwick, James O'Hara, Mary Quinlan, Virginia Reinburg, Kenneth Stow, Maria Antonietta Visceglia, and Patricia Waddy. I would also like to express my gratitude to those whose interest encouraged the project, Paul Gehl,

Peter Lukehart, Corinne Rafferty, Nancy Remley Whiteley, and Ann Wightman. Without the friends in Italy who offered hospitality and encouragement on so many occasions I probably could not have arrived at the end of this journey. *Grazie di cuore* to Renata Ago, Patrizia Cavazzini, Bruna Colarossi and Peter Horsman, Marina D'Amelia, Irene Fosi, Joan Geller, Orsola Gori and Renato Pasta, Angela Groppi, Fabrizia Gurreri, and Maria Antonietta Visceglia. I warmly thank Henry Tom of the Johns Hopkins University Press for his support and Suzanne Flinchbaugh, Brian MacDonald, Suzy Taraba, and John Wareham for their assistance.

The men I consider my Italian *maestri*, the late Marino Berengo, Giovanni Levi, and Armando Petrucci, perhaps did not realize the impact their attention to notaries would have on a distant American historian, but from them I learned to regard this unfamiliar profession with curiosity, awe, and respect. Their work has been an important part of my mental conversation as I wrote. This book is dedicated to Natalie Zemon Davis who first urged me to look at the Roman notarial records and first introduced me to many of my Roman friends. No one who has been lucky enough to know her has been untouched by the acuity, imagination, and sympathy of this remarkable historian, teacher, and human being. Her generosity of insight and instinct, her adventurous example, and her moral sensitivity have been an unfailing source of admiration and inspiration. I thank her for everything that she has given me. Finally, I owe a special debt to Nicholas Adams, *vir mirabilis et dilectus*, for his humor, love, and loyalty to the Roman notaries.

baiocco	base metal coin of varying value; in accounts worth one-tenth of a giulio
bolognino	another term for baiocco
carlino	silver coin replaced by the giulio in 1504
ducato d'oro della Camera	a money of account worth ten giulii; gradually replaced by the scudo d'oro during the sixteenth century
giulio	equivalent to ten baiocchi; valued at 2.9 grams of silver
grosso	one-half of a giulio
quattrino	by the mid-seventeenth-century a coin worth about one-fifth of a baiocco
scudo	coin worth ten giulii
scudo d'oro	a money of account valued in gold, not a coin like the scudo
testone	coin worth three giulii

Brokers of Public Trust

Introduction

Writing has a history. We know that story: how the ancient Mesopotamians etched marks on clay tablets, the Egyptians drew figures on walls, the Phoenicians invented a phonetic system of signs, and the Greeks added vowels. We know how the Latin alphabet originated, how its various scripts developed and were copied first in lead as movable type and then in electrical charges fired within our computers. We know, too, the story of the material vehicles that carried writing: the history of texts from those cuneiform tax records of Mesopotamia to the electronic correspondence of the early third millennium. And we know something about writers, especially those who had the good fortune to work after the birth of the author. While literary figures may loom largest in our history of writers, more humble users of quills and pencils have also found a place, as historians have sought evidence about the literacy and education of past societies. Writing's history has been a tale of technique and of expression —indeed, a triumphant tale recounting how technology progressed and the power of expression spread ever more widely.[1] This book contributes to the well-known story of writing and writers a type of text, the legal document, and its maker, the notary, which the tale has not yet been able to accommodate.

Notaries originated in medieval Europe in those Mediterranean societies peculiarly situated at the intersection of quickened urban commerce and rediscovered Roman law.[2] Their role in certifying contracts made them useful to Italian merchants, and fledgling communes in Italy borrowed them to make their unprecedented acts seem legitimate. But notaries were thought necessary to such transactions only because of the new forms of public authority and the new appreciation of written evidence elaborated in the medieval law faculties. So the notaries' historic trajectory was tied not just to the development of a commercial economy but to the fortunes of a specific legal tradition. In Anglo-American law, the notary was, and is, an insignificant functionary.[3] Notaries are still important today in countries where the influence of Roman or civil law has been strong: Scotland, France, Spain, Belgium, the Netherlands, and many parts of Latin America.

This genealogy may help to explain why notaries and their documents are absent from the history of writing in the English language but not why they fail to appear in studies of literate culture elsewhere. It is rather our approach to the history of writing, with its emphasis on technique and expression, that acts to exclude vast domains of writing activity and written artifacts from historical inquiry. We take the written record for granted, as if its necessity was self-evident and its form unimportant.[4] Yet every time historians discuss their sources, they tacitly acknowledge that the uses and modes of documentation vary greatly across time and space. What is recorded in writing depends not only on technical skills and cultural conventions but also on the structures and imperatives of religion, government, economics, and law. If we were to ask why some records survive and some do not or how nonwriters regarded and accessed writing services or why people chose one kind of record over another, the document would appear to us in its true light as an enigma rather than a given. If we were to ask such questions of those cultures where law and jurisprudence endowed the writing of a particular profession with special force, we would need to put that profession at the center of an investigation of writing practices. That is the notary's place in this study.

But first we must widen the lens with which we view writing practices in the past, and here we can learn much from the lively fields of book history and print culture. These have launched new questions about the messages conveyed by such physical data as format, page layout, and marginalia and have probed publishing and distribution circuits for insight into normally hidden dimensions of cultural history.[5] A fresh perspective that sees the book as a material object has invigorated the study of literary texts, enhancing our knowledge of their writers and readers, of how they circulated, and the varied uses to which they were put. We now look at books as much more than the sum of their contents, finding in them clues to a rich range of behavior, attitude, and practice.

As a physical artifact, writing can boast of a distinguished and indeed much longer tradition of expert attention than can the printed book. To medieval jurists, handwriting analysis was one of the canonical methods of establishing proof, and later graphological students opened up vistas not only on crime but also on character.[6] All those concerned about detecting forgery had to inspect the quality of ink, parchment, and paper, and scrutiny of the physical manuscript was fundamental to the modern disciplines of paleography, diplomatics, and codicology. So it is not so much that writing processes and vehicles have been ignored as that our focus has been too narrow. Establishing chronology, finding the best and earliest version of a text, or looking for the author's hand make a lot of sense if we are reading works of literature but are not necessarily pertinent to the vast quantity of writing produced for other purposes. Indeed, the very scale of our object of inquiry, the written document, even if we limited its range to the early modern period or to one country or city, would argue for a different methodology. Like scholars of print culture and the history of the book who also approach an enormous body of anonymous evidence, the historian of the document must ask broad questions about why, how, and by whom it has been shaped, used, and regarded over time.[7] These are the questions that I seek to answer for Rome between 1300 and 1700, a place in which the history of the notarial document and the notary remains oddly confused and obscure, but which could be equally fruitfully explored in other cities, countries, or continents with notarial regimes. Looking at the creation and use of records as something that demands explanation rather than something that goes without saying illuminates significant, often unspoken, assumptions about power in the past. As I hope to show in the Roman case, to do this we need to bring the history of the written artifact and the history of its artisans together and to bridge the professional gap between scholars of the Middle Ages and early modernists.

The notary is hardly an unknown or unstudied figure in Italian historiography, especially in the past forty years as social historians began discovering the riches available in the notarial archives.[8] Who could ignore the immense plunder of these sources, both the notaries' records for their private clients and their transcripts of court proceedings and institutional governance? And who, stowing away this booty, could fail to wonder about the men who had done all that writing? Some Italian scholars, particularly medievalists, did more than wonder. Building on the findings of an earlier generation of paleographers and diplomatists who had traced the origins of the notarial document, they chronicled the rise of the notarial profession in twelfth- and thirteenth-century Italy. They charted the efforts of notaries to organize themselves in corporate bodies and exposed the active collaboration by judges, jurists, and communal governments in securing their special status.[9] Their research left no doubt that, as a writer endowed with credibility (*fides*) by public authority, the notary in Italy was a product of the Middle Ages. Having established the crucial question of how Italian notarial documents came to possess this quality of public trustworthiness, however, medievalists perhaps understandably lost interest in the subject.

Nor have Italian specialists in the early modern period neglected the figure of the notary.[10] They have investigated in particular the ambiguous status of the profession as Italian society became increasingly aristocratic, but they have generally been more interested in the notary's clients than the notary himself, and they have not been at all curious about the notary's activity as a writer. In their defense, these historians have concentrated on what the notary wrote rather than the fact of his writing, quite understandably dazzled, if not overwhelmed, by the vast quantity of these documents and the minute details of every aspect of early modern life they reveal. They have eagerly sought to peer through the notary's texts to the social, economic, and political realities they record, largely indifferent to the processes by which the texts themselves were produced and preserved.

The writing of notaries was authoritative. Known as *scriptura publica*, public writing, it was a creation of political power.[11] Yet the notaries who produced it sold it to make a living and held various degrees of proprietary rights over the records they had penned. They combined aspects of public officials and, at the same time, self-employed professionals.[12] The notary stood at a curious junction between what we would call the private and the public spheres, though such terms would be anachronistic in the medieval and early modern world. He was a broker of public trust.

The case of the notary fits interestingly, though uneasily, into the history of the professions. In this book, I use the modern term *profession* when discussing the collective experiences and organizational life of Roman notaries in the late medieval and early modern periods, but perhaps the traditional term for those who earned a living in the same occupation, *arte*, would be more apt.[13] This was not a group defined in this period by academic credentials or a robust sense of vocation, though as a result of state initiative some did become a corps of limited membership and similar privileges. While the corporate profile of at least some of the Roman notaries did grow more distinct as they were assimilated into a previously decentralized judicial apparatus, many men who continued to identify themselves as notaries did not share in these changes. The foremost student of the modern notary in Italy is reluctant to describe his subject's ambiguous fusion of state official and free agent as a profession until the twentieth century, and I think his caution is justified.[14]

Because of the notary's close relationship with authority and because the political landscape of early modern Italy was so fragmented, any detailed study of the notary's writings before 1860 must be local. Although common legal notions underpinned his activity, city statutes, guild regulations, princely ordinances, and local formularies governed the specific mechanics of his craft, and in Italy each of these varied from one place to another.[15] In medieval Florence, the guild of lawyers and notaries rather than the state controlled the profession; in early modern Venice, the state set up the notaries' association and then completely dominated it.[16] The notaries and notarial documents of Rome have their own distinct history, not quite like those historians have chronicled in Genoa, Milan, Venice, or Florence, to say nothing of the countryside of Sicily or Lombardy. The uses made by clients and tribunals of notarial acts and rival forms of evidence also differed from place to place, conforming to the needs of a specific economy, society, political regime, and system of justice. To take just one example, Venice rejected the legal system in use elsewhere in Italy because of its commitment to a government run by aristocratic amateurs rather than trained lawyers.[17] Naturally, documentary culture in Venice reflected this decision. Because deep cultural and political structures underlay Italy's regional diversity, focusing on a kind of writing, scriptura publica, in a given historical setting reveals a great deal about broader social and institutional processes. The questions of what public writing was and of how it was produced in Rome between the late Middle Ages and the early modern period cut to the heart of the transformation of this city between 1300 and 1700.

Yet acknowledging the necessity of local studies of record keeping does not mean giving up more far-reaching insights, not just into history but also into historical method. Historians, like lawyers, take the notion of evidence for granted, forgetting that what a given tradition defines as evidence is itself a historical construction dependent on specific cultural, political, technological, and social practices. It is useful to step back occasionally and explore that process of historical construction so that we understand better our most cherished categories and assumptions. In the case of notarial documents, we still need to ask the basic questions, What made them different from other kinds of writing and why did people go to notaries? To reply that they were a form of legal evidence begs questions of why and how and under what circumstances—questions to which I hope this book will contribute some answers.

Historians also privilege the archives. Perhaps nothing is more sacred to the profession than its reverence for the documentary remains of human activity. The importance to researchers in various countries of what scholars generally think of when they think of notarial documents, acts drawn up for clients, ignoring for the moment judicial writings, is unquestioned.[18] In Italy, the few such acts that survive from the medieval period have been published in full and exhaustively studied, beginning with the earliest cartulary of Giovanni the Scribe in Genoa (1154–66).[19] In the fourteenth century, the number of extant volumes in the various archives of the peninsula's former states begins to grow, and by the fifteenth century in many cities they already exceed the compass of an individual scholarly career. The Florentine archives, for example, house more than twenty thousand volumes of notarial acts dating from before the mid-sixteenth century alone. Everywhere the surviving series then increase exponentially. Roman notarial archives, which as we shall see got off to a slow start, hold more than thirty thousand volumes dating from the fourteenth to the nineteenth century. Notarial records of civil and criminal judicial proceedings would, of course, add to this number. It is difficult for a historian not to genuflect before such a massive archive.

Yet the full story of *scriptura publica* cannot be written from the notarial archives alone. Just as the notarial act is not a "total" record of any given transaction and, indeed, can misrepresent the true nature of what actually happened in an exchange, surviving notarial archives may well distort our picture of what notaries were really doing.[20] In Rome, for example, working just from archival holdings and finding in them rich collections of contracts and wills, we would quite reasonably suppose that clients went to notaries impelled simply by the disinterested desire to record their agreements and last wishes. Knowing that an equally vast archive of notarial writing for clients' lawsuits has all but disappeared, however, restores balance to the picture of the notary's output and nuances our reading of clients' motivations in seeking out notaries. They might have taken the first step, which gives us the extant archive, as a precaution against the legal challenges of the lost archive.

Moreover, the archive cannot explain its own existence, which may have much to say about the interests of those in power or the reasons why people used or avoided notaries. Nor can the notarial records themselves tell us how they came into being or what their effects were or even how they competed against other types of evidence, written or unwritten. Of course, there is no question of the value of going directly to the sources and of handling the material object itself. Indeed, the thousands of extant notarial volumes in the Roman archives deserve more attention, not less, for they have many more secrets to reveal not only about their clients but also about the notaries and their documents.[21] Nevertheless, if we are asking questions about the process of documentation as a historically specific cultural practice, we must look for answers beyond the notarial archive. In this book, legal treatises, city and papal laws, account records, parish registers, and criminal trials have helped to shed light on what notaries were doing and how and why they were doing it.

The notaries of Rome are difficult to find when our story begins in the fourteenth century, but they were there and actively working, and over time their profile becomes more distinct and their writings better preserved. While it is essential to trace their evolution and the changes in political power that underpinned it, the core of this study is the physiognomy and practices of the profession that emerges in the late sixteenth and early seventeenth centuries with the sale of notarial offices. I have focused in particular on those notaries who served the inhabitants of Rome rather than the papal Curia or ecclesiastical officials because they were the most numerous and had the widest range of activity and clientele. Consistent with the historic division in the Papal States between spiritual and temporal government, there is a pronounced secular bias to this account in which the papacy usually plays the role of the state.[22] We will be chiefly following the notaries associated with the lay municipal government headquartered on the Capitoline Hill, men who wrote for private clients and sometimes for the judges of Rome's secular courts, where Roman law, not canon law, prevailed. The Capitoline notaries operated only in the civil sphere, because in the Middle Ages local notaries were not trusted to take impartial testimony in criminal prosecutions and the foreign magistrates who presided over criminal courts brought along their own record keepers. The chronological limits of this study respect the earliest surviving evidence, which dates to the mid-fourteenth century, and another documentary landmark in the early eighteenth century when the papacy makes its own extensive survey of the notaries and notarial records in Rome. Within the period 1300 to 1700, however, the most intensive transformations occur between 1550 and 1650, a fact reflected in the sources and in the argument of this book.

Our discussion begins with the theorists of the notarial document, the medieval jurists and early modern lawyers and magistrates who defined *scriptura publica* and who articulated its special character as writing. Public credibility, *publica fides*, the essence of the notary's art, drew on ancient Roman legal principles alchemized in the new law faculties of twelfth- and thirteenth-century Bologna. With their unprecedented debates about the nature of evidence, legal writers put into circulation the key concepts and terms that unified a notion of the notary and his activities across diverse local institutions and customs. In the second chapter, we consider the notaries of Rome in their manifold varieties and destinies as the city's center of power shifted from the municipality to the papacy over the course of the fourteenth to seventeenth century. Pope Sixtus V reduced the vaguely defined Capitoline notaries to thirty venal officeholders in 1586, at the same time giving them the opportunity to create their first significant professional organization. Over the next seventy-five years, this new institution gradually found its footing in the political, legal, and social landscape of baroque Rome, struggling against the odds to forge collective bonds and preserve its members.

If the probative value of the notary's documents owed much to the jurists, it owed an equal share to the second major source of law in Italy, statute—that is, the particular ordinances of professional corporations, cities, and princes. Of all early modern texts, notarial acts bore the closest relationship to public authority, which influenced not only their uses but also their material form. The evolution of Rome's laws shaping the two main types of notarial writing, business acts for private clients and judicial acts for civil tribunals, from 1363 to 1612 is the subject of the next chapter. Then we examine the preservation of notarial writings, one of their decisive advantages in the competition with other forms of evidence. Notarial archives came late to Rome, in 1507, 1562, and 1625, and they arrived in the fragmented and piecemeal way that characterized so many institutions in the papal capital. Both their successes and their failures are eloquent, however, telling us much about the play of forces engaged in making and keeping Roman documents.

The notary's ambiguous position between public power and private enterprise meant that, while he was privileged to manufacture a unique commodity, he also had to sell it to live. The fifth chapter looks closely at the basic unit of scribal production, the notary's household and office, as it operated in seventeenth-century Rome. It focuses on the business of writing, from purchasing a Capitoline notarial post and hiring employees to finding, and keeping, clients. In the final chapter we explore the tensions raised by the dramatic changes to Rome's documentary regime, especially between 1550 and 1650, as they surface in the late seventeenth century. The book concludes in the early 1700s with an internally generated assessment of the new disciplines that had been imposed on notarial writing over the course of the early modern period. The house-by-house investigation of the notaries' offices and the inspection of the city's two main notarial archives ordered by Pope Clement XI in 1702 affords us the chance to reflect on what the efforts of the state had accomplished and where they had failed.

The conceptual resources, material forms, political interests, and economic forces that went into the making of notarial documents in early modern Rome have something to teach us about the broader history of writing, both as object and as technique. We must cast our nets widely if we wish to understand what gives written artifacts their power. But we will catch very little if we do not also peer closely at the particularities of time and place in which writing practices operate.

CHAPTER ONE

The Jurists
Writing Public Words

While public writing as a practice dates back to the dawn of written records, the notion of public words, scriptura publica, was a legal fiction crafted by the jurists of medieval Europe and handed down to their early modern successors. It was not their only useful fiction, but it is one of singular importance for understanding the notary's distinctive quality as a writer, as was their idea of the public instrument, the written artifact with which notaries are so closely associated. The thinking of jurists about these topics from the time of the rediscovery of the legal texts of Roman antiquity in the early Middle Ages right through the early modern period matters to us not only because of its inherent interest but also because it powerfully affected European legal institutions.[1] University professors and lawyers teaching and writing about Roman law exercised a constitutive influence on legal developments in continental Europe to an extent unimaginable to denizens of lands where Anglo-American jurisprudence operates.[2] They were not the only source of law, as we shall see, but learned commentary on ancient texts of written law played a crucial role in defining the place of writing in theory and in practice. In the *ius commune*, the congeries of Roman and ecclesiastical (canon) law and medieval commentary that was their creation, the jurists constructed the legal processes and writing acts of continental society in long-lasting and culturally specific ways.

Before venturing into their preferred terrain, definitions, it is helpful to review the three major elements that came together to form this distinctive legal patrimony, the ius commune.[3] The body of Roman writings on law collected by the emperor Justinian in the sixth century, known again by the eleventh century, was a vital element, providing the materials on which the learned professors went to work.[4] The Justinianic corpus included several different genres of legal writing, the most important of which for medieval interpreters were the *Codex* or *Code*, composed of passages from imperial laws, and the *Digest*, a compilation of opinions of distinguished Roman jurists.[5] Equally crucial, of course, were the second elements, the professors themselves, a curriculum, and an institutional site for reading and commenting on authoritative texts. By the twelfth and thirteenth centuries, the *studium* of Bologna, one of Europe's earliest universities, had emerged as the preeminent place for studying Roman law.[6]

In their classrooms, glosses, and treatises, the teachers explained Justinian's books to students, a process that inevitably slightly changed their meaning as the jurists creatively brought ancient concepts to bear on contemporary practices and pressed their own institutions into Roman molds. So astute, sophisticated, and compelling were their readings that the principle became established, when trying actual cases on the continent, that only those sections of the *Corpus iuris civilis* that had received comment would be authoritative in court.[7] A third major element of the ius commune therefore was the rich tradition of learned reflection on the law, which lasted for more than five hundred years. By the late sixteenth century, the concept of scriptura publica that had been developed by the wide-ranging super novae of the 1200s and 1300s, such as Accursius, Popes Innocent III and Innocent IV, and the post-glossators Bartolus of Sassoferrato and Baldus de Ubaldis, was long established. Rather than follow the concept's development in detail through the Middle Ages, however, it is useful to focus on the stars of more limited intensity, like Giuseppe Mascardi (d. 1586), Prospero Farinacci (1544–1618), and Giovanni Battista Fenzonio (d. 1639), who illuminate its key features in early modern Rome. Convention called for each new author to review the opinions of his predecessors; thus, the tradition of citation, derided for its sterile technicalities by later reformers, in fact continually expanded the ius commune. So too did the unceasing necessity of bringing actual laws, statutes, into dialogue with the prestigious dicta of the academics.

The medieval jurists played a crucial role because Roman law did not concern itself very much with issues of evidence and proof. The commentators, whether protagonists or heirs of the profound transformation in modes of procedure around 1215 that shifted proof from physical tests like the ordeal to reasoned arguments based on data, elaborated this domain of law on their own.[8] They usually took one of two brief but well-known sections (titles) in the *Code* or the *Digest* on "De fide instrumentorum et de amissione eorum" as their starting point.[9] A comparison of the *Digest*'s treatment with that of the glossator Rogerius in the mid-twelfth century succinctly measures what a distance this pioneer had already traveled. Although the English translation of this section promises that it will treat documentary evidence, the first opinion quoted in the *Digest* does not even mention writing. " 'Instruments include all the evidence relevant to a case. Hence, both oral evidence and witnesses are regarded as instruments."[10] Unfazed by this Spartan fare, Rogerius elaborated: "Instruments are a type of proof. . . . An instrument is said to be all the evidence relevant to a case, but here particularly it means written instruments of which there are two kinds, one called public and one called private."[11] He then went on to describe what distinguished them, to detail the various types and uses of public and private documents, and to explain how each type ought to be supported if its truthfulness was challenged. Rogerius concluded that "because contracts are often written it must be said that a contract wants writing," making the dubious claim that Justinian's legislation bore this out. In fact, *Code* 4.21 and *Digest* 22.4 concern themselves more with ways to prove claims if you do not have a document than if you do. It was Rogerius—and, in succeeding generations, other jurists like him—who made the arguments for the importance of written evidence in establishing proof.

When Rogerius defined *scriptura publica* and *scriptura privata* he made distinctions as to their form as well as their uses. Formally scriptura publica came into existence in two ways, either as court records (*acta*) written in the presence of a judge or "as an *instrumentum* that a notary [*tabellio*] has made."[12] Scriptura privata by contrast is penned by *quis privatus*, a private individual. Rogerius did not discuss the distinction between a notary and a *privatus*, but we will need to do so. We have also to understand better what Rogerius and his successors meant when they termed the writing of notaries "public" and the product of their pens a "public instrument."

While the ancient notary or tabellio mentioned in diverse passages of the *Code* was an official writer of sorts, the tabellio to whom Rogerius referred in the twelfth century was different.[13] No longer just a vaguely defined imperial scribe, the notary of the Middle Ages had acquired a tighter identification with public authority.[14] So close was that relationship that notaries could count themselves, like magistrates, as "public persons."[15] As a *persona publica*, the notary's hand, too, was public, *manus publica*, and hence the work of that hand, scriptura publica, was an authoritative public document. The medieval notary's acquisition of *publica fides*, public trustworthiness, distinguished him not only from the ancient tabellio but also from official scribes often described as notaries in other legal regimes, such as that of Islam.[16] Observed while in conversation with private clients or scribbling in courtrooms and council chambers, the notary's writing activity might look identical to those of such scribes, but his written artifacts carried a different weight. No higher officer reviewed or attested them; they were guaranteed solely by his authority.

The records of twelfth-century Italy confirm that notarial writing had gained this special credibility. The formalities for authenticating personal transactions in writing, such as a sale or gift, changed subtly but significantly. Whereas the signatures of the notary and witnesses traditionally validated written agreements between individuals, in the course of the eleventh and twelfth centuries the witnesses' signatures drop away.[17] The signature of the notary alone was enough to render the document worthy of trust. This new character had nothing to do with his writing abilities or personal qualities, of course; it was the artifact of the legal fiction that he was a "public person."

As we have seen, Rogerius redefined the ancient instrumentum to mean a written document, applying it to both categories that he had been the first to distinguish, public and private. A private instrument, or scriptura privata more generally, was simply writing "whose purpose and form are private."[18] It was the handiwork of those without public authority, *privati*, who made a written record for their own personal ends. All sorts of writing might qualify, though he specifically mentioned those types, like receipts, discussed in the famous titles of *Code* 4.21 and *Digest* 22.4. By contrast, the public instrument was particularly associated with the notary. In the course of the twelfth century, simultaneously with their acquisition of publica fides, notarial records increasingly came to be called instrumenta rather than the early medieval term *carta*.[19] Although the new name owed nothing to Roman documents, it did add a suitable Justinianic dignity to words that had become more authoritative.

We can capture the jurists' mature formulation of the public instrument from the man with the most to say about how to make one, the prestigious Bolognese teacher of the notarial art, Rolandino dei Passeggeri (1215/17–97). The public instrument consists of two elements—the content of the negotiation (*negocii tenor*) and publication (*publicationes*).[20] The content is "the contract agreed and arranged between the contracting parties," such as a sale, dowry, or debt. Publication, somewhat more mysterious to Anglo-American readers, he defines as "those things that render the instrument public and authentic." "They are called the *publicationes* because they make the instrument public and authentic and worthy of trust and because they must be put in instruments and be written only by the hand of a public person, that is, the notary, who is a public person whose office is devised for the benefit of the public."[21] By Rolandino's count, the six items of information that made the instrument public, what later jurists would call the formalities (*solemnitates*), were the year, indiction, day, place, witnesses, and name of the notary. Subjects of the pope and emperor might add a seventh, the name and regnal year of their ruler.

Rolandino devoted many pages of his handbook to specific types of notarial contracts, a subject powerfully influenced by the Roman contracts in the *Corpus iuris civilis*. Worth emphasizing is the fact that, to be valid, their formal character was just as important as their substance. Rogerius has already alerted us to this equivalence when he defined the instrument by its "purpose and form." A hundred years later, the form had a reasonably firm physiognomy because over the centuries, although the jurists were not always of the same mind on whether there were six or seven or nine requisites for publication, they did agree that the notary's public instrument had to have certain formal features. In the opinion of some, he could be charged with the crime of *falsum* (forgery) if he omitted these.[22] A witness from the end of our period, Giovanni Battista Fenzonio, former chief magistrate of Rome's municipal tribunal, carefully enumerated the jurists' traditional requirements (nine in this case) but pointed out that publication formalities ultimately depended on local custom.[23] In seventeenth-century Rome, operative custom had pared these to the date and witnesses.

Rolandino's thirteenth-century manual for notaries divided their production line into three broad categories: public instruments, wills or testaments, and judicial acts.[24] The revolution in medieval justice epitomized by the outlawing of trial by ordeal in 1215 had put a premium on the written record of what judges saw, heard, and decided in court, and notaries armed with publica fides stepped in to provide it. Judicial acts must be in writing, the jurists taught.[25] Rolandino codified the new expectations that made notaries a vital part of the operations of judicial institutions in both secular and ecclesiastical settings. It was now obvious that, whether its source was a judicial record or a public instrument, scriptura publica was quintessentially, if not exclusively, the creation of the notary.[26]

Parallel to the expanded use of documentation in court proceedings was its increased use as evidence, as Rogerius had signaled when he had redefined instrumenta as written proof. While the new criminal trials that replaced the judicial ordeal had little use for writing because they required accusers and witnesses to confront the accused in person, civil disputes grew ever more dependent on it. Strongly influenced by the ritualistic features of Roman civil procedure, litigation became a highly formal series of set exchanges focused on documents.[27] Indeed, already in the mid-twelfth century, as we have seen, Rogerius assumed that written records, public or private, would be challenged in court and gave instruction in the ways to defend them. "If the truth of an instrument is questioned," he advised, "it can be proved by the depositions of witnesses or comparison of handwriting."[28] In the new culture of rational proof, most evidence had to be tested.[29]

The abolition of the ordeal had set the stage for a massive battle over the quality of evidence, a conflict that would keep jurists entertained and judges tormented from the twelfth to the eighteenth century.[30] The professors' goal was to define a clear and absolute hierarchy in which the authority of all possible kinds of evidence would be determined systematically. They hoped that this system of what came to be called "legal proof," would guide or, better, dictate to judges, leaving them very little discretion. However, the jurists were not by nature given to concord, so the clear and absolute hierarchy was in practice many contending scales assessing the merits of a highly fetishized concept.

The jurists classified their materials as "full" proof, "half" proof, or signs (*indicia*), which entered the discussion chiefly as indicators that torture would be needed to get more information. By the late sixteenth century, when the experienced ecclesiastical administrator Giuseppe Mascardi completed the most thorough treatment of the topic of evidence to issue from this extended debate, the categories were somewhat more refined.[31] In addition to seven types of full proof and four types of half proof, there were conjecture, signs, and *fictio*, which was "when falsehood is accepted as true in particular cases allowed by the law."[32] Seven, six, nine, twelve— the numbers did not really matter because the jurists did not agree.[33] After discussing a wide range of views, Mascardi put witnesses, documents, confession, evident facts, oaths, "reasonable" presumption, and reputation (*fama*) in the category of full proof, omitting inscriptions, letters with episcopal seals, precedent (*re iudicata*), and natural reason among others.[34] He classified as half proof the testimony of only one witness, handwriting analysis, scriptura privata, and conjecture (*praesumptio non ita urgens*). What he called "uncommon" types of proof, like duels, cold water, or a very odd test with an iron (*purgatio ferri candentis*), turned out to be mostly unacceptable to the church.[35]

Although many medieval jurists had placed *notorium*, that which was transparently obvious, at the summit of the ladder of evidence and some thought confession was highest, the real battle from the twelfth century on was between witnesses and documents.[36] Learned law both endorsed writing and allowed witnesses to prevail over it. Pronouncements for each side, sometimes from the same source, rang out for centuries. Pope Innocent III in the early thirteenth century and Baldus in the late fourteenth clearly favor witnesses and just as emphatically support written evidence.[37] Both Holy Scripture and the *Corpus iuris civilis* seemed to give the edge to witnesses (two or three), but the *Code* included one law that contradicted this: "In the administration of justice, documentary evidence has the same force as the depositions of witnesses."[38] When he reviewed the long debate, Mascardi expressed some perplexity, not to say fatigue, at the difficulty of deciding securely which should be preferred, witnesses or writings.[39] For our purposes, however, what was significant about the jurists' vexatious attention to the question is that it forced them to say a good deal about written evidence.

Baldus, whose theoretical treatment of proof was more extensive than that of earlier jurists, contributed significantly to the debate. The power of the public instrument, he wrote in his commentary on *Code* 4.21, derived from the authority of the writer, its formalities, and the fact that its content could be verified by the senses.[40] In his discussion of *Digest* 22.4.6, he answered the question, "Is an instrument presumed to be true?" affirmatively, adding "if it is public, . . . but not if it is private."[41] Two centuries later, approaching the problem from the perspective of an expert on crime, the Roman prosecutor Farinacci too had to consider in a dispute what weight the notary carried as a writer.[42] Citing many learned opinions, he claimed that as a rule the benefit of the doubt ought to go to the notarial record.[43] The instrument from the hand of a notary "carries three presumptions: that it is true, formal, and that everything in it occurred. . . . it has definitive force, ready execution, is said to be proof proven, [and] makes an apparent matter manifest, very evident, transparent and obvious to all [*notoriam*]."[44] Presumably the notary's public trustworthiness transferred itself to the public instrument so that it stood very high on the scale of proof.

The word *presumably* flags a key feature of the way the jurists conceived written evidence, however. Despite their disagreements, they concurred in thinking that the truth of documents was conditional. Even the public instrument had credibility (*fides*) only until it was disproved and in that regard was no different from scriptura privata.[45] One reason for their skepticism was the understanding of contract that they had inherited from Roman law, as an agreement between consenting parties. According to the *Digest*, "The point of writing is to prove the transaction more easily, but the transaction, if proved, is valid without it."[46] Baldus explained that writing implied an obligation, if such was clearly stated, but did not in itself constitute the obligation.[47] The real contract was the agreement between the parties; the instrument was merely the notary's record of that agreement.

If their legal heritage emphasized deeds over representations of deeds, the medieval jurists' debate about the hierarchy of proof highlighted the vulnerabilities of all such representations. So a second reason for their cautious attitude toward written evidence was that they had read all the arguments about the authority of oral testimony versus that of documents, and they saw that no form of proof, except the transparently obvious, escaped unscathed. Again, Baldus put the matter succinctly: "Proof is easier to support than to establish."[48] The public instrument had the weight of two witnesses, but a full proof required three.

Indeed, writing always required the support of witnesses.[49] The notary's record usually named two witnesses, but depending on the nature of the contract, more might be needed; following Roman precedent, testaments, for example, demanded a total of seven. Scriptura privata had to have three witnesses.[50] By the same token, the force of documents could be undermined or nullified by their witnesses, a problem that inspired feats of legal fancy among the jurists.[51] How credible is a public instrument denied by one witness of low status but supported by the other witness of higher standing? What if it is rejected by three witnesses, none of whom was present when it was formalized? If scriptura privata, such as a letter, receipt, or account book, is supported by the three living witnesses who signed it originally, does it have more, equal, or less force than a piece of scriptura publica whose two witnesses are dead? What if four witnesses to a will say it is false, but do not recall what was said at the signing, while three say it is valid and remember precisely the details of the setting, time, and words spoken? In his detailed treatment of proof, Mascardi tried introducing distinctions, a practical scholastic approach to the overheated question of witnesses versus written records. Some matters concerned documents, and in such cases oral testimony might be irrelevant; some made no reference to writing, and the two forms of evidence were equal.[52] However, if witnesses said an instrument was false, it could be rehabilitated only through other witnesses.

The unintended effect of this extended discussion of the hierarchy of proof was to reduce all writing, private and public, to the same level.[53] When pushed by the logic of their arguments, even proponents of public writing had to admit that in some cases scriptura privata might provide better evidence than a public instrument.[54] As we shall see, scriptura publica would have to look outside the classroom, if it wanted to retain its privileges. Yet, in posing their hypothetical "what if" questions about evidence, the jurists reflected the real life of the courtroom, to whose proceedings they frequently contributed legal opinions.[55] Moreover, their imaginative and critical interrogation of concepts had a significant, if indirect, impact on the writing practices of notaries and private individuals. Asking which document to believe led, as we shall see, to the close analysis of the written artifact produced by the notary and to the elaboration of a vocabulary for describing both the process of composition and the products of his pen. Although the actual practices of notaries provided the material, the jurists created the language for talking about public instruments, and through the statutes of cities and guilds, this language found its way into law and custom.

The notion that the notary and the testator or the contracting parties met together physically and that the notary formalized their wishes in writing operated to conflate act, the statement of wishes or the pact in the presence of witnesses, and artifact, the instrument or will that ensued. An instrument was said to be *rogated,* a term that scholars trace to the ritual of asking (*rogare*) the scribe to record the contract.[56] The authorizing notary who put pen to parchment was the *rogatario* or *rogatus,* and a later vernacular synonym for an instrument was *rogito.* The language, which predated the Roman borrowings of the twelfth century, implied that something social had happened to which the technical activity was subordinate. Medieval commentators were sensitive to this nuance in a transaction that after all took place between parties in the presence of a notary and witnesses. They preserved its performative dimension when they described a notarial instrument as being "celebrated," as if it truly were an event.[57] As a consequence, however, how the notary wrote received little attention from the theorists before the thirteenth century. To reconstruct the process of composition, historian Giorgio Costamagna turned not to theory, therefore, but to the rich evidence of practice provided by the early notarial archives of Genoa. From these sources he discovered that the notary who validated the act of the parties drew up the written artifact in three stages.[58] The notary followed a first draft (*notula*), presumably taken in the presence of the parties or very near in time to the transaction, by a more technical redaction in summary form (*imbreviatura*), and he climaxed the operation with an instrument "in public form" delivered to the parties. The making of a public instrument therefore entailed a sequence of steps that included an event, note taking on key details of that event (parties, witnesses, date, and place), a revision adding legal precision pertinent to the type of contract or testamentary formulas, and finally a signed version that clients took away.

While local practices varied in Italy, and the terms used in Genoa were not necessarily the same in Venice, Siena, or Rome, it is clear that notaries were writing a good many records that were not the final instruments "in public form." In the thirteenth and fourteenth centuries, the jurists began to wonder what the status of these earlier versions was; after all, they too were in the public hand of the notary and often had the essential formalities that the handbooks required. It was not an idle question because clients sometimes lost their public instruments and in some places, like Genoa and Rome, chose not to take them at all, assuming that the notary's second phase, the imbreviatura, was sufficient. If there were temporally distinct phases to the production of a public instrument and a variety of written artifacts issuing from each of these stages, however, the jurists had to sort out what authority these documents had. They had to develop language for talking about how to compare these versions, for deciding which was more or less valid, and for discussing future versions, or copies, which clients or heirs legitimately might request.

In the course of the fourteenth century the post-glossators, and Baldus in particular, commented in more detail on the products of the notary's pen. They deployed a vocabulary for this purpose centered on a set of terms—*matrix, protocollum, imbreviatura* or *abbreviatura, originale,* and *authenticum*—that enjoyed lasting success in the continent's legal discourse. The terms are essential to know not only because the jurists used them but also because they worked their way into statute.

The difficulty is that while they purport to denote scribal objects produced by notaries, they bear only a glancing relationship to the actual written artifacts of practitioners. This is the reason why they may have more than one meaning or may be employed in one city and not another or in the fourteenth century but not the sixteenth.[59] The jurists' language was fixed in the timeless and universal ether of the ius commune; notaries wrote on and with varied materials in specific places and times under diverse political and professional conditions. We explore these specificities in later chapters. For now it is our task not so much to match the professors' categories with physical objects as to grasp their conceptual import.

In fact, the notary's rough draft, what Baldus had termed the "earliest writing," hastily scribbled at the time of the transaction, would have been the most difficult of all phases to recover physically, for it was routinely struck through, thrown away, or lost.[60] The jurists thought more highly of these jottings than did the notaries, arguing that they captured the substance of the agreement between the parties (the contract) as well as those essential formalities (date, place, and witnesses) required in a public instrument. Their respect is reflected in the name *matrix* (Italian *matrice*) with which they rebaptized what the Genoese, who scratched them out, had called simply notes (*notula*). Always focused on hypothetical conflicts, the professors appreciated the matrix because if the veracity of the client's document was questioned, the "earliest writing" offered a way to check it. Farinacci quoted one authority who suggested that, "when the trustworthiness of an instrument is in doubt, go to the notary's notebook or sheet of paper on which the earliest writing of the instrument is made, as long as it is not so completely crossed out that it cannot be read."[61] In practice it would have been a rare notebook that survived to offer this useful evidence, but the jurists were concerned with solutions to legal problems, not practical problems, and in their defense it might have been a good thing if the notaries had saved their rough drafts more scrupulously.

As we saw earlier, the imbreviatura or abbreviatura (the terms seem to be interchangeable) was the second phase of the notarial redaction of an instrument. It involved the notary's specification of the technicalities of the contract or will, legal formulas referred to as the customary or abbreviated clauses (*clausulae consuetae* or *ceteratae*), which he added while recopying his first notes and the requisite formalities of date, place, and witnesses into another format.[62] When a client at a later moment wanted an instrument "in public form," the notary put it together from the information contained in the imbreviatura of the transaction. It was abbreviated to be sure, but it had everything legally necessary to be considered scriptura publica by the hand of a notary and carry public trustworthiness.[63]

The word *protocollum* or protocol could mean a single instrument or act but more commonly referred to a notebook or volume that contained the notary's whole output of imbreviaturae, usually in chronological order, for a given period of time. The protocol in this latter sense came to function as a guarantee of the authenticity of the notary's record both because it was understood as the proper place to keep it and because the temporal sequence of instruments hindered tampering (removing or adding acts) or falsification of dates. It was a key point of reference for the jurists when they talked about notaries. If it were missing, even the instrument in public form lost its fides. As the prosecutor Farinacci put it in the early seventeenth century, "Instruments without their protocols are suspected of forgery and do not prove anything."[64] His contemporary, the magistrate Fenzonio, closely followed tradition when he noted that if there was a discrepancy between a public instrument submitted by a litigant as evidence in a case and the record of the same transaction in the notary's protocol, the one in the notary's possession had greater credibility.[65] The protocol could even reinforce a public instrument that was missing key formalities.

The last, though optional, phase was the creation of the "public form" of the public instrument. The jurists actually did not say much about the mechanics of this stage, which mattered more to consumers (and governments) than to legal scholars. The notary provided clients willing to pay the extra fee with a version of the instrument, often on parchment, that bore his signature and his identifying symbol (*signum*) or seal, which they could take home with them.[66] Usually clients brought them "home" in order to present them as evidence in civil court, where they hoped the probative force promised to the public instrument could advance their suits.[67]

We come finally to the terms *original* and *authentic*, and we might well wonder how to apply these to the artifacts that we have just surveyed. Which version was the original—the notes that were as likely to be thrown away as saved, or the abbreviated version in the protocol, which the notary made some time after the actual transaction? Or was the original the version that the clients took with them, which they hoped would defend their rights or interests in some future contest? The notary had written all of these. Which were authentic? What was a copy, and what was its status in the hierarchy of evidence?[68] Did copies carry less weight than originals? In that case, what was the point of a sacrosanct protocol, if copies made from its contents were worthless? For clients who purchased notarial services, the point was to gain access to the words of a publicly authorized writer in a form that outsiders would believe. What form should that be? The questions pressed on the notaries, because the jurists put the responsibility for retaining the products of particular stages of their writing process on their shoulders, under threat of torture and criminal penalties.[69] Which products should they be sure to keep? The concepts had real-world consequences for clients and notaries, but they mattered to the jurists, too, because they cut to the heart of public writing.

After reproving most of his predecessors for confusing these terms, Farinacci announced that he would impose semantic order by defining them according to "our common way of speaking."[70] By this criterion, he declared the originale, the matrix, and the imbreviatura to be identical. Because two of the three categories varied in their material forms, this statement could not have been literally true. What gave it truth, what they had in common so as to make them interchangeable, was the early character of their inscription. They were the "earliest writing," a product of that moment that Baldus had pinpointed as critically important in his commentary on the *Codex*.[71] Farinacci admitted that the imbreviatura was not as "early" as the matrix but defended his claim on the grounds that it was just an abbreviated version of those first notes.[72] So, at least in Farinacci's early seventeenth-century Rome, the word "original" signified the moment of origin in all its primitive roughness, a fact the lawyer emphasized by describing the physical materials that bore the matrix. They were loose sheets of paper or little booklets (*liberculo*) to which the notaries gave dismissive names, like *broliardellum* or *bastardellum*. As we have seen, notwithstanding its unimposing appearance, the matrix or originale contained everything necessary to qualify it as a public instrument.

If *original* meant what was written down first, how should we understand the word *authentic* in a documentary context? The instrument "in public form" that the notary gave to the contracting parties at their request was *authenticum*. An authenticum was a copy, but it was a powerful copy, endowed with authority by its formal signature in a public hand and by the fact that it stood, as we shall see, in close relationship to the protocol.[73] It was this document that a litigant could take before a judge as proof of a claim; indeed, it was this copy that jurists taught ought to have the weight of two witnesses.

The fact that an originale and an authenticum, though quite different in their timing and aspect, had the same legal force ought to surprise us, but the jurists, both by what they said and by what they did not say, made it all seem quite natural. They pointed to the Janus-like protocol in the notary's possession as the pivot. Looking backward in the process, they claimed that the imbreviature in the protocol faithfully reproduced the parties' or testator's wishes as expressed in the original notes. The jurists did not linger over the fact that the imbreviatura, stage two, was a quite different text than the matrix it supposedly replicated. Facing the other direction, they affirmed the principle that no copy taken from the pages of the protocol, however authentic, carried probative weight unless the same instrument in the protocol backed it up. They did not mention that the heavily abbreviated version in the protocol (the imbreviatura) did not look at all like the authenticum, the copy "in public form." Their silences allow the material form of the public instrument, both physical and textual, to vary. Their words, on the other hand, stress its connection to the notary. To the jurists, the public instrument, at whatever stage of composition, never entirely let go of its author.

Because the notary carried such a burden of responsibility for his writing, we might well ask what the jurists thought about him. Was he simply the hand of authority, *manus publica*, and that was that, or did his humanity insert itself into their reflections? The answer of course is that to some degree the notary did force himself upon their attention, if only because the professors traded in the currency of all possible conflicts. While it was not until Baldus in the fourteenth century that a major theorist wrote specifically for notaries, commentators did address a limited number of legal situations that referred to their qualities.[74] These discussions focused on the notary's personal status, his knowledge of the facts he recorded, his expertise in his duties, his reputation and its effects, and his mistakes and misdeeds.

In contrast to governments and professional bodies, who, as we shall see in later chapters, imposed social and educational requisites on the aspiring notary, the jurists' demands were simple. The notary needed no more and no less than any person who qualified for a public position: he had to be a free adult male who had not been excommunicated or declared legally *infamis*.[75] As a human being of this privileged status, he ought to be able to arrive at truthful knowledge using his senses—in particular, his hearing and sight. It was not the notary's job, according to Baldus, to read the intentions of his clients as they made their wishes known at the rogation of the will or instrument.[76] Instead, he reported what they said and did. His charge was to hear them articulate those desires on their deathbed or to watch as the parties to a contract exchanged money and then to record accurately what he heard and saw. Unlike the Roman notaries themselves, who credited divine inspiration for their capacity to tell the truth, Baldus and his followers taught that the proper basis for a notary's knowledge of the facts was sensory.[77] The commentators drew illuminating contrasts between the office of a notary and that of a judge. According to Fenzonio, "the notary is called the judge's eye."[78] The notary represented what he saw and heard; the judge by contrast had to figure out what happened by interpreting the evidence presented.[79] The notary was supposed to use his hand as well, of course; at least one authority held that what a judge penned was not scriptura publica because "writing is not a judge's charge but a notary's."[80]

Consistent with the epistemological resources to which they had given him access, the jurists defined the notary's peculiar expertise narrowly. Although they went out of their way to specify that he know how to read and to write clearly, they did not necessarily expect him to have legal knowledge.[81] On what we might well regard as crucial technical know-how for a notary, the formulas of specific contracts and legal provisions known as the abbreviated or customary clauses, the professors said very little. They worried about when these could be added to an instrument and whether the notary had informed the clients about them, but they left their details to local custom.[82] They did not define the notary's expertise as skillful application of the right contractual language.[83] Quite a different matter was a public instrument missing its formalities of date, place, witnesses, and the like, for they regarded their inclusion as fundamental to the notary's job. Reviewing the authorities, Farinacci found that the vast majority believed that when a notary failed to provide them, he was presumed to have done so on purpose and could be criminally prosecuted.[84] If a notary was expert in his profession, "it is not plausible that he did not know which formalities to put into the instrument or testament and left them out."[85] Farinacci, the son of a notary, was slightly more indulgent. He praised the opinion of one jurist who thought that punishment ought to be administered only when it was a question of omitting the usual formalities that all notaries knew, such as having more than one witness or forgetting the year or the pope's regnal year. After all, he quoted approvingly, "a notary is not required to have the same expertise as a doctor of laws."[86]

The jurists' portrait of the ideal notary, a free male listener and observer who always remembered to include the date, place, and witnesses to a transaction, lacks only one finishing touch: a good reputation (*fama*). In the Middle Ages, reputation was so highly valued as evidence that the glossators considered it a form of proof.[87] Taking his cue from Baldus, Mascardi subtly demoted it as a category, but the concept remained influential.[88] Farinacci frequently alluded to the effects of a notary's bad or dubious reputation on the evaluation of evidence. Ill fame compromised the presumption of the ius commune in favor of the notary.[89] Even when a notary had not been convicted of a crime, notoriety could undermine the trustworthiness of his public words.[90] It had an impact on the judge's assessment of a disputed instrument, which lost credibility instead of gaining it from his authorship. It also opened the notary to criminal prosecution, for example, when a judge had to determine whether he had written or omitted something with evil intent or simply in error.[91] The jurists did not concern themselves with defining norms for the profession, but they did care about how the notary's reputation affected the probative value of his words.

This focus on the efficacy of the public instrument drove their interest in the notary's mistakes. As we have seen, if a notarial act was to count for something in a court of law, it had to be formally as well as substantively correct. Notarial error in either form or content jeopardized its validity, which in turn opened clients to legal harm and the notary himself to liability for damages.[92] Although the presumption of the ius commune was that errors in an instrument or will were not the notary's fault, the jurists liked to consider all possible contingencies. They were interested in how documents lost their probative force and keen to establish a means of distinguishing genuine mistakes from criminal alterations to the text, made either by the notary or by other malicious parties. Thus, they wanted to know, Was a given notarial document an actual instrument? Was it truthful? Would it prove in court?

Against the backdrop of these questions, the commentators paid close attention to the physical integrity of the instrument.[93] Farinacci in particular weighed the meaning of all graphic interventions, whether these changes were subtractions, by crossing out or scratching through, or additions, words slipped in between the lines or in the margins.[94] The jurists thought hard about whether and when the notary could correct an error in the instrument. Because it was legally valid in all three of its stages, he could not just throw it away and start over. Summarizing received opinion, Farinacci stated the general rule that the notary could not make a correction at all after the act had been rogated, though his dozens of elaborations and restrictions on this principle suggested otherwise.[95] Baldus had seemed more permissive, declaring that the notary could amend a mistake as long as it did not damage his clients' interests, but to judge from the many limitations he imposed, his pliancy was more apparent than real.[96] Opinions were divided and often contradictory. Because the jurists were committed to the idea that the original, imbreviatura and instrument in public form were identical, it was hard to allow the notary to fix mistakes, of commission or omission, as he redacted what in reality were three distinct texts.

At most, some commentators could offer two sources of flexibility. The first was the distinction between errors that had to do with his own office as notary (solemnitates) and those that pertained to the substance of the contract (names, things, boundaries), and the second was the intervention of a judge.[97] Even in the case of mistakes in the formalities, however, the jurists demanded a high level of scrutiny. If, for example, the notary had forgotten to include the indiction, which Baldus considered more obscure knowledge than the regnal year of the current pontiff, he could add it later, but it was quite a different matter when he omitted the date on a mortgage agreement.[98] The second source of flexibility was even less elastic. A notary who had noticed an error could notify a judge and perhaps the contracting parties, prove that the missing or incorrect data was in fact a mistake, and with their approval make the correction.[99] By the early modern period standards had, if anything, stiffened, with Mascardi and Fenzonio demanding that any changes be witnessed and recorded on the instrument.[100] Although practice probably did shift over time, it is worth noting that in 1398 the Roman notary Antonio Scambi, serenely oblivious to the jurists' shock and horror, simply corrected his mistake on a document with an explanation.[101]

After the doctors' austere defense of the integrity of the instrument, it may come as something of a surprise to learn that they were quite prepared to admit half measures. A suspicious document was not necessarily worthless. It might still have some credibility, and even if it failed to provide proof, it was a far cry from false.[102] The probative value of writing was relative, not absolute; a record disfigured by extraneous marks might still lay some claim to veracity. Nevertheless, as it slid down the scale of *fides*, it might well sink to the point of being judged invalid or untrue. At that point legal thinkers had to confront the question of the notary's culpability, not mere liability for damages but *dolus* or criminal intent. As Farinacci archly put it, "Let us move on to the falsehoods [*falsitates*] committed by notaries in several ways, would that it were not so."[103]

Law professors in the Middle Ages had inherited from the Romans the crime of falsum, a category of misdeed applicable to a rich range of deceptive practices. Roman law's falsum had a much broader register than the English term by which we are accustomed to translate it, forgery, embracing everything from altering documents and counterfeiting coinage to switching babies in the cradle.[104] As capacious as it was, falsum expanded even more in medieval and early modern Europe, sweeping in fictitious pregnancies, adulterated flour, and fake textile stamps, along with nefarious things done to writings, like opening, hiding, tearing, scratching, or burning them.[105] Obviously, any kind of document, whether in a private or public hand, might suffer malicious perusal, modification, or destruction, but falsum in Farinacci's exhaustive account encompassed some criminal behavior pertaining especially to notarial acts and to their authors.[106]

Contrary to what we might expect, forging public instruments was not high on the list.[107] The great Florentine lawyer Francesco Guicciardini showed profound insight into contemporary attitudes toward notarial documents when he noted that most false instruments were originally true.[108] It was only with time that the desire to change their provisions became irresistible, and when it did, notaries were far from the only suspects.[109] The jurists would have admitted that notaries sometimes falsified their texts, but it was the more challenging questions that interested them, like the legal status of real instruments rogated by false or putative notaries or the liability of notaries for invalid acts that were false.[110] In keeping with this taste for paradox, the first of the profession's misdeeds that Farinacci took up was the real notary who denied that he was the notary or, more precisely, said he had not rogated a particular instrument for a client and refused to give it to him.[111] A crime of this sort threw a society that entrusted the safekeeping of its contracts and wills to notaries into disarray, but the discussion allows us to see at a deeper level the distinction drawn between the man and the office. A notary might defend himself by claiming that he had drawn up the record as a friend (*amicus*), not as a notary (*tabellio*).[112] Mascardi explored this problem in some detail, pointing out that if a man who happened to be a notary signed his name to a document without mentioning that he was a notary, we could not assume that he had rogated it.[113] The public signature with its affirmation of the notary's office, however, allowed the presumption that the notary had signed as tabellio, not amicus. In his public capacity, unless he was old and forgetful, he was guilty of falsum if he did not bring forth the requested instrument.[114]

Some notarial misdeeds were straightforward even for the jurists. They largely agreed that failing to keep the protocol (or, more controversially, the matrix), leaving out the obligatory formalities, or drawing up illegal (i.e., usurious) contracts deserved punishment.[115] More contentious were those cases in which standard legal phrases failed to describe accurately what had taken place in a transaction. Two examples caught the special attention of the expert on crime Farinacci. Was the notary a *falsario* when he deployed the formulaic statement in a will that the testator had named his heir orally when in fact he had simply concurred with the notary's suggestion?[116] The purists defined falsehood as any alteration of the truth, and the statement was not literally true, so by one account the notary was indeed culpable. But the opinion prevailed that if the testator had nodded his agreement, the notary had done no wrong, nor should he be prosecuted unless the will as a whole had been invalidated.

A second, and thornier, problem was how notaries represented the act of paying in cash in their instruments. Was the notary guilty of falsum if he said the money was counted out (*pecunia numerata*) when it had been handed over but not counted, or counted but not in his presence, or counted and handed over but immediately returned? The variety of financial fictions that pass in review makes Farinacci's forty or so elaborations on the topic a cautionary tale for readers of notarial contracts but sharpens our understanding of the notary's own appearance in his texts.[117] Baldus argued that the notary committed falsum if he had merely witnessed someone putting money into a purse but stated that it had been counted. He counseled notaries to register the declarations of the parties in such cases (paying close attention to verb tenses) rather than make their own assertions. If the notary wrote that Titius said that the money in the purse had been counted, the notary would be off the hook if the amount in the purse was insufficient. He would be guilty of falsum, however, if he portrayed as a fact attested by his eyes and ears what was no more than a statement by Titius. The profession had to negotiate with some care linguistic conventions that emphasized the notary's textual presence and juridical doctrines that confined those representations to what the notary could see and hear.[118] Nevertheless, because proving falsum required close examination of an instrument's language, the alert notary could avoid prosecution if he erred on the side of more precision rather than less.[119]

Prosecution implied punishment, and here Farinacci, though never without a battery of cited authorities, may have created an original synthesis.[120] He acknowledged that the ancient penalties for falsum, deportation and confiscation of property, had given way to a system in which punishment was left up to the judge. "For the crime of falsum, there is no specific penalty because, since the kinds of falsification differ, the types of punishment vary according to the case and the type."[121] When the crime was serious, harmful to the state, or repeated, "such as a notary committing multiple falsities," culprits could face loss of a hand or the death penalty.[122] Loss of office and legal infamy (*infamis* status) followed upon the main punishment, and the guilty notary would also have to pay civil damages. Farinacci admitted degrees of guilt, however, arguing that, where culpability was slight, civil proceedings were more appropriate than trials for crime.[123] He would have relegated a dispute over the accuracy of a notary's description of a testator as being "sound of mind," which was legally essential for a valid will, to litigation.[124] In any case, the broad role he assigned to judicial discretion certainly permitted a spectrum of lesser penalties, chiefly fines.

Less nuanced than the jurists, Roman city law defined falsum committed by notaries, because they bore public authority, as public crime, which entailed specific procedures and penalties.[125] In the fourteenth century, notaries lost their office and paid fines (on pain of losing their right hand) as well as damages to the injured parties.[126] The fifteenth-century statutes added public humiliation to these punishments; the falsario had to stand on the steps of the senator's court on the Capitoline Hill before crowds summoned by the ringing of the town bell.[127] In seventeenth-century Rome, a complex grid of jurisdictions and growing state surveillance meant cases of notarial crime were more likely to be heard in papal than civic courts. As far as we can tell from still incomplete evidence from these tribunals, however, charges of false wills and instruments by notaries were rare.[128]

Both in legal doctrine and in local statute, notarial falsum embraced not only contracts and wills for private clients, what we call business acts, but also judicial acts written for litigants in civil cases or as part of a criminal proceeding.[129] Complaints that notaries in early modern Rome had manipulated judicial records, while not frequent, were at least as common as those for business acts. Backdating an entry in the office's judicial log (*manuale d'atti*), changing details on a legal notice, and falsely transferring a case from one court to another were just some of the abuses to which notaries could lay special claim.[130] One Capitoline notary who faced these and other charges, while still managing to hold onto his position for thirty years, was Flavio Paradisi.[131] Paradisi unquestionably had a touch of the flamboyant about him. In 1646 he accused an acquaintance of writing a defamatory placard calling him a cuckold (*becco*), but the case ended ignominiously when the court discovered that he had forged it himself.[132] The astonished defendant declared that if he had chosen to insult Paradisi he would not have called him a becco, "because I don't know whether he is one," but rather a falsario. "That trickster has been prosecuted in all the courts in Rome."[133] Of course, forgery was not the only kind of crime for which notaries might be prosecuted; extortion, cheating, and the whole normal array of misdeeds might apply just as well.[134] However, within the domain of falsum, although executions did take place in Rome, notaries seemed to have evaded them; the few convicted professionals of whom we have been able to find trace paid fines.[135]

Early modern jurists debated whether the penalties for falsum extended to falsification of documents by private individuals.[136] Rome's city law said that they did and levied the same fines on those who faked receipts and letters as it did on notaries who made false instruments.[137] However, because of their greater probative value in the economy of evidence, forged public instruments submitted in court carried double the penalties of falsified scriptura privata.

The learned commentators had significantly shaped the image, if not the reality, of the notary as a public writer, and their success in integrating a wide range of professional misconduct into the ancient crime of falsum sharpened that image both in law and in the popular imagination. As the story of Flavio Paradisi illustrates, to the public at large a notary who did wrong was a falsario, no matter what exactly he had done. The jurists were not hostile to notaries, of course, just more interested in each other, and in their serene indifference they made a final theoretical contribution of great value to the profession. This was their treatment of the role of custom.

As we have noted, the technical details of different types of contracts were called the customary or abbreviated clauses, and no legal writer thought that notaries needed any special knowledge of these formulas. It was enough that he employ those phrases that were commonly used. Usage or custom had a respectable pedigree. In the *Digest* itself we read that "custom [*consuetudo*] is the best interpreter of statutes," an opinion quoted approvingly by Fenzonio as he commented on those of the city of Rome.[138] But medieval and early modern jurists chiseled this doctrine to a fine point. According to Baldus notaries should observe local custom when drawing up public instruments, and Farinacci also noted that contracts varied by region and city.[139] Mascardi gave as an example of conjectures that we take for granted the notion that contracts had been written in the usual or customary manner.[140] In the view of Baldus, even deeply suspicious circumstances like a missing protocol or a false claim that money had been counted could be excused by local usage.[141] Such powerful theoretical support gave the notarial profession in each Italian city considerable flexibility in the conduct of its craft. In some places their practices flew in the face of the jurists' recommendations, but even where they conformed to general principles, local notaries could determine what kind of writing materials and formats, which formularies, and what style of signature to use. Guild and city statutes restrained this freedom to be sure, and custom itself was not without constraint. Farinacci made it clear that a notary was permitted to add during the second (imbreviatura) phase in drawing up an instrument only those customary clauses most uniformly, most frequently, and most recently found in contracts.[142] If his clients wanted to depart from common practice, the notary had to be very careful about which formulas he chose.[143] Nevertheless, with their liberal invocation of custom, the jurists had handed to the local profession a small sphere of autonomy and a useful tool.

The jurists did not have much to say about the fact that notaries earned a living from making scriptura publica. Their job was to comment on the written law and to mediate between texts and society, not to explore every facet of the operations of the legal system. They did not discuss the price of public writing nor did they regard it as anomalous that a free profession produced and sold documents imbued with public authority.[144] In his notarial handbook, Baldus stated tersely that a notary could not be compelled to give an instrument to the contracting parties without receiving his fee ("sine mercede").[145] Neither he nor the other theorists reflected on the logical or moral implications of turning evidence into a financial asset, much less on the notary's ambiguous position at the interface between public credibility and personal gain. When, however, in the late fifteenth century the popes began to sell notarial offices in Rome, a process more or less complete by 1600, the economic dimension acquired more robust theoretical underpinnings. Venal notarial offices were a form of property, *bona stabilia*, just like any other office put up for sale by an early modern state. The jurists were comfortable applying the usual norms of proprietorship to the papers and title of a notary's office; by right the owner of such property could sell, mortgage, or give away both protocols and title and could bequeath them to his heirs.[146]

The concept of public writing owed much to the accumulation of definitions and debates by generations of legal scholars between the twelfth and the seventeenth centuries, but quite clearly could not be left in their hands alone. They had fashioned an influential theory of evidence and a powerful new writer, the notary, from their reading of the *Corpus iuris civilis* and the needs of the medieval Italian cities. In the interests of judicial order, however, the cities themselves, and their successor states, had to transform the rich contingencies and hypotheses of the doctors into more certain and more enforceable rules. Statute, that is the laws of guild, city, and monarch, had a great deal to say about scriptura publica and the notarial profession in Rome, as we shall see in chapter 3. However, it would be a mistake to view legal doctrine and public regulations as entirely separate, for their relationship was a subtle dialectic. On the one hand, the jurists gave language to the writers of statutes, and the writers of statutes knew they could count on ius commune to cover anything they had failed to specify.[147] On the other hand, legislators in Rome as in other Italian cities were keen to corral the often-contradictory impulses unleashed by ius commune; they wanted to pin down ambiguities and settle conflicts. The differing way the two spheres of law envisioned what should happen when parties presented documents in court illustrates the complexity of their interaction.

As we have seen, in principle the jurists regarded any kind of writing, whether scriptura publica or scriptura privata, as efficacious evidence when supported by witnesses, more witnesses in the case of scriptura privata. But how in practice was one to make evidence effective? Notwithstanding its rhetorical flourish, Farinacci's claim that the doctors thought the public instrument "had definitive force [and] ready execution," was wrong.[148] In ius commune, according to the lawyer Luca Peto, who revised Rome's city statutes for publication in 1580, the public instrument did not have "ready execution," unless a debtor declared its contents to be true before a judge and in the presence of his creditor.[149] Writing seventy years later, Fenzonio agreed.[150]

The Roman statutes, which governed the conduct of all lay inhabitants regardless of what court they appeared in, broke sharply with learned law on the manner of mobilizing written evidence, whether produced by a notary or a private individual.[151] Strongly favoring writing over its rival, witnesses, they streamlined the procedures required for obtaining judicial action on the basis of documentation. The two-step process entailed the verification (*recognitio*) of the evidence submitted to the court and the issuance of a warrant to seize the goods or person in question (*executio*). In comparison to the penitent debtor imagined by ius commune, the Capitoline tribunal practiced a rougher justice. If a plaintiff submitted a public instrument signed by two witnesses, even if they were not present at the initial transaction, and their handwriting was identified in court as authentic, the document was legally recognized.[152] The statutes extended the same privileges to scriptura privata, if it was supported by the oral testimony of three witnesses or by handwriting analysis. Once evidence was formally admitted, municipal law authorized judges to act on it (*executio*) with dispatch. With very few exceptions (like false, simulated, or usurious contracts), after a ten-day period magistrates could simply enforce the terms of written agreements, both notarial instruments and personal receipts (*apoca*), with warrants of arrest or of seizure and confiscation of property.[153] This was as close to "ready execution" as anyone could wish—indeed, far too close for the comfort of Peto and Fenzonio.

Both Peto, author of a handbook to judicial process in the Capitoline court, and Fenzonio, who had once presided over the same tribunal, knew the Roman statutes well. In distinct ways and for varying purposes, both had been called to study them closely and to interpret their meaning for others. Fenzonio wrote with assurance about how the language of statutes should be glossed, strictly, following common usage, not the spongy dicta of the jurists.[154] Yet both were troubled by the gap that had opened up between "our statutes" and ius commune. Before judicial action, Peto would have interrogated the witnesses to a public instrument rather than merely identify their handwriting.[155] Fenzonio articulated the contradiction between doctrine and statute even more explicitly and was frankly amazed at the privileges granted to personal receipts.[156] In a lengthy comment, he attempted to soften what he termed the injury done to iùs commune by Roman city law.[157] The statutes did not really mean that the adverse party could not object to the evidence submitted, he argued, and he excused their liberal attitude toward scriptura privata as an effort to stop lawsuits over small debts.[158] The reluctance that these two prominent experts showed to give up the teachings of the learned law alerts us to its enduring power to nuance the rigor of statute as well as to fill in its silences.

Another mitigating influence on local regulators as well as a constant freshet of new juridical opinion was the Roman Rota, the highest civil appeals court in the Papal States. The twelve judges of the Rota were an exception in a general legal landscape that downplayed precedent; their decisions entered into the citation circuits of the jurists, and they were sometimes asked to make determinations about notarial documents and practices.[159] Farinacci and Fenzonio both refer to Rota cases, and Fenzonio collected more than two hundred pages of Rota judgments regarding the city statutes, some with important consequences for Capitoline notaries.[160] While judges normally did not have much room to decide questions of evidence, the Rota had its preferences, which may have exercised an indirect influence on the use of scriptura publica and scriptura privata.[161] But with such considerations we are leaving the domain of theory and entering the realm of practice, the world that will occupy our attention in the chapters that follow.

We have seen how medieval and early modern jurisprudence created and elaborated the concept of public words. It is time now to meet the profession that produced, sold, and preserved scriptura publica in Rome. Notaries made a personal living from their pens, but, as we have observed, their hands were imbued with public authority. Thus, it will not come as a surprise that perhaps no other group experienced as sharply the changing structures, relations, and operations of power that transformed Rome between 1300 and 1700.

CHAPTER TWO

The Profession

Defining Urban Identities

Notaries and Rome's Governments

Roman notaries must have been there earlier, but we see them at their work for the first time only in the fourteenth century. This is late by Italian standards. It is also paradoxical in a place where Europe's earliest corps of notaries was writing for the popes by the year 600.[1] The elusiveness of Roman notaries does not end in the fourteenth century either but continues until the end of the sixteenth century. Why is this? Although scholars believe scribes (*scrinarii*), later called notaries, provided services to Romans from the eleventh century on, the first surviving notarial act dates from 1344.[2] Perhaps eighty volumes of acts from seventeen notaries are all the trecento provides in toto, despite the importance of notaries in public life in that century and the towering figure of the notary Cola di Rienzo.[3] In the fifteenth century, notarial protocols become more abundant, and we have the first fragmentary text of a set of rules or statutes for an association of city notaries.[4] Yet close study of surviving acts reveals that a formal organization of notaries existed in Rome from at least 1297, and there may have been more than a hundred active notaries practicing there in the late fourteenth century.[5] Notaries who wanted to exercise their trade in Rome had to matriculate or become a member registered with the so-called college of notaries from at least the fourteenth century. No matriculation lists have survived.[6] Of other corporate records we have only one published edict in 1582 and a series of thirteen registers that begins in 1588.[7] The first extant text of statutes for the notarial college that is complete dates from 1618.[8] The absence of those usual sources which allow construction of notarial histories in so many other Italian towns, therefore, is a fact of the Roman archives, which we can hardly afford to ignore. But, then, medieval Rome itself mirrors this strange void, for of how many other Italian cities can it be said that there are no public deliberations, tax lists, judicial records, or family journals before 1500?[9] The destinies of the city's municipal structures and its notaries were tightly interwoven, as we shall see, and they share the same close encounter with oblivion.

The man whose occupational profile we draw in this chapter lived and worked in an urban community that itself changed dramatically in the period with which we are concerned. Between 1300 and 1700, its population grew fivefold. The Rome in which the notary Cola di Rienzo pored over his Livy and tried to inspire his neighbors with the hope of recapturing the greatness of the ancients had perhaps 30,000 inhabitants.[10] Between 1550 and 1600, its population doubled to around 100,000 and, after that spurt, edged more slowly to around 140,000 by 1700.[11] Such growth decade after decade arose from the arrival in Rome of "new men," young men from the mountain districts around Rome, from the other Italian regions, and from the rest of Europe, some of whom became notaries.[12] Slow social and economic change is also part of the story. A community whose liveliest entrepreneurs in the fourteenth century raised cattle and sheep was, by the seventeenth century, a leading center of European finance dominated by bankers from Florence and Genoa.[13] An intensely local frame of reference—rustic, mercantile, and feudal all in one— gradually gave way to a cosmopolitan, refined, and increasingly hierarchical set of aristocratic ways and values. If demographic, social, and economic shifts unquestionably refashioned Rome between 1300 and 1700, what drove change was the expanding Italian power of the papacy.[14] The major agents of transformation in this era, whose impact on the notarial profession would be dramatic, were unquestionably the popes.

The popes' absence from Rome in the fourteenth century permitted the belated elaboration of municipal institutions and the earliest city statutes with their first specific directives to notaries.[15] The return of papal attention and residence after 1400 led to the creation of an overlapping and competing set of state institutions and sources of law affecting the notarial profession in Rome. Papal presence also attracted notaries from all manner of lands to new jobs in the Curia, the papal bureaucracy, thus fracturing and complicating the formal organization of notaries into guild or corporation. The Renaissance popes made of Rome a jurisdictional landscape of extraordinary complexity in which notarial employment flourished. No one limited the number of notaries who could work in Rome, and the profession was open to all who were able to meet a set of basic qualifications. If the popes were not formally responsible for the open character of the notarial profession, they nevertheless profited from it and contributed to it by their needs. And in 1586 Sixtus V (1585–90) brought it to an end, converting the last and most numerous body of city notaries, the Capitoline notaries, into venal officeholders and limiting their number to thirty. By this decisive action the papacy completed its transformation of Rome's notaries, ushering in a new era in which the social and institutional profile of the Capitoline notaries sharpened but internal divisions within the profession as a whole also widened. Whether by their absence or their presence, the popes between 1300 and 1700 played a major role in defining what it was to be a Roman notary.

The notaries with whom we are most concerned are easy to distinguish when we meet them in the world that came into being after 1586. They are the thirty Capitoline notaries, attached to the civil judges of the Capitoline curia, also known as the tribunal of the senator, which was historically the city's secular tribunal for the laity. But when our sources begin in the mid-fourteenth century and throughout the fifteenth century, there are no Capitoline notaries; there are simply notaries—or, in the more precise Latin "notarii urbis," notaries of the city of Rome. In 1507, when the popes created a separate organization for curial notaries, they introduced a new distinction into this hitherto undifferentiated professional community. The notaries of Rome were perforce divided. We hear for the first time the designation, "notaries of the Capitoline curia," that is, notaries of the tribunal of the senator and the other smaller civic and guild courts on the Capitoline Hill, to distinguish them from the notaries of the papal Curia.[16] Was there a difference, other than of employment, between Capitoline notaries and Roman notaries more generally in the sixteenth century? If there was, it is not one that available sources allow us to detect with any certainty. But even to use the phrase "Roman notaries more generally" is to beg the question of how one defined a Roman notary: by birth or by the acquisition of Roman citizenship and property, as the notarial statutes had allowed since at least 1446? Even where boundaries should have been quite clear, as between curial and Capitoline notaries, we find some sixteenth-century notaries who identified themselves as both.[17] When I use the term Capitoline notaries in reference to the period before the Sistine intervention of 1586, therefore, I mean a broadly inclusive "notaries of Rome," which after 1507 carries the added connotation of the city of Rome as opposed to the Roman Curia.

The framework of local government that conditioned the activity of Roman notaries changed profoundly but subtly over the period 1300 to 1700. It was a process marked more by accumulation and shifts of authority than by clean breaks and abrupt departures.[18] When our sources begin in the 1360s, the municipality, if such a formal designation can be given that protean entity, was the de facto ruler of Rome, though the pope in Avignon maintained a presence through a deputy. The kaleidoscopic fourteenth-century civic regimes bequeathed to the city's future government the tribunal of the senator, a foreign judge who dispensed justice from a court on the ancient Capitoline Hill, and three conservators who were elected local officials also based on the Capitol. Six judges assisted the senator, four with civil jurisdictions and two for criminal cases.[19] In the Renaissance the municipal administration of Rome emphasized more insistently its ancient descent from the Senate and Roman People (*senatus populusque romanus*) and acquired a more stable and patrician character. By the sixteenth century it was common to refer to civic magistrates and councils as simply the Roman People, the Popolo Romano, as well as by the prestigious initials SPQR. The men who composed this People were landed gentlemen, cutting their former ties to local commerce in favor of investment in state office and finance, and the lay kinsmen of well-off, educated immigrants in the Curia.[20] The complex of civic institutions and rights symbolized by the Senate and Roman People and by the Capitoline Hill, its seat, endured after the papacy reasserted its dominion in the late fourteenth century and once more resided in Rome after 1420. It received articulation in a series of partially revised city statutes in 1469, 1494, and 1521 and in a complete and final revision of 1580, as well as in numerous papal privileges. These laws in combination with the learned tradition of the jurists defined the civil and criminal procedure used in the senator's court. Yet the Romans whose interests they protected found themselves over the next four centuries constantly renegotiating the meaning and reach of their institutions with the popes, with the new magistrates whom the pontiffs gradually added, and with powerful papal relatives.

Before 1586 Roman notaries shared the municipality's political fate but with a twist. In the fourteenth century, they may have actually exercised more political influence than notaries elsewhere precisely because communal traditions were so weak in Rome.[21] Once they had to contend with the increasing interference of active monarchs in the fifteenth century, however, they seem to have drawn, or been drawn, for the next two centuries more closely under the protection and control of the Senate and Roman People.[22] In any case, historically attached to Capitoline institutions, a good many Roman notaries—we do not really know how many— worked for the senator's court and for the municipality itself between 1300 and 1600. Notaries were prominent civic leaders in the early fifteenth century and continued to hold minor municipal offices into the sixteenth century.[23] Only toward the end of our period did the sovereign's pressure finally begin to loosen the former attachment.

The sovereign began pressing in the 1390s. Confronting a city that made its own rules and judged its own disputes, the papacy chose the domain of justice as the first over which to extend its lordly grasp. Notaries felt this at once, for in Rome they not only worked for private clients but also served as court clerks (*attuarii*) or what Italians call *cancellieri*. Several decades before Martin V actually returned the papal residence to Rome, his predecessors established three Roman tribunals with authority to try cases involving the clergy and papal courtiers, insisting that the tribunal of the senator had no jurisdiction over these categories of persons. Between 1391 and 1393, it was determined that the cardinal vicar would hear cases involving clerics, the auditor of the Camera those involving ecclesiastical courtiers, and the marshal of the Holy Roman Church those involving laymen who were papal courtiers.[24] Like that of the senator, all these courts had criminal and civil jurisdiction, and their jurisdictions tended over time to expand at his expense. The cardinal vicar's became the chief local court for spiritual matters, for the laity as well as the clergy; the auditor of the Camera's tribunal grew into the most important Roman court for civil litigation, again for laymen as well as ecclesiastics.[25]

The division of justice seekers into laymen (and women) and clergy was the sharpest stake the popes drove into the heart of civic institutions, but dividing "courtiers," that is, anyone employed by the papacy, from other citizens inflicted perhaps more insidious damage. In a dispute between two citizens, if one claimed a tie to the papal court, the conflict went before judges who were not, in theory, bound by city statutes. These steps in the 1390s initiated the process by which the popes over the next two centuries fragmented jurisdiction in order to protect those persons privileged by their clerical status or service to the papacy.[26] Eventually new papal tribunals and officials not only circumscribed but competed directly with the senator's tribunal, as the popes extended the powers of their judges over laymen while prohibiting laymen from ever judging clerics. A notable competitor was the tribunal of the governor of Rome, a papal magistracy created in 1436, which was given civil and criminal jurisdiction over anyone who lived in the city.[27] At the same time, the popes moved to assert the prince's monopoly of justice, and from 1404 appointed the senator to his post as the chief magistrate of the city's main secular jurisdiction.[28] Although the popes recognized the place of the Capitoline curia in the overall judicial apparatus of the city, they aimed to reposition it within a broader "state" system.[29] The demand for actuary notaries increased overall with this proliferation of courts, but the notaries who served the senator and his corps of six Capitoline judges operated in an ever-more complex political universe.

If the popes thus intervened to create multiple new judicial identities and to layer many new "institutions of state" over older municipal institutions, they were not the only reason why there were many different courts with many attendant notaries operating in Rome. Like officials elsewhere in Europe, administrative officers in Rome, whether they served the municipality, the papal Curia, the Apostolic Camera, a cathedral chapter, or a merchant's guild, all had some power to judge disputes and thus some form of jurisdiction. On the Capitoline Hill, for example, heads of guilds called consuls held courts (*consolati*) to hear cases connected with their trades. Also on the Capitol, the street masters settled conflicts over taxes for road repairs and the *maestri giustizieri* prosecuted those who damaged vineyards. Elsewhere in the city the great religious basilicas of Rome each had a jurisdiction of their own, and, of course, some wealthy immigrant communities, such as the Florentines, did too.[30] In Rome, when acting in their capacity as judges, officials always had notaries by their side.

The Making of a Notary

Formal training in the *ars notariae*, the art of writing notarial documents, seems not to have been available in Rome; medieval schools for notaries, which existed elsewhere in Italy, have not turned up. Some learned their trade from family members, and others from more experienced notaries; in addition, the 1446 regulations of the notarial college expected candidates to have studied city law on their own while working for a notary or attorney.[31] In the early sixteenth century, city statutes had increased the length of on-the-job training for notaries of the Capitoline curia from one year to three, although this was omitted in the final redaction of 1580.[32] The 1580 legislation imposed no period of apprenticeship but did specify that candidates for matriculation know the ars notariae and the sections of the statutes relevant to notaries.[33]

In a situation where professional practice supplied instruction, young notaries must have depended heavily on special handbooks or formularies with sample contracts and examples of the legal clauses needed for drawing up wills and instruments. The production of such texts, known generically as the ars notariae, was the proud accomplishment of the Bolognese in the thirteenth century.[34] The late medieval Curia strove consciously for a distinctive style (*stilus*) in its documents, however, and some of the very earliest legal works to be printed were formularies published in Rome for the use of curial notaries.[35] These appeared in many editions in the sixteenth and seventeenth centuries. A related genre, manuals of the formulas to be used in judicial documents, also contained examples for notaries to follow.[36] The Capitoline lawyer and jurist Luca Peto published such a formulary for use in the tribunal of the senator in 1567, and it ran to five editions before 1625.[37] Although no direct evidence has yet come to light, Roman notaries' libraries, as they did elsewhere, may also have included manuscript formularies.[38] Formularies guided local contractual customs. Both the opinions of the jurists and the legislation of city and sovereign acknowledged the authority of custom, or what we might better term the local profession, regarding the technical formulas deployed in notarial documents. The jurists deferred on many counts to custom, and the legislators said virtually nothing about the wording of notarial acts. For the clauses and phrases preferred in Rome the notaries must have passed on their "style" from one generation to another in the informal manner of workshop practices.

Notaries had to know their trade, but knowledge was not enough; they also needed the power to perform their duties. Someone with the right to create notaries had to grant this authority to a would-be notary in order for him to become a bearer of public trust. In medieval Rome, the sources of such authority were pope, emperor, and (until 1435) "urban prefect," a title based on a late antique Roman official, which notaries indicated by the use of such formulas of nomination as "by the authority of the sacred Roman prefect."[39] In practice, the power to create notaries was much more dispersed than this triad might suggest for the Holy Roman Emperor granted it to so-called counts palatine who exercised their "imperial authority" liberally. So numerous in fact were counts palatine, who could be ordinary citizens or even parish priests, that in their statutes of 1446 the notarial college warned their officers to check the credentials of counts palatine who claimed to possess this privilege.[40]

The popes in no way monopolized the creation of notaries, and some years after Martin V's return in 1420 we even find the conservators, chief magistrates of the Senate and Roman People, cited as the authorizing officials for investing new notaries.[41] In his 1507 legislation that endowed a new body, the College of Scriptors, with this power, Pope Julius II imagined that he was addressing some notaries elevated by imperial authority and others by papal or "apostolic" authority.[42] Eighty years later, Pope Sixtus V was considerably more precise, naming, among those with the power to authorize new notaries in the Papal States, apostolic protonotaries, counts palatine, and cavalieri [*sic*], communities, corporate bodies, archives, and individuals possessed of what was turning out to be a not very rare privilege.[43] Roman notarial records abundantly document the creation of notaries by apostolic protonotaries in the early decades of the seventeenth century, and this may have been the most common route into the profession in the capital at that date.[44] In 1631 Pope Urban VIII, ever hopeful that he could bring the chaotic notarial profession under the control of his state officials, attempted new legislation in the Papal States, though not in Rome and Bologna. Seeking to overcome the historic division between the power to create notaries and the right to test their capacity to do their job, he assigned overall supervision of the process to the prefect of the archives, an official whom Sixtus V had put in place in 1588. The opposition of the privileged was so strident, however, that Urban had to retract his innovation the following year.[45] Not until 1679 did his successors finally succeed, at least in Rome, in imposing a uniform procedure for creating notaries.[46]

In keeping with the feudal overtones of a grant of public authority to an individual, notaries received investiture from the counts palatine who created them. A notarial document recording the concession of "pen and inkwell" to a Capitoline notary in 1458 allows us a rare glimpse of this ritual.[47] Acting on imperial authority, of which he had written proof, the count palatine symbolically struck, then kissed the notary. The notary promised to write on clean paper, to keep the contents of the acts he rogated secret until their publication, and not to write falsely. The count palatine then administered an oath sworn on the Bible.

The "pen and inkwell" ritual also included a test of the notary's knowledge, for investiture was only the first of two essential steps in producing a valid practitioner. Counts palatine and other bearers of the authority to make new notaries gave ground to the profession itself when it came to evaluating the competence of would-be notaries. In Rome, the notarial college ordered its officers to ensure that counts palatine created notaries who did not engage in manual labor and who had been "examined and judged able in Latin and who had trained for at least a year with an attorney or someone knowledgeable in the notarial art."[48] Although customs varied from city to city, some form of registration or matriculation overseen by a formal association of notaries was common in late medieval Italy. By this process, the local profession judged the level of skill and the social suitability of those who would enter it.

A matriculation list of the "college of city notaries" is mentioned in the Roman statutes of 1363, although the college's documentation itself is almost nonexistent, and the earliest description of the matriculation process dates from 1446.[49] Those who wished to matriculate must have abandoned manual labor for at least four years and must conduct themselves decently and dress soberly.[50] They must own—and have studied—a copy of the city statutes, for the officers of the notarial college expected to test candidates on local law.[51] If they were judged suitable (*idoneus*) and approved by a two-thirds vote, they were entitled to pay a matriculation fee and to be entered in the membership rolls. The 1446 regulations make it clear that, while matriculation was required to exercise the notarial profession in Rome, it was not sufficient to work for the municipal government or as a court notary in the tribunal of the senator. For these duties a notary also had to be a Roman citizen or to have a residence in Rome.[52] Although the evidence is from the sixteenth century, citizenship may not have been very difficult to acquire; unlike in other Italian cities, in Rome newcomers were expected, and accommodated.[53] The 1446 notarial statutes sought to keep Capitoline posts in the hands of those whose property attached them to the community but, at a minimum, wanted all notaries who rogated in Rome to pass muster with college officers and know city laws.

This minimum was not easy to achieve in a city to which the papal court had returned with a seemingly insatiable appetite for notaries.[54] Expanding curial employment in the later fifteenth century drew bureaucrats, secretaries, scribes, and notaries from all over Italy and from many parts of Europe to Rome; occasionally such men might also find their way to the Capitol.[55] Not all of them expected to put down roots or even to stay for long; they came on the business of an international church, and many found work precisely because of their knowledge of the foreign tongues needed in the Curia or by foreign residents. The Roman notarial college may have intended to enroll them in its ranks, but it must have seemed apparent to the popes by at least the 1470s that large numbers of foreign notaries had managed to escape this corporate discipline.

Indeed, it was not obvious why curial notaries ought to be tested on their knowledge of the municipal statutes or matriculate with the Capitoline notaries, although Romans frequently resorted to curial notaries for their ordinary needs. Seeing an opportunity simultaneously to raise money and to impose order on this throng, Pope Sixtus IV attempted in 1483 to give a monopoly of curial business to seventy-two notaries who would purchase their offices.[56] Curial notaries cut out by this limitation induced the next pope to cancel the monopoly the following year, but the Sistine mold was decidedly the shape of things to come. Over the next century, the papacy was slowly and inexorably to refashion the entire notarial profession, curial and Capitoline, into a group of haves and a group of have-nots, a small number of venal officeholders and everybody else.

Pressed for funds, Julius II, nephew to Sixtus IV, revived his uncle's failed initiative in 1507. Establishing the College of Scriptors of the Roman Curia, a body of 101 venal officials, he placed the officers of the college, all prelates, in charge of a separate matriculation procedure for curial notaries.[57] By his action he not only drew a new boundary between curial and Capitoline notaries and set up a rival notarial corporation to the college of "notarii urbis" but unwittingly provided historians with their first quantitative data about the profession, albeit its least Roman portion. Julius's directives gave the auditor of the Camera and nine other so-called correctors (*correctores*), all qualified in canon law, the authority both to create notaries and to examine them. Those approved by the officers were registered in the matriculation list of the new Archive of the Roman Curia, which the pope set up in the same legislation.[58] Henceforth, there were two distinct matriculation lists in Rome, at least until Sixtus V limited the number of Capitoline notaries in 1586. Julius II was considerably less specific about the criteria for admission than the Capitoline notaries were, leaving the matter in the capable hands of the prelates who reigned over the College of Scriptors, but his text did insist that notaries "from any nation" could matriculate. By any nation, of course, a sixteenth-century Italian would understand "from any

city," for a man from Genoa was as foreign in Rome as a native of Lyons. Matriculation did not mean entry into the College of Scriptors itself, into whose ranks only
those able to purchase one of the 101 offices could ascend. Instead, it formalized
access to the notariate for the foreigners from elsewhere in Italy and Europe in a way
that had not previously been possible. Financially, the distinction between belonging to the College of Scriptors and matriculation in the Archive of the Roman Curia
was vast, though contemporary usage sometimes conflated the two.[59]

Thousands of notaries from all over Europe matriculated in the Roman Curia in
the sixteenth century and in ensuing centuries. Although the records are incomplete
and perhaps not yet fully discovered, they spotlight a multinational array of notaries
employed by countless foreigners doing business at the Curia.[60] For the years for
which we have data spanning the period 1507 to 1809, we find the names of almost
ten thousand curial notaries.[61] Extrapolating from the partial extant series, one
scholar suggests that in the sixteenth century seven thousand curial notaries matriculated. To this number he adds five hundred or six hundred "true" curial notaries, that is, notaries who actually worked for officials of the Curia and "who were
not required to submit to the formalities of matriculation."[62] The comment alerts us
to the fact that venal officeholders did not need to matriculate and that matriculation in the Archive of the Roman Curia was the very lowest rung of the professional
ladder for foreign notaries. Curial notaries without employment in papal bureaus or
tribunals must have lived from their profession only partially and sporadically,
finding work where they could among a varied lay and clerical, Roman and foreign
clientele.[63] It is tempting to imagine that the situation was similar for notaries
matriculated in the Capitoline list before 1586.[64] Perhaps they too numbered in the
thousands over the century, and perhaps for many of them matriculation meant
simply permission to work but did not guarantee a full-time career.

In other ways, matriculation was indubitably changing its significance for Capitoline notaries. One immediate effect of the sharpened boundary drawn by Julius II
around curial notaries was a clearer definition of their civic counterparts. To be
different quickly became to be privileged when, in his first act as pontiff in March
1513, Leo X restored the lost rights of the Senate and Roman People and exempted
notaries on the Capitoline matriculation list from Julius II's archival regulations.[65]
In a more gradual process, governmental authorities grew more interested in the
matriculation registry as an instrument of control over the profession. It was not
notarial college officers but civic officials, the conservators or their secretary, who
kept the matriculation list from at least 1508 on, joined in 1562 by the archivist of the
Archivio Capitolino, the civic notarial archive instituted that year on the Capitoline
Hill. Now the volume was also to include the signature and professional symbol of

the notary who had been admitted, to facilitate the authentication of his acts if doubts were ever raised about them.[66]

During the massive editorial revision of the Roman city statutes in the 1560s and 1570s, the criteria for matriculation underwent a notable shift, conveyed in the final edition published under Pope Gregory XIII in 1580. While the need to abstain from manual labor for four years and to know Latin remained from the 1446 regulations, the 1580 text added an age minimum of twenty years and demanded that notaries be sons of respectable parents who had trained them in proper behavior.[67] The vexed status of notaries in a time of heightened sensitivity to aristocratic virtues may well have influenced some of the new language.[68] Its insistence that to matriculate in the Capitoline list notaries must be Roman citizens or residents "considered Roman citizens according to the statutes," however, bespeaks a response to the pope's college for notaries from all nations.[69] While residence or citizenship had been required to serve as a municipal notary or to write for the tribunal of the senator since 1446, it had not previously been necessary for matriculation.

Creating a professional identity for curial notaries promoted a new emphasis on Roman identity among notaries who worked for a city clientele. We should not overstate the ethnic character of Roman identity, of course. The 1580 statutes permitted foreigners who owned a house and vineyard in Rome and who lived there with their household for three-quarters of the year to apply for Roman citizenship, and evidence from the 1580s indicates that it was liberally granted.[70] At least one notary serving the Capitoline judges had worked in Rome for decades before he bothered to go through the citizenship process.[71] Yet the shift in the 1580 text registered the presence of a different and rival notarial identity, buttressed by its own institutions and regulations, which, however loose they were in reality, contributed to a stronger sense of what it meant to be a Capitoline notary—or perhaps it might be more accurate to say a more restricted sense of what it meant to be a Capitoline notary. By the late sixteenth century, the papacy had somehow, through its jurisdictional exclusions and financial ingenuity, managed to turn the notaries of Rome (*notarii urbis*) into Roman notaries (*notarii romani*). Fittingly, it was the popes who gave them their new title, notaries of the Capitoline curia (*notarii curiae capitolii*), when they terminated the matriculation process in 1586, limited their number to thirty, and sold their offices.

Within the broad context shaping their political and professional lives, the city notaries of Rome created institutions through which they defined themselves. These institutions tell us a good deal about the status and strength of notaries in Rome's fluid and dynamic society, and they reflect faithfully the force of the alteration wrought by Sixtus V in 1586. We begin with the original college of self-employed notaries that preceded this great divide, before investigating the new college that emerged after 1586 as an organization of thirty venal officeholders, sharing little more with their forebears than the Capitoline Hill and the patronage of Saint Luke.

The College of City Notaries

By the early 1300s the notaries of Rome had forged a professional association, which they maintained until 1586. Yet the shape and texture of that late medieval association, which contemporary sources called the college of city notaries (*collegium notarii urbis*), wholly eludes us. This is not immediately apparent to the researcher who consults the inventories in Rome's state archive and discovers a multivolume series of notarial protocols from the fourteenth to the sixteenth century entitled the "College of Capitoline Notaries."[72] In fact, these protocols have no special connection to the notarial college at all, having been part of a former archive established in 1562 as a repository for the papers of notaries who had died without heirs. The notaries' organization itself never bore this title given it by modern archivists, although after 1586 it did become a college in the new sense favored by early modern popes, a body of venal officials known as the notaries of the Capitoline curia. By whatever title, before 1586 the professional organization of the city notaries walked with very light footsteps, leaving only the faintest traces in the documentary record.

References to specific officers of the notarial college like rector, corrector, and chamberlain (*camerarius*) next to signatures on acts dating from 1300, 1330, and 1348 are clues to the existence of a formal organization of which we have no other sign.[73] More evidence comes from the new regime that drafted the city statutes of 1363, which granted the notarial college power to choose its officials and delegated specific tasks to these officers regarding the papers of dead notaries.[74] The legislators closely guarded the process of copying documents from notarial protocols when, after the death of the rogating notary, they reverted to the possession of his heirs. These copies, *transumpta* or *transunti* as they were called in later centuries, were not simple transcriptions of the imbreviature in the notary's protocol but extended versions in which all the proper legal formulas were fully written out and abbreviations were eliminated. The 1363 statutes put the Capitoline curia in charge of this procedure but gave the notarial college the task of designating eight notaries from whom the judge would select two to verify that the transunto was accurate.[75] They also deputed college officials, on judge's orders, to remove any forced contract from the protocol of a deceased notary.[76] These fragments do not shed light on the inner workings of the notarial association in fourteenth-century Rome, but they take for granted that that there was such a body capable of work.

Our richest source before 1586 is another fragment. It describes itself as "other articles, orders, and revisions" to the statutes of the notarial college and follows the municipal statutes of 1469 in a unique manuscript transcribed at the city's orders in 1486.[77] This codex was the Senate and Roman People's official copy of its laws until the printing of a new compilation between 1519 and 1523. Although the revisions to the notarial statutes are dated 1446, we do not know when the statutes that they purport to revise were written and no text of these statutes survives. This is not the only allusion to notarial college statutes; the 1580 city statutes also refer to this ghostly document or documents.[78] The missing statutes may someday come to light, but their absence must be considered a part of the college's pre-1586 history. In Rome, even before Julius II divided up the notarial profession in 1507, city notaries could not have found it easy to conceive, express, or impose their collective will. Although they contain four rubrics taken over from the 1363 city statutes, the 1446 revisions are the first, and last, that we have that originate from the college before the 1580s. It was government, city and papal, not the profession, that was largely responsible for the increasingly intensive regulation of notaries in the fifteenth and sixteenth centuries. And it is a fine point to determine how independent the 1446 revisions could have been if we know of them only through a copy preserved by municipal authorities.[79]

By comparison to organizations of notaries in places like Bologna, Florence, Milan, and Genoa, the Roman college was weak, even before the popes created a rival association in 1507.[80] While there was no palace of notaries in Rome, and the city government obviously kept a close watch on the profession, organizational weakness was not necessarily an entirely bad thing for men who wanted to be notaries. The matriculation process, as we have seen, put only the modest social hurdle of not having done manual labor for four years in the path of aspirants and demanded no more training than one could acquire in a year's apprenticeship. There were no limits on the numbers who could practice and no requirement that they be Romans. The notarial profession was open in Rome. Easy access did come at a price, however, which was the powerlessness of notaries to defend their collective interests when they were threatened. The fourteenth-century municipal regime, in which notaries rose to public prominence and received laws favorable to the profession, gave way in the fifteenth and sixteenth centuries to a civic administration and a monarch more concerned to police notaries than protect them.

Yet the admittedly fragile evidence of corporate self-government, the revisions to the lost statutes of the college, do allow a unique glimpse of what mattered to the college of city notaries in 1446, and perhaps in following decades. Five notarial officers and a local lawyer or consistorial advocate, Andrea Santacroce, authored the text, they said, because divine light diffused to men through the writers of the Gospels put notaries under a special obligation to produce trustworthy documents, and many neglected this duty.[81] They wanted "to set in order the customary practices of the notarial office" so that anyone who intended to exercise that office would know how he must conduct himself, and so that their patron, the Gospel writer Saint Luke, would be honored and glorified.[82] The first decree, therefore, was that every October all notaries, all holders of law degrees, and all Capitoline judges and procurators (attorneys) would celebrate mass together on the feast of Saint Luke in the Church of Santa Maria in Aracoeli, with the college providing the candles.

The selection of Saint Luke as protector was not unusual for notaries; Saint Luke was also the patron saint of the guild of judges and notaries in Florence.[83] More informative perhaps was the choice of Santa Maria in Aracoeli for their yearly festivities. The Aracoeli was a Franciscan church and convent on the Capitoline Hill next to the palace where the senator held court and across from the Palace of the Conservators, the elected municipal magistrates. It was also the place where the fifteenth-century notarial college had its meetings, and where the notaries proposed to store the papers of their colleagues who had died without heirs. Because the Aracoeli was ritually associated with the Senate and Roman People, the notaries' location there situated them at the symbolic center of civic representation. Hosting a compulsory feast for all municipal legal professionals showed that the notarial college identified itself very closely indeed with the judicial activity that went on next door in the halls of the senator's palace.[84]

On Saint Luke's holy day, the college assembled in the chapter room of the Aracoeli convent to elect new officers. The text does not go into electoral details but indicates that some kind of *bussola*, or scrutiny system, operated because what it does say is that electors called *imbussolatori*, chosen by the assembly for four-year terms, should organize the election.[85] A bussola was the Roman term for a common electoral procedure in late medieval and early modern Italy in which designated electors drew up a list of approved candidates for office from which officeholders were then selected by lot. In Rome it was not unusual for collectivities, whether municipality, guild, or confraternity, to say very little about electoral procedures in their statutes, presumably so that they could be altered more freely. In its evasiveness about elections, the notarial college followed the codes of its broader community.

Although the statutes do not provide the number or titles of all the officials, they reveal that two "proconsuls," voted only by the officers, headed the college. The proconsuls were to call a meeting of the notaries on the last Sunday of every month and read the statutes aloud to them.[86] They had jurisdiction over "the men of the corporation" (*homines universitatis*)" and judged conflicts between them and outsiders in their tribunal in the senator's palace.[87] The proconsuls had the right to fine men of the corporation and also those who, like counts palatine, created notaries without the proper qualifications.[88] Along with officials called correctors and other unnamed officers, they tested candidates for matriculation on their Latin grammar and knowledge of municipal law and decided whether to admit them to the exercise of the notariate in Rome.[89] Together with the correctors, the proconsuls assisted the senator, whom we recall was a foreign magistrate appointed by the pope, in the delicate task of assigning specific notaries to the benches of Capitoline judges.[90] In late spring, during the week of the feast of Corpus Christi, the proconsuls and officers reviewed the notaries' annual volumes of acts to make sure they were put together properly and stamped them with the insignia of the college.[91] The 1446 statute revisions gave the proconsuls, correctors, and scribe (*scriptor*) of the college the task of protecting the protocols of notaries who had died, with the correctors to hold one of the keys to the locked chests in which these volumes were now to be placed for safekeeping. The officers could be penalized for being negligent in this duty, but they could themselves levy heavy fines on heirs who presented them with incomplete volumes and could share in the proceeds.[92]

The 1446 legislation emphasized the notarial college's determination to improve the writing and archival practices of notaries, both when they served a private clientele and when they sat in civil court. It contained important innovations, some of which admittedly were later abandoned and some probably not well enforced. The meager archival record makes it difficult to judge this effort to set the practices of the profession in order as a success. Yet the college's failure was not in its vision but in its enforcement mechanisms, a sign of its deeper impotence to control the conditions of notarial labor in Rome.

The information that the text supplies about the governance of the college must be read against this underlying corporate weakness. This is an association of officers. Within the restricted circle of the officers, few offices or duties are depicted with any precision, and of course the manner of selecting the officials is passed over in silence. Although it provided candles on the feast of Saint Luke, the college seems to have had no revenues. The text makes no mention of a treasurer or chamberlain, although notaries who matriculated did have to pay a matriculation fee, and that money must have gone somewhere. The officers divide up the fines. The relationship of officials to the generality of notaries is sharply hierarchical. Members are summoned to monthly meetings to hear the rules read aloud, and they attend a church service together once a year. Otherwise, they go before college officials when they sit for the matriculation exam, when they submit their volumes to be stamped annually, and when they bring charges against another notary or defend charges against themselves. Although it is true that the 1446 revisions are a fragment of a lost set of statutes, the fragment points to an organization possessed of few resources and composed of a small group of active leaders and, not surprisingly, a loose, poorly disciplined body of followers. Such a description makes the Roman notaries quite different from those of Bologna or Milan, but it may not distinguish them much from other professional and artisan guilds in late medieval and early modern Rome.

Although the college of city notaries has not left any other documentation, or at least none yet discovered, city laws and papal edicts from the sixteenth century record traces of its officers.[93] These are quite literally traces, perhaps a half-dozen individual names and a few miscellaneous references to titles. Two correctors participated in the city statute reforms of 1521, and two others emitted a printed edict in 1582.[94] The office of proconsul, evidently still at the apex of the college, seems to have been elevated out of the notarial ranks altogether and filled by the upper branch of the legal profession, lawyers who called themselves *advocatus*, not *procuratoris*.

The proconsuls and correctors appear to have transformed their role in the approval of court notaries for the Capitoline curia from advisers of the senator to equal partners. A directive alleged to date from circa 1508 and published in 1521 insisted that no actuary notary could sit at the bench "unless delegated by the senator, proconsuls, and correctors and other pro tempore officials of the said college and without their written authorization."[95] Judicial reforms undertaken by Pius IV in 1562 referred obscurely to a continuing important role for the correctors, although they hint that a bussola or sortition process was involved in the assignments.[96]

The conservators took charge of the notarial archive created at civic initiative in 1562, and the founding legislation for this new Archivio Capitolino made no mention of the college of city notaries. Yet it did give tasks in the administration of the archive to college officers, notably the correctors and their notary, which suggest that they were perceived as dependable bureaucrats.[97] They were to keep one of several registers of the fees paid for copies made of archive documents; they were to give receipts for any fees they collected; and they were to determine the fee to charge for it if the copy was very long. These archive regulations also required the notary of the correctors to sign the documentary inventories that heirs of notaries had to turn in and to record which instruments had been copied. It was a modest beginning to what would become over time a much closer connection to the archive.

In revisions to the city statutes in 1494, a significant alteration to the procedure for producing transunti, the extended copies of instruments in the protocols of deceased notaries, gave notarial officials a financial stake in this process for the first time. Since 1363 the college had been responsible for providing a list of eight notaries who could, under judicial supervision, verify that a document from a dead notary's protocol had been properly copied. The owners of the protocol, the notary's heirs, earned income from the transunto, as did the notary who actually made it, but the judge was explicitly prohibited from receiving anything for his role, and nothing was provided to the two notaries whom he had chosen to check the copy's accuracy. The statute revision of 1494 cut the share of the transunto fee that went to the heirs by one-third, and ordered that the remaining third be divided among the notary who did the transunto, the correctors of the notarial college who verified it, and the judge who gave the order.[98] Although the amounts might not seem significant to us, transunti fees loomed large in the post-1586 world of the Capitoline notaries. It seems likely that their interest can be traced back to this legislation of 1494, which placed them at odds with the heirs in a struggle that would go on for much of the next century.

The safeguards required for an authentic transunto must have seemed irksome to heirs and clients alike. After all, they interposed a judge and the notarial college between those who possessed the instruments and those who wanted copies, with all the attendant delays and expenses middlemen always caused. It was much simpler to locate and pay the owner of the protocol and hire a notary to make the transunto, although this meant no one checked its accuracy. Civic reformers fought this abuse, denouncing in legislation of 1521 "many who acquire the privilege of making transunti of instruments from the protocols of dead notaries without observing the necessary formalities."[99] Complaints obviously continued because in the 1550s Pope Julius III intervened in defense of the "jurisdictions" of the Capitoline notarial college in the face of heirs who ignored the statutory transunto procedure.[100] This was an unusual example of papal support for the privileges of the college, that is, of its officers' right to a percentage of the transunto fees.

It is true that in 1562 when the conservators, on behalf of the municipality, sought to take physical possession of the protocols of dead notaries from the heirs and place them in the Archivio Capitolino, they said nothing about a judge or notarial officials. Instead they permitted the archivist to make transunti and promised heirs "the whole fee" from copies.[101] They did not maintain this posture, however, for the 1580 statutes upheld the meticulous observation of the transunto formalities dating back to 1363 and 1494. Not surprisingly a subsequent edict of the notarial college officers in 1582 did too.[102] The 1580 statutes specified how the judge and officials would divide up their third of the transunto fee, which was the same price charged for a public copy from a living notary. The judge issuing the order and the scribe (or archivist) who actually made the copy each received fifteen bolenenos (baiocchi), the notary of the correctors received half that amount, and the "residuum" went to the correctors to be used for the "fees and expenses of the college."[103]

The decade of the 1580s was a watershed for the Capitoline notaries, who found their traditional ways of working changed drastically by the introduction of venality by Sixtus V in 1586. Though there is no evidence to suggest that anyone knew what was coming before the papal election of 1585, something was stirring in the world of the Roman notaries in these years. The footprints deepen a bit, and we have a few more sources on the notarial college, even rare words from its officials. The edition of the city statutes published in 1580 broke sharply with legislative habit in Rome and provided a global revision of the laws that had accumulated since 1363. It also altered the composition of the tribunal of the senator, a focal point for the college of city notaries.[104] The process of revising and publishing the statutes may have reflected a deeper activism on the part of the local landed classes, whose members identified themselves with the Senate and People of Rome, or it may have prompted greater civic and corporate self-awareness. Whatever the reason, in the early 1580s the notarial college took a few steps out of its almost complete obscurity.

The 1580 city statutes, in a logic prepared for centuries, contained a full range of rules for notaries, though some of these had first appeared as self-regulation by the college. Just as the 1446 legislation of the college had incorporated several provisions verbatim from the city statutes of 1363, the 1580 edition took over the text of 1446 with only a few, albeit significant, modifications. The new city laws retained the college governance, matriculation procedure, notarial dress, and forbidden recreations of old, adding a prohibition on carrying a sword.[105] The notaries still hosted an annual mass on the feast of Saint Luke for the city's legal profession. There was somewhat more precision about titles of officers, though not their mode of election; proconsuls, correctors, a notary of the correctors, and syndics would serve the college.[106] As we have seen, the correctors now handled finances, keeping the college's share of the transunti fees and spending them on gifts of wax for the eminent guests at the Saint Luke's festival.

The 1580 legislation granted the notaries the power to draft their own statutes, subject to approval like other Roman guilds by the conservators and senator. It departed strikingly from those they had drafted in 1446, however, in adding judicial oversight where college officers had previously acted on their own. In the tribunal, where the proconsuls had enjoyed the right to pass judgment in conflicts within the profession and between notaries and outsiders, they could now hear cases only if a Capitoline judge also participated.[107] The text indicates that proconsuls and correctors exercised this jurisdiction together but understates the legal presence because it does not say that by this time the proconsuls were in fact lawyers, not notaries. It was the custom in early modern Rome for guilds to have courts to decide controversies relating to their trade, but it was unique for lawyers and judges to play such a large role in them. Similarly, in matters that seemed strictly professional, for example, how much a lengthy court document would cost to copy, the correctors made the decision along with the judge in the case.[108] Despite the fact that the fifteenth-century text was the first to give close attention to the writing notaries did in court, judges were not as pervasive in the 1446 statutes as they were in 1580. The new city laws leave the unmistakable impression that the judiciary was now more interested in what the Capitoline notaries were doing. Perhaps that was why they required the proconsuls, correctors, and senator to make a "rigorous" background check of "the way of life and morals" of any Roman notary wishing to serve in the Capitoline curia.[109]

The other notable difference from earlier regulations was the notarial college's expanding role in the operations of the Archivio Capitolino. While the founding legislation gave the correctors little more to do than sign transunti receipts, the 1580 statutes record their supervision of the entire process by which the dead notary's papers arrived safely in the archive.[110] Clearly, the city magistrates had discovered that they could not make a notarial archive work without the participation of the notarial college. And the college, profiting from the greater certainty of collecting its portion of the income from copies kept in an archive, pitched in, a fact recognized in this legislation.

The most persuasive sign of the greater vigor of the college after the new city statutes is a printed edict from the proconsuls and correctors dated 16 December 1582, the only known edict they ever published.[111] Because the action of emitting proclamations was in itself a well-recognized claim to authority in early modern politics, their published orders bespoke the officials' stature within the Capitoline arena. If we were to judge what mattered most to college officers at this point in history from a unique document, and we have so few sources we can hardly do otherwise, it would be the archive and the court. With its half-dozen commands to archivists and heirs of notaries, the printed edict confirmed the notarial college's de facto jurisdiction over the Archivio Capitolino. With an equal number of directives addressing the conduct of notaries and their staff in the senator's tribunal, it proclaimed the college's power to discipline judicial writing. Two duties added since 1580 made the correctors responsible for approving the *sostituti*, notarial employees often seen acting for their bosses in the Capitoline curia, and for checking annually the bound volumes of judicial documents notaries produced at the benches.[112] At the same time, the college's edict repeatedly invoked the authority of the city statutes, treating them as the final word on how Roman notaries behaved and wrote. The higher profile of notarial college officers meant not the independence of the professional body, therefore, but its dependence on the Senate and Roman People and its subordination within, and contribution to, the machinery of Capitoline justice.

If this hypothesis is correct, we can better understand how the college of city notaries had slowly become the college of Capitoline notaries. An article of the 1580 city statutes informed notaries that they had three choices if they wanted to work in their profession in Rome: to matriculate on the Capitol, to matriculate in the Curia, or to serve another Roman court.[113] For those like Ottaviano Saravezzio, who in 1584 inscribed the initials O.S.N.C., "Ottaviano Saravezzio Capitoline Notary," beneath his professional symbol at the beginning of his protocol, the choice of an identity was clear.[114] In a city where jurisdiction was so fragmented, no professional body could monopolize employment. By the 1580s the college certainly understood that what strength it had lay in its relationship to the tribunal of the senator.

The Thirty Capitoline Notaries
Foundations, 1586–1612

On 29 December 1586 Sixtus V limited the number of notaries serving the two civil judges in the tribunal of the senator to thirty and announced the sale of these offices for five hundred scudi apiece. The pope's legislation created a college, as the new corps of venal officeholders was called, of Capitoline notaries endowed with an array of privileges to entice buyers.[115] With his one stroke, Sixtus set aside the centuries-old traditions of the city notaries and nullified those portions of the municipal statutes that supported them. The possibility of matriculating as a Roman notary vanished along with the former notarial college and its officers.[116] Sixtus, a famously activist administrator, transformed the conditions of labor for the majority of city notaries and laid the foundations of a new identity for the fortunate few. Yet changes of the magnitude Sixtus envisioned could not be fully enacted overnight. It took more than twenty years for the market to absorb their implications, and during that period his successors in effect renegotiated their terms with the notaries. Only after two decades of testing by the new Capitoline notaries was the legal and economic infrastructure that would support their future existence completed.

Within two months of Sixtus V's election on 24 April 1585, rumors began circulating that he was going to reduce the number of Capitoline notaries to twelve, but the Senate and Roman People seem not to have heard about it until early January 1586.[117] Then they learned that the decision was a fait accompli, and the pope had already expedited the *motu proprio* that would result in the sale of all the notarial offices in their civil courts. Despite the bleak prospects, the conservators led a delegation of citizens to Sixtus to protest the interference and to induce him to cancel it in exchange for a financial contribution to the papal bread bank, the Annona. For almost eight months it looked as if their efforts had succeeded, but in August the conservators reported again to the civic councils that the pontiff wanted to turn the Capitoline notaries into twenty-six venal posts to be sold for five hundred scudi each. They hardly needed to add that they saw his action as harmful both to individual notaries and to the Roman People, that is, the municipality, but when it was not possible to halt it, they were more successful at cutting a deal for the latter than the former. In November the pope agreed to pocket only the initial proceeds himself and to donate subsequent sale revenues to the Roman People in order to reduce the civic debt. Municipal resistance overcome, the final orders for the sale of thirty offices were issued at the end of the following month.

Although there was no reason to predict the seizure of the Capitoline notarial offices by Sixtus V in 1586, it did not occur entirely in a vacuum. Venality in the Curia was a long established custom by this time, which peaked under Sixtus V.[118] Moreover, the first papal attempts to sell non-notarial offices in the Capitoline administration went back at least to the pontificate of Sixtus IV.[119] The Senate and Roman People resented such assaults and fought to get their offices back when a new pope was elected, but a pattern of papal depredation of the municipality certainly existed. Sales of notarial offices were also nothing new. Beginning with Sixtus IV the popes had put notarial offices in the Curia up for sale, as we have seen, and in what has been called the first major effort at reform of the notariate in 1556 Paul IV sold all the criminal notarial offices in the Papal States.[120] Then, too, only a few years later Pius IV imposed a cap of twenty on the number of notaries serving the senator's tribunal, though we lack evidence of its enforcement.[121] Before Sixtus V, however, no pope had extended his reach so far and so decisively into the operations of the city notaries.

Like Julius, Sixtus V had tremendous ambitions for the papacy, which impelled him to search creatively for revenues and to ignore the protests of those reluctant to provide them. He was also an audacious governor on many fronts, not the least of which was his complete reorganization of the departments of the Curia, whose modern structure still owes much to his innovations.[122] Although his motives in transforming the Capitoline notaries into venal officeholders were financial, Sixtus slammed his full apostolic power down on other notaries too, fearing that poorly drawn and badly kept notarial documents could unravel the fragile tissue of society. Having made several attempts to set up ecclesiastical archives, in September 1588 he instituted the first public notarial archives throughout the Papal States, except for Rome and Bologna.[123] The new order that Sixtus imposed on the city notaries of Rome, therefore, participated in his broader vision of government and justice, and of the sacrifices he felt his subjects ought to make for it.

In certain key respects Sixtus's intervention assimilated the Capitoline notaries to the notaries of the papal tribunals, redefining them essentially as writers of judicial acts, *actuarii* in the technical terminology, or court notaries. He declared that fifteen notaries would be assigned to each of the two civil judges of the Capitoline court.[124] These judges were known as the first and second *collaterali*, and together they handled all the litigation before the senator's tribunal. Their jurisdiction extended over all laymen resident in Rome who were not connected to the papal court and all civil matters, including dowry agreements, wills, and the guardianship of minors.[125] In redefining the Capitoline notaries as court notaries, Sixtus did not assume they would only serve litigants, but undoubtedly expected that they would also rogate business acts, like contracts and wills, for a private clientele. His objective was to sell these notarial offices, so it was not at all in his interest to restrict their sources of income. Thus, the thirty Capitoline notaries could operate a normal nonjudicial notarial business and enjoy the exclusive right to produce the documents needed for lawsuits in the senator's tribunal. He also permitted them to work for guild tribunals.

If these moves paralleled those of his predecessors long accustomed to selling curial offices, in some respects Sixtus preserved, and in fact solidified, the distinctiveness of the Capitoline notaries. Because the pope saw the thirty Capitoline notaries as so many investment units, he allowed purchasers to put in place substitutes capable of doing a notary's work. In order to exercise some control over the skills of these substitutes, however, he had to give the profession a role, and for this purpose he established a formal association or college of the notaries actually exercising the thirty offices. The pontiff assigned them the task of examining, approving, and swearing in substitutes, that is, notaries like themselves. The college also had the right to decide on rules for its governance, subject to review by the collaterali judges, to have officers with new names like *decano* and *mensario*, to use an official seal, and to make records.[126] A more robust association of Capitoline notaries than had ever previously existed would spring from these rudimentary beginnings in the Sistine legislation.

In an odd, and perhaps not entirely coincidental, reflection of precisely the two main interests of the old notarial college that he had abolished—tribunal and archive—Sixtus donated the Archivio Capitolino to the new college. To the chagrin of the city magistrates, he gave the notaries the "total care, rule, and administration" of the archive that had once belonged to the Roman People, and would again under later pontiffs.[127] In place of the oversight of the abolished correctors, transunti from the archive would now need to be verified by two notaries in the college, one from each of the two collaterali. The pope also decreed that the documents of notaries who had lost their jobs because of his legislation go to the Archivio Capitolino after they died.[128]

Sixtus tried to drape the college in some of the trappings of prestige that were supposed to count for much in the public life of Rome. Like curial officials, the thirty Capitoline notaries would receive gifts of wax from the pope at the annual feast of the purification of the Virgin; they would enjoy the privileges of Roman citizens and a place in processions ahead of other notaries. More substantially, the pope gave the college an income, or rather several sources of revenue, to be pooled in a common fund (*massa*) and shared among members. The college had the right to collect from its thirty member notaries one-quarter of the fees they were paid for judicial acts and one-quarter of the transunti fees from instruments they held in their offices. It was also owed one-third of the transunti fees from instruments kept in the Archivio Capitolino, and the entire fee for transunti of judicial acts that had found their way to the Archivio Capitolino.[129] In addition, Sixtus gave the college the proceeds of the office of notary of the *maestri giustizieri*, the civic vineyard tribunal.[130] Each month a college officer was to distribute the combined total of massa equally among the thirty notaries. Finally, the pope bestowed two forms of judicial privilege upon the thirty Capitoline notaries. He promised the college the convenience of summary justice by the senator's tribunal should it be sued, and he significantly raised the bar for removing a notary from a civil case from that specified in the 1580 city statutes.[131]

These trappings seasoned the goods to advance the pope's financial goal of adding fifteen thousand scudi to his treasury. Once purchased from the papal Datary, buyers could treat Capitoline notarial offices as they treated other forms of nonmovable property, including leasing them, reselling them, or, in the famous Roman device of the *società d'ufficio*, breaking them up into portions and selling the portions to partners. Sixtus's legislation explicitly permitted sales to foreigners and minors. Sales of offices in Rome took one of two forms: they were either *vacabile*, in which case the government had continuing rights to sell them once they had been vacated by death or resignation, or *non vacabile*, in which case they were fully the property of the purchaser, who could pass them on to his heirs at death. The complex politics of his seizure of this particular city asset, however, meant that Sixtus had to devise a more complicated ownership formula. He declared the thirty offices of the Capitoline notaries non vacabile for three years, and then partially vacabile after that.[132]

The motives for such a policy may be clearer than the mechanics. Buyers paid more for offices that were fully heritable, and initial sales by the Datary could be expected to be brisk. But the pope had promised the Roman People a share in the plunder of the Capitoline notaries. By making future sales of the offices, actually one-half of each office, vacabile, Sixtus intended to ensure a continuing revenue stream to the municipality. Perhaps without intending it, he had now also made shopping for notarial offices dependent on the favor of the conservators.[133] Indeed, if we can trust the story told by the owners of office 18 in 1591, in the era before venality their grandfather had received his Capitoline notarial office from the pope.[134] By selling them off, Sixtus may actually have shifted patronage resources from the papacy to civic officials.

In consequence, the pontiff was forced to treat the Capitoline notaries somewhat differently from the venal notaries in the papal and ecclesiastical courts, whose offices tended to end up as vacabile, meaning ownership reverted to the state treasury. This distinction deepened in October 1612 when, perhaps at the prodding of the Capitoline notaries themselves, Pope Paul V (1605–21) offered even more favorable terms to purchasers of Capitoline notarial offices. Paul declared the thirty offices fully non vacabile, that is, entirely the property of the purchaser or purchasers, to be sold, resigned, and bequeathed at will.[135] Now the market, not patrons, would determine who acquired these posts. The pope ordered the conservators to grant letters patent for an office whenever they were asked, upon payment of "the usual regaliis," and told the papal Datary to expedite the concession under the same conditions.[136]

If there were any doubts that after 1612 purchasers had complete liberty to do as they pleased with their Capitoline notarial offices, they were put to rest by a decision of the Papal State's highest appellate court in 1620. The Roman Rota confirmed that not even the popes could interfere with the free exchange of this particular commodity.[137] The papal concession of 1612 was a fateful turn of events for the Capitoline notaries. The freedom buyers now enjoyed to trade in Capitoline offices turned out to be a mixed blessing, if a blessing at all, for the notaries themselves. It challenged the cohesion of their nascent professional association and, in the long run, undermined their bargaining power with the papacy. But however ambiguous a privilege, it would condition their existence profoundly for the next 234 years.[138]

In early modern Rome even free property came with strings attached. Sixtus had promised the Roman People some of the income from office sales, and Paul V did not forget the city's needs. He ordered the college to pay from the monthly massa 400 scudi a year to the municipality for the upkeep of the two Capitoline palaces, the senator's palace where their court sessions were held, and the Palace of the Conservators where the archive was located.[139] At the same time he confirmed a decision apparently made by the notaries in 1604 that required a minimum massa contribution of 1.50 scudi (15 giulii or 150 baiocchi) a month.[140] The pope specified that if their individual judicial fees and transunti did not equal that amount, the Capitoline notaries had to provide it from their other income.[141] Massa were in effect like feudal dues; they were charges upon the income of the offices, which owners had no choice but to pay, despite their full and free possession of their property. Investment in the Capitoline offices thus resembled investments not only in the countless venal offices of the Curia but also in Roman real estate, so frequently encumbered by *censi* or mortgages and dues of various sorts.

It did not take long for the market to respond to Paul V's restructuring of the municipality's share in the Capitoline offices, and within a few years it was clear that making them non vacabile had succeeded perhaps too well. Buyers and sellers behaved with such complete freedom that new papal orders in November 1617 complained that no one was bothering to notify officials when an office changed hands.[142] There was also the small matter of those fees owed to the conservators and to the papal Datary for required paperwork that buyers and sellers were ignoring.

Paul V regarded the notarial college as the proper tool to enforce the mechanisms by which he had planned to keep civic and papal officials informed about who actually held title to the thirty Capitoline offices. So in this intervention of 1617 he required the college to pay for forty-six copies of his orders and to deliver them personally to twenty notaries, two-thirds of the membership, who had failed to go through the proper steps in gaining title.[143] The pope gave purchasers of Capitoline notarial offices two weeks from the date of the instrument of sale to notify the college mensario and two months to pay what they owed to the conservators and the Datary or face a huge fine of three hundred gold ducats.[144] The new regulations make quite clear therefore that neither the college nor the authorities exercised any control over the sale itself.

Because the premise of venality was that anyone could own an office regardless of whether he or she was capable of exercising it, it had surprised no one that many of the hundred posts in Julius II's College of Scriptors, for example, ended up in the hands of institutions and women.[145] Similarly, Sixtus had spoken openly of foreigners and minors acquiring the Capitoline offices. Having made the offices completely the property of their owners, Paul V confronted the fundamental contradiction of venality, that it was very difficult to keep track of owners, and even harder to know, let alone discipline, those to whom they contracted or subcontracted the duties of office. The pontiff understood this. In his massive reform of the papal and civic courts in 1612, he had commanded that anyone who wanted to lease, rent, or turn over a notarial office to an administrator must have written papal permission and the approval of the individual by the judges of the tribunal in question.[146] Despite the language of buyers and sellers in his orders to the Capitoline notaries in 1617, therefore, Paul was more interested in identifying the notary in whose name the office was to operate, the titleholder, than the actual owner or owners.[147] It was the titleholder who was of greatest interest to the notarial college, too, as it struggled to collect the money needed each year to ensure free sales of the thirty Capitoline offices. It was essential to know who owed contributions to the common fund, and the distribution among the colleagues of the new member's fifteen-scudi entry fee was not unwelcome either.[148]

How much influence did the college exercise over the choice of suitable men? The Sistine legislation stated that it was to examine, approve, and swear in those presented by the owners. By contrast, Paul's 1612 judicial reforms made the "superiors" in the relevant tribunals responsible for approving their own court notaries. The Capitoline notaries' first extant statutes (1618) since Sixtus had imposed venality failed to mention the judges and implied that their own role was decisive.[149] They listed four necessary steps for admission, the first of which was for the notary to gain the approval of the college for his "way of life, habits, trustworthiness, and suitability."[150] The insistence on this last point in their revised statutes of 1652 suggested that it may not have been happening, as did the new fines they threatened for signing a document in the name of a notary who had not been formally admitted.[151] The text of 1652 emphasized that applicants must come in person and that the college could reject them, unless of course they were the sons or heirs of predecessors.[152] While we lack the meeting minutes for the early seventeenth century that would allow us a glimpse of how the college vetted would-be titleholders, we do have evidence that some complied, at least with the last three steps in the procedure. They obtained letters patent from the conservators and apostolic letters from the Datary and submitted these documents to the college's mensario.[153] They also paid their admission fee.[154] It must remain an open question, however, how much actual control the college exercised over who would become a Capitoline notary in the era of venal office holding.

Some of the men who belonged to the notarial college in the early seventeenth century owned their offices outright, but most probably did not. As we shall see in chapter 5, we find these thirty offices defined by every conceivable type of business arrangement, lease, partnership, salary, and hybrids of these. At times, the relationship between those who contracted to do the work of a Capitoline office and the notary in whose name it operated cannot even be determined. It was this diverse and shifting raw material that had to sustain a college of the notaries of the Capitoline curia in the new era of venality. Moreover, collegial life was not a luxury but a necessity, especially after 1612. The inexorable obligation to provide those four hundred scudi each year to the municipality gave the titleholders no other choice. But the Capitoline notaries had not needed the impulse of the liberation of their offices in 1612 to urge forward their professional association. The college's documentary record, though thin, begins in 1588, just two years after Sixtus's radical intervention, and, although no statutes of the fledgling association survive before 1618, that record leaves no doubt of their collective activity. The venal Capitoline notaries apparently lost no time in building up the structures they felt they needed to defend their professional interests.

Structures, 1586–1674

Not until 1652, when the thirty Capitoline notaries revised the rules of their common governance for the second time in forty years, did they show much interest in the records of their collegial life. At that time they ordered copies of the privileges and legislation of the college to be inventoried and deposited in a special locked chest.[155] The gesture signaled that they knew they had a history, albeit one that began only in 1586, and that if they wished to have a future they would need the documents to prove it. It is puzzling that notaries, professionals who made their living by preserving memory, should have come so late to this awareness, which sank in slowly over their first six decades. How slowly is suggested by an archive, which, though admittedly richer than that left by the college of city notaries, is sparse. The first extant statutes of the new college (1618) survive in a unique and much damaged manuscript and the second set (1652) only in later editions, one from around 1711 and the other from 1831.[156] In addition to the two statutes from the first half of the seventeenth century, we have thirteen other volumes dating from 1588 to 1833.[157] The earliest are six registers of the collection of massa contributions, which with many lacunae begin in 1588 and cease in 1681.[158] We know that the college's secretary took down the resolutions of the monthly meetings in a separate volume, but we do not have these meeting records before 1667.[159] To put it another way, from the first ninety years of the college's life, we have only what amount to intermittent treasurer's accounts and, of course, the statutes of 1618 and 1652.

Yet these sources do tell us something about the resources and vexations of the Capitoline notaries in the formative period of their association, their sense of identity, their relations with different centers of power in baroque Rome, and their collective direction. What they do not tell us is also instructive. Unlike those of their fifteenth-century forebears, the seventeenth-century statutes are silent about their members' work. As we shall see in subsequent chapters, governments so thoroughly dominated public discourse about the Roman notaries' two most important activities, writing and preserving records, that these texts had little to say about the documents their offices produced. The sources are eloquent, nonetheless, about what it took for the Capitoline notaries to survive, even as privileged notaries, in the complex interface they inhabited between tribunal and market, authorities and clients.

THE EARLIEST YEARS, 1586–1618

Sixtus V had told the notaries in 1586 that they could write statutes to govern their collective life, subject to approval by their judges.[160] Is it possible that they waited thirty years to do so? I think not, though we do not have them, and we have only one or two oblique references gesturing to their existence.[161] However, a close reading of the two earliest massa account books covering the period 1588 to 1607 leaves no doubt of a group that, though feeling its way in many respects, could act forcefully. The college of notaries of the Capitoline curia might be new, but it appears to have come into the world expecting combat and prepared to mobilize all the political resources available in early modern Rome to advance its agenda. If these resources did not include written rules for self-government, the notaries managed themselves with unusual discipline and effectiveness.

The thirty Capitoline notaries did not like something—unfortunately, we do not know exactly what—in the legislation that Sixtus had written establishing their venal offices. They may have begun agitating to change it while the pope was still alive, but they won their point almost immediately after he had died in August 1590. The official "correction" to the Sistine orders came within weeks of the election of the short-lived Pope Gregory XIV (1590–91).[162]

The common Roman political dynamic in which the legislation of one pontiff was undone by his successors worked to the disadvantage of the Capitoline notaries in the case of the Archivio Capitolino, however. The conservators, the civic officials who had originally set up the archive in 1562, saw its control wrested away by Sixtus's decision in 1586 to give it to the new college. Biding their time they won their rights back under Pope Clement VIII (1592–1605) in 1594.[163] At length, a compromise gave the conservators, on behalf of the Roman People, jurisdiction over the archive but conceded its actual management, expenses, and revenues to the Capitoline notaries. The college paid eighty scudi in 1602 to formalize this arrangement, but not before the conservators had posted an inscription over the entrance of the archive insisting on the public's right to obtain copies at a reduced rate.[164] The notaries would fight this injunction.

Although what was corrected in 1591 eludes us, the struggles with the conservators manifested the notaries' anxiety in these early years over the extent of their powers and thus their ability to generate income. Jurisdiction, which may have been a purely symbolic good to some Roman contenders, meant the livelihood of court notaries.[165] The question of which judges decided which cases had practical economic consequences for their notaries, and in a city of fractured judicial resources like Rome, few sparked more conflicts. Although by their nature the massa accounts reveal little about the content of these disputes, they show that the Capitoline notaries tangled with other courts over jurisdiction repeatedly, for example, in 1590, 1596, 1606, and 1607.[166] In 1607 they even permit us to know who their adversaries were: the great papal civil justice court, the tribunal of the auditor of the Camera and, close to home on the Capitoline Hill, the protonotary of the senator.[167] Litigation was the favored means of carrying on power struggles over jurisdiction, or indeed other issues, and these sources document regular retainers to attorneys, fees to lawyers for reviewing their arguments, payments to scribes for copying evidence and petitions, and payments to porters for delivering them.[168] Hiring carriages for them, Capitoline notaries also mobilized the senator and the collaterali judges to intercede with the pope or influential cardinals on their behalf.[169]

The Capitoline notaries may or may not have had statutes in these early decades, but they certainly had officers and a regular means of electing them. Payment for a bussola or list of candidates for office in 1596 makes this plain.[170] The mensario who kept the massa accounts on which we depend for the early history of the venal college may have been a post that rotated monthly. The term of the secretary appears to have been a year, with a replacement chosen annually in October on the feast day of the college's patron saint.[171] The office of decano, whom later statutes would identify as the most senior notary in the college, must have changed only on death or retirement.

Even more significant evidence of the Capitoline notaries' robust association than having officers, however, was spending money. In 1602 they raised the funds necessary to regain control of the Archivio Capitolino by forgoing the monthly division of the massa payments that they had put into the common purse.[172] But signs of a conscious policy of investing for the college's future needs emerge in 1604, when, in tandem with imposing a minimum massa payment on each member of 1.50 scudi a month, the notaries opened a bank account and began to purchase shares in the public bond market.[173]

Because the meeting minutes of the college are missing, the arguments that persuaded the majority to shift the basis of massa collection from a proportion of judicial fees to a flat rate remain a mystery. The new policy meant that in theory the mensario could count on collecting 45 scudi a month, a sum that generally exceeded the variable amounts the notaries were contributing a decade earlier.[174] Instituting a minimum contribution increased their individual financial burden so they must have had good reasons for doing so. It also meant that eight years later, when Paul V freed up their offices in exchange for the annual provision of 400 scudi to the Roman People, the Capitoline notaries knew they could pay it. While we do not know whether they had their eye on that prize in 1604, they clearly had earmarked the money they were depositing in the local *monte di pietà* for purchases of bonds (*luoghi di monte*); they bought one for 120 scudi in November 1604 and four more in 1605.[175] By passing up the monthly distribution of massa, as they had in 1602, they accumulated further funds in their bank account.[176] Why? Tantalizing but enigmatic evidence that they purchased or redeemed an interest in one of the thirty Capitoline notarial offices between 1605 and 1607 does not really answer the question, and the massa records for the crucial period around 1612 are lost.[177] What we can safely conclude, however, is that in their first twenty years the thirty venal officeholders who worked for the civil judges on the Capitol had fought quite a few battles and had won some victories. The Capitoline notaries had quickly forged a sense of collective purpose and a common strategy. Given this bond, it is not surprising also to find in 1606 the first payments for masses to be said for the souls of their deceased colleagues.[178]

The crucial turning point of 1612, when Paul V made the notaries' offices fully heritable, may well count among the achievements of the new college, although we have no direct evidence. We do know that their acquisition of the municipality's share in sales of their offices required the Capitoline notaries to commit themselves as a body to paying every year the sum of 400 scudi to the Roman People. The convergence of a free market in Capitoline notarial offices with a substantial regular financial burden, however, set contradictory pressures in motion for the college. Dependable massa collection was essential, for in theory, if all thirty titleholders paid the stipulated monthly minimum, the college would raise 540 scudi annually, more than enough for its obligation. But it was now more difficult to know who was responsible for making payments, because, as we recall, within a few years of the legislation two-thirds of the notaries had not completed the paperwork on their purchases. Despite repeated injunctions, the college still had not succeeded in tracking titleholders by 1674. Moreover, business trajectories varied considerably, and not all offices were equally profitable. Indeed, constant efforts to defend the jurisdiction of the Capitoline curia from competitors and to preserve the price structure of public instruments in the face of papal reforms suggest that thirty may have been too many notaries for all to prosper. Collectively, the Capitoline notaries had done well in their first twenty years, but over the next century some income sources declined, and others fluctuated worrisomely.

At the same time, subtle political processes gradually cut the venal Capitoline notaries off from their old civic patrons, the Roman People. In 1612, the same year in which their offices were freed, papal efforts to improve justice in the Roman civil courts led to landmark legislation disciplining notarial writing. Although Paul V's reforms never denied the separate jurisdiction of the tribunal of the senator, the Capitoline notaries did not escape the long arm of his new documentary regime. Where power compelled, it also attracted, and over the course of the seventeenth century the political focus of the Capitoline notaries shifted slowly but inexorably away from the Capitol and toward the Vatican. In that magnetic field, they found themselves without strong protectors and with little bargaining power.

The two sets of statutes created by the college in the decades between 1618 and 1652 and the papal privileges they secured in 1674 testify to the efforts of the venal Capitoline notaries to adjust to the complex conditions in which they operated in baroque Rome. Only dimly grasping the forces that shaped these conditions, they struggled to keep their professional association viable. Their statutes illuminate the strategies and the strains of piloting a leaky vessel through the fierce crosscurrents and strong undertow that marked this formative period.

DEFINING THE TERMS, 1618–1652

Parchment cost them one scudo, illuminations of the crucifix and the notaries' patron Saint Luke took another ten, and the scribe's wages probably added around two scudi per copy more.[179] The sum the Capitoline notaries spent on the first extant statutes of the college was about a third of their massa collection (forty-five scudi) in a good month. Elegant gold script on the title page and chapter titles of the sole surviving copy, though no illuminations, point to the special status of the manuscript, which bears the autograph approvals of the two collaterali judges in 1618.[180] It is twenty-six folios with twenty-nine articles, covering patrons, officers, meetings, admission to the college, and, of course, the obligatory massa.

The Capitoline notaries held their meetings the first week of each month in the Archivio Capitolino, located near the courtyard in the Palace of the Conservators. There they sat together around a table, with the seating arrangement carefully fixed in the 1618 statutes and a little less rigid in those of 1652.[181] Titleholders had to display the volume in which they entered judicial citations to the mensario before the meeting, and if they were up to date with their massa payments, they received a small "distribution" for attending, always exactly the same amount as everyone else.[182] The massa registers show that, even with the incentive of the distribution, it was rare to find all thirty notaries in attendance.[183] Yet, usually at least half were there, and the money was not unattractive; Erasto Spannocchia of office 15 protested when he missed a meeting because he had been told the wrong time.[184]

When the thirty Capitoline notaries looked around the table each month it was likely that the question on their minds was, Who had paid his massa and who had not? The question was complicated, as we have seen, by the fact that it was all too easy for the market in offices to ignore the formalities insisted upon by pope, city, and college and leave the colleagues in ignorance of precisely who should be at the table. But it was not just the owners or titleholders they did not know about who undermined the common fund but also negligent, tightfisted, or impoverished members they knew well. Each felt the failure to pay massa personally because those attending the meeting went home with a smaller distribution, and the collectivity also risked coming up short on its yearly obligation to the municipality. The college was not completely without remedies to compel massa contributions. In the 1630s it successfully sued at least two owners of Capitoline offices, neither of whom were titleholders, and received substantial back payments.[185] Litigation was slow, however, too blunt an instrument for regular use. It was more efficient to create a sense of colleagueship, to invoke the Gospels and the traditions of Rome, and to set up as best they could an associational life that fostered the common good. This was the central task of the statutes the Capitoline notaries wrote and revised in the first half of the seventeenth century: to counter the centrifugal force of venality and a free market in offices by pressing home the imperative need to act as one.

The statutes of 1618 give the impression that men who routinely recorded the meetings of countless organizations in Rome did not themselves know how to conduct one. Apparently, they learned over the next several decades. In 1652 the articles instructing them to propose items for discussion one after another, to bring up a new topic only after the previous one had been settled, to delegate business that could not be expedited at one session to a committee, and to vote on a measure only after it had been thoroughly discussed were gone.[186] The 1652 statutes worry more about discord than confusion at meetings, and especially about strong disagreements between members or with the college's collective decisions.[187] They dictate all kinds of measures to keep the peace, including elaborate protocols for showing respect to the most senior notary in the college, the decano, who ran the meetings and had the right to speak and vote before anyone else. So fulsome is the language about the reverence owed to the decano in the text of 1652 that it may be a clue to the motivation behind the statute's revision, for Leonardo Bonanni assumed the decano's position that year following sixteen years under the leadership of Tranquillo Scolocci.[188]

The statutes of 1618 set forth the duties of ten officers, a third of the total members. It must not have been easy to fill the posts because there were penalties for refusing office, and in 1652 the college dropped the minimum qualifications for officers from three years of membership to two and from twenty-five years of age to twenty.[189] The decano served for life, but the other college officers were elected in various ways. The mensario was extracted during the monthly meeting to serve a one-month term, but because the extraction was to be made "one after another according to seniority among those present," it was hardly left to chance.[190] If the decano's authority represented the college's homage to hierarchy, the strict rotation of the mensario's job signaled its commitment to collective governance. In addition to such mundane tasks as notifying members of the time of the meeting, the mensario had to settle disputes between colleagues and, with the judge's blessing, between them and their clients.[191] The treasurer, called the *depositario*, whose role grew more important over these decades, was the third major official.[192] While before 1620 each mensario seems to have kept track of who paid in massa during his monthly term, the 1630s massa register shows that the depositario, whose term was open-ended, had taken over this responsibility.[193] Reflecting the delicacy of his assignment, the members elected the depositario by a two-thirds vote.[194] The mensario was paid 1.20 scudi for his monthly service, and the depositario 18 scudi per year.

Less important officers were chosen each October by lot for a one-year term.[195] The college's secretary was among these, as well as two syndics, who had the duty of reviewing the depositario's accounts and making sure all officials had passed their records on to their successors.[196] In a sign of the strong identification of the college with the Archivio Capitolino, four other elected officers had responsibilities for the traditionally lengthy and expensive process of authenticating transunti, which we have seen were the instruments copied from the protocols of deceased notaries. While this task might appear to have occupied almost half the college's officers, it could not have been very onerous. A hired archivist took requests for transunti (and a deposit) from the public, made sure customers handed over the judge's authorizing warrant, looked for the original on his shelves, made the actual copy, and collected fees for the whole process.[197] Aided by helpful formulas written into the notarial statutes, the secretary formalized the procedure with considerably more dispatch, if no less expense, than in previous centuries.

The evidence of accounts and statutes shows that the Capitoline notaries were firmly embedded within the physical as well as legal space of the tribunal of the senator. The notaries apparently did not welcome the order that they pay the regular costs of sweeping their courtroom in the senator's palace. Whether it was the conservators or the senator himself who made the assignment, the matter eventually fell to the senator as chief magistrate to enforce. After he threatened legal penalties and after six months of wrangling, the sweeper's wages appear for the first time in the massa accounts of April 1595, a monthly entry that continues unflaggingly through the surviving volumes.[198]

In addition to cleaning their judges' courtroom, the Capitoline notaries also paid for its repairs. In 1618 they donated four new doors and a *spalliera* behind the collaterale's bench.[199] Across the piazza in the Palace of the Conservators, they provided a welcome fund for building upkeep with their annual four-hundred-scudi payment, and they furnished and supplied the archive on its ground floor. This material connection to the Capitoline Hill had a ritual and political dimension, too. Although as individuals these notaries came from diverse locales and worked in offices scattered around the city, as a collectivity they linked themselves closely to Roman civic traditions.

Embracing their *romanitas*, they proudly described themselves in their statutes as keeping court records for the Senate and People of Rome and imitating the ancients in the respect they showed for the senior (playing on the root for the word senator) members of the college.[200] The college took part in the new senator's *possesso* or inauguration procession.[201] Retaining Saint Luke, patron of their pre-1586 forebears, the thirty Capitoline notaries continued the custom of celebrating his feast day in October by hosting a solemn mass at the church next to the senator's palace to which they invited their judges and the rest of the officialdom of the Roman People. The Latin sermon, the music and chant, the flowers and candles all came at a price, but the Capitoline notaries paid it so that they could demonstrate their profound gratitude not only to Saint Luke but to the municipality.[202]

When giving gifts of chickens, sugar loaves, and candles to the judges at Christmas and Ferragosto and calling on their aid when they needed favors, the Capitoline notaries behaved like proper clients in the civic patronage network.[203] Nor were they just going through the motions when they spoke of thanking civic officials for their many "grazie," which included Christmas presents of pepper, wax, sweetmeats, and gloves.[204] The conservators helped obtain the release of their hired archivist Antonio Campora when he was imprisoned by order of the cardinal protector of the *neofiti* (new converts to Catholicism) in 1615, and the civic councils defended their privileges in 1608 and 1622.[205] In 1616, as in 1596, 1606, 1607, and undoubtedly at other times, the collaterali judges interceded for them with papal officials.[206] When the notaries presented extra Christmas capons to one of the judges for doing double duty while his colleague's office was vacant, their gratitude was appropriate, for without his extra service half of their members would have lost their fees from judicial work.[207]

Admittedly, the course of patron-client relationships did not always run smoothly. The conservators' attempts to make available cheap copies of the documents in the Archivio Capitolino ran into stout resistance, and they ignored the notaries' request for a permanent room in their palace.[208] For their part the senator and collaterali sometimes disciplined the Capitoline notaries, as a group or individually. We have seen that in 1617 the senator made them pay for the orders to their members that reminded them to expedite their titles to their offices properly, and the collaterali may have forced fraudulent notaries to sell their offices, as was rumored in one case.[209] Papal policy increasingly pressed judges to stop abuses by their notaries. But for the most part the foreign-born magistrate who served as senator and the collaterali judges, drawn from those upwardly mobile lawyers of the peninsula seeking careers in the papal bureaucracy, resembled allies more than adversaries. Even the popes acknowledged this when, as a mark of special favor, they guaranteed the Capitoline notaries summary justice from the senator.[210]

The political realities of the papal capital taught the wisdom of having ecclesiastical as well as civic patrons, beginning with Saint Luke, of course, but moving swiftly to a cardinal protector. We catch only a few glimpses of these men, usually receiving Christmas gifts, but they were clearly chosen with an eye to influence and wealth. The Roman cardinal Girolamo Mattei (1547–1603), who had been auditor of the Camera before his elevation, may have been the Capitoline notaries' first protector. They lobbied him to defend their jurisdiction in 1596.[211] The noted art patron Cardinal Benedetto Giustiniani (1554–1621), from a fabulously rich Genoese banking family, was his successor.[212] A 1618 petition from Marco Tullio dell' Huomo of Capitoline notarial office 16, who was desperately trying to put together a legal defense team after spending several months in prison, illustrates the kind of aid a cardinal protector might be called on to provide.[213] If their own collaterale judge Marco Antonio Gozzadini was the man Pope Gregory XV (1621–23) made a cardinal, the Capitoline notaries must have been overjoyed by the news and very likely chose him as protector after Giustiniani's death in 1621.[214] We lose the scent when Gozzadini died just two years later, but sometime between 1641 and 1652 they selected the great-nephew of Sixtus V, Cardinal Francesco Peretti (1595–1653).[215] The 1652 statutes make clear that, on the politically sensitive question of who would be cardinal protector, the notaries must be in open and perfect accord.[216]

Apart from the protector, the only other cardinal to receive regular gifts from the

Capitoline notaries over the years was the cardinal prefect of the tribunal of the Segnatura di Giustizia and his auditor.[217] An enduring relationship with these officials began under Sixtus V. The pope, eager to send legal business to the newly venal Capitoline notaries but also to distribute it evenhandedly, specified that when the cardinal prefect remitted cases from the Segnatura to the Capitoline curia, they be assigned in rotation.[218] The notaries welcomed the "commissioned cases," as they were known, and their relationship with the Segnatura di Giustizia continued to expand. By the eighteenth century, and perhaps before, it was customary for them to read citations one day a week at the judicial audience held by the prefect's auditor.[219] The ritual gifts thus marked an important node in the patronage networks of the college.

As for the popes themselves, the sources are a bit too meager to assess how the thirty Capitoline notaries regarded their sovereigns, the rulers who dictated the very conditions of their professional existence and whose legislation we examine elsewhere. Zealous papal attention to notarial writing and archival practices over the period 1560 to 1630 certainly shifted the focus of the Capitoline notaries from the Capitol to the Vatican. Sixtus V and Paul V were undoubtedly perceived as benefactors to the men who purchased these offices, though Paul's judicial reforms struck intrusively into their writing practices in ways that must have been trying. Urban VIII (1623–44) may also have annoyed them with his new archival demands in 1625, although we have only the evidence of silence, but relations with him and his Barberini relatives could not have been a simple matter. Signaling their awareness that civic power was not enough to protect their jurisdiction, the Capitoline notaries sought Urban's guarantee that the *caporioni*, elected leaders of Rome's fourteen districts (*rioni*), should choose as notaries only men from their ranks.[220] It is likely that the special Christmas gift of twenty-eight scudi received by his agent on the Capitol had something to do with that favorable treatment.[221]

When it was his turn, Urban VIII asked the college to contribute the large sum of two hundred scudi to his unpopular war with the Duke of Parma in the 1640s, giving the notaries only ten days to collect the first installment.[222] By small steps like these the Capitoline notaries were drawn inexorably into the papal judicial orbit, joining the notaries of the papal courts in what was becoming de facto, if not de jure, a single state system. Perhaps it was not a coincidence, therefore, when the Capitoline notaries allied with the notaries of the auditor of the Camera in a successful suit to defend their respective jurisdictions as courts of first instance in debt cases in a judgment handed down by the cardinal chamberlain in 1636.[223]

Because their college not only guaranteed the inheritability of their offices but also helped them to negotiate the status and power hierarchy of baroque Rome, the

Capitoline notaries had an incentive to keep it solvent. In the first twenty years of venality, they succeeded in accumulating a small capital, as we have seen, by winning back from the Roman People the right to income from the Archivio Capitolino and by setting minimum massa contributions. By the middle decades of the seventeenth century, however, the confident financial trajectory of the early years wavered. Following the trail of revenues from archive and massa, we see that after 1612, instead of being able to put money away, the college had all it could do just to collect what it was owed.

Of all their links with the civic past, none was more material for the venal notaries than the Archivio Capitolino, which contained the protocols of Roman notaries going back to the fourteenth century. Willingly seeking responsibility for the upkeep and storage of these records, the Capitoline notaries clearly considered what remained to them after the share of the heirs, one-third of the fees from transunti, to be a valuable asset. To attract customers, the 1618 statutes stipulated that the archive was to be open in the morning while the Capitoline courts were in session.[224] How well founded were these hopes? Early accounts do not record the new college's income from the archive systematically, and amounts fluctuated widely from month to month. In June 1598, for example, transunti brought in eleven scudi and the next month twenty-five scudi.[225] Yet a picture does emerge. The massa book of 1615–20 shows that copies netted on average ninety-seven scudi a year, probably somewhat less than in the 1590s but still significant for a group that had to find a minimum of four hundred scudi annually.[226]

This income did not come free, however, and in the decade after 1612 the Archivio Capitolino cost the notaries quite a bit.[227] Surprisingly, because the archive had lost its main constituency when Sixtus V made the Capitoline offices venal, it needed more space.[228] In 1614 the civic councils granted the college conditional use of a second room in the Palace of the Conservators for the protocols of the notaries who worked for the first collaterale.[229] The college paid to make it suitable for an archive and asked unsuccessfully to keep it in perpetuity.[230] In addition to the renovation, in 1616 the notaries covered the cost of binding fifty-one old protocols and buying a leather volume in which to inventory the archive's contents. In 1618 they purchased new locks, and in 1619 more shelving. In 1637 the Archivio Capitolino again needed new keys and in 1638 a small ladder.[231] Another expense was their hired archivist, whose position the 1652 statutes formalized, though in practice it had long predated them.[232]

The painful logic of a capital consisting of notarial records, however, as Romans had been realizing already for some time, was that its value tended to decrease over time.[233] Fewer people needed copies of a will or a censo one hundred years after its rogation than fifty years and so on. The depositario's accounts show that the college's annual revenues from the Archivio Capitolino had declined to around sixty scudi by the 1640s and the figure was even lower by the 1670s.[234] By the early eighteenth century, the Capitoline notaries regarded the archive as a useless burden, struggled to rid themselves of it, and failed only because of forceful papal intervention.[235]

Disappointing returns from transunti deepened the college's dependence on regular massa contributions, which ought, if everyone had paid the minimum, to have provided 540 scudi a year. Because the amount of massa (above the minimum) owed by individual Capitoline notaries was based on their earnings from judicial acts and transunti, the college enforced collection by having the mensario review each office's register of these documents (the *liber expeditionum*) monthly.[236] The 1618 statutes instructed members to use a bound volume with numbered pages for this purpose.[237] The massa records of the 1630s, the first we have from the hand of the more stable depositario rather than the rotating mensario, rarely show anyone paying more than the mandatory minimum of 1.5 scudi. Taddeo Raimondo of office 25, who contributed on average 4 scudi more each year than the minimum, was an exception, as was the depositario himself, Paolo Vespignani of office 28.[238] Even those who eventually paid the minimum, however, did not necessarily pay it every month, and long arrears were registered for many Capitoline offices, especially those in the hands not of titleholders but of subcontracting lessors or administrators.

Fines might have been one way to compel timely massa payments, but the college accounts reveal only one such entry, in July 1616, when two notaries paid the very small penalty of ten baiocchi.[239] By the 1630s the college seems to have abandoned fines in favor of denying delinquents the meeting distributions or Christmas gifts, or shaming them by making them ineligible for college offices.[240] Litigation was the backup method of enforcement.[241] While the accounts from the 1640s show less than a 5 percent shortfall in massa totals, the Capitoline notaries were alarmed.[242] The 1652 statutes made significant changes to this crucial income source.

First, the college increased the fines it apparently did not levy to three scudi for incorrect or late payments and ten scudi for appealing against an order to pay.[243] Then, to bolster income from massa, the 1652 statutes also added for the first time since 1586 a new type of document. Targeting an enthusiasm of Roman investors, the new charges fell on paperwork needed for trading shares in the public debt.[244] Other measures increased the powers of the depositario to oversee the whole process of collection.[245] They also demanded that the liber expeditionum record what massa were owed for each pertinent document and required signatures verifying compliance.[246] Finally the statutes enhanced the college's ability to force payment from delinquents by insisting that as part of admission formalities new notaries execute a public instrument obligating them to pay massa.[247] The instrument's purpose was to remind members that they might face legal action for failing to put in their monthly contributions. The 1652 statutes explicitly authorized the college to sue titleholders, owners, or administrators for massa debts before either Capitoline or curial judges. They also declared that judges in either jurisdiction had the right to place administrators in notarial offices in order to obtain back payments.

Tightening up its income, the college also wanted to use a revision of its statutes to strengthen bonds among its members. "It is fitting that the notaries of our college hold our writing and instruments in common."[248] Because notaries were of all people the most likely to seek individual profit from documents, the declaration introducing article 31 of the 1652 statutes seems somewhat surprising. The article bolstered esprit de corps, however, by confirming the long-standing custom by which Capitoline notaries and their children could obtain any business or judicial act they desired without charge, even after they had relinquished their offices.[249] The ability to litigate for free was indeed a nice privilege in seventeenth-century Rome. The college built ties through aid to members too, setting aside time at each monthly meeting to listen to the needs of the indigent, sending loaves of sugar to a colleague who was ill, or making loans to the hapless Dell'Huomo in prison.[250] The statutes expected Capitoline notaries to attend each other's funerals, and the college paid the bills.[251]

Paul V's 1612 judicial reforms had decisively ended any illusion that the notarial profession itself was responsible for seeing that judicial acts and business contracts were properly written and kept, although the pope had left the new college the former college's right to inspect protocols annually.[252] In their incarnation as venal officeholders, the Capitoline notaries showed no interest in monitoring production standards and generally avoided any role in disciplining each other's writing practices. They defined professional misconduct now not as fraudulent instruments but quarrels; what mattered most to them was collegial harmony. Their fears were not without foundation if we look, for example, at contemporary France. The statutes prohibited words and deeds that injured colleagues in or out of the meeting, actions that jeopardized their common interests as a college, and protests over massa or meeting decisions.[253] Insisting on respect for seniority, but not exclusively, they reminded members that no one's vote was to be disdained.[254] Thus, they punished infractions of collegiality less with derisory fines than loss of voice and vote, forfeiture of monthly distributions and Christmas gifts, and finally banishment from meetings.[255]

More artfully, however, the revised statutes of 1652 sought every means possible to remove the sources of internal strife. Because relocating might increase competition for notarial business in a specific area, they insisted that the Capitoline notaries not change their quarters without the concurrence of the whole college.[256] The college's successful efforts to gain a monopoly of notarial service to the fourteen district caporioni might have led to "avarice and ambition" among members. The 1652 statutes assigned notaries to rioni by a strict rotation, though they acknowledged that it might not always be easy to persuade the caporione to accept the notary they had selected for him.[257]

Sixtus V had made much of granting the venal Capitoline notaries the privilege of a higher standard of proof when litigants sought to remove them from a case "on suspicion." Writing in the 1630s, the former senator Giovanni Battista Fenzonio emphasized that litigating parties had to give the judge explicit reasons, not just allegations, when seeking to dismiss one of the Capitoline notaries.[258] The notaries looked at the matter differently. Whatever the reasons, one of them was going to lose the fees and another was going to gain them. To diminish the pain, the 1618 statutes gave one-third of the lost fees to the notary taken off the case.[259] By 1652, "taught by experience" about the conflicts arising in these situations, they decree that both notaries would share the proceeds equally and that both would sign the official records.[260]

As this problem reveals, no threat to brotherly fellow feeling could compete with that posed by the Roman judicial system itself from which the Capitoline notaries drew their livelihood. The college's many efforts to mitigate competition for the fees of litigants show how fiercely notaries fought for these fees. The 1652 statutes addressed in detail the question of how to decide which notary got the case when warrants had been issued in the acts of several.[261] Another article, which might appear at first glance to be an attempt at judicial reform, was in fact motivated by the wish to keep members from trying to undercut each other. It specified that in cases where property had been seized or a person incarcerated, presumably for unpaid debts, only the notary who had provided the initial summons could write the ones for release.[262]

Given how much was at stake, the college eventually resigned itself to the prospect that there would be times when colleagues would sue each other over their court cases. The 1652 statutes supplemented the informal mechanisms by which the mensario or the meeting itself settled disputes with special procedures for litigation within their own ranks.[263] These were all the more necessary because the judges, whom of course they knew intimately, liked to send these cases back to the college to resolve.

Keeping their own house in order was a priority for the thirty Capitoline notaries because they needed to stand together in the challenging Roman environment in which they worked. By indicating what they most wanted to control, the 1652 statutes hint at what they had the most trouble controlling. The real sore spots were admission to the college, approval of those who leased or administered offices for titleholders, disputes with clients (especially litigants), location of their offices, and assignment of notaries to the caporioni.[264] They reserved their highest fines, twenty-five scudi, for infractions related to these issues, as well as for removing documents from the archive.[265] In each of these domains, try as they might, the college of the notaries of the Capitoline curia did not have the last word. It had to bow to superior forces, whether in the form of the market for venal offices, patrician privilege, or judicial oversight.

THE CRISIS OF THE 1670S

Twenty years out, the new measures of 1652 designed to increase massa contributions and make them more reliable appear to have succeeded. The register begun in October 1667 recorded the unvarying entry of 540 scudi a year, just what it should have been if each notary had paid the annual minimum of 18 scudi.[266] But other evidence belies the soothing figures. In 1670 college members hoped the Roman People would cut the annual payment in consideration of the lengthy vacant see, which had shut down the courts from 9 December 1669 to 11 May 1670.[267] Along with venal notaries from other tribunals, the Capitoline notaries asked to have their numbers reduced early in the reign of Pope Clement X (1670–76).[268] In September 1672 they deputed an attorney to attempt to collect massa arrears from someone who had not paid for ten years.[269] At a meeting called by the pope, they sent delegates to complain about loss of judicial business that resulted from infractions of their jurisdiction.[270] And finally, in April 1674, they sought papal help to confront the failure of titleholders to pay massa and, more profoundly, to inform them of who properly held title to the thirty Capitoline offices.[271] By July the pope had complied with a chirograph granting them much stronger legal powers of compulsion and setting forth what must have been their own view of what was going wrong.

According to this text the college could not obtain the four hundred scudi required each year for the Roman People from its members and had to resort to borrowing.[272] Structural problems long afflicting the Capitoline notarial offices were to blame. Because, like all venal offices, they circulated freely, they fell into the hands of clerics and ecclesiastical institutions that could not be sued in the tribunal of the senator or became the dotal property of daughters that was legally protected from creditors. Notwithstanding the threats to litigate in papal tribunals launched in the 1652 statutes, privileged persons in Rome apparently did not heed the regulations of a notarial college.

In addition, it had proved impossible for either the college or the papal and civic authorities to compel the buyers and sellers of Capitoline notarial offices to keep them perfectly informed of who held title to these posts.[273] Even if owners sincerely urged the men whom they intended as titleholders of the offices to follow the cumbersome series of steps needed to register their titles and gain admission to the college, neither they nor anyone else knew whether the new titleholders had done so. No one oversaw the whole process, and notaries avoided delays and expense by ignoring it. By raising the bar in the 1652 statutes and demanding that new notaries legally obligate themselves and their heirs to pay massa, the college may even have added to the motives for evading title formalities. According to Clement X, who must have been speaking from the college's own script, the organization was destitute because owners countered its attempts to litigate by waving their legal exemptions, and titleholders completely ignored its existence.[274]

Clement's 1674 chirograph invalidated privileged exemptions and allowed the Capitoline notaries to proceed legally "manu regia et more camerali" against those who had not properly expedited their titles. The college now had the authority to seize the documents of anyone who had failed to complete admission formalities and take them into their own custody in the archive. With the senator's approval, college officers could go even further, auctioning off the offender's office, removing its records, and placing it under an administrator. The college was not required to make any formal accounting of its administration of the office in these circumstances, and if any litigation ensued, the senator, presumably sympathetic to his notaries, would be the ultimate arbiter.[275]

So pleased were the Capitoline notaries with their new legal powers that they ordered that the chirograph be printed and given to all thirty, with the original to be kept in the chest of their important documents in the archive.[276] It was a victory, and one that allowed them finally to set all the structures of their professional association in place. Perhaps it was also effective; seven years later, the college managed a temporary increase in massa payments for nine months.[277] But the negotiations with Clement X, whether over reducing their numbers or increasing the college's legal clout, could not have made it clearer that in the post-1586 era the fortunes of the thirty Capitoline notaries were in the hands of the papacy.

CHAPTER THREE

The Laws

Shaping Notarial Pages

Was there something incongruous, even contradictory, about the way the notary straddled the boundary between personal gain and public duty, between profit and truth? In the medieval universe that had created him, the answer was no. The notary was like so many in that world who bore in their persons some small share of someone else's authority, traced back, ultimately, to lord or king or emperor or pope. To his medieval contemporaries, the notary was similar to others, not unique. The figure of a man whose business was marketing public trust was not so different from that of a man who sold promises of pardon in the afterlife as to provoke undue concern.

Yet those same governments that had bolstered and benefited from this new type of public writer did find other aspects of his activity troubling, particularly in light of the ambiguous ruminations of the jurists. So they legislated, hoping to narrow the array of possibilities that the learned doctors had spread before them. Laws to shape, alter, improve, restrain, or otherwise influence not only who became a notary and how much he charged for his wares but also how he practiced his trade testify to their efforts. Imagining widely varying ways to police the artifacts of the notary's pen, the Italian communes of the North and Center pioneered these statutes beginning in the 1200s.[1] With a delay of a century or so, the city of Rome and its notarial college followed the same path.

Like the city-states, Italy's medieval monarchies were also constructed of notarial parchment and did not forget their origins. The kings of Naples and Sicily were equally suspicious of the entrepreneurs of public trust and almost as free with their rules. By contrast, the popes, as deeply committed to parchment as any rulers, evinced little initial interest in regulating notarial activity. To be sure, the evidence is meager, and the political grip that might have generated it tenuous, especially in the fourteenth and early fifteenth centuries. City law and the profession's own customs and rules governed Roman notarial practices while the popes were in Avignon and long after their return in 1420. Only gradually, as Renaissance pontiffs grew worried about the notaries serving their own institutional bureaucracy, did the papal government intervene in any significant way in the writing habits of the Roman notaries and their clients. Slowly at first, but with gathering purpose, the papacy in the sixteenth and seventeenth centuries muscled in on the documentary turf once supervised exclusively by the Roman municipality and the notarial college. By 1700 the popes had thoroughly reshaped the ways that records were made and kept not only by notaries serving the Curia but also by those, like the Capitoline notaries, who worked for the rest of their subjects.

The legislation aimed at the notary's pages between the mid-1300s and the late 1600s illuminates how Rome's changing and overlapping layers of government thought about documents and what that thinking meant for notaries. Admittedly, laws are an illusory form of evidence, purporting to describe what they can only in fact prescribe. The process by which a new regulation influenced actual contracts or judicial acts was slow, uneven, and marked by ongoing interpretation that bore it ever further from its port of embarkation.[2] We have long been taught that law may be better evidence of the intentions of its authors than of the practices of its targets. On this account, legal sources are essential for reconstructing the concerns and wishes of those who had ultimate power over public writing in Rome. But the evidence of statutes is useful for other reasons, too.[3] It alerts us to realities that we would miss if we depended only on chance archival remains for our picture of the Roman notary and his work, helping to balance, for instance, the unequal fates of his writing for private clients and that for the courts. Then, too, the letter of the law can reveal points of contact we might not otherwise discern in a context in which abstract juridical concepts tended to float above the documents on the ground. In the last analysis, however, what distinguishes notarial writing from all other kinds of writing, then and now, is precisely the way it is regarded by those in authority. To understand public writing, therefore, we must follow their gaze.

The rule makers, whether of the city, the profession, or the state, cared about the character of notaries and the fees they charged but fixated particularly on their papers. Over the course of three centuries municipal, guild, and papal laws sought to shape the material text by their dictates about the page, its container, the means of access to its contents, its reproduction, and the spaces in which it was located. This is not to deny the role of notaries in the confection of their acts for some regulations simply generalized existing working methods, and, as we have seen, the words on the page were largely left to them. Rather, it is to argue that legal and institutional pressures bore down on their texts in ways that affected the documents' appearance, cost, and utility to consumers. Because they were hardly prepared to fund his services out of the public purse, Rome's early modern rulers, first civic and then papal, tightened controls on the notary's writing, while hoping that he would continue to profit from it. His ambiguous status straddling truth and enterprise suited their purposes perfectly.

Let us turn now to Rome in the year 1363, a community in control of its own destiny with muscular groups of local landowners, merchants, and artisans eager to suppress the barons, and the popes far away in southern France.[4] As we saw in the preceding chapter, the moment did not last; by the 1390s the popes were again firmly dictating policy to their Roman subjects. While they held the power, however, the Romans of the fourteenth century did what the citizens of other free cities in Italy were long accustomed to doing. They wrote down the rules by which they would govern themselves, found the men and treasure that would make government effective, and spelled out the way justice would proceed in their territory. The most important evidence we have of their accomplishments is the Roman city statutes, whose influence over all subsequent local law far outlived the regime from which they issued. Commonly dated to 1363, the statutes are in fact a layered and composite text with fragments of earlier and later materials.[5] Here we find mention of the two great classes of notarial writing, business acts or the contracts, wills, and dowry agreements made by fourteenth-century notaries for their private clients, and judicial acts, the records made by notaries for court proceedings, either civil litigation or criminal prosecutions. Because in this book we are following Rome's city notaries, not the foreign notaries in the train of the senator who registered criminal proceedings, we are concerned only with the civil courts.[6]

Most of what survives in the Roman archives today, mainly from a later period, are examples of the first type of notarial document, business acts (*atti negoziali*), a fact that has led us to think of notaries' writing almost exclusively in terms of contracts or public instruments. These are the rich sources that have captured the hearts of historians in many fields over the past century, and rightly so. But it was justice that was the main preoccupation of the city government in 1363 and of its statutes. Civil judicial procedure was the subject of the first of the statutes' three volumes in 1363, criminal justice was the topic of the second, and everything else deemed necessary to urban self-government was lumped together in the last volume. The writing that notaries did for citizens seeking remedy in the civil courts, judicial acts (*atti giudiziari*), was equally if not more important to the legislators of 1363, and indeed to their successors in Rome, as were public instruments.[7] It may well have been more significant to their clients, then and later. Those in authority always distinguished between judicial and business acts, though penned by the same notaries, and they are still separated in the Roman state archives today.[8] Many fewer judicial acts remain.[9] We may be reluctant to believe that public justice depended so heavily on private enterprise or, to put it another way, that brokers of public trust played such a prominent role in court proceedings. For all these reasons it is easy to miss the fact that the political authorities of medieval and early modern Rome thought of notaries first and foremost as operatives in the judicial system. Civil justice was the driver, and the motivation for regulating notarial writing usually arose in connection with legal reforms.

Yet we would be mistaken to draw too firm a boundary between these two dimensions of the notary's activities. In both he wrote at the request of paying clients and to further their goals. In both he worked in a context richly informed by the jurists' thought about evidence.[10] Moreover, there were more substantial links between the two kinds of writing. For those who authored the 1363 statutes, civil justice was defined by whether creditors would be paid.[11] The notary's provision of evidence in the form of business acts dovetailed neatly with the judicial acts demanding, transferring, and acting on written documents that he also supplied. Nevertheless, both our habits and those of the legislators argue for treating the notary's public instruments and his civil judicial records separately.

Business Acts
The City Statutes of 1363

Public instruments appear pervasively in the 1363 statutes' articles on civil procedure. While the jurists had debated the relative merits of witnesses versus documents, the municipal regime of the fourteenth century could not imagine peacefully settling conflicts without the records authenticated by notaries. Thinking about litigation led the statute writers directly to writing, which they assumed would be produced, disputed, and proved or disproved in court. Public instruments were not the only type of written evidence favored by Rome's city law. Scriptura privata in some forms, even unsigned personal receipts (*apodixa*), shared the same privileged status.[12] But the statutes taught creditors that, if they were armed with notarial instruments, they would have the best chance of a favorable judgment and with it the right to throw their debtors in jail, confiscate their goods, and collect what they were owed.[13] Having decisively registered its preferences, this legislation spoke in a selective and unsystematic way about business acts, aiming to strengthen them at those points where either the jurists or everyday life left them vulnerable.

Nothing made this plainer than their treatment of the crime of falsum. In sharp contrast to legal theorists, the statute writers provided Roman notaries with generous latitude to forget what they had heard or seen with their senses and to add or subtract it to a document at a later moment.[14] Where the medieval commentators pointed out the possible flaws in notarial writing practices, Roman legislation weighed in to give them the benefit of the doubt. The statutes created a very high bar for accusations that notaries had falsified records. Plaintiffs had to prove clear malice behind the notary's changes to a text and the litigant's deliberate intention to exploit them to harm his adversary.[15] Correcting or filling in what was missing or wrong in a public instrument was not, by this reading of city law, a notarial misdeed but rather a practice to be encouraged. Was the credibility of a document shaken by alterations, omissions, or additions in the hand of the notary? No, was the emphatic answer of Rome's fourteenth-century governors, who threw their support behind notarial writing even when it erred.

Given these sympathies, it comes as no surprise that, when a notarial document was challenged in litigation, city law backed it very strongly. If a public instrument was produced as proof in a lawsuit and the adversary claimed under oath that it was suspicious (*suspectum*), the senator as chief magistrate should summon the notary who had made it and the party who had submitted it as evidence.[16] To defend its credibility, the rogating notary had simply to show the judge the volume in which the imbreviatura entry for the instrument was recorded. The contrast with the treatment of scriptura privata was telling. Private receipts were certainly acceptable as evidence, but, if contested, the only way to prove their trustworthiness was by comparing the handwriting on the suspicious sheet.[17] This method was prey to much greater uncertainty of interpretation and outcome.

Charges of forged or suspect evidence might easily arise in the fray of litigation, but the notary's life cycle posed a threat of a different kind to his papers. Because they were his property, the volumes passed to his heirs. The Roman statutes did not specify, as laws in some places did, who could inherit notarial documents, but they did try in some fashion to protect their integrity and that of the copies made from them after the notary's death.[18] Inevitably that meant not merely prohibiting their destruction but restricting their commercial circulation as well: "No one may buy or sell the protocols of dead notaries, nor tear them up, nor hand them over to others, either freely or for a price, to tear up or put to any other illegal use." In this, as in all articles of the statutes, the prime method of enforcement was fear of penalties. The senator, alerted either by open or secret denunciation, was authorized to proceed against anyone suspected of destroying notarial protocols and to levy harsh fines on those convicted.

Equally delicate was the problem of access to business acts when they were in the hands of the heirs but might be needed by clients. The Roman statutes set the rates that could be collected by the owners of notarial protocols for finding and showing an instrument by a deceased notary to someone who asked to see it.[19] If the public copy of the instrument was also required, a "good and suitable" notary should be employed to extend it from the imbreviatura, within eight days, at a fee also fixed by the statutes. Although Rome's laws called on the Capitoline court to supervise the process, they authorized the notarial college to designate a group of expert notaries from whom the judge should choose two to check "diligently" the copy or transunto thus produced.[20] All three should sign it to guarantee its identity with the original agreement.[21] The 1363 statutes were always sensitive to the possible uses of notarial documents in court, and therefore alert to the need for litigants to meet the deadlines for their suits despite the death of the rogating notary. If a litigant needed the copy in less than a week, the judge should set a shorter period for the hired notary to complete his work. If he did a poor job, the statutes, fully attending to ius commune in this instance, affirmed that "a person's rights [*ius*] may not be lost because of a defect in the instrument."[22]

City laws also defended business acts against notarial misdeeds. Once the statutes' high threshold of proof was met, they punished the notary who made a false document (*cartam*) with a huge fine and loss of his right to practice; if he failed to pay the fine within ten days, he could lose his right hand.[23] Knowingly producing a false instrument as evidence in court was subject to only slightly less severe fines. The statutes forbade more mundane deceptions as well. Contracts or wills might be superseded or rendered null for many reasons, and when that happened, they were usually crossed out (*cancellare*), with a large x, but retained in the notary's volumes. Notaries were not allowed to strike out any instrument in their volumes, unless so ordered by the party who had undertaken the transaction in the first place.[24] In addition, the city upheld the legal force of notarial instruments made prior to the moment in which a notary, or one of the witnesses to his instrument, was formally challenged (*diffidatus*), though not afterward.[25]

Yet the municipal government sometimes imagined good reasons to destroy business acts. Its statutes reflected the fundamental Roman law principles underpinning valid contracts—that they were freely entered into and truthful representations of the facts. Therefore, the senator could order a notary to delete from his volume any instrument to which one of the parties had been forced to consent. If such compulsion came to light after the original notary had died, and was proved by the testimony of "five good men," the senator could ask the officers of the notarial college to remove the offending document from the notary's protocol.[26]

The 1363 statutes had little to say about the actual production of business acts, but their modest interventions alert us to possible weak points in contemporary practices as well as to the influence of ius commune. At the time of the initial transaction between notary and client, the lawmakers instructed the notary to copy *in quaternutio suorum protocollorum* the substance of what he had heard and the names of the witnesses before leaving the place of rogation.[27] The "substance" and witnesses are, of course, the jurists' legal requisites for a valid notarial instrument, as we saw in chapter 1. Should we infer that in their haste some notaries were forgetting these crucial details? More likely, they were scribbling them on whatever loose sheet they had at hand and perhaps failing to keep these rough notes or to recopy them in a more organized fashion. Civic authority here promoted a different, though probably also current, practice, of having the notary carry a notebook (*quaternutio*) to record his acts.[28] Quaternutio is evidently a fluid term in late medieval Rome, for we read three different words in this same passage in the extant statute texts, three variants in four manuscripts.[29] While we do not know for certain what the quaternutio of the statutes looked like, they may have been the similar to the quarto-sized booklets made of a rough rag paper known as *bomicina*, which survive.[30] However, these survivors may represent a later scribal phase in which the notes for each imbreviatura were recopied in chronological order, and often with more detail.[31] When such quarto notebooks were stitched together they formed a composite volume, usually referred to by late medieval notaries in Rome as a *liber* (book) but called by Roman statute writers, following the jurists, a *protocollum* (protocol).[32]

By demanding that notaries use notebooks early in the process of redacting a business act, the municipal regime encouraged a particular form of written memory that would shape decisively the subsequent evolution of both Roman notarial documents and the legislation policing them. Undoubtedly Roman notaries were themselves responsible for the initial choice of the codex form of the quaternutio over its chief rival, the pierced and stitched pile or *filza*, which was confirmed by this 1363 legislation. Notaries in the busy port of Genoa, by contrast, experimented with both notebook and filza and ultimately found the filza form more efficient for rapidly drawing up a large number of contracts.[33] The regulations were significant, however, not only because they approved a specific material vision of the Roman protocol, one in which the volume composed of notebooks was the norm, but also because of their clear insistence that even the first rough notes of a contract be recorded with an eye to their preservation. City laws thus attempted to firm up the foundation beneath the public instrument, so that the notary would be in a position to produce the supporting evidence he needed to prove its reliability if he were challenged.

Ever mindful of court deadlines and of the damages to suits for missing them, the legislators urged notaries to respond within three days to a client's request for a public copy of a business act. They also specified a tougher physical medium for the public copy, the version of the instrument that circulated, than for the protocol; notaries were to use parchment or *carta de corio*, paid for by the client, rather than rough rag paper.[34] Notwithstanding the solicitude for notarial records thus displayed, the statutes were remarkable also for their reticence. As was the custom in medieval and early modern Italy, they had nothing to say about how notaries were to prepare or keep their volumes.[35] They were silent about the conventions used to formalize documents. They did not legislate, with one exception, on the presence or absence of signatures or symbols at any phase in the redaction of the notarial act.[36] And at a time when Bologna, Modena, Reggio, Mantova, Ravenna, and Venice had already compelled their notaries to submit either copies of imbreviature or fully extended transcriptions to special government offices, Rome merely ordered them to inscribe promptly an abbreviated version of a transaction in a particular scribal vehicle.[37]

The regime that expressed its desires and anxieties about documents in the 1363 statutes was friendly to the interests of notaries and conceded them a large measure of independence.[38] Their autonomy in creating valid instruments was complete; no judges supervised or signed the contracts or wills that notaries drew up for their clients. Their business acts were privileged evidence in court. The statutes made it difficult to accuse them successfully of falsehood and attempted to shore up their records at moments of structural weakness, such as when they passed out of the physical possession of a living notary. While laws promoted the practice of taking early notes in notebooks and defended the customer's interest in obtaining a public copy of an instrument in a reasonable amount of time, they left almost all the other details of redacting, compiling, and keeping their business acts to the notaries themselves.

Were these important practices subject perhaps to the rules of the notarial college itself? In the absence of evidence, in the form of either statutes or abundant intact notarial documents from the fourteenth century, we cannot be sure, but the silence of the sources is not without eloquence. Would we be left with fewer than a hundred notarial protocols from the entire trecento if Rome, like Bologna and other north Italian cities, had required notaries to deposit a copy of their acts in a special public registry? Yet the Roman government was not alone in the free hand it gave to notaries and their heirs in the late Middle Ages, for the majority of Italian cities lacked such registries. Like those of many cities, Roman laws generally had as little to say about the disposition of notarial records as they did about other forms of income-generating private property, such as cattle or houses. Was this an odd fate for what some jurists had celebrated as "proof proven"? Perhaps, yet we have also seen that the 1363 statutes did distinguish the notary's volumes from other kinds of property in two important respects: they could not be destroyed and they could not be bought or sold.

Legislation of the Fifteenth and Sixteenth Centuries
THE NOTARIAL *REFORMATIONES* OF 1446

Roman legal and notarial sources grow steadily more plentiful in the quattrocento and cinquecento, though they remain spotty by comparison to other Italian cities.[39] By demanding that clerics be tried in their own courts according to canon law, the popes had succeeded in driving a fresh, or refreshed, set of distinctions through urban society some three decades before Martin V arrived back in Rome in 1420. This meant a dual legal system, a proliferation of judicial institutions, and a fragmented professional world for Roman notaries with consequences affecting their documents.

Against this complex backdrop, rules governing business acts might now originate from multiple authorities: the city, the notarial college, or the papacy. We seem to hear from the notaries themselves in the most important surviving evidence from the fifteenth century, *reformationes*—that is, revisions—to their association statutes dating from 1446.[40] While the timing and agency of the text may be more complicated than first appears, these regulations had unquestionably acquired authoritative status by the second half of the fifteenth century. The revisions exist in a unique copy commissioned from a prestigious scribe in 1486 by the Roman municipality as part of a compilation of city laws, which was used as evidence in legal proceedings until 1519.[41] We may not have the original statutes of the college, which these thirty-four rubrics "reform," but we do have the city government's authorized copy of the rules the Roman notaries had adopted by the mid-quattrocento. They penetrate much more deeply into notarial writing practices than the 1363 city laws.

Although virtually all the passages about the notary's pages that appear in 1363 are repeated, fresh additions further enhance the stature of the protocollum. Notaries were now subject to criminal prosecution if they failed to record a transaction (*rogitum*) in their protocol, which expanded the definition of the crime of falsum considerably over that of the 1363 statutes.[42] In line with ius commune, Roman statutes were positioning the volume as the ultimate legal repository for a valid business act. Not surprisingly, therefore, the notarial statutes of 1446, for the first time of which we know, tell notaries exactly how they are to construct their protocols. A "well-bound" volume should be made each year. On its cover, or perhaps its first page, the notary should put the date, the pontifical indiction, his signature and symbol, and the number of sheets within.[43] Going beyond the traditional threats of fines, the college added a novel means of enforcement. Notaries were to bring their new volumes (*libri*) to notarial officials annually during the week of Corpus Christi to be imprinted with "the stamp of the college of notaries."[44]

Although we know very little about how—or whether—these policing measures functioned in fifteenth-century Rome, they leave little doubt about the privileged material and legal position of the protocollum. What this meant for the status of any particular notarial act was plain and echoes the thinking of the jurists. According to the profession's own rules, a business act must appear with its key contents and formal elements bound within a collection of all the notary's instruments for a single year. The public copy, on the regulation parchment, was an option available to clients who wanted to pay for the extra labor and materials, but the validity of the act depended on what was written in the volume possessed by the notary. Not much was said about earlier phases of writing apart from the 1363 injunction to jot down the main details of a contract in a notebook before leaving the site of the transaction. The 1446 notarial statutes were almost completely silent about whether the record should be left as an imbreviatura or should have its abbreviations filled out in a fully extended version, about any phases of recopying, and about what ought to become of any rough notes. Up until 1580, custom would regulate these practices. The profession emphasized instead gathering the notebooks of business acts within a particular kind of textual container, one marked by a distinguished juridical pedigree, the bound and labeled protocollum.

One regulation did intrude deeply into notarial writing practices in 1446 by dictating the number of lines and letters notaries had to write when they made copies for clients. In addition to rogating transactions, notaries counted on income from reproducing documents, and they charged a standard "copy fee" per page. Concern about the cost of civil justice motivated the legislation, which was directed at copies of court cases called *registra*, but the 1446 college statutes casually extended it to copies of business acts as well. For each ducato he was paid, the notary must hand over forty-eight pages of writing with twenty lines (*versus*) to a page, and at least eight words or thirty-two letters to each line.[45] We do not know how or whether these mandates on scribal labor were enforced, but they are the first signs of a pattern in which the authorities' desire to control judicial documentation spilled over onto business acts. New disciplines arising in association with litigation thus stretched out to grasp contracts and testaments.

Another harbinger in the 1446 statutes, though strictly limited in its application, is our earliest Roman legislation requiring that the abbreviated version of the contract be fully extended, that is, written out without abbreviations. This requirement was meant not to be a general practice but rather to head off future quarrels on those occasions when two notaries jointly rogated an instrument or worked on the same lawsuit. The two were not to separate until they had agreed on the substance of the text and recorded that common understanding by fully extending the imbreviatura. As insurance, they were also to attach their rough notes to the instrument; one notary was to sign this text, and the co-notary to keep the signed copy in his protocol.[46] The practice of fully extending business acts in Rome may have begun within these special cases; notaries of the quattrocento and cinquecento increasingly did it more generally, although it did not become mandatory until 1580.

Scrutiny of the protocols of living notaries brought fresh attention to the handling of the business acts of dead notaries. With the 1446 rules, we see the first tentative efforts to create, for some of these protocols at least, a protected final resting place, notwithstanding their continuing qualification as private property, the possession of the notary's heirs. The profession focused in particular on those records mostly likely to disappear after a notary's death, protocols inherited by persons or institutions lacking intimate ties to the notarial profession. While repeating the 1363 provisions, the 1446 revisions also broke significant new ground.[47] Heirs must notify the officers of the notarial college within two days of the notary's death "and show them all the volumes." Making clear that it was their responsibility to gather up any loose instruments that might have been lying around, the laws penalized the heirs if the protocols did not contain an entire year's writings. Within a week of the notary's passing, the officers were to lock these documents in a chest with two keys, retaining one key and giving the other to the heirs. If the heir was a notary himself, he was allowed to take the chest to his house, though he would not have been able to open it without the second key belonging to the college officials. As in 1363, the notarial college officials, under judicial supervision, retained their responsibility to check any public copies made from the imbreviatura of a dead notary.[48]

The key, though short-lived, innovation in 1446 was that heirs who were *not* notaries could no longer keep in their physical possession the notarial documents they owned. Instead, "for the preservation of the writings" they had to permit these locked chests to be placed in the sacristy of Santa Maria in Aracoeli, the church that served as the ritual center of both the municipality and the notarial college. This passage is the earliest Roman evidence of the notion of a dedicated space, an archive, for the city's notarial records. Admittedly, it was an archive conceived less as a place of consultation than as a treasury of precious objects.[49] The 1446 college regulations envisioned gathering and keeping these volumes in a church sacristy, a secure location where costly vessels, plate, and vestments were stored, and they emphasized locking them tightly, as if their value lay in being there rather than in being read. Yet the notaries' palpable archival sensibility marks a preservationist's advance over the measures articulated in the 1363 city laws, which dealt with the worrisome fate of a notary's business acts after his death by prohibiting their commerce or destruction.

Did the sacristy of Santa Maria in Aracoeli fill up with chests of documents in the later fifteenth century? Although further research might enlighten us, it does not seem likely. The proprietary interest of heirs in protocols was too strong and the college's enforcement mechanisms too weak. This regulation was reversed by Pope Alexander VI in 1494 and superseded by rules less favorable to the preservationists and more favorable to the heirs of notaries.[50]

THE CITY STATUTES OF 1580

Almost a century after the manuscript containing the notarial college's 1446 revisions to its statutes was penned, the Roman city government, with papal approval, issued a new version of city law that significantly altered the notary's business acts. The statutes of 1580 resulted from an effort within the civic administration to confront the gaps that had opened up between law and reality.[51] Led by lawyer Luca Peto, the administration sought to reflect more accurately how the municipality actually functioned in the new era of papal dominance. From the mid-fifteenth century on, the pontiffs had showered decrees upon the Romans, and Peto systematized this haphazard accumulation into his careful revisions.[52] Peto's rendition was so successful that the 1580 edition was to endure as the final synthesis of Rome's local law until 1847. Because in 1507 the pope had created a separate association for curial notaries over which the municipality had no authority, the new statutes applied only to the Capitoline notaries—that is, those matriculated in the college of city notaries. Four articles of book 1 of the 1580 statutes summarize the former rules on notarial documents and show us the innovations of the sixteenth century. While the revised articles bore titles harking back to the 1363 and 1446 statutes, they rearranged and restated the older elements and explicated novelties with new precision.

The bound and labeled protocollum retained its superior legal position, but it was quite a different kind of volume from what it had been in the fifteenth century.[53] Its most important change was to include only the *mundum* or complete texts of the business acts that notaries had rogated rather than the abbreviated versions that had characterized the imbreviature. The protocol of the 1580s' legislators was more uniform than its ancestors. "Each year the notary should put together his protocol[s], as many as he wishes, which should consist of numbered sheets, well joined and bound together, in which the instruments that he has rogated should at least substantially be recorded *in mundum* within a month of the day they were rogated."[54] The 1580 statutes imagined that there might be not one but several bound protocols from a single notary in a given year. If the 1446 college regulations had left some ambiguity about numbering pages, it was now clear that each sheet should be numbered. Though they no longer mentioned the internal quaternuti, or notebooks, their description of the protocol, "bene compactis et ligatis," implied that it was still composed of elements joined together.

Earlier legislation, whether from the city or the notarial college, while emphasizing that notaries should not leave the site of the contract without recording the legal essentials of the transaction, had said nothing about successive transformations of these notes before their appearance in a bound volume. The abbreviated versions of the testaments or contracts that clients expected to find in the notary's protocol had been legally and materially sufficient in the fourteenth and fifteenth centuries.[55] Legally, they constituted the crucial evidence that the notary had recorded a valid agreement or will; materially, they functioned as the clay from which a fully extended public copy of the instrument could be shaped, if a client asked for it and paid the extra charges. By the late sixteenth century, however, abbreviated texts were overtaken by a fresh input of ius commune and perhaps by new writing habits, which repositioned them in city law.

The imbreviatura of the 1580 statutes was no longer the last stage in the production of a valid instrument but a midpoint. Rome's laws now mandated that the notary take one further step.[56] As always he must make notes (*notulae*) before the parties left his presence.[57] These notes must be entered into his imbreviatura, which was for the first time in Roman legal sources referred to by the term from learned law, matrice. Finally, in a timely manner he must prepare a mundum version, which was the fully extended text with its abbreviations spelled out. Enforcement methods were unchanged: the threat of fines plus inspections of protocols by college officers, now however shifted to the week after Christmas. The key role of Luca Peto in rewriting the 1580 statutes may explain why the jurists' term matrice now entered Roman legislation, but the demand for full transcriptions of acts has no obvious source apart from the notaries' and their clients' own changing practices.

Once synonymous with the protocollum, the imbreviatura was so no longer. Consequently, despite its new association with the juridically resonant concept of the matrice, its material destiny was uncertain. This is made plain in a passage that, while ostensibly addressing the case of a business act rogated by two notaries, in fact illuminated notarial writing practices more generally.[58] What was to be done with privileged evidence, like signatures, that would have to be recopied as the transaction went from the abbreviated to the mundum version? If the parties to an agreement or the witnesses had signed in the imbreviatura, the notaries should "diligently preserve it." The implication was that retaining the imbreviatura was optional. Should they fail in diligence, it was of no grave concern because the full version in the protocol would "mention the signature as it appears in the matrice." The language of the 1580 statutes reflects the new subordination of the imbreviatura, now synonymous with the matrice, to the protocol with its full mundum texts of instruments and wills.

The protocol retained its preeminence as the authoritative vessel in which valid, and indeed annulled, business acts must find their place, yet the nature of the texts it contained had changed significantly. These were now fleshed out versions, with all the "etceteras" filled in. "[Notaries] can extend the abbreviated clauses in the matrice, according to their style, in the protocol and [in the] public instrument."[59] By style the legislators here meant the customary legal formulas, which, as the jurists recommended, were determined by local formularies.[60]

While leaving composition largely in the hands of the notary, therefore, the laws strengthened the role of the protocol as a repository, which could be consulted for a complete history of what had happened to the instrument. City authorities pushed notaries in the direction of ever-more meticulous inscription of their own document-handling practices. As in the past, removing an annulled act from a protocol was prohibited, but now notaries were also instructed to indicate its fate in the margin of the contract and to include the names of witnesses to the act of cancellation.[61] Generalizing a practice that individual notaries had certainly maintained much earlier, the laws instructed notaries to make a marginal notation next to the instrument in their protocol whenever they issued a public copy of it.[62]

The municipal authorities also pressed for timely production of business acts—a more difficult goal once protocols were to hold completely transcribed instruments and wills. No deadlines had previously existed for writing a transaction in the imbreviatura; now notaries had to make the mundum version within a month.[63] The temptation for notaries to collect their fees and halt their labor with the bare legal essentials, which had after all been the customary writing practice before the sixteenth century, died hard. Henceforth the Roman authorities would endlessly repeat the rule that notaries fully extend their abbreviated matrici by the legal deadline. Yet the 1580 statutes increased to a week the amount of time clients had to wait for public copies they had requested.[64] While notaries could delay responding to clients' demands for public instruments, they faced new deadlines in preparing the texts that went into their protocols.

Finally, the city government that had sponsored the creation of a public archive for the acts of deceased Capitoline notaries in 1562 stiffened the procedures it had initially permitted for making copies or transunti from these records. The 1580 statutes restated the elaborate legal formalities that were first set forth in 1363.[65] Only copies made in accordance with these provisions, they declared, would carry the same probative value as the originals.[66] They also guaranteed that revenue from transunti would continue to flow to the notarial college.[67]

Following more than two centuries of civic and professional legislation business acts in Rome had assumed a form that would prove enduring. After 1580 it would no longer be the municipality, however, but the papacy that would promote changes in the ways notaries wrote and kept wills and instruments for their clients. Although they were not the last word on the notaries' pages, the statutes of 1580 were the final dispositions on notarial documents issued by the city government. Less sympathetic to notaries than the 1363 statutes, they nonetheless envisaged a significant role for the college of city notaries in the policing of that part of the profession over which they had jurisdiction. Pope Sixtus V's decision of 1586 to sell their offices transformed the profession by tightly attaching Capitoline notaries to the tribunal of the senator, and of course it rendered the role of college officers, as set out in the 1580 statutes, obsolete. After 1586 the thirty new Capitoline notaries, owners or lessors of notarial offices, found themselves increasingly taking orders directly from the pope or officials and commissions of the Curia like the notaries of other courts in Rome. In the course of an intensive effort to improve the functioning of these courts, Pope Paul V emitted legislation in 1612 that made slight physical alterations to the notaries' pages but radically reconfigured the ways they were handled and conceived. Together with the institution of venality under Sixtus, this legislation laid the foundations for a changed documentary regime in Rome. The breaking wave of Paul's reforms swept the Capitoline notaries along with all the other notaries in Rome into a new era.

The Reforms of Paul V

The papal commissioners who worked from 1608 to 1610 to write the laws known to later Romans simply as the "riforma di Paolo V" intended not so much to disrupt the usual ways notaries wrote business acts as civil litigation papers. The target of the reform was the judicial system, and notaries figured prominently in its provisions because of their place in that system.[68] Yet, if the two types of documentation, business acts and judicial acts, were conceptually and functionally distinct, one of the most significant innovations of the 1612 legislation was to intensify the links between them. In the process of making justice work better in Rome, the papal commission unintentionally affected business acts as well.

Although many rules were holdovers from the past, the reform committee compiled an array of unprecedented detail; there are 127 regulations in the chapter on notaries (ch. 19) and 27 more in the chapter devoted just to their judicial acts.[69] Some of the reforms were clearly responses to new problems arising from making the notarial offices venal, like the difficulties the authorities now had keeping track of which notary exercised a particular office or regulating practices in enlarged offices where lower staff did the notary's traditional work.[70] Other measures, reacting to the city's dynamic finance sector in these decades, attempted, fruitlessly, to keep notaries out of new kinds of credit operations.[71] Reflecting this more impersonal system of exchange, notaries were now legally required to know the true identity of a party to a contract or find at least one witness who did.[72] The majority of the provisions, however, in one way or another expressed the state's wish to render writings potentially necessary to civil justice more visible. Office income from all documents, business and judicial, was now to be recorded carefully in the receipt book (*liber receptorum*), the better to see what rates the notaries were charging.[73] Similarly, the abolition of the fee for looking at instruments and the new requirement to put indexes in protocols made it easier for people to find their notarial records. Via dozens of similarly minute provisions, many focused on the ways notaries handled business acts, the papal authorities painstakingly dismantled the very obstructions between documents and clients that notaries who owned their offices might well have preferred to maintain.

Some of the new regulations grew out of the recognition that notaries simply were producing more, or longer, documents. Paul V's reforms ordered that instruments be gathered together every three months and allowed three months to make the mundum versions, though Giovanni Battista Fenzonio argued that Capitoline notaries were subject to the shorter deadline of the 1580 statutes.[74] The legislation also required that every protocol have a table of contents (*indice*). Because of their need to find a specific act easily, Roman notaries had been creating such indexes long before 1612; Nardo Venettini, active between 1382 and 1428, provided meticulous examples in his protocols.[75] The papal commission showed its interest in making the consultation of notarial documents easier by thus generalizing such practices. A similar motivation may have prompted the state's distinctive treatment of last wills and testaments, which were now to be bound separately from other business acts, once opened after the testator's death.[76]

Some innovations arose from the larger size of venal notarial offices, in which the titleholder who lent his name to the office could not possibly perform on his own all the scribal labor demanded by his judge and his clients. The 1612 legislation faced this fact with some hesitation, repeating the 1580 city law that Capitoline notaries must write the judicial acts of their court themselves, but adding stipulations that members of the office staff who recorded proceedings be approved by the judge.[77] It was less ambivalent regarding business acts, allowing sostituti to rogate instruments provided they sign them at the end.[78]

By far the most radical changes affecting business acts were greater access to simple copies and abolition of the *visura* fee. Both policies built on city and papal initiatives that went back some decades and now reached maturity. The 1612 legislation reinforced a practice mentioned in a papal list of notarial fees in 1562, which permitted clients to pay a lower rate for what were called "simple copies" of their contracts and wills.[79] A simple copy, in contrast to a public instrument, lacked the formalities of the date and place of the transaction and names of witnesses and notary; it was not even signed. Simple copies did not constitute judicial proof, and their use in court was explicitly forbidden. This less formal and cheaper type of notarial documentation was elaborated somewhat in the city statutes of 1580, which replaced the flat rate for simple copies with a rough sliding scale.[80]

Paul V's commission gave the matter much more attention than had the 1580 statutes, showing a clear desire to make simple copies available despite evident objections from notaries.[81] The law now insisted that notaries provide simple copies of instruments at the copy rate, if their clients wanted them, though it exempted what must have been one of the more popular types, testaments. The fees for simple copies remained lower than for public instruments, but the 1612 legislation introduced a more refined sliding scale with an increased number of categories and higher amounts in some categories. Although the state made concessions to notaries in some of these provisions, it decisively upheld the right of customers to purchase a cheap version of their business acts from the rogating notary.

The papal reformers did not stop there. In its most significant break with local tradition Paul V's legislation went on to abolish the visura, the fees that clients had since the fourteenth century paid notaries to see their own documents.[82] Henceforth clients could view the instruments that had been rogated by their notary or submitted to him in a civil action for free, as well as obtain a simple copy of them at the reduced rate.

Taken together, the two measures broke down barriers that Roman authorities had historically allowed notaries to erect between clients and the legal records of their business transactions. The new papal legislation did not overturn the notaries' property rights in these papers, but it cut off some of their traditional income and imposed a more diversified product line upon them. While the notaries might own the documents, the papacy intervened in 1612 to insist that customers be able to see them freely and that they be permitted to take away what were in essence "consultation" copies.

What could account for this deliberate policy of enhancing access to the notaries' protocols? Again, the answer lies in the links to litigation. To men intent on improving a legal system that privileged written evidence, it must have seemed only logical that subjects be guaranteed access to such evidence. But what was the logic of allowing simple copies of business acts to circulate, copies that in theory could not be submitted as evidence in a case? Perhaps so that clients could show them to their attorneys for legal advice? Whether this was in the minds of Paul V's reformers we do not know, but decades later Roman notaries would complain bitterly that clients' *procuratori* had indeed exploited these innovations at their expense.[83] In any event, the source for the abolition of the visura for instruments in 1612 must surely be the principle, first articulated in city legislation of 1521 and repeated in 1580, that notaries were to exhibit judicial acts to the parties and the judge without charge.[84] For Capitoline notaries, the reform legislation registered the new reality that ever since 1586 had brought their two streams of documents, business acts and judicial acts, into closer and closer contact. We turn now to that second stream of notarial writing, almost obliterated from the archives but crucial to understanding *scriptura publica* in early modern Rome.

Judicial Acts
The City Statutes of 1363

Pushing back again in time to the fourteenth century, we are struck by the prominence of civil justice in the politics of the day. One of the first demands of the popular reform movement led by the notary Cola di Rienzo in Rome in 1347 was that lawsuits be settled within fifteen days. Despite Cola's violent overthrow in 1354, the statutes of 1363 bore the imprint of many of his political goals.[85] They certainly attempted to devise procedures that would carry a plaintiff from complaint to judgment in no more than two weeks. Rome's popular regime saw notions of good government and speedy civil justice as closely connected, as would its papal successors.[86] Notaries were key agents in the processes of civil justice, and efforts to police their judicial writing practices can be detected even in this very sympathetic 1363 constitution, though to appreciate them we need to know something about how a lawsuit took place. Although litigation records do not survive for this period, book 1 of the city statutes focuses entirely on civil procedure, and its more than 120 articles provide the raw material for such a reconstruction.[87] How might we imagine such a suit unfolding in the Rome of the 1360s, and what role did notaries play in this process?

It might have happened like this. An irate creditor storms up the Capitoline Hill to a notary's bench, brandishes the instrument of *obligatio* that states what his debtor owes him, summons him to appear in court to pay or face the consequences, and leaves the instrument (always in public form) with the notary. A process server (*mandatarius*) searches out the debtor's residence and hands him the summons (*citatio*) or, in his absence, reads it aloud so that it can be heard in the neighborhood. He then returns it to the notary, who writes on it the date of the announcement. The debtor who shows up before the judge to face these claims (evidently many did not) may ask for a copy of the instrument, which the judge's notary must give him within two days. The plaintiff then has ten days to disprove the evidence. If he has raised doubts (*exceptiones*) about it, the judge can grant three extra days for the parties to make their arguments, a period when witnesses may be questioned by the judge or notary. Failing to disprove the creditor's document, the debtor faces distraint of his goods or person in payment of the obligation. Before the creditor actually collects, however, he will likely need several more court papers: the decree of seizure, the record of the distraint, the record of delivery of the goods to the creditor, the quashing of the obligation. The debtor for his part, whether his property is sequestered or he himself imprisoned, will also need warrants (*mandata* or *mandati*) from the notary of the case, if only to get his goods or his person released.

Based as they were on ius commune, which since the twelfth century had demanded that notaries record trials, Rome's 1363 statutes take for granted the judicial services of notaries.[88] Like procedure elsewhere in Italian civil courts, litigation on the Capitol was primarily an affair of documents, a network of intersecting and interacting citationes and mandata, all issued by notaries.[89] The statutes do not describe the civil notaries in any detail, referring to them in passing as the notary of the case (*notarius cause* [sic]) or notary of the acts (*notarius actorum*) or simply by the ancient term *tabellionis*.[90] We learn by chance in the following passage that notaries were delegated to specific judges. "In addition, . . . a notary who has been assigned to the office or bench of any judge in the Capitoline court cannot serve as attorney [*procuratore*] for anyone during the period in which he is serving at that bench."[91] Although we know that they earned fees for their judicial sentences based on the value of the amounts in dispute,[92] we know nothing about how many Roman notaries operated as court officials, for how long, or how they were selected.

Friction between notaries and litigants is what the statute writers lubricate with their legislation. For example, because one of the notary's main jobs was compiling the dossier of documents submitted by the contending parties, the legislators insist that when he lost an instrument, he must remake it at his own expense and compensate the parties for any harm that his negligence may have caused them.[93] Another annoyance to consumers was the notary who lagged in giving them copies, either of evidence or of witnesses' responses to questions, within the strict deadlines of Roman civil procedure. Under threat of fines, the law gave notaries two days to make a copy of a document that had been submitted by the parties and eight days to produce a transunto of an instrument from the protocol of a dead notary.[94]

Because oral testimony was often key in lawsuits, clients might well suffer—indeed, the whole judicial system could come to a halt—if judges and notaries delayed their examination of witnesses. The statutes threatened them with penalties if they tarried. Clearly assuming that notaries would not just read questions and record the witness's replies but would listen and follow up if necessary, the legislators of 1363 reserved their most detailed instructions for the topic of witness testimony.[95] Notaries were to report what the witness said "fully and explicitly" and not simply write "so and so said such and such." If the witness was not precise in his answers, they were to ask how he knew what he claimed. Merely stating that the witness had agreed that a particular statement was true without discovering the reason for his knowledge would net them a fine and invalidate the testimony, which would have to be taken again. Oral testimony had first to be textualized in order to play its role in the high-stakes game of proof. This was the job of the civil notary at the fourteenth-century Capitol.

Legislation of the Fifteenth and Sixteenth Centuries
THE NOTARIAL *REFORMATIONES* OF 1446

After its return in 1420 the papacy intervened more vigorously in the judicial affairs of its Roman subjects, and, while upholding the jurisdiction of the senator's tribunal, made clear its restriction to lay inhabitants. In 1469, in the name of judicial reform, Pope Paul II forced revisions of the city statutes to emphasize this point.[96] The sovereign's new energy seems to have propelled others in Rome to pay fresh attention to the mechanics of the judicial system, too.[97] The notarial college's statute revisions of 1446, which we recall were part of the official manuscript of the 1469 city statutes, for the first time indicate how the notaries at the benches of the Capitoline judges were to be chosen. And, in striking contrast to the few chance comments about judicial acts in the 1363 city statutes, the notaries devoted a good deal of attention in their own text to how they should write at those benches.

Allocating notaries to the court was the first task. As chief magistrate of the Capitoline tribunal, the senator within a week of beginning his six-month term was to meet with the officers of the notarial college to assign notarii actorum to the civil judges.[98] No numbers were given, but the qualifications were more than simply having matriculated. As we saw in chapter 2, to exercise a civil judicial office, notaries must also be Roman citizens, or owners of a residence in Rome, and untainted by a bad reputation.[99] The requirement that they be of local origin or interest distinguished them from their colleagues handling the criminal cases of the senator's tribunal. It gave employment to Roman notaries but made them vulnerable to the perception of illegitimate influence on the proceedings, because it was hard for contemporaries to imagine that a native son could be completely fair to friends and enemies alike. These competing values made the notary's good reputation, a standard theme of the jurists, all the more essential.[100]

In parallel to its attention to the protocol of business acts, the 1446 college legislation focused on a physical container for judicial acts. Judges should ensure that the notaries at their benches wrote all judicial acts in one book.[101] It is probably to this book that the regulations were referring when they stated that notaries must keep a large, bound folio-sized volume called a *manuale* or *bastardello* with the names of the senator and the judge, the date, the notary's signature and symbol, and the number of sheets stamped with the seal of the college. Before leaving their seat, notaries were expected to record there "all judicial acts, as best they could, at least what was done [*effectum*] and the essence of the act [*substantialia*]."[102] When making copies (*registra*) for the parties from the manuale, he must synthesize (*reducere*) them precisely, giving the sense of all the original evidence, instruments, witness testimony, and other documents submitted to the court.[103] We have very little material evidence of civil litigation from the fifteenth century, but a few manuali of acts have survived, the earliest from 1458. Civil notaries, like criminal notaries, also used filze, stitched piles, to hold together the documents they received.[104]

The notary had to make copies of the summaries within the manuale to give to the contending parties. Litigants who wanted these so-called registra, as we saw earlier, could pay a set fee that guaranteed them a specific number of pages of text: for one ducato, forty-eight pages, with twenty lines of writing on each page, and at least eight words or thirty-two letters to the line.[105] The 1446 notarial college regulations made it plain that the job of the civil notaries was to write and especially to make copies. While judges were sitting, they declared, notaries were to keep silent and write.[106] Even if the judges left their posts, court notaries could not wander around the palace; they must remain in their seats writing so that they "and their copies" could be found.[107] By law, if perhaps not always in practice, those copies had to be produced within short deadlines, and notaries who chatted and stretched their legs were not going to get the job done.

Writing was a powerful weapon in litigation, of course, and the regulations of the notarial college sought to deflect deep suspicions about whose interests court notaries were actually serving. Procurators, as attorneys were called, were not allowed to select the actuary notary for their case. Only judges had this right, and they were to distribute the cases among their notaries following a prearranged order.[108] Yet the boundary between the activities of representing the parties (procurators) and of writing the summons, testimony, and sentences of the case (notary) was difficult to patrol. Anxiety about possible collusion between those performing the two roles surfaced more insistently in the 1446 regulations of the notaries than in the city statutes; perhaps it was a sign of a profession on the defensive in the new atmosphere of judicial scrutiny.

Proper conduct ought to have been very clear. Three separate rubrics declared that actuary notaries could not represent litigants before their own judge, and others forbade them as well to "follow" any attorney and to write for them "in their houses."[109] Yet ambiguities abounded. Rubric 34 of the same text stipulated that, to learn their trade, young men should work for a year for a notary or a procurator, in whose house they might well be found writing. Sometimes clients deputed their notaries to serve as their procurators either for a single case or for all of them.[110] And what are we to make of the rule that ordered notaries not to speak at the bench unless the procurator of the case was absent, in which case they could fill in (*sup-plere*) for the missing attorney?[111] Perhaps this was just scribal error; when the 1580 statutes repeat these lines they change them to one of the missing litigants.[112] Yet the inference is inescapable that notaries knew the procurators' job well enough to stand in for them, that notaries who were not on judicial duty could legitimately act as procurators, and that notaries working for one judge might switch roles to bring a case before a different judge.[113] If all of this was permissible, the line between notary and procurator was a very fine one, and the potential for abuse, at least in the perception of some litigants, great.

Fees, of course, were another source of conflict with clients, who bore all the costs in civil proceedings. The fact that notaries collected and distributed the money owed to court personnel, including judges, exacerbated tensions. What people paid for justice was a matter of intense concern to the popes, who, almost as soon as they took up the reins of power in Rome, began issuing public announcements of judicial fees.[114] Yet in this internal set of rules for the notarial college, notwithstanding its quasi-official status, fees for judicial acts were not yet subject to firm regulation or convention. The 1446 text swings between setting fixed rates for judicial acts and leaving room for discretion, on the part of either notaries or their judges. As we have seen, a notable innovation was setting the rate for and amount of writing on copies of judicial records for the first time.[115] In charging for the judicial acts themselves, notaries were exhorted to conform to a list of fees that took up two pages of the manuscript.[116] On the other hand, they were also instructed to treat litigants who were widows or poor people more mildly than other justice seekers.[117] Finally, to heighten the confusion, the text further stated that judges should determine the payments owed to their notaries.[118] Such ambiguity on the sensitive point of access to justice would prove intolerable to the papacy in the century to come.

CIVIC INITIATIVES, 1494–1521

Over the course of the quattrocento and cinquecento, the fate of the Capitoline notaries was linked closely both to changes imposed by the pontiffs on the senator's tribunal and to the political fortunes of the municipal government. As both the court and the administration of the city of Rome felt the ground shift beneath them, they gradually reached out and grasped a different kind of role for themselves within the strongly monarchical regime that the Renaissance popes had established. The senator's tribunal slowly assumed its place as one among many local courts, though one in which civil cases loomed large.[119] The municipality sharpened its profile as the special patron of local lay institutions, including the Capitoline notaries. Meanwhile, the judicial uses of notaries' pens attracted keen new scrutiny from the pontiffs at a time when they had come to view their own princely role as quintessentially judicial.[120] Thus, a complex set of forces bore down on the writing city notaries did for litigants over the period between the revision of their college statutes in 1446 and their transformation into officers of the court by Sixtus V in 1586. While a paucity of sources and of scholarly studies makes tracing a precise picture of the evolution of civil justice in the fifteenth and sixteenth centuries difficult, key legislative initiatives affecting notarial writing are clear.[121] The most important of these were additions to the city statutes in 1494 and 1521, Pope Pius IV's new laws on the Roman court system in the early 156os, and the ultimate revision of the city statutes in 1580.

In their 1494 revisions to the city statutes, which may not actually have been printed until 1523, the municipal elite made a few changes to civil and criminal procedures in the tribunal of the senator.[122] While they had a dramatic legal effect on the preservation of business acts, their impact on judicial writing was limited to hastening witness testimony. Where the 1363 statutes had urged prompt interrogations, notaries now had a deadline of ten or fifteen days depending on the number of witnesses; they had another five days to provide litigants with copies of this testimony.[123] The 1494 legislation does contain a clue to the obscure process by which actuaries were chosen to question witnesses: by lot from a selection list composed of "ten upright and expert notaries" from the first civil tribunal and six from the second. Explaining the new precision about the mode of sortition was undoubtedly the fact that the notary who took the testimony had the right to the entire fee for both interrogation and copies.[124]

Some of the same men responsible for rewriting the 1494 city statutes pushed reforms of civil justice more prominently in another version of 1521.[125] In the background was the reality of much more competition for judicial business now that papal tribunals like that of the auditor of the Camera were increasingly active. Blaming the flight of would-be litigants to other courts on the slowness of Capitoline procedures, the civic council session of 21 January 1521 sought papal approval to speed up litigation.[126] The council deputed a committee of civic officials, lawyers, and three officers of the college of city notaries to propose specific remedies, which won Leo X's support and were printed on 28 September.[127] Not surprisingly, given the legislators' irritation with court delays, several of the fifty-six articles addressed notarial writing practices, and the final article was a lengthy repetition of past directives to the Capitoline notaries.[128] Unremarked was the fact that since 1507 statutes emanating from the municipality no longer disciplined all Roman notaries but only those attached to the senator's tribunal.

Given the long-standing suspicion of the intimacy of notaries and attorneys, and the 1446 prohibition on notaries' writing in their houses,[129] it is interesting that the statute writers actually increased the amount of time that court notaries were to train with procurators from one year to three years (art. 43). Although this was dropped in subsequent legislation, it is a strong sign of the civic leadership's belief in 1521 that the Capitoline tribunal needed more expert notaries, as well as of the general fluidity between the two domains of judicial activity. Other changes attempted to press notaries to get their work done quickly. If the witnesses had been cited to appear for questioning and the questions from the accused had not yet arrived, the notary should go ahead and ask his own questions (art. 6). Judges should remove from the case any notary who dawdled in obtaining testimony (art. 7).[130] The 1521 reforms even looked into delays caused by illegible handwriting. They required that copies of court records be written in italic (rather than gothic) letters, a sign that readability was already closed identified with this script, which became widely used in Italy in the course of the sixteenth century (art. 10).[131] Their final injunction to the Capitoline notaries encouraged them to write their documents "elegantly and in an orderly manner," if they wished to win eternal praise.[132]

While the new statutes emphasized notarial speed, they also made it clear that litigants could demand more writing from notaries than ever before. In the final article of the 1521 revisions, the authorities reiterated a set of notarial regulations dating from 1508. These describe a new kind of court copy, the *extractus*, which forced a good deal of labor out of court notaries in a short period of time. If the suit concerned goods or property worth at least twenty-five ducati, at the party's request and upon receipt of a deposit the notary should make a "formal and orderly" extractus of all the written evidence submitted and actions taken in the case.[133] The client's procurator had three or four days to read the extractus, which the notary was then charged with recovering.[134] Meanwhile, he was to produce a full transcription of the witness interrogations and attach these to the extractus before handing the complete dossier over to the judge for his decision. All this was to be accomplished within eight days of receiving the deposit, on pain of a year's suspension from his office. This same legislation was also the first to state explicitly that documents submitted in a lawsuit over more than ten ducati could not be returned until the case was settled, unless the notary made and retained an accurate copy and a judge authorized the restitution. Again, what is noteworthy is the increasing number of occasions in which judicial acts had to be copied, notwithstanding the Roman authorities' wish to speed up civil justice.

THE REFORMS OF PIUS IV (1561–1564)

The civic elite's effort to address deficiencies in the senator's tribunal in 1521 was not its last, but it was not to try again until the 1560s, just when the popes, like other European monarchs in this period, were seizing the initiative for improving judicial operations. Between 1561 and 1564, Pius IV singled out for "reform" all major papal tribunals in Rome from the Rota to the auditor of the Camera, as well as all the "ordinary tribunals," that is, the many other courts operating in the city.[135] In a pattern we have already observed with the Roman city government, judicial reform prompted the state to intervene in notarial activity.[136] In the legislation on ordinary tribunals *Cum ab ipso*, published 30 June 1562, notaries were reminded once again not to act as procurators in their own court (no. 71).[137] They were not to work for more than one tribunal (no. 70), and they were not to live in the house of their judge (no. 19).

The Capitoline notaries found themselves the target of five of the seventeen injunctions aimed at notaries. Most startling, as we have seen, was the maximum limit of twenty notaries, who were to write exclusively for the civil judges of the senator's tribunal (no. 64).[138] Along with the notaries of the papal tribunals (of the governor, Borgo, Savelli, Tor di Nona, Ripa, and Ripetta), the Capitoline notaries could not leave their posts without written permission from the pope (no. 59). Pius IV reminded them not to charge more for judicial acts than the fees set in the city statutes and, somewhat ominously from the perspective of civic jurisdiction, to follow the rates established for the civil notaries of the governor's court in cases where no fees had been set (no. 65). Accompanying the half-dozen or so laws the pope issued to improve operations in the tribunals were the first detailed tables of rates for civil and criminal judicial acts by notaries in "ordinary" papal courts.[139] These too were intended for Capitoline notaries, "in cases where their statutes did not provide" them. In recognition of their control over an important patrimony of instruments and contracts, Capitoline notaries were the only notaries whose heirs had to notify an official, the secretary of the conservators, when they died (no. 68).

Pius IV had met with notaries before promulgating his legislation, but by comparison to later papal judicial reforms, especially those of Paul V in 1612, his attention to them was modest.[140] Yet, what little he said about the Capitoline notaries showed that he regarded their judicial activity as very much subject to his will. This he demonstrated not only by the radical step of reducing their number to twenty but also by setting default rates for their acts and requiring them to obtain his approval of their departure from the Capitoline court. Nevertheless, Pius did leave to municipal officials the selection of the twenty notaries, and he did acknowledge the authority of city laws over their fees, niceties that not all of his successors would observe.

It was not the first time that the papacy had imposed rules on the Capitoline notaries, of course; Julius II had done so, albeit briefly, in 1507. Pius IV's efforts were more systematic, however, and heralded the practices that would remake Roman justice over the next fifty years.[141] The details of his legislation provide clear evidence that the Capitoline notaries, despite the technical autonomy of their court, were being brought steadily within the papal ambit. What is not obvious is the attitude of the Roman civic government toward this development. Less than two weeks after *Cum ab ipso* was promulgated, a meeting of the public council on the Capitol heard a complaint from a civic official that abuses by notaries and procurators were causing "great expense to litigants" in the tribunal of the senator.[142] Over the next year and a half, simultaneously with Pius IV's efforts, the civic authorities prepared reform proposals of their own for the senator's court. This project was part of a wave of municipal initiatives in the 1560s that would lead to two new archives as well as a building program and revised statutes for the Capitoline administration.[143] The patrician families whose interests reigned there may have been trying to reassert privileges they felt the pontiff was ignoring. Or perhaps they welcomed Pius IV's intervention and took it as an opportunity to press for further changes, some of which eventually surfaced in the new city statutes of 1580. The municipality showed no such inclination when it came to improving criminal justice, seeing this as a matter completely in the hands of the pope. They were less reticent about civil justice, perhaps because these were disputes about their own dowries, testaments, and property.[144]

The pope's efforts of the early 1560s to improve the tribunals of the Curia and the city raised more explicitly than earlier civic laws the inherent problem of the cost of judicial writing.[145] The list of fees for judicial acts had grown steadily since the fourteenth century, testifying to the elaboration and proliferation of different types of court documents. Yet a princely ruler wanted his subjects to have access to justice in his tribunals, despite the economic realities. Whether in city or curial courts, the legal system that depended so completely on documents, and that required those seeking justice to be able to pay the expense of making them, was clearly caught in a vise of contradictory pressures. Pius IV's new laws had actually addressed documentation even before they had turned to the courts themselves; a motu proprio of 22 November 1561 targeted the way curial notaries prepared registra, copies of court cases made for the parties.[146] Seven months later in its reform of city tribunals, *Cum ab ipso* declared that notaries could make registra only when the amounts in dispute exceeded two hundred scudi in value and not "in cases involving wages and destitute people or similar, in which one is to proceed summarily [*executive*]." [147] The push to eliminate judicial writing went further when *Cum ab ipso* prohibited any documentation at all in cases where parties were contending over no more than two scudi. When litigating over such small sums, unless there was a good reason, the judge should try the case and give his judgment orally.[148] In a move driven by the contradictions rather than being the master of them, the pope concluded the lengthy official list of notarial rates for instruments and judicial acts in 1562 by declaring that notaries were to accept nothing "from poor and destitute people who are unable to pay."[149] In a more practical gesture, however, as we saw earlier in this chapter, this very list had been the first to publish lower rates for simple copies of notarial instruments.[150] As difficult as it was within the existing notarial regime to overcome the fact that writing cost money, the papal reformers were keen to find innovative, though not always coherent, ways to do it. This theme would resurface in the great reform effort of the early seventeenth century.

THE CITY STATUTES OF 1580

If the Capitoline notaries had received glancing blows from papal laws directed at all notaries in the 1560s, they could count on being the exclusive focus when the municipality revised the laws used in its own jurisdiction and published them with papal approval in 1580.[151] Because the Capitoline court followed its own legal procedures, rooted in the ius commune traditions embedded in the 1363 statutes, from which those used in the newer papal tribunals diverged, the 1580 statutes necessarily commanded the close attention of Capitoline notaries.[152] Drafted in the 1560s and 1570s by the Capitoline procurator and jurist Luca Peto, who knew the notaries from a lifetime of personal experience in the senator's court, the new text directed several articles to their judicial activities.[153] Taken as a whole, the 1580 statutes consolidated past innovations rather than breaking new ground as they did with business acts.

As we saw earlier in this chapter, the revised city laws streamlined the senator's court but maintained its profile as an important civil jurisdiction for lay Romans. The six judges of old were reduced to four: the senator, who had both civil and criminal jurisdiction; one additional criminal judge; and two other civil judges, the first and second collaterali, who were served by the Capitoline notaries. Peto's revision did not limit the number of court notaries or tell us how they were chosen for their duties, though the text of 1580 does refer to a bussola, which might have been used for drawing lots as was the case in 1494.[154]

The statutes did describe the prerequisites for the job, sticking closely to those laid out in the notarial regulations of 1446, and it may be that any notary who met the criteria and was admitted to write by the senator and the officials of the notarial college could serve. Actuary notaries had to be Roman citizens with a residence in the city and on the matriculation list kept by the secretary of the conservators.[155] The senator and officers of the notarial college must examine them "rigorously" on their suitability and adequacy for the job, certifying this in writing. The text of 1580 nowhere suggests that there was a fixed number of actuary notaries, and Peto corroborates this flexibility elsewhere.[156] The statutes' insistence on background checks by the college of city notaries also indicates that the profession maintained some control over the selection of actuaries and that city authorities viewed this role favorably.

Lawsuits no longer took, even in theory, two weeks but, at a minimum, two months.[157] The new statutes repeated the 1521 revisions and Pius IV's legislation in demanding that actuary notaries in the senator's tribunal perform their duties themselves and not have an employee or sostituto substitute for them.[158] Harking back also to 1446, the 1580 text insisted that notaries were to attend their judges in silence, diligently writing.[159] The prohibition dating to 1363 was renewed yet again: on no account were they to act as legal representatives for anyone bringing a case in the Capitoline court.

The statutes addressed in a way different from that in the past the potential damage a notary could wreak on a legal proceeding if he was not perceived as impartial. Unlike the 1446 notarial college regulations, these said nothing about judges delegating notaries to particular civil cases. In fact, from other evidence we know that litigants themselves selected the court notary they wished to use.[160] So the 1580 legislation provided new recourse if the defendant was suspicious of the notary employed by the plaintiff—measures that were softened subsequently by Sixtus V.

Before a lawsuit was formally contested, the notary could be removed from the case on mere suspicion.[161] If the suit was already underway, a higher standard prevailed: the litigant had to state a reason to suspect the notary, and the judge had to approve the notary's exclusion. If the parties disagreed on a new court notary, the judge was to extract by lot the name of a notary "from the bussola of all notaries in his tribunal." Any evidence submitted to the first notary was to be transferred to the new notary without payment. According to these statutes, a notary removed from a case because he was "suspect" instantly lost his office in all Capitoline tribunals.[162] If in violation of the law he maneuvered himself back into the case, he would be liable to the penalties for the crime of falsum.

The three kinds of judicial writing that drew special attention in the 1580 statutes —the manuale or official record, the copies, and the witness interrogations—were all types targeted by earlier regulations. As in the past, notaries were enjoined to record each day's acts, at least in essence, in the manuale before leaving the tribunal. New was the demand that these be bound every six or twelve months.[163]

The extent to which money dominated the production of court documents was ever more obvious, both from the growing fee lists for distinct types of judicial acts[164] and from the bans on payment for certain services. Notaries made a living from payments clients made to view business acts, at least until 1612, and it must have seemed perfectly reasonable to them to treat judicial acts similarly. Legislators had a different view of access to documents in a court context. Reiterating a measure from 1521, they prohibited court notaries from charging the judge or contending parties for looking at a judicial act.[165] Nor could they take money from litigants for showing them evidence submitted as part of the suit.

In a familiar theme, copies were to be delivered as quickly as possible, within two or three days if they were not lengthy. To police their compliance more forcefully than in the past, actuary notaries were to record the date when they delivered the copy in the manuale. In theory at least, if they took longer than three days, they could be removed from the case. The 1580 statutes incorporated and refined the early sixteenth-century innovations in the ways notaries produced and circulated copies of court documents. They retained the deadlines and procedures for making the extractus in cases involving more than twenty-five gold ducati but insisted on more meticulous copying. To the older language they added that "all acts [be] transcribed literally as they appear in the manuale, adding or extending nothing."[166] The statutes set a rate per sheet for these copies but did not increase the number of lines or letters demanded of notaries from those first set in the 1446 notarial regulations.[167] All copies were always to have the same number of letters, words, and lines, on penalty of fine. Apparently there was some notion of how many pages could be copied in the eight days allowed by the law, for the statutes permitted the judge and notarial college officers to set an alternative deadline if the documentation was more than four hundred pages long. Fifty pages a day, we can infer, was the maximum expected of the scribal hand.

By the sixteenth century the privileges extended to notarial instruments submitted in a Capitoline lawsuit had been tempered somewhat since 1363; instead of "ready execution," they required support from witnesses before they could be put into effect.[168] Whether they questioned witnesses at home or before a judge or further afield, Capitoline notaries could expect routinely to conduct interrogations.[169] The 1363 city statutes had instructed court notaries in some detail about how to take witness testimony in civil cases, and this was now yet more central to litigation. With their continued discussion of such examinations, the statute revisions of 1494 and 1521 contributed to this development.[170]

The 1580 statutes reasserted much that was familiar. Tradition dictated that notaries put all questions submitted by the parties to the witnesses and write down everything that they said "explicitly, completely, and without abbreviation [*per extensum*]."[171] Notaries were ordered not to use vague formulations, and if the witness himself was uncommunicative in his replies, to warn him that he must describe what had happened specifically and thoroughly. "If the witness does not want to say more than that the question is true, then his deposition will prove nothing," the statutes reminded readers. More surprising, though consistent with the wish to cut litigation delays, was the new language that shortened from ten days to two the deadline for taking testimony, on pain of removal from the case.[172]

On balance, the 1580 city statutes legislated no major changes in judicial writing practices equal to those for business acts. Instead they emphasized the work that had gone on before, especially in 1446 and 1521. The citizens' legislative push on civil justice had crested in the early sixteenth century under the pressure of what was new competition from papal courts; by 1580 all seemed, deceptively as it turned out, stable.

A similar impulse to emphasize rather than revise old rules operated in the edict published in 1582 by the officers of the city notarial college.[173] While the judicial activity of Capitoline notaries, and their sostituti, drew the greatest attention, its sixteen articles usually referred back to one or another passage in the 1580 statutes. One alteration was a new method of enforcing the binding of judicial acts (art. 14). It was mid-December, and college officials reminded all notaries working for the tribunal of the senator that they must present their bound and indexed manuali of judicial acts as well as their protocols for inspection in two weeks' time.[174] The most significant deviation from the 1580 statutes was, as we saw in chapter 2, the recognition that sostituti were in fact writing for the Capitoline courts. The greater message, of course, was the submersion of the notaries' own process of regulation within that of the municipality.

The image of the Capitoline court notary that emerges from the 1580 statutes is one in which technical demands and legal responsibilities were highly developed, but conditions of employment vague. Six years after the promulgation of this final statement of Roman municipal law, Sixtus V, as we have seen, broke with text and tradition by making the Capitoline notarial offices venal, fixing their number at thirty, and assigning fifteen notaries to each of the two collaterali.[175] Having been transformed into officers of the senator's tribunal, the renamed notaries of the Capitoline curia were henceforth defined by their role as writers of judicial acts. If their assignment to the civil judges had been haphazard in the past, and we know so little about it that even that is a guess, now it was articulated and formalized. Offices were allocated once and for all to one of the two civil judges. The radical changes affecting the status, duties, and college of the Capitoline notaries, however, had little immediate effect on their writing practices, which continued for a time to be governed by the 1580 statutes and the traditions of ius commune. Sixtus V's innovations altered their relationship to the judicial system, but the court reforms of Paul V in 1612 had more impact on their judicial acts.

The Reforms of Paul V

The most far-reaching papal effort to systematize judicial practices in the early modern Roman courts, *Universi agri dominici*, Paul V's constitution reforming curial and city tribunals, was published in March 1612.[176] It was the fruit of two years' labor by a curial commission established in 1608 but first proposed under Sixtus V, which was known as the "special commission for the reform of the tribunals."[177] Before his election to the papacy as Paul V in 1605, Cardinal Camillo Borghese had worked under Clement VIII on proposals for improvements in the judicial system that had never come to pass.[178] Like a number of his predecessors Paul seized the opportunity of his election to advance an agenda developed, and thwarted, in an earlier pontificate. The justly famous "riforma di Paolo V" was immense in its sweep and detail, dwarfing the legislation of Pius IV of the 1560s upon which it built, but was also conceived much more imaginatively as a unified judicial apparatus.[179] Given the enduring patchwork of jurisdictions in city and Curia, this mighty but poignant effort at comprehensive reform had a touch of the fantastic about it. But it was a fiction powerfully wrought in its scope and scale, which would remain a touchstone for decades to come.[180]

The reformers took up every court in Rome from the papal Segnatura to the river-trade tribunals of Ripa and Ripetta, and every dimension of the justice system from prisoners' food to judges' fees. No official escaped them, but notaries drew particular attention, and their judicial acts were the only documents to receive a chapter of their own in the new legislation.[181] In the remarkably comprehensive vision of the reform commission, notaries occupied the largest place not because they were at the top or even the bottom of the judicial hierarchy but because they supplied the system's lubrication, its flow of paper. As we have seen, so focused was the commission on notarial pages that it even legislated on business acts, which had no direct bearing on the courts. Its primary interest, however, was judicial acts, especially those for civil courts, because legislation of 1608 had already targeted notaries working in criminal jurisdictions.[182] In the view of the reformers, notaries were central agents of justice, even if it was justice pursued by individuals against each other. It was they who, with the aid of scribes, produced the countless types of warrants, kept the numerous documents submitted in cases, recorded all legal actions, and performed various other tasks in and out of courts and prisons. Making the writing practices of the actuary notaries its focus, the state sought to correct in some cases, modify in others, and establish the means of continuing surveillance in general.

The pope needed neither consent nor justification for seeking to improve his courts, and the commission made notably fewer gestures toward the special status of the Capitoline tribunal than did Pius IV in the reforms of 1562. Nevertheless, it recognized the force of the city statutes at several points, invoking them particularly if they set notarial fees or if they offered a higher legal standard than that promulgated in the 1612 constitution.[183] Like all legislation in papal Rome, the "riforma di Paolo V" did not dismantle existing laws but poured a new layer upon them, which like lava inevitably flowed over the notaries of the Capitoline curia. The reforms sought to cut down on scribal labor in litigation, to link evidence and judicial records more tightly, to keep civil justice open to the poor, to increase oversight of notaries and enforcement mechanisms, and to suppress abuses of the judicial system that were peculiar to notaries. The Capitoline notaries would feel their effects in both protocols and manuali.

Pius IV's tribunal reforms from the 1560s had already displayed signs of concern about what it cost to litigate, and Paul V's legislation on notarial instruments sought to make clients' access to their business documents cheaper. Not surprisingly, Paul's reforms of judicial acts aimed at a similar goal. They raised the limit on disputed amounts that had to be tried orally from two to five scudi and increased the number of words court notaries had to fit onto a page.[184] The line unit had shifted from words and letters to syllables, and now court registra, the case records made for litigation involving substantial amounts of property, had to contain twenty-four lines, not twenty, with twelve syllables each.[185]

Paul V's reforms contained novel if highly technical strategies for reducing notarial costs by economizing on the amount of writing notaries needed to do. In principle no document could be considered evidence if it were not written in the registrum or extractus of the case.[186] In practice the reform legislation suggested many ways to meet this criterion without endless repetitive transcription, in effect allowing brief versions to "count" legally. Papal orders once entered in the registra could be referred to subsequently by the relevant folio number (no. 9).[187] When a public instrument was submitted as evidence in a case, its content should be "succinctly" summarized, not reproduced in a full mundum version (no. 11). When swearing in multiple witnesses, notaries had to write out the oath only once (no. 13), and similarly, when mentioning the names of the judge or the litigants in the record, their titles had to be listed only one time (no. 14). The records of a case in one tribunal did not have to be rewritten if the case was transferred to another court (no. 1). These and similar provisions illustrate precisely why litigation had grown so expensive, and how the state hoped to alter writing practices so that it would become less so.

A second thrust aimed to preserve documents and make them easier to find. Here the consequence of many small measures was to intensify connections between the two sides of the notary's writing activity—business and judicial acts. Mimicking the index required in the protocol, for the first time, a table of contents or *rubricella* was required for judicial registra. The rubricella, however, was more elaborate than the protocol's table of contents; it was to serve as a thumbnail sketch of all the documentation in the proceedings, providing the tenor of each act and judicial decree, and a brief summary (*reique gestae summam vel indicem*) of the instrument, with the full date and names of the contracting parties.[188] For the first time, notaries were instructed to keep witness interrogations and judicial sentences in separate volumes, neither as loose sheets or spiked piles (filze) nor as annotations in the manuale of judicial acts.[189] With these additions, actuary notaries were henceforth responsible for maintaining three separate series of court records, as well as the filze of evidence submitted.

The reforms were very specific about how notaries were to handle evidence. It was not, or no longer, enough to scribble on the original summons and throw it into a desk (*pulpitus*). Notaries had two days to note documents turned over by the litigants in the manuale and thread them into a filza.[190] Notable are the twin desires to privilege the manuale as the key location in which to record the fact that a given document had been submitted in the case and to keep this loose material together in a separate but orderly way. The quality of the material support, the paper itself, also drew more attention than ever before; there was no question of using anything other than paper, but it ought to be "good paper, not stained or absorbent."[191] Paper quality and penmanship were also particularly mentioned when notaries took the cheaper kind of witness testimony, "summary" questioning, as opposed to the more detailed (and costly) *articuli* and *interrogatoria*, as the questions from plaintiffs and defendants were called.[192]

Most striking were minute instructions about signing court documents and marking references to other documents on them. Clearly, Paul V's legislation aimed to intervene in a network of linked documents to establish which officials were responsible for them. For example, the notary who received back a summons that had been delivered by the process server to the defendant must have the messenger sign it and must put his own name on it before entering it in his judicial acts (no. 22).[193] Notaries were instructed to identify the public instrument or private receipt that underpinned a particular warrant[194] by placing the date of the document on the warrant (no. 13). Conversely, the notary should record the judicial act terminating a financial arrangement (*disdetta*) on the original instrument setting up the partnership as well as in his manuale (no. 38).

The effects of the 1612 reforms were to connect business acts and judicial acts more closely together via new scribal practices of marking, referencing, and annotating. The reform commission strove to improve the judicial work of notaries by creating habits that later moderns would call "red tape" or "bureaucracy" but that could equally well be described as more efficient cross-referencing, indexing, and linking. For the Capitoline notary, who since 1586 was defined as a notary for the tribunal of the senator, the activities of drawing up instruments and of issuing warrants would entail constant sorting, searching, and filing between the two categories of writings.

As we have seen, the 1612 tribunal reforms broke with tradition to allow clients to see their notarial instruments for free and encouraged wider use of cheaper types of documentation, like simple copies. The poor who sought civil justice received relief in the form of a two-pronged policy. The poor themselves were allowed to have whatever court documents they needed for free, and their lawyers were permitted to *view* any documents at no charge.[195] It would be up to the judge to decide whether an individual qualified as "poor," and witnesses called to testify about poverty were to be interrogated at no charge.[196]

Enforcement had always been a weak link when the city, college, or papacy promulgated rules for notaries. It was rare to set up policing mechanisms, as the notarial college did in 1446 when it required notaries to bring their protocols each year to be stamped by its officers. If they said anything at all about enforcement, municipal or papal laws tended to put the job in the hands of the notary's judge. By contrast, Paul V's reforms emphasized enforcement, strengthening the judge's disciplinary role and introducing novel types of control. They instructed judges to reject registra and extractus that the notaries had made improperly and to compel them to redo them. The reforms set severe penalties for noncompliance—fines of a thousand gold ducati and loss of one's notarial office. To underscore their rigor, they authorized the two highest papal magistrates in the city, the auditor of the Camera and the governor of Rome, to proceed against lax notaries even without a complaint from litigants.[197] Lest those in venal offices in nonpapal courts think they could escape, the reform legislation explicitly mandated enforcement by the senator, chief magistrate of the Capitoline court. "The senator and [his] other judges are required to make all who are under their jurisdiction and correction, all notaries, archivists, and others in the Capitoline tribunals, observe all the provisions of the law on pain of the prescribed penalties . . . even those notaries who are officeholders [i.e., owned their offices]."[198] While judges were also to settle disputes over notaries' fees, the papacy did not expect them to police all of these practices alone.[199] Repeating a provision from the 1582 edict of the old notarial college, annual inspections of the bound volumes of judicial acts remained the privilege of the officers of the Capitoline notaries.[200] The notaries still had some measure of collective responsibility for proper preservation of their judicial writings.

The 1612 legislation initiated a few apparently minor technical changes in writing practices that had far-reaching consequences for enforcement. No blank pages were permitted; notaries were ordered to draw a line across any blank page or part of a page in any notarial volume so that nothing could be added on the empty space.[201] Tables of contents—the index for protocols and the new rubricella for court registra—were not just handy finding aids but a means of checking whether a document had been removed or added to the volume.[202] Similarly, the receipt book, which was now required in order to record every exchange of fee for service in the notary's office, could become supporting evidence if documents mysteriously disappeared, or appeared, in the manuale or protocol.[203] It is not clear whether the papal reformers intended to control notarial fraud with these innovations, but they certainly had the effect of facilitating criminal investigations. To the evident goals of making all phases of litigation more open to scrutiny by higher magistrates and to improving justice by increasing transparency among lower court officials,[204] we should add deploying new tools for detection of misdeeds by notaries.

The curial reform commission was not unaware that litigants felt, and were, vulnerable to the men whose pens provided the crucial stream of documents that made up a lawsuit, and they tried to name and suppress abuses peculiar to notaries. The very first regulation in the section on court notaries repeated an earlier law demanding that a vernacular list of fees for judicial acts be posted prominently in the notary's office.[205] Reflecting realities changed by venality, the 1612 laws added something new to the now centuries-old rule against notaries serving as procurators in their own tribunals; procurators and lawyers were for the first time prohibited from owning or investing in a notarial office.[206]

As mentioned earlier, the reforms were somewhat ambiguous about how much judicial writing the staff who worked for a court notary could perform. They elaborated on legislation of 1562, in effect allowing employees[207] approved by the judge to take witness testimony and write up judicial acts. This indulgence was not extended to the Capitoline notaries, however, who were specifically enjoined to serve their judges personally, at least in their courtroom.[208] Here the reformers were on thin ice. The prohibition against judicial writing by employees does not square with the 1582 edict of the Capitoline notarial officers, which regulated the conduct of sostituti in court or, more importantly, with Sixtus V's founding legislation of 1586, which permitted substitutes.[209]

Finally, the commission attempted to curb the slippage of judicial powers to court notaries and to outlaw their many strategies for extorting money from litigants. Notaries were to read all summons aloud to the judge and not to issue decrees or warrants (literally, *termini*—that is, the deadline by which an action had to be completed) on their own authority. They were to obtain a judge's signature for every *mandatum* and not to charge extra for doing so.[210]

Judicial writing gave notaries many opportunities to cheat litigants, and the reform legislation of 1612 furnishes a suggestive, if far from exhaustive, catalog of such practices. If they are paid for a copy of a court document, notaries must provide it.[211] They were not to delay delivering the judge's sentence on the pretext that they had not been paid.[212] Forcing the defendant to accept copies of the evidence if he did not wish to have them was unlawful.[213] Similarly, compelling litigants whose cases involved fewer than twenty-five gold ducati to put down a deposit for an *extractus* (copy) was illegal, because an *extractus* of the case was obligatory only when larger sums were in dispute.[214] Legal grounds for distraining property included the sworn oath of plaintiffs that defendants were about to flee the city or were squandering the goods in dispute. Notaries were ordered not to accept such oaths from extraneous parties and not to issue distraints unless duly authorized.[215] In their obsessive detail, these prohibitions painted a vivid picture of what contemporaries meant when they complained about the "abuses" of notaries.

The question of how effective the reform legislation of 1612 was lies beyond the bounds of this study, largely because the question presumes what would have to be proved—namely, that the papal commission had identified the correct problems in and solutions to the existing court system.[216] Upon hearing in spring 1608 that the pope planned an overhaul of the civil tribunals, Rome's news writers scoffed, recalling that investors in these offices had foiled earlier attempts at reform.[217] Unlike the contemporary French monarchy, the papacy had maintained the role of notaries in courts, converting them into owners or lessors of a financial investment; it now had to deal with the consequences. Yet there is no question that something changed after 1612 and that those who spoke about notarial practices in the decades to come thought of this legislation as a turning point. "You used to be able to get a notary for two bits," grumbled a procurator, bitter about the cost of the new laws.[218] Down through the seventeenth century, voices from trial records, letters to papal officials, and reports of curial committees all refer back to the "riforma di Paolo V" or simply "la riforma."[219] With its unprecedented attention to the smallest pulleys and levers of the great machine of papal justice, the 1612 legislation indubitably accomplished at least one result—to raise awareness of how documents were handled among notaries, their employees, and their customers.

Paul V's reforms climaxed almost three centuries of government intervention in notarial writing practices in Rome. From the sophisticated civil court procedure with its assumptions about the probative role of documents that we find in the 1363 city statutes to the minute techniques of cross-referencing demanded of notaries in the 1612 papal legislation, the hand of authority pressed ever more firmly on the notary's pen. But the notaries who drew all this legislative attention were not the same in 1612 as they had been in 1363; they were fewer and more visible. The Capitoline actuary notary of the city statutes of 1363—indeed, of 1580—was difficult to identify. The notaries to whom Paul V addressed 154 articles of reform were easier to name; they were those who worked for Roman tribunals, all of whom by 1612 were "officials," that is, holders of venal offices. Fitting seamlessly among them following Sixtus V's restructuring were the notaries of the Capitoline curia. Control of notarial writing had increased exponentially since the fourteenth century, while a smaller number of notaries than ever before fell within the ambit of the law. New legislation focusing on judicial acts targeted those professionals who had been transformed via venality into court officials.

Of course, it did not have to happen this way. Judicial reform might have shunted notaries out of the tribunals and created new groups of officers to staff them, as it did in France. The fact that early modern notaries held their ground in the Italian courts may well reflect the continuing strong influence of the medieval jurists in the justice systems of the peninsula. Conversely, the notaries' judicial role enhanced their association with public authority and the image of their writing as trustworthy.

In Rome, although civic draftsmen made a distinct contribution, the papacy was the prime architect of these legal changes, which were driven by its powerful identification with the judicial system and by its efforts to integrate and dominate the fractured mosaic of Roman courts for which it was itself responsible. In the long run, clients came to prefer the privileged few, the court notaries—or, as a seventeenth-century jurist put it, "the notaries with offices"—for their business acts as well as their lawsuits, but we must not let their dominance of the record obscure the broader reality.[220] The writing practices of the bulk of notaries were of little interest to popes like Pius IV or Paul V who were bent on judicial reform. For legislation affecting all notarial documents, we have to look beyond the courts to the protracted and tortuous struggle to create archives for Rome's notarial records.

CHAPTER FOUR

The Archives

Creating Documentary Spaces

From the late sixteenth century, the Capitoline notaries presided over a notarial archive of a limited sort, as we saw in chapter 2, and a hundred years earlier had been the first public body to take any responsibility at all for the preservation of notarial acts in Rome. Though they did not sustain this initial effort, both the papal and civic governments eventually caught hold of the notion and over the course of the sixteenth and seventeenth centuries made physical control of documents the basis for extending power into new domains. Notarial archives were a distinctly early modern phenomenon in Rome, which owed most to the popes, though something also to the municipality. To this day, Roman notarial archives remain indelibly marked by the jurisdictional peculiarities of the place and time in which they were initially set up. Although they did not necessarily function as their founders intended, the new documentary spaces created in this period introduced novel ways to access and manipulate writing to Roman notaries and to their clients. They also affected the handling and significance of documents more broadly as scriptura privata joined scriptura publica within their purview. Yet before tracing these developments and their consequences in detail, we need to situate them in a historical and theoretical context that allows us to appreciate the unique features of the archival regime that came into existence in papal Rome.

The medieval jurists extolled the trustworthiness of notarial writing, but their hierarchy of proof acknowledged that writing of any sort had some kind of value. In the final analysis, what notaries wrote could muster only the probative force of two witnesses. This force was not negligible, and the consolidation of the profession attested to its power, but in practical terms notarial documents would not have kept their edge over rival forms of evidence simply because they were written by notaries. Their decisive advantage lay in their power to prove even after all witnesses and the notary himself were dead. To make good on this potential, the documents had to be preserved.

Preservation might have been left up to the contracting parties, but this was not what happened in Rome, or Italy more generally. Clients, who as we have seen did not routinely purchase a public copy of an instrument or will, expected to return to the notary if they needed to see their old agreements or get copies of them, and the notary collected a fee for each and every later transaction. The economic logic of his position gave the notary a strong material interest in keeping track of the records he had made for his clients, though not those he made for a tribunal or government bureau. As we have seen, the law recognized the right of the notary's heirs to the income generated by this peculiar form of property. Despite this logic, some Italian states, beginning with Bologna in 1265, did not entrust the safekeeping of notarial documents to notaries but instead set up city government agencies to preserve them.[1] In doing so, they sought to tip the delicate balance in the notary's dual nature as entrepreneur and authority toward the latter. These cities did not challenge his proprietary interest in his client's acts, but they did interfere in his business by requiring him to allow a duplicate set of records to be made, which could be placed under city protection.[2] The community, they declared, also had an interest in the preservation of notarial records. We shall call this response the *public registry model.*

Initially, Rome and Florence, along with Genoa, Milan, and Naples, followed what we shall term the *professional model,* in which the notary was his own primary archivist. In this model local governments did not set up their own documentary depositories but rather issued increasingly detailed laws about how the notary was to preserve his records. Taking their cue from the jurists' arguments that no business act was valid unless the notary had a record of it, these rules compelled Roman notaries to make an annual bound volume, whose manufacture was supervised by officials of the notarial college. This protocol, as we have seen, became the chief site of surveillance, a textual container upon whose proper forms the trustworthiness of the notary's writing largely depended. Where the government guaranteed the survival of notarial documents by means of notaries rather than a public bureau, its legislation targeted especially the most vulnerable moment in the life of the protocol, the moment of the notary's death. In 1446 the Capitoline notaries had directed that the records of deceased notaries without heirs in the profession should be kept in locked chests in the sacristy of Santa Maria in Aracoeli. Yet such a rule, even before its retraction in 1494, seems not to have cut deeply into traditional practices, for we find notaries leaving their papers to confraternities, and widows or mothers of notaries bequeathing them to family members.[3]

Beginning with Julius II, clearly inspired by his uncle Sixtus IV, the popes struck out on their own unique path. Julius broke sharply with the professional model in 1507 by selling notarial offices in the Curia and attempting at the same time to create a documentary depository at the Vatican. The depository failed for many reasons, not the least of which was that important categories of notaries, including the Capitoline notaries, did not have to use it, but it did promote the idea of a public archive in a city that lacked such a notion. In some sense, Julius II's unsuccessful archive underpinned the city's initiative in 1561 and 1562 to create a depository for the protocols of dead Capitoline notaries, the Archivio Capitolino. The popes did not give up, however, and their efforts to combine venality and a public registry did eventually bear fruit in another form under Urban VIII when Rome's first general notarial archive was established in 1625.

Public notarial archives were far from the norm in early modern Italy. They were resisted successfully by both clients and notaries in the Viceroyalty of Naples, in the Republic of Genoa, and in the state of Milan.[4] Forceful princes imposed them in Tuscany in 1569, in the Papal States (except Rome and Bologna) in 1588, and in Rome in 1625. But despite their similar origins, the Tuscan and the Roman archival regimes could not have been more different for the grand dukes eliminated the proprietary nature of notarial writing, while the popes preserved it.[5] The tension inherent in the notary's dual identity as businessman and public authority was thus maintained in early modern Rome, yet the papacy eventually found a two-pronged way to protect notarial documents. One prong was the sale of notarial offices that were attached to public tribunals, and the second was the requirement that all notaries—curial and Capitoline, officeholders and free agents—make copies of their instruments to be deposited in the new Archivio Urbano. Under what we might call the papal model, therefore, preservation of records, at least in theory, was guaranteed both by the investor's desire for a return on his investment and by the existence of duplicates in a state bureau.

Let us now look more closely at the evolution of documentary spaces for notarial acts in Rome as they came into being and operated between the mid-fifteenth and the mid-seventeenth centuries. We track the new institutions chronologically, as they were initiated within the fragmented jurisdictions of Rome, Curia, city, and finally state. We begin with Julius II's Archivio della Curia Romana, followed by the Archivio Capitolino of the Senate and Roman People, and conclude with the Barberini's Archivio Urbano.

The Archivio della Curia Romana

Capitoline notaries had taken the first tentative steps to preserve the records of dead notaries by the mid-fifteenth century.[6] Not long after, the popes showed that they too had concerns about how notarial documents were being preserved, though it was those produced in their own bureaucracy, not in the city, that provoked them. In 1483 Pope Sixtus IV, worried that foreign notaries drawn to work in the reactivated departments of the papal Curia in the fifteenth century would depart from Rome with their records, envisioned an ambitious registry for curial notaries.[7] As we saw in chapter 2, he set up a college of venal notarial officeholders in the Curia, hoping to pour the proceeds from selling their offices into his treasury. On the archival side, Sixtus gave this college the job of transcribing in registers the notes of all notarial documents rogated by curial notaries, which were to be brought each month to the archive. Instruments issued in public form would require the signature of a member of the new college. From their first attempts to regulate notarial archives, therefore, the Renaissance popes chose to operate through a distinctive combination of venal office and public registry.

Nothing much came of Sixtus IV's radical initiative, which was abolished by his successor the following year, but it planted a seed that bore fruit when his nephew became Pope Julius II in 1503. Julius's bull *Sicut prudens* of December 1507 re-created the Sistine college of venal notarial offices in expanded form as a 101-member College of Scriptors of the Roman Curia and, as we have seen, set up an admission procedure for other curial notaries.[8] With breathtaking grandeur, he also established a notarial archive that would record the acts of living and dead notaries, those in the Curia and those in the city, both contracts and judicial documents, at least from papal tribunals. The founding legislation of what became known as the Archivio della Curia Romana, or Archivio di Curia for short, offers a sweeping and original, though not very clear, vision of vast scope. For political, financial, and institutional reasons, it never attained its promise, but in truth no Roman archive has ever achieved the universality Julius II attempted in 1507.

The audacity of the Julian archival project lay in taking up Sixtus's plan for a public notarial registry that would keep a record of current work as it was being done rather than focusing only on the fate of documents after a notary's death. Taking aim at the foreign notaries who congregated around the papal court, Julius directed them within a week to bring the signed notes (*notae*) of instruments that they had rogated to the new archive to be checked against their protocols and registered.[9] He grappled with the unprecedented public access to documents that such a registry might unwittingly provide by trying to devise a way for contracting parties to keep their agreements in a "secret book" in the archive. In a move beyond even the ambitions of the 1612 reformers, he ordered notaries of papal tribunals to turn over the registra of all completed court cases within two years to be inventoried and preserved, unless or until the judge or the interested parties wanted them back.[10]

Another indication of the boldness of Julius's legislation was that it imposed new document-handling procedures on notaries outside the Curia. The pope's reach extended over the Capitoline notaries without the slightest gesture to their traditional autonomy or to their patron, the Roman city government. Ignoring existing archival provisions, Julius decreed that the protocols of any deceased notary without a son to carry on the paternal career should be deposited in the Archivio di Curia.[11] Similarly, he ordered that the contracts of all foreign curial clients, which would include those rogated by Capitoline notaries, be brought for registry in the newly designated "public archive and decent place" in the Vatican Palace.

Yet for all its brave and expansive vision, the Julian archival project stumbled on jurisdictional realities, the implications of venality, and operational details. The law excluded from the registry notarial agreements made between Roman citizens, which was the bulk of the business of Capitoline notaries; after Julius's death in 1513, his successor exempted the Capitoline notaries altogether from the 1507 bull as part of a package of privileges conceded to the city government.[12] Julius also made an exception for business acts drawn up by notaries in papal tribunals, who, the bull pointed out, were venal officeholders. Because one of the pope's motives in setting up the College of Scriptors was to raise seventy thousand scudi for the costly military campaign he had just concluded in Bologna and for the new basilica of St. Peter's, he was compelled to appear to respect the property rights of the purchasers of venal offices.[13] He could not afford to legislate for the protection of their documents in a way that interfered with their possession of them.

What the Archivio di Curia lacked most, however, was an institutional infrastructure that was up to the task of registering all this notarial activity. There was much to be done, whether for living notaries, who were to bring their notes every week to be entered on the books, or for the protocols of deceased notaries, which might be quite safe but useless if they could not be found again in the archive. A system was needed for indexing these protocols, along with the personnel to undertake it, and for the complicated business of making and checking transunti, the extended instruments of dead notaries.[14] Julius had expected the officers of the College of Scriptors, ten *correctores*, all high prelates, to oversee these tasks, but someone still had to perform them. In the early years, it is clear that someone did. Today in section 66 of the Archivio Urbano, three series of registers, more than a hundred volumes composed by the staff of the Archivio di Curia, cover the years 1507 to 1550.[15] Papal orders in 1569 that the college hire notaries, however, indicate that by then it lacked vital manpower.[16]

Most necessary, of course, were funds to make the archive function. Venality did not prove a good source of revenue or labor for the archive, for the College of Scriptors turned rapidly into an investment opportunity rather than an occupation.[17] A good deal of mystery surrounds the actual operations of the Archivio di Curia before its absorption in the Archivio Urbano in 1625, for whatever documents it accumulated between 1507 and 1625 have since been redistributed along paths sometimes difficult to follow.[18] Some foreign notaries consigned their protocols before leaving Rome, although Julius II had oddly omitted to order this in his legislation. In addition, the volumes of sixty-three notaries belonging to the College of Scriptors in the sixteenth and early seventeenth centuries are among the holdings of the Archivio Urbano, as are those of several hundred other curial notaries.[19] One of these curial notaries was Antonio Campora, archivist for the Capitoline notaries and a private notary active in Rome between 1604 and 1631. He is responsible for several protocols from the early 1620s, which bear a stamp consisting of a cross and the letters AC, indicating inspection or deposit in the Archivio di Curia at that time.[20]

Julius had made the powerful papal auditor of the Camera responsible for the Archivio di Curia. The auditor's occasional edicts commanded the public to turn over the documents of dead or absent notaries and ordered private notaries on the Curia's matriculation lists to bring their documents to the archive within a week.[21] Without money or staff, and with many important papal offices exempted from its jurisdiction, however, the Archivio di Curia may have been largely ignored by its default clientele, the thousands of private curial notaries whom it was set up to control. The Archivio Urbano was the follow-up to Julius II's great vision of an all-encompassing Roman notarial archive, and, as we shall see, it was organized along very different lines.

The Archivio Capitolino

In the 1440s the college of city notaries tried to safeguard the documents of notaries who had died by forcing heirs who were not notaries themselves to turn them over to the college. The officers directed these orphaned protocols to locked chests in the sacristy of Santa Maria in Aracoeli on the Capitoline Hill.[22] A church sacristy may not have been the site of choice for regular research, but the notaries did not view the records of their deceased colleagues as sources of information. The Capitoline notaries, and the heirs who remained the owners of the writings even though they were not in their physical possession, saw notarial acts as sources of revenue. The city statutes of 1363 had set the rates that heirs could charge for finding and showing instruments to those who wanted to see them, and, as we saw in chapter 2, transunti, legal copies made from the protocols of dead notaries, generated small but satisfying streams of fees for centuries.[23] The notarial college thought a sacristy an appropriate location for locking up what it regarded as treasure—or, to be more precise, someone else's treasure.

However logical the choice of site, the college was writing an unprecedented role for itself. While city laws had taken notarial acts under their special protection at least since 1363, this was not a physical but a juridical guardianship. The college of city notaries might claim to govern the profession and its practices, but how far this right extended to interfering with the property of notaries' heirs was not certain. The intervention signaled an anxiety about the dispersion and loss of records so pressing that the college would ignore legal niceties and impose novel constraints on heirs. What it imagined was hardly an archive, though its concern with preservation was explicit; the college made no provision for inventories, for access, or for a curator or archivist. Translated into modern terms, it was a vision closer to a bank vault than a public library. Yet it was the notarial profession's first collective step toward such a notion, and it preceded that of either papal or municipal authorities by many decades.

The heirs of notaries must have complained, for the college's regulation of 1446 was decisively overturned by new rules under Pope Alexander VI in 1494. The change occurred as one of a number of revisions to sections of the city statutes on civil procedure.[24] The requirement to consign documents to the notarial college for safekeeping in the sacristy of the Aracoeli vanished. The law now declared that once a detailed list (*repertorium*) of their contents had been produced, the deceased notary's protocols were to be locked in a chest and turned over to the free disposition of the heirs.[25] This was not complete freedom, because the heirs were liable if clients' interests were damaged by their negligence, but it was a striking reversal of the college's policy of 1446.

It would be wrong to infer that the college of city notaries necessarily opposed the change, however, for it was accompanied by two other innovations that it may have welcomed. As we saw in chapter 2, the 1494 legislation codified for the first time the claims of the notarial college to a portion of the fees that heirs received for transunti made from their protocols. In exchange for physical possession of the notarial documents they had inherited, the heirs now had to concede a third of their earnings to the notary making the copy, to the judge overseeing the request, and to college officers. In addition, the statute revisions introduced a useful new technique by which officials could keep track of notarial acts in the form of the *repertorium*.[26] The repertorium was a list of the names of the contracting parties, the type of contract, and the date of each instrument in a notarial protocol. The notion, if not the reality, of such lists, which were to be kept separately from the documents themselves, would become a fixture of notarial policing in the centuries to come.

Yet for all their subtlety, the 1494 laws signified a setback for documentary conservation. In hindsight, and with our suspicion of the great losses of notarial volumes that took place in late medieval Rome, we must lament the decision to give back to the heirs of notaries who were not notaries their physical power over the records.[27] The policy stood for almost seventy years, reiterated explicitly at the time of another important revision of civil procedure in the Roman city statutes of 1521. The 1521 legislation confirmed in every detail the provisions made in 1494 for the protocols of deceased notaries.[28] Not until the 1560s did the municipal government repent of its indulgence and lobby successfully for the creation of a notarial archive under its control on the Capitoline Hill. Housed in the Palace of the Conservators, this would become known as the Archivio Capitolino to distinguish it from Julius II's Archivio di Curia.[29] It would remain on the hill even after Urban VIII instituted the general notarial archive in 1625 and would be administered more or less willingly by the Capitoline notaries until 1880.[30]

City council decrees show that a proposal to set up a notarial archive under municipal auspices won support in several meetings in May 1561.[31] The committee delegated to work on the project—one notary, two procuratori, and a lawyer—gained council authorization for its suggestions in November, and in March 1562 another committee reviewed and approved the new rules for the archive.[32] While Pius IV's judicial reform legislation of 30 June 1562 does not refer to the archive, it does set up a new mechanism for informing city authorities when a Capitoline notary died. It required heirs to notify the secretary of the conservators within two weeks of the notary's death and of what documents he held, commanding the secretary to keep this information in a special volume.[33] On 12 September the pope bestowed his assent on the planned archive, and the city magistrates publicized it in a vernacular edict of 23 December 1562.[34]

Ignoring the existence of the Archivio of the Roman Curia, the Roman municipality declared its goal of preserving the documents both of Capitoline notaries who died and of "other [deceased] Roman and foreign notaries."[35] Although the edict contained an intriguing order to living notaries to turn in a monthly list (*rubricella*) of their current contracts, its primary purpose was to gather the papers of notaries who had died. In their choice of the vernacular, their tone, and their policies, the authors of the legislation were mindful that their most important audience was the heirs who possessed these papers. They gently if condescendingly lamented the conduct of the heirs, "for the most part people of little wealth, women and children, and others who have not the slightest familiarity, knowledge, or regard for these documents." The owners gave them away or sold them or took them home when they left Rome for their native lands. The magistrates tried to arouse compassion. Such negligence caused harm to people remarkably like the heirs themselves, "the poor, children, and women who lose their possessions because they do not know to whom or where to go to find their documents."[36]

Understanding that force would not accomplish their purpose, city officials attempted to entice heirs to give up their documentary patrimony by promising them more secure returns. The dispersion and loss of notarial acts were bad for the heirs, they pointed out, because then they received no income from them. The new archive would remedy this problem. They repeatedly reassured heirs of their rights to fees from copies, and devised elaborate bookkeeping procedures that would make the transunto process transparent to them.[37] New furniture would protect their documents, and generous archive opening hours would permit access to heirs each morning during the hours the Capitoline courts were in session and for two hours every afternoon.

Perhaps because they were so intent on persuading heirs of the benefits of submitting to the new regulations, the authors of the 1562 edict neglected to mention the legal formalities required for the making of transunti from the protocols of dead notaries. They did not say that a Capitoline judge and notarial college officers had to approve these copies, as stipulated in city statutes of 1363, 1494, and 1521, and as would be repeated in those of 1580. Naturally they also omitted all reference to the fact that since 1494 officials were entitled to one-third of the heirs' fees for this approval.[38] The edict assured heirs that they and their successors would collect "the entire ordinary fee" for their instruments, though they did not say what this was. The archive itself would charge users minimal rates for its services: a maximum of one giulio to look for a contract and no more than two carlini for the labor of copying it.

As in the past, at least since 1494, heirs must inventory the protocols they had inherited; when they delivered them to the archive they must allow the archivist to make his own copy of the list in his special volume of inventories. The edict said nothing about binding loose instruments into protocols and, indeed, assumed that they would arrive in stitched piles and bundles. A clever system of drawers in the large armoires (*armarij*) commissioned for the new archive would neatly solve the problem of loose papers. Seeking always to persuade the heirs of how well the archive would protect their interests, the authors of the 1562 legislation promised that each deceased notary would "have his own separate drawer [*cassetta*] for his heirs and successors" with his name in capital letters on the locked drawer. Although its archivists could not maintain this rule without some adjustments over the centuries, the acts of deceased notaries in the Archivio Capitolino were still organized by cassetta at the time they were inventoried in 1704.[39]

The chief municipal authorities, the conservators, were the "superintendents and *patroni*" of the archive, responsible for its administration and for its needs. They had to make sure that the documents of deceased notaries arrived, even if all the enticements of the edict's rhetoric and terms failed.[40] The 1562 legislation alluded to officers of the college of Capitoline notaries, but gave them no formal responsibilities for the Archivio Capitolino. It said nothing about how the archivist was selected.[41] In a curious duplication of the job of the secretary of the conservators, the archivist was instructed to keep a "matricola Capitolij," a book in which all Capitoline notaries "and other Roman notaries" would sign their names and draw their particular symbols.[42] They would pay three giulii for the privilege of being thus "admitted" to the new archive.

The Archivio Capitolino had been operating for only a few years when the patrician landowners who dominated the municipal government conceived of a new role it could play, which, if it had come to pass, would have considerably expanded its scope. A key legal device for protecting the integrity of landed estates was the entail or *fideicommessum*, which had spread widely among the landowning elites of sixteenth-century Italy.[43] Entailed property could not be sold or alienated by heirs and was thus legally restricted (*vincolato*). The conservators reported to the civic councils in July 1568 that offspring who wanted to ignore these legal constraints were finding notaries willing to write contracts that permitted them to dispose freely of entailed property, in violation of the fideicommessa imposed by their ancestors. As a remedy for such abuses, they suggested that all fideicommessa be recorded in the Archivio Capitolino.[44] Such a move would have been a first step toward a public registry for the acts of living notaries, making the archive far more than a repository for the instruments of dead notaries. Whether or not the recommendation was implemented in 1568, a subsequent order from the governor of Rome to notaries to turn such documents over to him suggests that it was not. The concerns that prompted it were still lively enough sixty years later for the Archivio Urbano, which was in fact Rome's first public registry, to create a separate series for fideicommessa in 1631.[45]

When the Rome city statutes received their final revisions and were published in 1580, they contained a number of changes affecting the Archivio Capitolino, which can be read as a critique of its operations in the first two decades. The 1580 statutes gave a prominent role to the officers of the notarial college in the risky period following a notary's death and increased documentary controls by the profession at the expense of the heirs. They also reintroduced distinctive treatment of the sons and grandsons of notaries, which had been eliminated in 1494. Within three days of the funeral, the officials of the notarial college were to lock the deceased notary's protocols in a case (*capsa*), unless he had left a son or grandson who was either himself a notary or "able and willing" to become one.[46] In a shift from 1562, the scribe or archivist of the Archivio Capitolino, not the heir, was within a month to make a repertorium of all these protocols with the number of sheets in each. He was also to record all loose instruments with the date and names of the contracting parties. The heir received a copy of this inventory, while the notary's papers remained in the archive. The archivist reversed this procedure when the heir was a Capitoline notary, giving him back all the documents of the dead and retaining the inventory.

As we have seen, the 1562 edict establishing the Archivio Capitolino had ignored the legal procedures for making the public copies of business acts extended from the imbreviature of dead or absent notaries. In 1580 the authorities made up for this omission with a vengeance. They retained from the 1363 statutes collaboration between the Capitoline court and the notarial college in overseeing this complex process, though they streamlined it somewhat.[47] Most importantly, building on the insights of 1494, they spoke in detail about the fees that an ever-expanding number of officials would receive from transunti. Now four different officials had rights to a share in the proceeds: the judge overseeing the procedure, the notary of the Capitoline notarial college, the scribe or archivist who actually wrote out the transunto, and the notarial college itself.[48] Clearly it was no longer only the heirs who had a stake in the papers of dead notaries. One thing city authorities had learned since 1562 was that a notarial archive could not thrive without sources of revenue and without officials who had a material interest in its operations.

Two years after the publication of the city statutes, the officers of the college of city notaries showed how deeply they were involved in its administration by printing a series of regulations that included several on the Archivio Capitolino.[49] These refined some of the key features of the 1580 legislation but took a much more severe tone toward heirs than twenty years earlier. Cajoling them into giving up their ancestors' notarial records was no longer necessary; now they must shoulder some of the costs and be prevented from cheating the archive. Heirs who were not notaries were now subject to some of the new document-handling practices recently imposed on the notarial profession. College officers insisted heirs bind and number loose instruments and provide them with an indice, a table of contents, before they were deposited in the archive. If after a month the deceased notary's papers were still not bound and indexed, the archivist could do it at the heirs' expense.

The officers also emphasized for the first time the need to keep secret the contents of the archive, although this may have been a way to justify new restrictions on heirs' access. When establishing the Archivio di Curia, Julius II had been sensitive to clients' desires to keep their property arrangements to themselves, although he had devised a clumsy method to accomplish this.[50] The locked drawers of the Archivio Capitolino, apparently sufficient in 1562, seemed less so in 1582. Now notarial officials ordered the archivist to wall the documents off physically and not to let anyone see them without written authorization (a mandato) from a judge and college officers. The archivist was to enclose the large cupboards whose drawers were filled with notarial protocols in a "claustrum seu steccatum" and to prevent their contents from circulating. If papers had to be removed from the archive for any reason, the archivist must obtain written permission from notarial officials. College officers also emphasized the 1580 legislation that no copies of any type might be emitted without the legal formalities required for transunti.[51] They explicitly prohibited heirs, even sons, and those who had purchased or leased documents (*cessionari seu emptores*) from making transunti from the protocols of deceased notaries without the necessary signatures and demanded that anyone asserting such a privilege provide them with written proof. To counter the impression that these measures might be aimed at hiding income from the heirs, however, they ordered that all transunti expedited be noted on a public "tablet" (*tabella*). This was undoubtedly a simpler device than the three sets of books required in the early years of the archive.

Although this edict makes it clear that the notaries' college was actually managing the Archivio Capitolino in 1582, city officials, as we have seen, were since its inception its governors. When Sixtus V transformed the Capitoline notaries into venal officeholders in 1586, he ignored these claims of the Senate and Roman People and handed the archive to the thirty new titleholders, who were given its "total care, rule, and administration."[52] The civic magistrates profited by his death to regain their rights, though they effectively returned its care and governance to the college after 1601.[53] The next challenge to the college's jurisdiction did not come for more than a century, and when it did, it came from an unlikely source, the college itself.

It would be useful to know more about actual archival operations in the Archivio Capitolino in the late sixteenth and early seventeenth centuries, not least because it contained a few of the city's small number of surviving medieval notarial volumes. These were in the archive by 1704, the date of the earliest extant inventory, although we do not know exactly when they arrived.[54] Recent research has uncovered the existence of archival markings that definitely predate the 1620s, when they were cited by a writer who used the Capitoline protocols for genealogical work.[55] This tells us that someone had tried to establish a system for finding documents in the Archivio Capitolino. As we saw in chapter 2, in 1618 the Archivio Capitolino was to be open mornings during court sessions; in 1652 hours are not mentioned except to prohibit access after the ringing of the Angelus.[56] No light and heat were allowed at any time.

Of course, the notaries of the Capitoline curia themselves, as venal officeholders, were exempted from any requirement to consign their own documents to the Archivio Capitolino. The notion of the office as a vendible commodity included its protocols and court manuali. Sixtus V had charged college officers with making an inventory of the records left when a Capitoline notary died, but the recipient of this inventory was no public institution but rather the next notary to lease or purchase the office.[57] Paul V's reform legislation of 1612 reiterated this exemption "for those who buy offices," while ordering the heirs to protocols of any other pre-1586 Capitoline notaries to deliver up their inherited documents.[58] In this way, a modest trickle of volumes continued to flow into the Archivio Capitolino until the Archivio Urbano was established in 1625.

On the eve of Sixtus V's grand archival intervention in the rest of the Papal States in 1588, which ordered the creation of notarial archives in every town, Rome had two notarial archives, both limited in their reach. The Archivio di Curia theoretically functioned as an ongoing registry of notarial documents made by living curial notaries, as well as a deposit for the papers of those who had died, but in practice it fell far short of that. The Archivio Capitolino defined itself more narrowly and more traditionally as a repository for the records of deceased pre-1586 Capitoline notaries without heirs in the profession (widened after 1586 to include bequests of those who had lost their places). It may well have been living up to that restricted task adequately. Unwilling to disrupt the new arrangements with the Capitoline notaries and willing to ignore the deficiencies of his curial notarial archive, Sixtus exempted Rome, along with his second largest city, Bologna, from the duty of instituting local notarial archives in 1588.[59]

Like his neighbor Grand Duke Cosimo I of Tuscany, Sixtus V viewed a state takeover of notarial archives as a potential moneymaker for the fisc.[60] At the same time, the pope made an eloquent case for the close connection between the preservation of documents and the well-being of the propertied classes. To Sixtus, justice meant "maintaining [subjects] in their possessions," and to advance that goal he wanted to set an archival example to princes everywhere. He pointed out that even "nationi barbare," meaning those outside Europe, had public archives.[61] The promise of the Sistine vision took thirty-five more years to embrace the city of Rome, but when it did so, it gripped ferociously. In 1625, in the third year of his pontificate, Pope Urban VIII took the radical step of creating a "general" notarial archive that erased the distinctions between curial and Capitoline notaries and revived the Julian notion of a public registry. Over the next twenty years, the pontiff and his nephews gradually added even wider duties to these until they had established what was in effect a new, if short-lived, department of state supervising the entire notarial profession and its products.

The Archivio Urbano

After a buildup of several months, the founding legislation of the new archive, to which the pope gave his own name, trumpeted forth on 16 November 1625.[62] Like that of Julius II, it was a bold experiment that did not turn out quite as planned, but unlike those involved in the 1507 project, the authors of the Archivio Urbano plotted every detail on every coordinate to provide it with a solid infrastructure. Few if any institutional interventions of the long Barberini pontificate from 1623 to 1644 rival the scope and complexity of its conception, and indeed its meticulous execution, at least in its early years. The pope and his most trusted aides, the Barberini family cardinals, invested a great deal of effort in trying to bring off their experiment, which never enjoyed in later reigns the same warm papal attention. Yet, although there was much that was new and much that was distinctively Barberini about the Archivio Urbano, it arose within a broader context of interventions by the papacy in the handling and care of public documents, both secular and sacred. Between 1565 and 1625 the popes attempted to create many kinds of new archives in their dominions, and they succeeded in establishing most of them. In this period the records of churches, religious orders, the college of cardinals, and the papal administration itself joined notarial acts as objects of state solicitude.

Julius II's Archivio di Curia was, of course, a precedent, and later popes also cited proposals from the time of Pius IV, but the pace quickened after the Council of Trent, when Pius V established ecclesiastical archives throughout the Roman Catholic Church.[63] Church income depended on accurate knowledge of church property, which could be attested only by thorough and well-kept documentation. Knowledge of properties yet to be acquired lay particularly in the hands of notaries, so in 1568, 1576, and 1585 the cardinal responsible for the ecclesiastical institutions of Rome asked them for information on all legacies or gifts their clients had made to religious and charitable bodies.[64] While the cardinal vicar did not establish a rival archive to those of the Curia and the Capitoline, his orders heralded a new concern about how testaments were preserved that reappeared a generation later in the Archivio Urbano. Sixtus V's legislation on notarial archives in the Papal States in August 1588 followed his two earlier initiatives, one in April 1587 calling for a general archive at Rome for all religious institutions and another in June 1588 creating individual archives in Rome for each of the religious orders.[65] Paul V, whose court reforms took such keen aim at documents, rounded up the records of his own administration and gave them new quarters in the Vatican Library, while sternly ordering the staff to keep his notaries away from them.[66] Urban VIII himself, within a month of creating the Archivio Urbano, founded an archive for the college of cardinals in the Vatican Palace.[67]

From the outset Urban VIII presented the new notarial archive as a continuation of the efforts of Julius II—indeed, of an even more ancient church tradition of maintaining public archives. In fact, as a Florentine Urban VIII would have been familiar with the state notarial archive established by Grand Duke Cosimo I in 1569, which undoubtedly influenced his plan.[68] Like Sixtus V, though without the arresting reference to the example of uncivilized countries, the pope enumerated the benefits his subjects would enjoy from keeping contracts and wills in good order. Chief among these were preserving social peace and family patrimonies, the security of dying wishes, and a vision of justice pleasing to property owners. Existing Roman notarial archives failed to provide these benefits, he claimed, because they "had fallen into disuse or were deficient in many [details]."[69]

The novelties in this initiative were not rhetorical, therefore, but political and bureaucratic. The pope named the most powerful man in his entourage, his nephew Cardinal Francesco Barberini, as the protector of the new archive and placed a fellow Florentine and Barberini client, Camillo Perini, at its head.[70] The pope's brother, Cardinal Antonio Barberini the elder, also known as the Cardinal Sant'Onofrio, published all the regulations governing the Archivio Urbano between September 1625 and June 1626 in the name of his nephew. In contrast to both Julius II and Sixtus V, Urban put his closest advisers in charge of the new notarial archive. Most tellingly, like Cosimo, he kept it under his direct control rather than leasing it out to a state contractor as Sixtus had done with the notarial archives of the Papal State in 1588.[71] The pope appointed Perini to the post of conservator of the Archivio Urbano and elevated him to the rank of prelate, a crucial marker of status at the papal court.[72]

Rome's celebrated handwritten newsletters, the *avvisi*, reported on these developments on 24 September and 4 October 1625.[73] The public first learned in detail about the Archivio Urbano from a vernacular edict dated 1 September 1625, which was pasted up one month later on the walls of the cardinal chamberlain's head-quarters at the Cancelleria near the city's great market square, the Campo dei Fiori. This *bando* with its thirty-six "provisions and orders regarding the new archive" was followed by several shorter additional instructions on 13 October and 14 November 1625, all released before the pope's legal authorization of the archive on 16 Novem-ber.[74] Within these thirty-six initial regulations, we can discern strenuous and at times inventive efforts to contend with old problems that had shipwrecked the Archivio di Curia when it attempted to become a "general" notarial archive and to address the new conditions of venality prevailing among Rome's public notaries. At the same time, they laid the groundwork for stronger state control of the notarial profession in the city and also for broader supervision of documents written by private individuals.

City news writers, particularly attuned to the audience likely to be affected by this novel archive, summarized the thirty-six regulations, pointing out that "notaries representing the four major tribunals must serve [in the archive] on a rotating basis and those who have purchased their offices may continue to rogate *instrumenti perpetui* provided that they bring them within a specific period of time to the archive; other notaries will have to be examined and will have to post bond."[75] With a slight air of surprise, they go on to report that the provisions are "aimed solely at the public good"; the interests of venal officeholders will be protected because archive officials will not be permitted to compete with them and archival fees will be very low. The news professionals rehearsed what struck the most obvious chords with their readers. The Archivio Urbano did not intend to undermine the income-generating power of notarial documents or the proprietary nature of the venal notarial offices; henceforth, private notaries in Rome could work only if authorized by the archive; and only certain types of contracts were subject to the new legisla-tion. They captured the significant news for Roman officialdom, though they did not grasp or perhaps appreciate the bureaucratic ingenuity behind the headlines or the pain of the new habits the archive would attempt to instill.

Although the news writers did not say so, the Archivio Urbano aimed to collect copies, not original notarial acts. Unlike the Julian Archivio di Curia, which em-ployed scribes to transcribe into registers the notes handed in by notaries, the 1625 regulations expected notaries to make their own verbatim copies of the originals in their protocols and deliver them to the archive. Nor did the creators of the Archivio Urbano in fact want copies of all notarial acts but only of certain broad categories, especially wills, transfers of real property and loans made against land, and certain kinds of powers of attorney, far fewer than those sought by Julius II and Sixtus V.[76]

Such long-term credit instruments were termed "perpetual" because they were not contracts for limited periods of time. Short-term leases were excluded, for example, as well as business partnerships and pacts for agricultural work.

Testaments were a high priority for the Archivio Urbano, but they were also a troublesome documentary quarry. Wills might be dictated to a notary and thus find their way into his protocol, but often testators wrote down their last wishes themselves and handed the paper over to the notary for safekeeping. If clients delivered sealed wills to their notaries to preserve until their deaths, the archive could hardly require notaries to break these seals and copy their secret contents before such time. Moreover, priests as well as notaries might record or receive these documents. Even in the many cases where the notary had rogated the will in the presence of the testator and witnesses and entered it in his protocol, he still faced the difficult task of protecting the testator's privacy should he submit a copy of the will to the archive. Accepting the need for secrecy in handling wills, the Archivio Urbano mandated an elaborate system of cover sheets with symbols and numbers instead of names.[77] If no copy of the will arrived at the archive before the testator's death, the 1625 rules demanded that notaries deposit a copy after death within ten days of opening the testament.

Once archived, many safeguards encircled the document. Wills could be opened only upon receipt of a death certificate and in the presence of the rogating notary, who had to bring along the original for an archive official to check against the copy. Naturally, the heir paid the archivio a percentage of the total amount of the legacy for this service, although it was unclear what advantage he or she drew from it (art. 22).[78] The new regulations had carefully exempted testators from their strictures; people could make wills wherever and however they wished. The power of the state fell on the notary and, to a lesser extent, the priest; if a testament came into existence with their aid, they had the legal responsibility to make it available to the Archivio Urbano either before or after the testator's death. To secure compliance, the 1625 provisions declared that testaments, however safely kept in a notary's protocols, would not prove in court unless they had also passed through the hands of the archive staff (art. 22). They sweetened this by giving direct relatives who were heirs a slight discount on fees and allowing them to take possession of inherited property before going to the archive, provided they get there within two weeks.

In addition to loans secured on real estate, to wills, and to gifts between the living, the Archivio Urbano sought to keep track of certain types of powers of attorney.[79] By such measures, the Barberini gave a rare hint that they were concerned about not only mortgages but also other kinds of credit operations, a growth industry in contemporary Rome. While Sixtus V had demanded that documentation of any kind of loan be deposited in the notarial archives he set up for the rest of the Papal States, the Archivio Urbano had to craft more-subtle language. In Rome, policing sophisticated credit instruments required naming not the form of debt but the document that empowered a third party to broker one. A special target of the legislation, therefore, was powers of attorney issued either in the papal territory of Avignon or outside the Papal States (art. 11). Previously, holders of such documents who intended to use them in Rome visited a Roman notary so that they could be formally recognized; now, in addition, they must first register them in the Archivio Urbano. The 1625 rules warned notaries who worked for the *monti*, the public loan funds in Rome, not to accept any foreign power of attorney unless it bore the stamp of the conservator of the archivio, and they declared that any payments based on such documents would not be honored. Adding further emphasis in a special follow-up edict of 13 October 1625, Camillo Perini reminded all cashiers, bankers, treasurers, and merchants not to pay out money to bearers unless the foreign power of attorney had been archived.[80]

The founders of the Archivio Urbano were aware that many written agreements were not guaranteed by the public trust of the notary, and from the outset they extended their reach also to scriptura privata. In the initial regulations for the Archivio Urbano, they invited "anyone who would like to preserve any sort of document, be it public or private, to give it to the archivio, paying one giulio for this privilege, and two giulii per sheet for a transunto or authentic copy" (art. 30). The invitation turned out not to be optional; the next article made it plain that if a written agreement fell within the definition of perpetual contract, regardless of who wrote it, a copy had to be brought to the new archive or it would be nullified.[81] These controls on scriptura privata exceeded those of Sixtus V, who had instructed people with written obligations (secured on real property) that were not penned by a notary to have them registered, but not retained, in a special volume in the local archives of the Papal States.[82]

Thus, copies of wills and perpetual contracts, the prime targets of the Archivio Urbano, had to be deposited regardless of whether they were in scriptura privata or scriptura publica. As we have seen, the new rules also invited Romans to archive any other writing they wished it to keep.[83] At a certain level Rome's first copy archive, which seemed to focus on notaries, actually treated all writers equally, acknowledging the new writing practices spreading through urban society. Whether their preservation in a public archive lent additional credibility to personal documents, however, was a matter of debate among the jurists. Despite Mascardi's endorsement, Nicolò Passeri, author of a 1615 treatise on scriptura privata, remained unconvinced.[84] Only with further research in judicial records will we know whether Urban

VIII's grand project provided scriptura privata with the equivalent of the notary's protocol, a place of safekeeping buttressed by claims of legal authenticity.

For all its detail there were signs that the "provisions and orders for the new archive" of 1 September 1625 were a work in progress. Having with great energy and some precision specified the kind of documents they wanted for the Archivio Urbano, the authors ordered notaries not only to turn in copies of the desired instruments but also to keep the originals in a distinct set of volumes in their offices. Moreover, they told them in the future to send a brief summary "of all other instruments" that they rogated every three months to the archivio. The "brief summary" should state the name, surname, and city of origin of the contracting parties and the monetary value and type of contract. This was in article 20. By the end of the text in article 34, they had evidently thought better of provoking such an avalanche of information. Notaries should indeed make a summary list of all their instruments, but they should keep it in their office awaiting orders to show it to whomever the conservator of the Archivio Urbano designated.[85] Belatedly awakening to their general silence on short-term loans, the authors of the provisions abruptly ended by exhorting notaries to record all resales of censi and società d'ufficio, and the trail of documentation that attended these loan operations, in yet another volume in their offices. They did not ask for copies.

The Archivio Urbano may have been feeling its way clumsily with respect to its archival mission, but it solved the delicate problem of protecting the rights of notaries to the income from their instruments with consummate skill. Because the papacy was responsible for selling the notarial posts in the city's tribunals in the first place, it had every reason to be solicitous of the interests of those who had invested in its judicial system. At the Archivio Urbano, users could relish the ease of looking for documents "in only one archive," but that was all they could do. The rules strictly prohibited archive staff from rogating instruments and from making copies, activities for which clients had to pay the original notary.[86] They threatened transgressors with a huge fine of five hundred scudi. The staff was enjoined not to undertake the remunerative writing of a notarial business but to respond promptly to the requests of parties who turned up at the new archive asking "to compare and archive instruments and documents and to see the catalogs." The archive catalogs permitted users to determine to which city notary they should repair to obtain a copy of an instrument. The limitations on the new institution ensured that notaries with venal offices would not find it threatening, and indeed, although much later we hear complaints from the Capitoline notaries, there were no contemporary protests.[87]

The Archivio Urbano never intended to be just an archive, however. It aimed to impose a more far-reaching discipline on the notarial profession, which was felt most immediately by the notaries without venal offices or connections to tribunals, Rome's more numerous but less powerful group of private notaries. As we saw in chapter 2, in the sixteenth century notaries could not operate in Rome unless they were matriculated on the list of either the Archivio di Curia or the Capitoline notaries. Foreign notaries were to sign up with the Archivio di Curia and local ones with the Capitoline. The Archivio Urbano took over the matriculation functions of both institutions, continuing that of the Archivio di Curia and resurrecting that of the Capitoline notaries, which had ceased in 1586 when Sixtus V converted their functions into thirty venal offices.[88] Now private notaries of whatever nationality must submit to an examination by archive officials and must post a bond.[89] The new measures aimed to suppress the practice of "casual" rogation by notaries who worked informally for other notaries, declaring that anyone on hire who was not an authorized sostituto on the staff of an office could no longer legally produce instruments for clients (art. 14). The Archivio Urbano would serve as the repository for the acts of registered private notaries, who had ten days to submit a mundum copy of wills and gifts, and twenty days for other business acts (arts. 16 and 17). The restrictions against making copies by the archive staff seem not to have been extended, or at least not as forcefully, to private notaries (arts. 28 and 30). Oddly, the 1625 regulations said not a word about turning in the protocols of deceased notaries, the documents that had attracted the very earliest protective legislation in the fifteenth century.

Urban VIII dreamed of having only one archive in a city where there had been two notarial archives for almost a century, from which major groups of notaries were exempt. Only by riding roughshod over long-held traditions could he forge the unity he so valued. No more explicit sign of his determination to make the Archivio Urbano a truly general archive could there be than the presence of both the leading curial notaries and the Capitoline notaries at its helm. The pope's founding legislation had endowed the conservator of the archive with many privileges and with an ample civil and criminal jurisdiction.[90] The most ingenious organizational feature of the new archive, however, was its intention to draw its staffing from the ranks of all notaries with offices. Ignoring the historic distinctions between the Capitoline and curial notaries, and overlooking the differences of jurisdiction and procedure that characterized the tribunal of the senator and those of the papacy, the 1625 regulations imposed a common set of responsibilities on four groups of notaries. They ordered the notaries of the auditor of the Camera, the notaries of the Camera, the notaries of the tribunal of the cardinal vicar, and the notaries of the Capitoline curia each to send an officer to serve for three months in the Archivio Urbano.[91] The role of these experts, or their authorized sostituti, was to check that the copies turned in as demanded actually conformed to originals, to make indexes and catalogs of the contents of the archive, and to help users find documents in the catalogs. Along with the conservator, these four were also to administer the tests to private notaries who sought permission to rogate in Rome. Did this innovative staffing mechanism ever actually function? No evidence has yet come to light, and perhaps it remained only an administrative fantasy.[92] Even as a dream, however, it signified that with the Archivio Urbano the process of fusing fragmented courts and notaries begun by Paul V's reform of documentary practices had taken another step forward.

From the outset, its creators conceived of the archive as a way to locate documents as well as to store them, and the 1625 regulations made the correct shelf order of the volumes and the manufacture of "finding aids" a priority. Within the rooms of the archive they mandated the division of materials by tribunal, so, for example, the instruments delivered by the notaries of the auditor of the Camera would be kept together, shelved in alphabetical order (by notary) and in numbered volumes. Each volume was to have a rubricella "with the indication of the type of contract, such as *venditio* and so forth, as seems best to the conservator, so that each document may easily be found."[93]

Perhaps the most lasting achievement of the Archivio Urbano was the creation of catalogs, which, in a semantic expansion from the word's usage in 1494 and 1580, were now referred to as *repertorij*. According to article 9, "distinct *repertorij* and indices should be made of all the names and surnames of those who in the future make wills and any other testamentary bequests, both free inheritances and those subject to entail, primogeniture, or other legal constraint."[94] Although only wills and gifts between the living were mentioned, the staff exceeded these commands by adding catalogs of the names of contracting parties in all the instruments they collected. One of the most interesting experiments they undertook, though they abandoned it by the early 1630s, was the creation of alphabetical lists by clients' surnames rather than the usual contemporary practice of alphabetizing by Christian name. Thereafter, baptismal names were the point of entry into the Archivio Urbano's holdings.

In the first generation of the archive's existence, the archivists produced more than fifty volumes of such repertorii. Clients who had made wills or gifts over a period of five to fifteen years were gathered together in distinct volumes; names of those initiating other types of instruments were divided into volumes by tribunal. For the years 1625 to 1627, for example, there were two volumes listing the names of contracting parties in the instruments of the Capitoline notaries and two in those of the notaries of the auditor of the Camera. "Miscellaneous notaries," which likely meant the private notaries, had separate catalogs. Armed with the Christian name and an approximate date, users could search the repertorii of the Archivio Urbano for the record of a particular contract and the name of the notary in whose office they could find it. Once they had located it in the notary's protocol, they could return to ask the archive officials to compare the original and the copy so as to be certain there had been no alterations in the original.

Shelves, binding, wages, rent—who would pay the costs of setting up and running this ambitious new state notarial archive? It needed an income, even with the unpaid labor of the four notaries borrowed from the major city tribunals, which, as we have seen, may or may not have been forthcoming. The Archivio di Curia had been theoretically financed by sales of offices in the College of Scriptors, but these revenues had been diverted into the hands of investors. The Archivio Capitolino paid its expenses through fees generated by copies (transunti) made from its holdings, a source ruled out in principle at the Archivio Urbano. Sixtus V had leased out the notarial archives of the towns of the Papal States, solving the problem of funding by shifting it to the banker who purchased the contract. Urban VIII passed the costs onto the notary's clients at the point of production. He confirmed the usual copy rate in Rome for the copy to be brought to the archive and set new fees for archiving it. Archiving fees were relatively low; they advanced on a sliding scale of one grosso (five baiocchi) per one hundred scudi in value to a maximum of eight scudi on real estate sales and a maximum of two scudi on all other eligible contracts, including wills.[95] The notary collected both sets of fees from his customers at the initial moment of rogation.

Because of the volume of their business, Capitoline notaries and the notaries of the auditor of the Camera had three months to deliver copies and fees; other notaries with offices had two months. Testaments, as we have seen, had shorter deadlines. Obligations in scriptura privata paid at exactly the same rate as notarial instruments. Private notaries had twenty days to make the copies and turn them in, paying along with the archive fee an extra tax of one grosso per sheet of the original, presumably because the Archivio Urbano was serving in lieu of a protocol. The archive invited anyone to bring in any document he wished for safekeeping, paying one giulio (ten baiocchi) for the privilege. These funding provisions would not prove sufficient. Lacking a source of income in its holdings, the Archivio Urbano was forced to rely for its revenue stream on the diligence and alacrity of the notaries, and they proved neither diligent nor prompt. After Camillo Perini departed in 1633, the archive was farmed out, but this failed to remedy its financial woes.

Such problems lay in the future, however. In the fall of 1625 the Barberini seem to have thought of everything to guarantee the success of the Archivio Urbano, both as an archive for the kinds of agreements they thought most likely to provoke disputes and as a more general means of supervising the notarial profession in Rome. They had freshly rented quarters near St. Peter's, many copies of the new regulations dispersed around the city, and a trusted familiar in charge. As Perini opened for business in the Palazzo Alicorni, perhaps he began his work by arranging the hundreds of volumes of original protocols and registers he had inherited from the Archivio di Curia.[96]

By the following summer the Barberini cardinals knew that the Archivio Urbano needed more legislation, to plug loopholes in the founding texts and to expand its authority over financial transactions, and in a single day they issued three separate edicts. Claiming that residents were trying to evade the new archive by slipping outside the walls and rogating acts in the surrounding district, they ordered notaries of the district to turn in a copy of all pertinent instruments in which even one of the contracting parties lived in Rome.[97] While repeating the kinds of contracts they wanted archived, they lengthened the list of types of powers of attorney they now wanted to include. Archive officials also made up for the extraordinary omission of solicitations to those holding protocols of deceased notaries, for so long a staple of notarial regulation. On 30 June 1626 they finally commanded that the documents of notaries who had died be delivered to the Archivio Urbano.[98] Two weeks later, Pope Urban VIII asked bishops throughout the Papal States to search their dioceses for the instruments of deceased notaries and threatened to excommunicate anyone who knowingly hid them.[99] He was right to suspect that religious entities might be reluctant to turn over the contracts that proved long-standing possessions and rights to an archive that seemed like merely the latest gesture of papal grandiosity. Some resisted for many more decades, and one Roman church clung to its oldest notarial protocols until the twentieth century.[100]

The most intriguing novelty in this burst of new orders, however, was the Barberini's attempt to use the Archivio Urbano to penetrate into the most advanced sector of the local economy, finance. The spread of the so-called *società in accomandita*, which had first appeared in Rome in 1613, particularly disturbed them.[101] While the founding legislation of the archive had targeted long-term loans secured on real estate, it had had very little to say about the records of other types of credit operations. As we have seen, it did no more than try to track the use of powers of attorney issued abroad. Yet Rome was one of the busiest and most inventive financial markets of early modern Europe. It restlessly sought new ways to make money beget money, whether selling offices in the papal Curia in the fifteenth century, inventing public bonds in the 1520s, or fashioning more recently a unique short-term credit instrument, the *società d'ufficio*.[102] Indeed, the fortunes of many religious and charitable institutions, as well as thousands of individuals, were bound up in these instruments. Although the Archivio Urbano had not been established to control such exchanges, the Barberini now tried to adapt it to do so.

In contrast to partnerships, where losses were equally apportioned, lenders in the società in accomandita limited their losses to what they had invested. In the days before the limited-liability joint-stock company, these appealing terms drew a wide range of investors, mobilized by middlemen who put the deals together by joining those who wanted money to those who had it. The economic and legal world imagined by the notarial instrument placed creditor, debtor, notary, and witnesses in a common space to make and observe a binding agreement. The reality of seventeenth-century investing was creditors and debtors who would never meet in person, with agents in distant cities seeking the best rates in a fast-paced and fluid market.[103] Notarial instruments might document some phases in these partnerships, but agents were just as likely to fix their deals in scriptura privata, in merchants' account books, letters, or notes. In their third edict on 30 June 1626, the Barberini cardinals demanded that participants in any società in accomandita contract, whether notarized or not, deliver it to the Archivio Urbano within thirty days, on pain of losing the protections they had negotiated.[104] This penalty made them liable for a proportion of the entire business losses rather than the amount to which they had actually agreed.

The middlemen drew the heaviest suspicion. Unchecked and unsupervised, they dashed about brandishing powers of attorney and promising sums of money to unknown borrowers with whom creditors had no relationship. The pope, the edict declared, "wanted to remedy the troubles that arise between merchants who do not know the condition of those with whom they do business and make them more secure."[105] The way to do this was to try to keep track of the brokers, the men who committed other people's money and left no identifying marks on it. Whether they operated by scriptura privata or went before a notary, the agents must provide the Archivio Urbano with a copy of every document authorizing or removing them from their financial speculations.

Such regulations, had they operated, would certainly have slowed the pace of exchange, binding money and its handlers in fresh bands of red tape. Moreover, because they were retroactive in their application, they would have overwhelmed the new archive with a storm surge of temporary powers of attorney of unstable substance and brief shelf life. Like many of the archive provisions, they were also difficult to enforce. How could state officials detect whether middlemen were complying with the rules? How long would it take for them to litigate successfully the cases in which partners were made fully liable for all debts rather than for their contributions to the total? Società in accomandita contracts vanish from later legislation, and we do not know how many were archived, if any, or how many temporary powers of attorney. What is significant is that, within eight or nine months of its foundation, its creators had come to see the Archivio Urbano as more than a general notarial archive and a means of controlling Roman notaries. It now appeared to them as a tool for disciplining the most unruly, or innovative, sectors of the local economy.

Evidently, the archive's sponsors considered their handiwork complete as of the summer of 1626, not anticipating the obstacles that would force many changes in their original arrangements in the years ahead. In 1629 Andrea Brugiotti, the printer holding the lease of the Apostolic Camera's printing press, published most of the legislation about the Archivio Urbano, including the three edicts of 30 June 1626 and that of 15 July, as a forty-page ottavo booklet equipped with a detailed index.[106] The little pamphlet, supplemented every few years by posters announcing the latest revisions in the regulations, was an instrument for educating the profession and the public in new archival practices.

The Capitoline notaries may well have obeyed. In the 1630s the account books of the widow of Capitoline notary Lorenzo Bonincontro record payments for copies and for archive fees for the instruments produced in her late husband's office, though admittedly they were tardily delivered.[107] Researchers will discover archiving marks in the margins of many original post-1625 business acts indicating that they had been shown to the staff of the Archivio Urbano at the time the fee and the copy were turned in.[108] Many carefully numbered volumes of copies sit to this day in the Archivio Urbano. Capitoline notary Angelo Giustiniani, for example, has seven volumes of business acts there dating from 1625 to 1644, plus three volumes of wills; for Leonardo Bonanni, who rogated until 1667, there are twenty-three volumes of copies.[109] The copies are far fewer than the three protocols of original instruments produced by the offices of Giustiniani and Bonanni each year, but the archive had never intended to collect all notarial acts. Although some of the minor points in the 1625 legislation seem to have been totally ignored, one of its major objectives was not.[110]

Some private notaries also obeyed, finding that the new controls boosted their legitimacy and compensated for the lack of an office by providing clients with a public notarial archive. One of these was Eugenio Salvetti, who, after a twenty-five-year career working in various notarial offices in Rome, posted bond and was approved by archive officials.[111] Thereafter, he rogated in his own home and sent in his copies to the Archivio Urbano. The acts of private notaries who died could now also be located with greater certainty, which, in theory at least, ought to have magnified their appeal while they lived.[112]

Romans quickly learned how to exploit the Archivio Urbano. The nieces of a wealthy fishmonger, astounded to have been cut out of his will, brought criminal charges against his heir in 1635 and demanded to see the signature on the testament located in the archive.[113] Because the will was in the protocol of a deceased curial notary, the women knew they had an original to which to compare the contested version. Useful to lay persons pursuing criminal verdicts, the archive was also helpful to the notarial profession in unexpected ways. Robbers broke into the office of Capitoline notary Tranquillo Pizzuti in 1628 and hauled away a number of his documents. Pizzuti petitioned Camillo Perini and Cardinal Francesco Barberini to allow him to make copies of some twenty stolen wills from the copies deposited in the Archivio Urbano.[114] Exercising his powers as the general guardian of notarial documents in the city, Perini himself offered a reward for information about the theft.[115] More informally, when notaries ran into each other at the archive, they had a chance to hear the latest professional gossip and to exchange stories and warnings about shady deals and untrustworthy employees.[116]

Camillo Perini discussed the Pizzuti theft personally with Urban VIII.[117] Although the Barberini kept close watch on the Archivio Urbano after his departure in 1633, the government's grasp inevitably relaxed once the Apostolic Camera began leasing it to a private contractor and supervision was handed to the treasurer general. The treasurer's was a venal post held by one of the highest prelates in the Curia, usually in this period from a wealthy Genoese banking family; it was unlikely to reproduce the intimate engagement of a trusted familiar. The treasurer did inherit Perini's full jurisdiction; he was the supreme judge over all Roman notaries, he ensured that the contractor ran the archive properly, and he enforced the edicts commanding notaries to turn in their copies.[118] Perini's replacement as conservator, Giulio Donati, lost these powers and had to obey the orders of those in higher authority.[119]

The bureaucratic descent of the Archivio Urbano after 1633 was complicated, and somewhat offset, by its uninterrupted political support from the Barberini cardinals. While the treasurer general had nominal authority over the archive, its protector Cardinal Francesco Barberini continued to publish its regulations and made his own auditor responsible for seeing that they were obeyed.[120] He declared that only his auditor should pass judgment in disputes over archive fees or rules. Such jurisdictional confusion in high places signaled opportunities for conflicts lower down. In 1639 the auditor of the Camera, not far below the treasurer general in the curial hierarchy, challenged the Archivio Urbano's control over the process of examining and approving notaries. Brandishing Paul V's legislation, he reasserted the privileges of the College of Scriptors to certify the suitability of the employees of notarial offices and to discipline the writing practices of sostituti.[121] All the while these tensions were playing themselves out, the finances of the archive were revealed to be precarious, if not actually ruinous.

The first lease of the Archivio Urbano was intended to run from 1633 to 1642, but its lessor, Alessandro Gentile, defaulted after only three years.[122] In 1636 the first of a long series of contractors from the diocese of Fermo, Francesco Felice, paid 1,400 scudi a year to manage the archive with the hope of bringing in at least enough income to repay his investment and with luck turn a profit. In 1645 Rodomonte de Nobili, a veteran of the Roman courts, succeeded him with another nine-year lease.[123] A major change in the way archive fees were collected in 1646 must have improved the Archivio Urbano's earnings because Rodomonte's brother Antonio paid 1,562 scudi for the nine-year lease in 1654, and this amount remained constant in the following contract.[124]

Our evidence that by the 1630s the archive was encountering recalcitrant notaries and could not force compliance with its directives comes chiefly from the published edicts of governmental officials like Cardinal Francesco Barberini. These sources may exaggerate resistance. In the time-honored tradition of pacts between early modern states and the private contractors to whom they leased public functions, like tax collecting, the state's role was to compel obedience from subjects so that the contractors could carry out their duties. Officials put out the commands and threatened the punishments on printed posters that were stuck up at major city squares, while financiers actually managed the business. If the business, whether it was banking, the flour tax, or archival fees, failed to prosper, the state could find itself without any investors willing to do its job. Papal officials had every incentive to depict the Archivio Urbano enterprise as profitable and, once they had struck deals with private contractors to run it, to portray any disappointment in those profits as a failure of subjects to obey the rules. The evidence of their edicts must be read in the light of these economic realities.

Yet even unpublished sources, though from a curial milieu, point to problems in the way the Archivio Urbano was operating.[125] Notaries, it appeared, were not archiving their instruments, as they should have been. In 1637, a year into Felice's new contract, Cardinal Francesco Barberini issued a revised list of twelve "provisions and orders regarding the Archivio Urbano," with sharp criticisms of the notaries and bold new enforcement mechanisms.[126] The original orders of 1625, the cardinal protector claimed, had been partly neglected and partly disputed, "in order to impede their execution," and he intended to clear away these obstructions. In his view notaries were failing to bring their copies to the archive within the prescribed deadlines because their office employees were not extending the instruments from their matrices in a diligent and timely fashion, and he gave them one month to do so (art. 2). More importantly, he tried to find a way to compel future diligence by knowing precisely what pertinent contracts the notaries were producing. The 1625 regulations had set up vague and contradictory procedures for doing this, which the cardinal protector now clarified. He instructed notaries to keep a daily roster of eligible contracts and foreign powers of attorney, showing not only the name of the contracting party but also that of the sostituto in the office who had rogated it, in a volume to be signed by archive officials (art. 3). Such a book would belong officially to the Archivio Urbano, though it would reside with the notaries and be distinct from the receipt book ordered by Paul V's reforms. This seemingly innocuous innovation, if it had lasted, would have transformed the relationship between the state and the notaries. While since the fifteenth century Capitoline notaries had exhibited their protocols to their own college officers each year, neither they nor any other notaries had previously been required to bring anything to government officials for signature or inspection. By such barely perceptible gestures, the Barberini sought to fashion of their new notarial archive an instrument to replace corporate discipline with that of the state.

Another new enforcement measure extended earlier instructions given to bank cashiers also to notaries, ordering them not to honor foreign powers of attorney, wills, or gifts between the living, unless they bore the imprint of the archivio (art. 5).[127] Cardinal Barberini attempted to put an end to quibbles about just which instruments were included in the legislation. For the first time, he defined perpetual contracts as those lasting longer than nine years, and he elaborated on all the types of possession contracts (always of real property) of which he wanted copies (art. 6). He reiterated that scriptura privata agreements must be archived, giving their holders one month to comply (art. 7).

The cardinal protector also repeated his orders of 1626 that the protocols of private notaries be delivered to the Archivio Urbano within two weeks of their death (art. 12). In the sole exception to the prohibition on copying, he permitted archive staff to make, and presumably levy fees on, transunti of these original acts and said nothing about the rights of heirs to any residual income from them. If this was indeed the practice at the new archive, it was a significant breach in the principle of the proprietary claims of notaries to the future income from their business acts. Private notaries had now lost these rights; only the venal officeholders retained them.

Two special problems with the archiving of wills had surfaced since 1625. In addition to parish priests, hospital employees, the secretaries of charitable institutions, and even notaries working for criminal jurisdictions took down testaments for the dying, and the cardinal reminded them all that they were subject to the same obligation to deliver these to the Archivio Urbano (art. 4). He rectified an omission in the founding legislation by authorizing the conservator of the archive to open sealed wills within two months of the death of the testator, on presentation of a death certificate, even if no one came forward to make the request (art. 8). In fact, in 1628 Perini had opened sealed wills dating from 1578 to 1625, without this specific authority.[128] Churchmen evidently believed that those testators who had no potential heirs clamoring to execute a will were especially likely to have bequeathed their property to charitable and devotional institutions. Barberini's 1637 amendment did not go to the heart of the difficulty of which the cardinal vicar had warned as early as 1576. How were officials to know who had died so that they could try to find their wills? As we shall see in chapter 6, the problem remained intractable, despite a drastic intervention by Clement XI in 1703.

While most of the twelve provisions issued in 1637 represented elaboration or refinements of the founding legislation of the Archivio Urbano, the cardinal protector broke new ground when he announced that he wanted to enforce Paul V's orders dictating the binding of instruments into protocols every three months. Making no attempt to hide the wider disciplinary purposes of the archive, he empowered the staff "to review [*rivedere*] the offices" of Roman notaries and to punish transgressors of the norms of 1612 (art. 9).[129] It was the first mention of the possibility of inspections of notarial workplaces by the agents of the Archivio Urbano, and it expanded their mandate well beyond the archive. Cardinal Barberini authorized them to check the offices, protocols, and instruments of any notary in any tribunal as well as those without offices to ensure compliance with all previous papal regulations (art. 10).

The cardinal was right to see a logical connection between the goals of the Archivio Urbano and the document-handling practices of notaries. If the padroni of offices forced their employees to have every new contract extended in its mundum version and ready for binding within three months of the transaction, as earlier laws required, the mechanics of archiving the copy would be relatively simple. The notary's office could simply send someone with the protocol and a copy of the mundum to the Archivio Urbano for checking, payment, and consignment. If notaries did not keep track of the work rhythms of their sostituti and giovani, however, "neglect and delay" in extending the matrici would occur, which Cardinal Francesco Barberini blamed for the failures of the new archive.

Like other radical features of Barberini legislation, however, the inspection of notarial offices by the agents of the Archivio Urbano seems to have remained a dead letter. We have no evidence that it occurred under either Urban VIII or his successors. These seeds did eventually germinate, but it took sixty-five years and major changes to the soil and climate of papal government for them to do so.

A year and a half before Urban VIII's pontificate came to an end in 1644, the cardinal protector issued a third revision of the "provisions and orders" for the Archivio Urbano, which took a different tack toward its troubles. Demonstrating that his archive was in danger of leaving no legacy in state administration, Cardinal Barberini's January 1643 edict attempted to shore up its powers by bringing it more closely under his personal control.[130] Without changing any of the rules affecting its contents, he reorganized its structure and further expanded its authority to intervene in notarial practices outside its walls. His chief strategy was to shift the conservator's former jurisdiction to his own auditor Giulio Cenci, to whom a newly created subordinate with the title of archivist answered.

The cardinal's auditor had the right to see that notaries were extending their instruments from their notes, binding them into protocols, and keeping a separate list of the eligible contracts owed to the archive, and he could order the archivist to visit the offices to check for compliance. It is the first time that the term "*visitare*," meaning a thorough, on-site investigation, appears in Roman notarial legislation.[131] An ingenious new method of enforcement allowed officials not only to inspect documents in the notaries' offices but to carry off those that had not been archived, to hold them for a month while the delinquents satisfied their obligations, or, failing that, to copy them at the notaries' expense. The cardinal's auditor received all the legal faculties he might need to enforce archival rules and settle fee disputes without delay.[132] He also inherited the conservator of the archive's power to approve private notaries who wanted to rogate on their own.[133] The cardinal protector treated the archivist, nominally responsible for managing the Archivio Urbano, as a lowly subordinate, warning him in a public edict to preserve the acts in his care, not to overcharge users, and not to make copies from his holdings. His auditor could order inspections of the archive itself and impose penalties on the archivist.

Turning to the Roman notaries, Barberini offered yet another amnesty for recalcitrants, allowing them two months to turn in their copies or face the stated penalties. He insisted on the general rule, however, that notaries and their sostituti extend their notes "into a clean version ready to bind" within one month. For the first time, they were also directed to retain the matrice for one year from the date of the transaction, "because experience shows that both the circumstances and the [particular] qualities of the contracts are forgotten if there are delays in extending the original notes."[134]

By January 1643 Urban VIII's government faced far more severe challenges than sloppy notaries, however, as the papal nephews led a costly and unpopular war against neighboring states, and the pontificate waned with the pope's health.[135] Cardinal Francesco Barberini's method of strengthening the Archivio Urbano in the final years of his uncle's reign only served to identify it more closely with the Barberini, which weakened its prospects in a post–Urban VIII regime. To these political vulnerabilities the archive added the further liabilities of contested jurisdiction and unreliable revenues. As we have seen, several leading officials of the Curia disputed its powers and, despite the inclusion of major groups of papal notaries in its regulations, other important curial notaries, like those of the Dataria, were still exempt. For an institution whose management was farmed out to private entrepreneurs, both these conditions meant lowered income, not only from uncollected fees but also from the inability to prosecute transgressors effectively.

Two years after Innocent X replaced Urban VIII as pope, and one year into a new nine-year lease of the archive, the treasurer general Lorenzo Raggi at last asserted his prerogatives and made dramatic alterations both to the founding legislation and to Cardinal Francesco Barberini's later innovations.[136] Raggi's edict of 31 October 1646 marked a turning point as decisive as that of Perini's departure from the Archivio Urbano in 1633, but in truth it was the Barberini's fall from power that ushered in a new era. The treasurer's most significant modification was to change the way that archive fees were paid. For twenty years clients had given notaries the money to take to the archive along with the copies of their documents. Raggi pointed out that under this system notaries had no incentive to deliver either fees or copies, which helped to explain the now familiar "neglect and delay " in extending their instruments and bringing them to the archive. He shifted the payments to the clients. Henceforth, clients were to go to the Archivio Urbano bearing a note from their notary that described the nature and value of the contract and hand over the archival fee themselves (art. 2).[137] Archive staff would return the notes to the clients after entering the information in their registers, then await the arrival of the actual copies from the notaries. The notaries and their employees still faced the same deadlines for bringing the copies along with the originals, bound in numbered and indexed protocols, against which they would be checked for accuracy (art. 3). The 1646 regulations did away with Barberini's 1637 policy of having notaries keep a separate volume, signed by the archivist, listing eligible contracts; it was hardly necessary if archive officials themselves were making such a register. Instead, the treasurer re-emphasized the faithful recording of all business in the notary's receipt book, a practice introduced by Paul V's reforms (art. 4).

The 1646 edict on the Archivio Urbano reiterated the original 1625 obligations to archive wills and scriptura privata agreements. It also repeated the list of types of instruments subject to the archive, innovating in only one particular (art. 9). Previously powers of attorney issued outside the Papal States had been the target, but now copies of all powers of attorney, including those written without a notary's aid, had to be deposited. Raggi continued to make an exception for those authorizing litigation and, in a notable new privilege, those issued on behalf of cardinals and the highest officials of the Curia.

Significantly, the treasurer backed away from the novel enforcement methods Cardinal Francesco Barberini had tried to introduce. Gone was any mention of investigations of the notarial offices by archive officials. Indeed, high-level archive officials, whether conservator, archivist, or auditor of a powerful cardinal nephew, had themselves vanished from the regulations, along with the cardinal protector. Instead, Raggi had resuscitated medieval methods of compulsion, apparently hoping to entice secret denunciations of transgressors by the prospect of rewards. All fines collected, he declared, would be divided three ways among the accuser, the contractor, and the Apostolic Camera (art. 10). He deployed this tactic to snare the most lucrative of notarial acts, wills, by levying a penalty of one-quarter of the value of a bequest upon heirs who did not pay the archive fee and offering a third of that to the person who turned them in (art. 6).

While the treasurer general's new regulations for the Archivio Urbano were conservative by comparison with his predecessor, he had clearly benefited from two decades of institutional experimentation. They gave him the luxury of assessing results and making adjustments. Putting the onus on clients rather than notaries to deliver fees to the archive worked, at least to assure the archive's income. Rodomonte de Nobili, the contractor holding the lease from 1645 to 1654, must have collected more than the fourteen hundred scudi he invested because the Apostolic Camera increased the price in subsequent leases.[138] Nevertheless, the post-Barberini archival regime was distinctly less ambitious than that of Urban VIII and his nephews. Reassured about its income, those responsible for the Archivio Urbano had no reason to seek constantly for new ways to force changes in notarial writing and document-handling practices, even when such changes simply meant compliance with rules long on the books. More problematically, the modifications of 1646 may have repaired the finances of the Archivio Urbano at a rather high price. Notaries still had no incentive, and now little compulsion, to turn in their copies.

The archive settled into its new modus operandi. After the Barberini pontificate, the pace of government edicts regarding the Archivio Urbano slackened. There had been at least nine under Urban VIII; there would be only four during the remainder of the century.[139] Pope Alexander VII waited until 1659 to order a follow-up to the treasurer general's 1646 regulations, and when he did, he simply repeated them almost verbatim.[140] Only a close examination of the thousands of volumes in its holdings would reveal whether the Archivio Urbano's collection of copies flourished or languished with less attention from the popes. As we shall see, papal investigators in the early eighteenth century pinpointed enduring loopholes and claimed that notaries owed thousands of documents to the Archivio Urbano. The archive moved to various city locations during the course of the seventeenth century, finally settling down in the somewhat remote Vatican Palace.[141] Was this a metaphor for its marginalization in city life?

Urban VIII's copy archive in Rome may not have fulfilled the great dreams he and his nephews nurtured for it in the 1620s and 1630s. It may not have gathered all the copies of the documents it sought from notaries or ordinary subjects; it may not have controlled all private notaries working in Rome; it may not have disciplined writing practices in the notarial offices around the city. Its ambitions illuminate what early modern governments could imagine, however, as well as what they had to settle for. The Barberini had confronted the problem of enforcement of notarial legislation in new ways. They envisioned a department of the state that would centralize surveillance of notaries and compel obedience to existing laws using novel methods of inspection and compulsion. When Urban VIII and his successors were incapable of endowing such a bureau with the resources and personnel needed to fulfill these aspirations, the Archivio Urbano ended up as a mere archive, a minor annoyance and occasional convenience for the bulk of notaries and their clients.

Although it left no legacy in state administration, Urban's effort had left an important legacy of another sort. In Rome, where there had never been a general public registry of notarial acts, private economic agreements had never before drawn such sustained government interest. Urban VIII's radical scheme did for business acts what Pius IV and Paul V had done for judicial acts. As these earlier popes had imposed uniform regulations on notaries in the city's many different tribunals, Urban imposed common rules on all notaries, ignoring age-old distinctions between Capitoline and curial notaries, and between venal officeholders and those in private practice. Moreover, he established the precedent by which a single official of the papal government, first the conservator of the archive and eventually the treasurer general, dictated norms for writing, handling, and keeping business acts. Whether or not the papacy could force notaries to obey the archive's rules, the common rules had transformed a fractured profession's relationship to the state. They had made all the varied practitioners of the notarial trade responsible not just to investors, clients, employers, or colleagues but also to the papal government.

Conclusion

The striking concentration and quantity of legislation reviewed in this and the preceding chapter transformed the notary's pages and their spaces in Rome between 1450 and 1650. While the notarial profession and the municipality played a role in getting these changes underway, the papal government was by far the most resolute innovator, particularly after 1550. The results are manifest: increased surveillance of notaries, either by judges or via the Archivio Urbano; centralized document collection, through both venality and the establishment of public archives; and eased consultation of records through a wide array of measures ranging from abolishing the visura fee to mandating indexes in every protocol. But if the effects of the great state interventions on scriptura publica are clear, their motivations are less obvious.

One possible explanation is the general imperative of state building undertaken by absolute, centralizing monarchs. The papacy was strengthening its control of all facets of its subjects' lives in these centuries, and their documents naturally appeared in its crosshairs. Regulation of notarial writing flowed from this exercise of power. A subtler version takes papal concerns about its subjects' litigiousness at their word and reasons that making notarial documents harder to lose or falsify would reduce disputes and lawsuits and enhance social order.[142] Another hypothesis is the modernization thesis in which some bureaucratic processes are deemed inherently more rational than others; the state naturally gravitated toward these as it "developed" in the early modern period. Creating public notarial archives reflected, and fueled, this drive toward modernity.[143] A final theory stressing the importance of credit relationships to the early modern economy argues the need to establish a hierarchy among debtors based on the strength of their claims.[144] Here the popes bolstered notarial acts so that they could compete more effectively against oral testimony and scriptura privata in the Roman market for evidence.

While there are valid, or at least plausible, elements to all these explanations, the papal model is notable for introducing venality into the broad picture of notarial activity, and venality complicates our reading of motivation. Beginning in the 1470s, the popes clearly demonstrated their willingness to sell off curial notarial offices for gain; having squeezed out as much as they could manage by the 1580s, they willingly sold the notaries of other administrations. An undated memorandum that circulated in the Curia probably around the time of Sixtus V's establishment of notarial archives in the Papal States promises that controlling notaries will be lucrative for the state.[145] The centralizing and modernizing monarchs saw notarial documents and notaries as fiscal plunder. Once the popes had sold whatever they could, however, the independent forces of the market and the logic of venality powerfully circumscribed their ability to control notarial practices. As we have seen, they tried investing in a state-financed disciplinary mechanism, which might have acted as a counterweight, but they could not sustain it. Perhaps it is no accident that their legislation intensified at the very moment when venality absorbed all but the last remnants of a free profession. If talk was not exactly cheap, normative discourse was at least an investment they could continue to make.

Also complicating the question of what drove the state's transformation of notarial pages and spaces is the fact that the policies of centralizing and modernizing monarchs were not always coherent. If they had only regarded notaries as sources of profit, the popes ought to have done everything possible to shore up their income so that the offices would bring higher prices. Instead, as early as the 1560s, they were actually lowering the price of using notaries by forcing diversification of their product line through the creation of simple copies in lieu of the more costly public copies. Abolishing the fee for looking at business acts in 1612 cut into notaries' earnings too. We have argued that concerns about the functioning of their judicial system led the pontiffs to look for ways to economize on writing done by notaries both in and out of court. There were obvious tensions between the papacy's dual goals of profiting from venality and cutting the cost of notarial services, inconsistencies that made the enterprise of brokering public trust a risky business. As we shall see in the next chapter, men in seventeenth-century Rome who sought to make a living by producing scriptura publica had to operate within these new and contradictory conditions.

CHAPTER FIVE

The Office

Building Scribal Lives

Public writing depended for its existence on a robust apparatus of legal principles and, increasingly, an array of disciplinary mechanisms. Without the bedrock of Roman legal conventions, ideas of proof and public office would not have taken the forms that they took in Italy's notarial regimes, and without the attentions of those wielding power, whether in Rome or elsewhere, notaries' words would have been worthless. Yet more than just a set of authoritative notions and persons, scriptura publica was also a writing practice or, better, practices. Hands and minds acted to create notarial documents, and to understand public writing, we must know something about its producers, the conditions of its production, and the commercial matrix in which it was consumed.

The dramatic papal interventions of 1550 to 1650 ensured that public writing remained a business and that notaries continued to traffic in public trust in order to make a living. As we have seen, the popes solidified the fundamentally entrepreneurial nature of the Capitoline offices; by cutting numbers and making notaries buy their posts, they raised the economic stakes. After 1586 the notaries of the Capitoline curia wagered goodly sums on the hope that they could cover the cost of a purchased office and make a profit. The risks of miscalculation were real; bankruptcy meant jail and dishonor. The fact that they were trading in paper that was so intensely legislated, while the source of its value to their clients, opened notaries to the added threat of judicial sanctions. The legal stakes were not inconsequential. Even if papal authorities failed to detect wrongdoing, outraged investors and customers were quick to call them to account. Venality altered the conditions of notarial production, enhanced the possibilities for gain, and heightened the dangers of loss.

While it is true that Sixtus V had created a corps of thirty privileged notaries to serve the Roman citizenry, the market for their wares was far from secure. Scriptura publica in early modern Rome faced steady, perhaps increasing, competition from other types of evidence. Writing by private individuals was flowing under, around, and above public writing in an ever-widening stream. Much of this river of words frankly imitated notarial discourse, though not in the Latin language of the law.[1] Romans did not necessarily want to go to notaries; for some kinds of contracts, they may even have grown more reluctant to pay for a notarial act.[2] Some exploited alternative sources of scriptura publica, establishing proof, for example, by taking the records they had written themselves to a judge to certify.[3] Others exercised the option, sanctioned by some jurists, that allowed them to state their desire that their scriptura privata document have the same force as a notarial instrument.[4] On price alone it was hard to argue with them.

Ordinary writers had learned from notaries the practice of documentation, the habit of written receipts, promises, and agreements. Merchants had recognized this very early, and Roman city statutes from the first treated scriptura privata with respect. Despite the absence of good measures of literacy, it may well be that an increasing number of Romans could write, and, if so, they were most likely to write in connection with some type of economic exchange. Even those who could not write, understanding the economic, legal, and cultural value placed on written records, found ways to gain access to them that did not always pass through the hands of notaries.[5]

One resource the Capitoline notaries could throw into the balance, of course, was their command of some of the portals to the civil justice system.[6] To obtain alternatives to public writing, customers often turned to the civil courts, and when their court of choice was the tribunal of the senator, they ended up doing business with the Capitoline notaries. Other factors, too, pushed Romans very frequently toward the courts and, thus, often into Capitoline offices. But there were thirty Capitoline notaries to pick from, and the city offered other tribunals, all of them by the seventeenth century staffed by eager venal officeholders. Notaries had to compete for litigants. Despite the oft-quoted complaints about the abuses of court notaries, the judicial economy of baroque Rome did not provide an easy living for its professionals.

Against the background of high stakes and precarious profits, the Capitoline notaries had to find the capital to purchase an office; hire, train, and pay a reliable scribal labor force; come to terms with the fresh laws and archival demands imposed by the papacy; and satisfy enough clients to stay in business. The trick was how to make people believe their writing was trustworthy and worth the price in the risky, competitive conditions in which venal officeholders operated. The challenges were new in the first half of the seventeenth century, following Paul V's judicial reforms and his grant of fully inheritable offices and Urban VIII's establishment of the new archive, when the young notarial college was still struggling to organize itself. They played themselves out in the notary's office, the space to which we now turn. This was a financial investment and a physical location, a workplace and a household, a courtroom and an archive. The writing that went on within and without its walls claimed to have special force, to be a kind of writing different from its rivals in the early modern market for proof. By what material practices, social relations, and economic exchanges did it sustain these claims to credibility, and how were they received? To find out, we will look, as closely as the reticence of notaries permits, at the men of the Capitoline curia who made their living from scriptura publica in the decades between 1612 and 1652.

Acquiring an Office

Notaries with venal offices who could count on a steady stream of work from a tribunal stood at the apex of the profession in seventeenth-century Rome. A 1703 inquiry identified a total of sixty-one such offices, of which the Capitoline notaries represented a half.[7] From the 1480s on, the popes had gradually reshaped the profession of notary in Rome into those with offices and those without. Thanks to their eagerness to gain income and tighten controls over the judicial system, this process was largely complete by 1630 and the professional landscape had assumed its final premodern contours.

What did this notarial setting look like in 1630? While the thirty offices of the two Capitoline collaterali were the most numerous, they were not necessarily the most prestigious or remunerative. During most of the seventeenth century, that honor probably fell to the ten notaries of the tribunal of the auditor of the Camera.[8] Yet, unlike the Capitoline notaries whose offices were fully inheritable from 1612, the notaries of the auditor of the Camera could purchase but not bequeath their offices.[9] Next in size came the nine offices of the Apostolic Chamber, which were leased rather than sold; these "notaries of the Camera," as they were known in the seventeenth century, were reduced to four in 1672.[10] The court of the cardinal vicar (Vicariato) also relied on four notarial offices.[11] The seventeenth-century popes increasingly tended to treat these four groups of notaries somewhat differently from the other venal officeholders. As we saw in chapter 4, Pope Urban VIII described them as "colleges" when he assigned them duties in the new notarial archive that he established in 1625. Later pontiffs continued this practice of forcing responsibilities for the profession as a whole upon these four groups of notaries. Strictly speaking, a college, to Urban VIII as well as his predecessors, was nothing more than a collection of venal officeholders. They might have some collective interest in protecting their investment but few other points of contact. Of these four colleges before the 1670s, only the Capitoline notaries developed a fully elaborated association complete with statutes and officers.[12]

With some exceptions a single notary leased most other offices; this was the case for the tribunals of water and streets, Borgo, agriculture, the downstream river port of Ripa, the Florentines, the building committee (*fabbrica*) of St. Peter's Basilica, and the hospital of Santo Spirito.[13] A notary who leased an office from the College of Scriptors acquired judicial work for the papal tribunal of the Segnatura in 1659.[14] The very active criminal court of the governor of Rome shared one notarial office among several notaries and also had two notaries for civil cases. Nor were the thirty Capitoline notaries the only notaries serving civic magistracies. The protonotary of the senator worked on civil cases and another notary wrote for the senator's criminal cases, while both the judge called the captain of appeals and the elected conservators had notaries. The case of the notaries of the Rota, the papal appeals court, was more complicated. Until 1671 each of the twelve judges on the Rota had the services of four notaries, for a total of forty-eight, but without formal offices. Rota business was not brisk enough to sustain so many notaries, and in 1671 the number was reduced to four, to whom their predecessors' documents were turned over.[15]

While sixty notarial offices may have operated in a city that grew from 120,000 to 140,000 between 1620 and 1700, there were far more than sixty notaries in Rome, though it is not easy to say exactly how many more.[16] We generally know only the names of the notaries with offices, yet scholars sifting through parish registers and trial records constantly unearth otherwise unknown notaries. Although we have no quantitative data on this unorganized profession as a whole, it is obvious that most notaries in Rome did not have an office. Most probably worked in someone else's office or on their own as private notaries. The sheer variety of notaries we encounter in Rome underlines this point. Not counting the notaries who actually worked for officials in the papal Curia, foreign curial notaries at any one time must have numbered in the hundreds.[17] The Roman Jewish community supported for many decades the services of its own notaries.[18] The papacy designated specific Christian notaries to write up the contracts of the Jewish moneylenders, perhaps in order to monitor their interest rates, and also assigned a notary to the cardinal protector of new Christian converts (*neofiti*).[19]

Even more telling are lists of candidates for two elected notarial offices in the municipal government, the notary of the syndics and the notary of the *pacieri*, for the years 1623 to 1643.[20] Of 148 notaries on these lists over the two decades, only 25 were Capitoline notaries. Who were these other men who had managed to secure nomination to civic posts but of whom there is no other systematic trace? Some of them at least were the successors to the old pre-1586 city notaries, men who now took jobs as *sostituti* in the offices of the notaries of the Capitoline curia and in other Roman offices or who did private free-lance notarial work. Although we will never know how many such men made a living from the notarial profession in Rome, the number could not have been negligible.[21] If we did not believe the evidence of the variety of hands at work in the protocols of the thirty Capitoline notaries, we have confirmation in the efforts of the papal authorities in the 1620s to bring them under state control.

By contrast to the shadowy world of the private notaries, we can name the titleholders to the thirty Capitoline offices in almost unbroken succession from around 1600 until the 1880s.[22] Names are helpful, indeed essential for any research in notarial documents, because records were (and are) filed by the name of the rogating notary. But notaries effaced most information about themselves in the business contracts and litigation proceedings that they wrote up for their clients. To learn something more than their names, we must look for the thirty Capitoline notaries in other sources, in the records of other notaries, college accounts, civic registers, confraternity archives, parish censuses, and even trial transcripts. These tracks lead us into the places where public words were written in baroque Rome and introduce us to the men who made a living from writing them.

Our sample, taken directly from the names on the volumes produced by the thirty Capitoline notaries in the year 1630, yielded thirty-one notaries, because there were overlapping personnel in office 14.[23] Although we cannot know for sure how many owned their offices outright and how many leased them under various partnership or employee relationships, Capitoline notaries tended to hang on to their offices. Twenty-five in the 1630 sample kept them for eleven years or more, and eight lasted for more than thirty years. Judging by the number of volumes of instruments, which is only a partial indicator of business activity because it excludes the judicial side of the notary's work, longevity in office was good for business.[24] Stability brought more clients, and offices with a rapid turnover of titleholders or, worse, a series of leaseholders or temporary administrators suffered. One venerable Capitoline notary of the period, Giovanni Battista Ottaviani, blasted the practice of subletting and insisted that office 13, which had once belonged to his brother-in-law and which he had headed successfully for forty-one years, be sold immediately after his death.[25]

Capitoline notaries in 1630 were not necessarily Romans by birth.[26] Only one of the seventeen for whom we have information was a native Roman, Lorenzo Bonin-contro, perhaps not coincidentally the most prestigious and wealthiest of his cohort. Even if all fourteen for whom we lack data were born in Rome, however, more than half were not. Some arrived from as far away as Avignon, Milan, and the Romagna. Most followed the well-worn paths of migration to Rome from the spiny center of the Papal States—from small towns like Calvi and Collescipoli, and larger ones like Cività Castellana and Acquasparta—or from the hill towns behind Carrara and Sarzana in what was then Tuscan and Genoese territory. The immigrants likely arrived as teenagers; when we know their ages, we find them acquiring their Capitoline offices when they were in their early thirties. The Roman-born Bonincontro, from an ancient notarial family, was younger, only twenty-four; Ottaviani, who had to wait for his brother-in-law to die, was an older forty-three. Roman identity never demanded Roman birth, of course, and Sixtus V had included among the Capitoline notaries' privileges the right to Roman citizenship.[27] Some newcomers evidently took this to heart because we find in their wills the Milanese Francesco Arrigone, the Orvietan Angelo Canini, and the Genoese Ottaviani calling themselves Roman citizens.[28]

Despite the fact that their offices were fully inheritable and the college did lower some bars for offspring seeking admission, few successors to the sample notaries were obvious kinsmen. We have personal information on successors in half the cases, and they include three sons and a nephew plus three other men who bore the same surnames as their predecessors. Though some immigrants, like Ottaviani, married into Capitoline offices, the large number of newcomers in the 1630 sample tells us that access did not depend exclusively on family connections. Many of the thirty Capitoline notaries perfectly mirrored the typical immigrant to Rome in this period—a young man from central Italy—rather than issuing from a closed circle of local notarial families.[29]

Was being a notary a noble profession? Even a judge as elevated above the status fray as Giovanni Battista Fenzonio, the former senator of Rome, thought that this was a vexed question, and all over seventeenth-century Italy it ignited passionate debate.[30] Fenzonio solved the problem rather cagily by explaining that in Rome a rich notary with a reputation for integrity, who lived suitably, was "certainly" eligible for the public offices that signaled nobility.[31] It was an easy answer, because he knew that in Rome, unlike most Italian cities, there was no juridical definition of noble status.

More to the point, therefore, is where the Capitoline notaries of 1630 stood in the city's informal status hierarchy. Thirty men do not easily dissolve into a single social assessment, all the more so when generalizing about someone like Giovanni Francesco Gargario, who held his office for two years, and someone like Ottaviani, who held it for forty-one. Yet some generalization is possible. Although the thirty Capitoline notaries were undoubtedly favored among the city's notaries, we look vainly for the marks of recognition that distinguished Roman gentlemen. Being elected to civic office as caporione or conservator was perhaps the most public sign of acceptance for someone without an aristocratic title in baroque Rome.[32] Neighborhood gatherings of patrician Romans determined who would draw up the list of candidates for these offices.[33] Capitoline notaries might be addressed as "signor" rather than the more plebeian "maestro," but except when the official actually had to be a notary, they hardly ever occupied elected civic office or attended meetings of citizen councils.[34]

Lorenzo Bonincontro was the exception. He was elected caporione for the district of Trevi in October 1626, and even after his three-month term was over, he showed up at several important meetings of the public and private councils in 1628 and 1630.[35] Bonincontro did not hide his profession. While active as titleholder of office 18 from 1605 until his death in 1634, he also leased the office of notary of the conservators between 1616 and 1625 and was elected notary of the syndics in 1624.[36] But Bonincontro was a wealthy man whose household was organized quite differently from other Capitoline notaries. He could live in a manner the judge, or his gentlemen neighbors, would have deemed suitable for civic officials in baroque Rome; most of his colleagues apparently could not.

We know disappointingly little about the cultural or intellectual interests of the notaries in the sample.[37] Their participation in the artistic and literary life of the city is thus far undocumented. While notaries in other times and places might take a leading role in public debate or city politics or might express innovative if clandestine religious opinions, the Capitoline notaries of 1630 do not. Some of them at least were pious men. Lorenzo Bonincontro built a chapel dedicated to the Madonna della Pietà in the Franciscan convent of Sant'Isidoro.[38] Giovanni Battista Ottaviani left a bequest to his confessor as well as money to more than a dozen Roman churches for masses for the repose of his soul and those of his godparents and kinfolk.[39] But others, like Angelo Giustiniani, who found catering to the whims of his ecclesiastical clients trying at times, may have been more tepid in their devotions.[40] Making a living was not easy for some of these men, and perhaps the pressures of investors, clients, and competitors, to say nothing of papal regulators, flattened their aspirations and kept them fixed on business. To understand better how these forces operated, we need to explore the economics of obtaining and running a Capitoline notarial office.

How did notaries put together the resources to acquire Capitoline offices? Though scattered, the evidence reveals that strategies were complex. Few, at least in the mid-seventeenth century, had the good luck of ten-year-old Cesare Camilli, who in 1636 inherited the office his father had begun by leasing in 1628.[41] Short of a legacy, the options were to lease, sublet, administer, or purchase, and virtually all of these modes could be arranged not only by individuals but also through partnerships.

Ownership was not a straightforward matter in any case. When a court inquired as to whether Angelo Giustiniani owned office 11, his employee replied that yes, he owned it, but did not know whether he owned it "freely."[42] After Tranquillo Scolocci's death in 1652, his widow received "possession" (*possesso*) of his office, in which her dowry had evidently been invested, for three years.[43] During that period, she certainly collected the earnings of office 26, but to call her the owner would require nuances altogether lost in modern usage. While the courts might uphold the freedom of buyers and sellers to trade in Capitoline offices without the intervention of the authorities, they could not remove the charges, claims, and obligations that encumbered those very entities. These were intrinsic to this richly ambiguous form of property.

Some Capitoline offices belonged to wealthy Roman patricians who leased them to professionals who gained title and admission to the college. Giovanni Battista de Fabijs owned office 8; Lelio Barisiani, office 27; the Vitelleschi brothers (Ippolito and Paolo Emilio), office 17; and Marcello Muti, office 24.[44] In 1630 the titleholders to these four offices were Capitoline notaries Felice Antonio de Alexandriis, Salvatore Melli, Marcello Cortellacci, and Giacomo Attilio. They may well have held their offices on terms like those we find outlined in the lease for office 20, which Guido Camilli signed in August 1628.[45] If so, we can infer that investors in Capitoline offices had read the laws carefully, knew the kind of risks they faced when putting capital into a notary's business, and wanted to shift those risks as far as possible to the leaseholder.

In 1628 office 20 was in the parish of Sant'Eustachio, although Camilli would soon move it to the Corso near the Arco di Portogallo. Camilli, who had worked for the late titleholder Palmerino Speranza, made his contract with Speranza's children and three other investors who included the noble Pirro Mattei and the prelate Giovanni Andrea Castellano.[46] Its precise clauses about how he managed the office and treated its documents were intended, as the lease intimates, for an eventual titleholder, and indeed Camilli did become a Capitoline notary.[47] He paid the owners fifteen scudi a month on a yearly lease that would be automatically renewed unless they notified him of termination.[48] As was customary, Camilli was responsible for all the office's expenses, from the rental of the space and wages, food, and board of the staff to its paper and candles. The investors specifically instructed their leaseholder to follow the document-handling practices mandated by Paul V's judicial reforms, from extending all instruments to binding them between strong covers. They demanded that he fully record payments in the receipt book and keep the judicial accounts (*liber expeditionum*) "as they do in similar offices." The contract also insisted that Camilli and his employees meet the deadlines and pay the fees required by the Archivio Urbano. Camilli was to guard the records of his predecessors, which were detailed in an accompanying inventory, and to make sure that the office was never left unattended. Doubtless aware of a notary's peculiar financial vulnerabilities, the owners warned Camilli about the quality of the security he accepted in lawsuits and urged him to take good care of the money, precious objects, and financial instruments (*cedole*) left on deposit with the office.

By contrast to a titleholder, even one who leased, those who rented or administered Capitoline offices that operated in someone else's name were much further down in the pecking order. A rental agreement from 1626 allowed a certain Giacinto Paulino to sublet Marco Tullio dell'Huomo's office 16, or perhaps only its nonjudicial portion, for a year for a monthly rent of eleven scudi.[49] Like Camilli, he was responsible for paying all the office's expenses and was liable for any money deposited with the office. Although she was much less meticulous in her demands than the investors in office 20, the owner of office 16 did insist that Paulino accept no sureties worth more than fifty scudi without her approval. Interestingly, her contract with Paulino permitted him to locate the business anywhere in Rome that he wished, a clause the Capitoline notarial college would certainly have rejected.

Although we rarely hear about men like Paulino, subcontracting and administering Capitoline offices was not uncommon. Sometimes it was a transition status, as an employee of the office moved up or a previous subcontractor became a titleholder.[50] Sometimes the titleholder, whether or not he was an owner, might not be able to manage the office that operated in his name or, for the moment, there might be no titleholder. An administrator managed office 16 in 1618, for example, when Dell'Huomo was in jail, and in the late 1630s Ottavio Franceschini administered office 20 for the youthful Cesare Camilli.[51] A vacancy in office 12 in 1622 is probably the reason we find two partners, coadministrators, listed in the parish census in a household that was evidently the notarial office.[52] Sometimes offices remained in the hands of a changing cast of administrators for years, a situation that made it difficult for the college to collect massa and, to judge from Ottaviani's comment, caused trouble in other ways.[53]

Buying the office might be the ultimate goal, but few aspirants seem to have been able to come up with ready cash to reach it. Admittedly the evidence is limited to chance archival discoveries, for, as we have seen, the market not the state controlled the sale of Capitoline notarial offices. Of course, this also means there was no set price. We have the instrument of sale for office 21, which was bought by Francesco Arrigone in May 1628.[54] In addition, we have information about the sale of office 18 from the private account books of Lorenzo Bonincontro's widow, the price of office 16 quoted in Paulino's rental agreement, and the trial testimony of one of Angelo Giustiniani's employees. The figure of 4,000 scudi for office 11 suggested by Giustiniani's scribe in 1632 was undoubtedly exaggerated.[55] The owner of office 16 said it was worth 2,850 scudi in 1618, Arrigone paid 3,250 scudi in 1628, and Ginevra Bonincontro sold office 18 between 1637 and 1639 for 3,493 scudi.[56] At 2,850 scudi Dell'Huomo's office may have been relatively cheap in 1618 because of the title-holder's unfortunate absence. By contrast Bonincontro's office price of around 3,500 scudi likely represents the higher end of the range; it had certainly been one of the most reputable and busiest of the thirty, though by 1637 it had already passed briefly through another notary's hands. The details of the sales of office 21 and office 18 show that notaries often purchased Capitoline offices on the installment plan.

Arrigone bought office 21 in 1628 from Francesco Grillo, who was the son of a Capitoline notary and briefly titleholder himself. It was located in Grillo's home near the Trevi Fountain, and seems to have remained there after the sale. Arrigone put down 300 scudi in cash and promised another 950 scudi within the next few months; he paid 6 percent interest on the balance of 2,000 scudi, which was due within four years.[57] The purchase of office 18 was more complex. Notwithstanding the prohibition against divisions in the 1618 notarial statutes, Lorenzo Bonincontro's office had in fact been divided, presumably after his death in February 1634.[58] His successor, Giulio Grappolini, obtained three-quarters of office 18 on unknown terms and a certain Antonini rented the fourth quarter for 82 scudi a year.[59] Grappolini died in June 1637 before completing his payments, so the owners of office 18 were still Bonincontro's two young children. As their guardian, their mother contracted the sale of three-quarters of the office with the next titleholder, Francesco Pacichelli, in December 1637. Pacichelli paid an initial sum of 193.75 scudi and a week later completed his down payment with another 500. He agreed to pay Ginevra Bonincontro 5.5 percent interest on the remaining 1,900 scudi. In January 1639 Pacichelli purchased the fourth part of the office from the Bonincontro children for an additional 900 scudi, on the same terms as he had contracted initially. The total price for office 18 was 3,493 scudi plus interest, and Pacichelli was still making payments on it five years after he started.

These examples remind us of how difficult it was to raise a large amount of capital in an economy that seems to have been in a chronic liquidity crisis.[60] For all the hyperactivity in the Roman financial markets, cash, or *pecunia numerata* as the notarial instruments called it, and even cedole (funds in paper form) played a limited role in exchange. In credit-dependent Rome, where it might take years even to collect wages, partnerships helped to generate capital for many kinds of enterprises.[61] Some of these were notarial business ventures, such as Antonio Ferraguti and Virgilio Cellio's purchase of office 8 in 1614 and Cleante Cortellacci's lease of office 17 in 1631, in which he invited Mario Rangiani to be his partner.[62] Although this was not always the case in partnerships, Cortellacci was the titleholder, but both he and Rangiani performed notarial duties. In some cases, a partnership between a titleholder and his successor marked the transition between two owners, perhaps while installments on the purchase price were coming in. In office 21, Francesco Arrigone evidently made this kind of arrangement for several years with Francesco Grillo, who was not active professionally, while the owner of office 12, Angelo Canini, took his handpicked successor, Carlo Novio, as a partner before his death in 1649.[63] While not partnerships in the same sense, marital property also helped to finance the acquisition of Capitoline offices, a reminder of the centrality of the notary's household to his business.[64]

Whether as lessor or owner, a man who wanted to be a titleholder brought his professional qualifications and some capital to the transaction; what did he receive in exchange? The short answer was furniture and documents. The furniture was occupationally specific. Francesco Arrigone's purchase included *pulpiti,* a type of desk preferred by notaries, and *rastelli,* which in this context might mean racks or shelves.[65] Pulpiti were high desks with stools; each had a cover that could be closed with a key and internal compartments that could also be locked. Rough drafts (i.e., matrici) of instruments as well as loose fully extended copies that had not yet been sent to the binder were sometimes kept under lock, as was the paper distributed to the staff. Other office contracts mentioned stools, benches, and cupboards.

Even more crucial than furnishings to the definition of a notarial office, however, was its *scripturae* or documents. Arrigone bought three types when he purchased the office at the Trevi Fountain: bound volumes of notarial instruments, bound volumes of judicial acts, and stitched bundles of supporting evidence accumulated in the course of litigation (*filsi iuribus productis et rogatis*). The inventory of more than a hundred volumes attached to Guido Camilli's lease gives some idea of the quantitative dimensions of a Capitoline office's archives. In 1628 his office, number 20, contained sixty-five protocols, dating from 1548, and fifty-four manuali, dating from 1567, in addition to some smaller documentary series.[66] Later inventories suggest that the size of Camilli's collection was not at all unusual.[67]

As Armando Petrucci has argued, the sixteenth century marked an important expansion in the notion of the office as it came to signify the physical site of state activity, and in Rome the venal notarial offices nicely illustrate this process.[68] The geography of notarial services shifted significantly in the last quarter of the cinque-cento as the thirty Capitoline notaries began to settle down at specific locations. By 1630 many could be found at addresses that would endure for the next two hundred years. In the sample these included Lorenzo Bonincontro's office 18 at the corner of the Corso and Vicolo dei Mancini (now Vicolo del Piombo), and those of Giovanni Battista Ottaviani (13) at SS. Apostoli, Francesco Arrigone (21) at the Trevi Fountain, Torquato Ricci (1) next to the convent of S. Maria in Campo Marzio, and Marcello Cortellacci (17) on the Trastevere side of Ponte Sisto.[69] Angelo Canini's office 12 in the present-day zone of the imperial forums had been occupied earlier by his pre-decessors and remained there under his successors in 1702; Angelo Giustiniani's office 11 in Via del Gesù was also in the same street in 1702. Romans likely conjured up quite specific topographical associations when hearing that someone had nota-rized an act in Bonincontro's or Canini's or Giustiniani's offices. Although we do not know all 1630 addresses, Capitoline notaries seem to have concentrated in the Tiber bend and along the Corso, avoiding the outlying districts.[70]

Nevertheless, as we have seen, some contracts with owners allowed Capitoline notaries the freedom to exercise their profession anywhere in Rome. In this still fluid period of the early seventeenth century, therefore, changes of address were not unknown. We have noted that Guido Camilli moved the office he leased from the neighborhood of Sant'Eustachio to the Corso in the late 1620s.[71] Giovanni Agostino Tullio's office 4 was next to the priests' residence at Sant'Andrea della Valle in 1624 and at the Piazza della Pigna twenty years later. In 1616 Piazza Mattei hosted two Capitoline offices, but after this situation led to trouble, Felice Antonio de Alex-andriis, who took over one of them in 1617, moved it to the present Via del Semi-nario near the Pantheon. The second office, which was in quarters rented from the Mattei family, remained around the corner at the piazza "of the elm" until the nineteenth century.[72]

How was this physical stability achieved when, in the purchase and lease con-tracts we have reviewed, "office" clearly did not refer to the space of the notary's activities? Although the exceptional Lorenzo Bonincontro owned the quarters used by his office 18, most Capitoline notaries did not have freehold ownership of their places of work. Instead, specific contractual clauses gave them a life interest in a combined residence and workplace on which they paid rent.[73] In practice, it was hard to distinguish this kind of arrangement from ownership, especially when a property had acquired the contractual identity of a notarial office and thus could be rented only to Capitoline (or other) notaries. By 1652 the notarial college was actively promoting such topographical permanence, regarding it as a serious economic threat if titleholders shifted locale without the consent of their colleagues.[74] Their attention to place turns ours toward the notary's household, where the business of public writing focused. While Capitoline notaries might rogate as many acts in their clients' shops and homes as in their own offices,[75] and their employees ran constant errands all over Rome, the household was the center of documentary production.

Working as a Household
Employers

In 1630 Capitoline notaries usually lived where they worked, and so did their employees. The titleholders ran offices with a staff of one or two to a half-dozen men, and censuses record that these workers frequently slept and ate under the same roof as their employer. Because we have little evidence of formal contractual relations between the notary and his employees, their presence together in a common household helps to situate them among the middling sort in city society. Roman designations of the notary's place of business as a *banco* underscored the parallel between a notarial office and a workshop, though it was more common to find the term *officio* or office used to indicate a notary's location.[76] A household at a Capitoline notary's address might well include three or four young men, a servant or two, and sometimes a wife and children.

In contrast to the majority of Romans who lived in households comprising only family members, most Capitoline notaries for whom we have such information lived either with their kin and employees or simply with fellow employees.[77] An example of the first type was Guido Camilli's residence on the Corso in 1630, which included his wife, his four-year-old son, his sister, and two notaries who worked for him.[78] In a city that demographers have signaled for its pronounced "male" character, however, it was the second type, the household of unrelated adult men, which was most distinctively Roman.[79] In 1630 Angelo Giustiniani's office was home not only to the forty-eight-year-old bachelor himself but to all five members of his notarial staff, men in their twenties to sixties, as well as two servants.[80] A variation on this pattern was the head notary who lived very close to his place of business, while his staff worked, ate, and slept at the office. This was the case with Marcello Cortellacci, a Trastevere notary who lived alone except for a female servant, while his nearby office was home to several employees. It was also the case with Angelo Canini, a widower with four children whose office had a separate entry in the parish censuses of the 1630s and 1640s that showed four to six men ranging in ages from seventeen to thirty-eight living together.[81]

Few Capitoline notaries lived like Lorenzo Bonincontro in a household with brothers and no employees. In 1629 he was listed in the parish of SS. Apostoli with his wife, two young children, two unmarried brothers, and four servants.[82] On the other hand none of the Capitoline notaries, sharing quarters as they did with a staff of two to five employees, could equal the households of some notaries of the auditor of the Camera, who may have lodged a dozen office workers under a single roof.[83] We will look at a few Capitoline notaries and their families in more detail and then situate them more broadly within the spectrum of the notarial profession in Rome. While these cases are not a scientific sample, they are a suggestive sampling of individual notaries of the Capitoline curia around 1630.

In that year Giovanni Battista Ottaviani (c. 1551–1636), proprietor of office 13 at SS. Apostoli, was not the most senior, but he was one of the oldest members of the college. Born around 1551 at Villafranca lunigiana in the diocese of Sarzana, the border region between Tuscany and the Republic of Genoa, he had come to Rome and married Hortensia Vola, daughter of a Capitoline notary, succeeding his father-in-law and then his brother-in-law in the same office in 1595.[84] At seventy-nine, Ottaviani presided over a household that no longer included his adult children, Girolama, the nun Maria Angelica, and the attorney Bartolomeo Ottaviani. Girolama, born around 1601 and still living at home in 1623, had married Giovanni Francesco Morelli in the interval; her sister was in the convent of S. Lorenzo in Panisperna; and their older brother Bartolomeo, who as a forty-year-old had been residing in his father's house in 1629, may have died. The household consisted of Ottaviani's wife, Hortensia; a female servant of around fifty named Sulpitia; and five men aged between nineteen and twenty-seven, at least four of whom clearly worked in the notarial office. The parish priest of SS. Apostoli was unusually loquacious in 1630, so we find Nicolo and Ottavio identified as "sostituti" and Marco labeled "scriba." Giulio Cesare Tosone from Montefalco at twenty-seven was the oldest of the employees; while others came and went, he remained a constant fixture in Ottaviani's household until the older notary's death in 1636, and it was Tosone who succeeded him in office 13.[85]

Angelo Canini was a generation younger than Ottaviani and at an earlier moment in his career and family life cycle. In 1630 Canini (c. 1583–1649) had been holder of office 12 in the Monti district of Rome for seven years, though he had been working as a notary since his youth. Born in Fabro near Orvieto, Canini migrated to Rome as a boy in 1595 and studied with the Jesuits for two years; at fourteen he began as a *novizio*, the first step in the office hierarchy, with Capitoline notary Biagio Cigni, who ran office 29 from 1592 until 1621. In 1623 Canini purchased his own

Capitoline office and moved to its site at the Arco dei Pantani, not far from the Church of Sant'Adriano, the ancient Senate House, in the Roman Forum. He had already been married for some time to Maddalena Bruschi with whom he had four children: Pietro Antonio (born between 1610 and 1616), Giovanna (born c. 1618), Michele (born c. 1621), and Albano, born the year of the move to the Pantani. In the parish census of 1631 when we meet the Canini children, ranging in age from eight to twenty, their mother was dead, and they lived with their forty-eight-year-old father and a female servant.[86]

Over the next eighteen years, the core of this household remained remarkably stable; in his thirties, Canini's son Pietro Antonio finally married and brought his young wife Anna Rainaldi and his mother-in-law to live in his father's house. His two younger brothers, both destined for the priesthood, never left. Their sister Giovanna, who was gone by the time she was twenty, had returned to her father's house with her husband five years later in 1643, though she died soon afterward. In 1648 Angelo Canini headed a household of ten people that now included not only his surviving children, a granddaughter, the mother of his son's wife, and a female servant but also a nephew and two brothers, both in their twenties, whose relationship to Canini is unclear. When he made his will in April 1649, Canini designated his oldest son as heir. He requested burial in his parish church of S. Maria in Campo Carleo, where his wife and daughter were previously interred, and he made careful arrangements to support his son Albano, an archpriest of Castel Gandolfo, and his son Michele, should he too wish to become a priest and remain in his older brother's household. Because Canini was already in partnership with Carlo Novio, his successor in the notarial office, the way was clear for this thirty-eight-year-old notary to take over his senior partner's practice in 1649.[87]

Angelo Giustiniani (c. 1582–1644?), head of office 11 next to the palace of Cardinal Muti in Via del Gesù, was of the same generation as Canini, though he had become a notary at twenty and acquired his Capitoline notarial office a decade earlier than Canini when he was around thirty years old. Like Ottaviani and Canini, Giustiniani, who came from Acquasparta in Umbria, was an immigrant to Rome. He had worked as a sostituto in office 11 before becoming titleholder in 1611.[88] Although we know little about his background, his younger brother Vittorio had also moved to Rome, become a notary in 1610, and served the tribunal of the Rota until 1639. Giustiniani's household, as we have seen, usually included four or five office employees who slept two to a room in the upper reaches of the notary's combined office and residence and ate their meals together; in December 1631 the young notary who would succeed Giustiniani fourteen years later, Giovanni Matteo

Massari from Velletri, joined this group. A female servant did the cooking and cleaning for the men, and sometimes a manservant who tended the horse and worked in the notary's vineyard lived there too.[89]

Unlike Ottaviani and Canini, Giustiniani seems never to have married. During the early 1630s his notarial office was the subject of a criminal investigation in which innuendos surfaced about his sexual life, including suggestions that he was carrying on an affair with his servant Letizia. If true, Letizia's heart seems to have been stolen away by one of Giustiniani's employees, and she had left by 1633.[90] Therefore, we do not know who the mother was of the three small children whom the parish priest of S. Stefano del Cacco recorded in the censuses of 1639 and 1640 as Giustiniani's "figli naturali." The oldest, Domenico, was apparently born around 1633, and the two younger, Pellegrino and Pellegrina, were born in 1636 and 1637.[91] Although Giustiniani did not follow his colleagues' path to legitimate marriage, his delay in having children until he was in his fifties was not unheard of at a time when notaries seem rarely to have married, if at all, before their late thirties. Given Rome's distinctive sex ratio, his family of illegitimate offspring may also have had parallels in other Roman households.

Lorenzo Bonincontro (c. 1581–1634), holder of office 18 from 1605 to 1633, represents the Capitoline notary at the apex of wealth and prestige.[92] While the cases we have seen thus far illustrate the broad middle range, Bonincontro's household shows us the elite end of our sample. Atypical—because he was born in Rome, he was the son and grandson of Capitoline notaries, he took part in civic political life, and he married an heiress—Bonincontro conforms to the image of the notary forged in places and periods where the profession was more exclusive and more powerful than in early modern Rome. A prominent figure inevitably leaves more traces than his colleagues, and indeed we do know more about Bonincontro and his family than about most Capitoline notaries; this is due in part to the chance survival of a series of account books kept by his widow after his death in 1634.[93] These illuminate the tenor of life in a wealthy notarial family as well as many otherwise obscure facets of the notary's business. We have already noted Lorenzo Bonincontro's status as a gentleman. His domestic setting played an important role in communicating his unusual social distinction.

Born in Rome around 1581, Lorenzo Bonincontro was the son of Faustina Orlandi and Marc'Antonio Bonincontro, a Capitoline notary active in the 1580s. By 1605, when he was in his mid-twenties, Bonincontro had taken over the notarial office associated with his father. His brother Camillo, a doctor of laws also apparently born in the early 1580s, held one of the civic offices connected with the university in 1606 and again from 1613 to 1619, while a second brother Francesco, born around 1590, was a priest. As we have seen, both brothers, then in middle age and unmarried, were living with Lorenzo on the Via del Corso in 1629. In February 1629, following litigation initiated by Camillo a few years earlier, the brothers had agreed to cede all their rights to their parents' property to Lorenzo in exchange for yearly allowances and payment of certain debts. Both brothers died within the next two years.[94]

Lorenzo Bonincontro seems not to have married until he was in his forties. Although we do not know the exact date of his marriage to Ginevra Zeloni, who was fourteen to twenty years his junior, their oldest child Anna Maria Faustina was born around 1627 and their son Marc'Antonio a year later. The match with Ginevra Zeloni brought Bonincontro a wealthy wife, for after her brother's death she became sole heir to her father Zelone Zeloni, a successful Roman attorney with landed property in his native Tuscany. Through her mother, Francesca Capogalli, Ginevra was also linked to a family with deep roots in the Roman notariate; Capogalli notaries were active in Rome from the fourteenth century onward. The marriage seems to have been a success on the emotional as well as the financial front, for Lorenzo called Ginevra his "very dear and beloved wife" in his will and, at his death in February 1634, made her guardian of their children.[95]

The Bonincontro household was unquestionably prosperous, drawing income not only from the notarial practice but also from real estate investments, loans and bonds, venal offices, and from the sale of grapes and mulberry leaves from its lands. Lorenzo was a notary who wore a diamond ring and had his own coach; his widow bought new livery for her male servants every two years; their children were tutored at home rather than sent to school. Ginevra employed a staff of domestic servants that ranged from three to five people, a coachman, and a man to tend the family's two vineyards. A list of the keys to her house, where even the oven had a lock, implies the value of its contents and suggests the numerous rooms occupied by this extended family and its staff. In addition to the Corso residence, Ginevra purchased and renovated a second house near Trajan's Column to which she and her children may have moved after Bonincontro's death.[96] Although some Capitoline notaries were men of substance, very few had the resources of Lorenzo Bonincontro and his wife.

The elderly Ottaviani and his three middle-aged colleagues may well give a more accurate impression of family life among the middle and upper range of Capitoline notaries than among the lower end. Notaries who remained in their offices for decades, as they did, almost inevitably produce more biographical information than those, like Giorgio Giorgi from Avignon, who graduated from Bonincontro's office to his own Capitoline office in 1629 but held on to it for only four years.[97] Moreover, we need to ask, even if we cannot fully answer, the question of what place these families occupied in relation to other Roman notaries. Two examples from outside the sample group and opposite ends of the professional spectrum help to situate the Capitoline notaries more broadly within the context of the early seventeenth-century Roman notarial profession. One, Felice de Totis, represented the man whose successful career enabled his family to leave the notariate behind and reach decisively for higher, gentlemanly status within his lifetime. The other, Virgilio Lusanna, symbolizes the notary with artisanal roots who, despite attaining a Capitoline office, risked falling back among the artisans from whom he came.

Felice de Totis migrated to Rome from Città Castellana in the Tiber valley. Although we do not know when he began his career, he was established enough by 1607 to serve in the elected civic post of notary of the *pacieri*. By 1614 he had begun to lease one of the nine notarial offices of the Apostolic Chamber, which he held until 1633. Then De Totis moved into tax farming, a far more lucrative activity than notarial exertions; from 1637 to 1642 he leased the right to collect one of the two major municipal sources of revenue, the wine tax known as the *gabella dello Studio*. Although this particular contract seems to have ended unhappily for De Totis, who bowed out of the lease after a jail term, his social ascent was not jeopardized by this misfortune for he had secured a crucial foothold in the papal curia for his son, Monsignor Carlo Vincenzo de Totis. When the elder De Totis made his will in April 1648, he did not mention his notarial origins. Instead, he strove, with the help undoubtedly of the rogating notary, his former colleague, to pour onto the pages all the knowledge he had acquired of how to preserve family property in an ecclesiastical city. Like cardinalatial families, curial families in Rome, especially newly minted ones, adopted the practice of placing clerical sons in charge of their lay brothers and sisters. Felice de Totis enjoined his other five children to obey their brother the monsignor, to whom he gave responsibility for educating them and for administering the family patrimony. Although he made his second son a principal heir along with Carlo Vincenzo, De Totis forbade any division of the inheritance by the brothers until after the monsignor's death. While grudgingly providing for his lay son, he tried to circumscribe this young man's access to the family wealth in every way possible, and he left all decisions concerning the dowries of his four daughters to the monsignor. De Totis had enjoyed the satisfaction of leaving his children in a more elevated social position than he had inherited; now launched in the Curia, they were indeed poised for further ascent. In the view of the dying notary, however, their future could be guaranteed only if the monsignor was allowed complete freedom to deploy siblings and patrimony for the family's advance. Here we see the fulfillment of the hopes for social mobility that must have attracted many of Rome's immigrants in the seventeenth century, though few could equal De Totis's success in raising a provincial family from curial notary to prelate in just two generations.[98]

A Roman native likely born in the late sixteenth century, Virgilio Lusanna stands at the other end of the social and professional spectrum from Felice de Totis. His father was a tallow chandler in Piazza Giudea, near the main gate to the Roman ghetto, who had managed to place his son in a novitiate in a Capitoline notary's office. After some time, Lusanna was able to purchase Capitoline notarial office 8 in Piazza Mattei, a few minutes' walk from his birthplace, which he held from 1600 to 1607. From 1608 on, he remained in the neighborhood and, exploiting his wide acquaintanceship in the quarter, continued to work at the margins of the notariate for another twenty years.[99]

Lusanna married the daughter of a Milanese immigrant and had several children; his wife's dowry was more than nine hundred scudi. One of Lusanna's sisters was married to an estate agent for the large Roman hospital of Santo Spirito; another may have been married to a barber; and a third was married to a rope maker, who was his neighbor on the Piazza Mattei. Although this last brother-in-law was unable to read and write, he had financial investments of more than four hundred scudi, so we should not assume he was an impoverished rope maker. The social milieu from which Lusanna sprang was clearly that of the independent Roman artisan and tradesman. These were men of property, though of uneven literacy, whose clever sons might well parley elementary Latin and arithmetical skills into an office apprenticeship and become estate stewards or notaries.[100]

Lusanna's grip on his Capitoline office was not secure, however, and in the decades after he gave it up in 1607 he made a living as a private notary in the most precarious ways possible. He had a desk in the office of his successors where he registered acts in their name, and, if even a few of the accusations leveled against him in several trials were true, skimmed money from his clients in fraudulent money-lending operations.[101] We do not know how large a patrimony, if any, Lusanna was able to pass on to his heirs after all his fines and court fees were paid, but we can be sure that it did not include a notarial office or his own good name. It is difficult to imagine that his children were able to climb out of the ranks of the master artisans and tradesmen.

Having looked at a sampling of notaries who headed offices in the middle decades of the seventeenth century, we have seen that employers had at one time been employees. Sharing as they did the experience of working for a titleholder, they had all been part of a labor force, which, though all but invisible, was absolutely essential to the productivity of the venal offices. We turn now to the obscure world of the men whose hands were chiefly responsible for the records that we now read: the employees of the thirty Capitoline notaries.

Employees

Only Capitoline notaries could sign public copies of the acts rogated in their name, but for the bulk of their documentary production they depended on the pens of their employees. Without these men, it would have been impossible to earn the fees that kept a venal notarial office going. They rogated transactions both inside and outside the office, extended the rough drafts into full transcripts, created the table of contents for each protocol and manuale that returned from the binder, and made copies at clients' request. On the judicial side, the staff wrote out and filed summons in lawsuits, recorded the audiences at which litigants or their attorneys presented their documents, carried warrants to judges for signing, and kept the accounts of all judicial acts expedited by the office and of all payments received. They stood guard so that the office was never left unattended, and they ran countless errands in an era when the only means of communication were either face-to-face or by messenger.

Demand for scribes was elastic and turnover relatively high in baroque Rome. "You hire a hand when one leaves or is fired," a notary's servant testified.[102] As we have seen, the Capitoline notaries might have as few as two clerks or as many as five. Papal authorities reluctantly acknowledged that the sale of notarial posts had increased the size of the office work force and given it a distinct hierarchical structure. Although still insisting that Capitoline notaries serve their judges in person, for example, the 1612 judicial reforms recognized that a "principal notary," caponotaro or padrone, headed the office, and a staff, designated by the terms giovane and sostituto, worked for him.[103] The entry-level position was that of novizio, in which a youth spent a year learning the notary's art.[104] To rise to the status of a sostituto, the young man had to be formally created notary, which empowered him to rogate business acts.[105] In later decades, when papal disciplinary orders targeted the sostituti and giovani directly, they showed that the state well understood who was actually producing notarial documents in the venal offices.[106]

Thus, the late medieval tradition of informal, largely on-the-job training for young notaries continued in early modern Rome. No special academic center for notarial studies existed, and even apprenticeship contracts were rare. When we find notarized agreements to teach a youth the "art and profession of notary," they are not between parents and employer but between an orphanage and a notary. In exchange for instruction, meals, and clothes the orphan apprentice promised to serve his new padrone for three years.[107] Exceptions apart, the more usual work arrangements must have been oral, not written.

Boys destined to be notaries in Rome where documents were written in Latin had acquired some knowledge of the language in school, as Angelo Canini did when he studied from ages twelve to fourteen with the Jesuits.[108] It was uncommon for a would-be notary to attend university lectures in logic, as Giacinto Gallucci claimed to have done in Macerata.[109] Because many of the young men who worked in Capitoline offices came from small provincial towns within a day or two's journey of Rome, they must have acquired their Latin from local schoolmasters. They learned the details of the notarial craft as novices in the offices of established notaries in their hometowns or in Rome, usually entering as Canini did while still in their teens. Once they had become giovani, they could expect to earn around 1.50 scudi a month.[110] The more ambitious could hope after a few years for a salary of 2 scudi a month once they advanced to the rank of sostituto and were allowed to rogate instruments and, despite the 1612 legislation, process the office's judicial business.[111] In addition to wages, which were paid at such lengthy intervals that we might almost consider them a form of forced savings rather than a regular income, padroni often recompensed their employees by other means. As we have seen, many young and not-so-young men shared a table and roof with the rest of the notary's household.

Information on the economic and social background of the young men who worked in the Capitoline offices, while scattered and anecdotal, suggests that they were recruited from families of varied means. Thanks to the trial of one of Angelo Giustiniani's sostituti between 1630 and 1633, we have a relatively full picture of the staff in office 11 on Via del Gesù.[112] Giacinto Gallucci testified that his father in Montegiorgio (Fermo diocese) owned financial instruments and real estate worth thirty-five hundred scudi. Ettore Alberti, a twenty-three-year-old giovane from Velletri, told the court that he himself owned a house and a vineyard in nearby Segni worth four hundred scudi.[113] Their colleague Bartolomeo Benedetti of Tarano, on the other hand, was so poor that his flesh showed through his threadbare clothes; he had to borrow a cloak from Alberti when he went on an important mission to try to save his job.[114] When asked, most of these young men said they lived on their earnings as notaries, though Gallucci admitted that he asked his father for money when these were insufficient.[115]

Precise comparisons between immigrants and native sons are hard to come by, but if we can judge by the contrasting backgrounds of two Romans who became Capitoline notaries, Virgilio Lusanna, son of a tallow chandler, and Lorenzo Bonincontro, son of a Capitoline notary, variety was the general rule. In an active trading center like sixteenth-century Milan, novice notaries gravitated to the offices of men who shared the same mercantile background as they did.[116] In baroque Rome with its commerce in parchment, we cannot yet say whether analogous occupational affinities influenced employment, but migration patterns may have. It might be a coincidence, but three of the five employees in Giustiniani's office in April 1630 came from villages very close to each other, no more than five miles apart, in the Sabine hills. The market for scribal labor seems to have been too unorganized for Giustiniani, or any other Capitoline notary, to have hired on the basis of hometown ties. Recommendations from trusted colleagues were a more likely source of pertinent information on recruits than common *patria.*[117] But informal networks among immigrants may have alerted these young men to potential openings in notarial offices, so that they might present themselves when vacancies occurred.

Vacancies occurred frequently.[118] Most employees, especially those in their teens and twenties, did not stay long with any given notary; six or seven month stints were not unheard of, and parish census data suggests that two years was common. The interrogations of Angelo Giustiniani's staff by the governor's tribunal provide details about the peripatetic early careers of several of these young men.

Bartolomeo Benedetti, the defendant in the case, had worked in the profession for five years when we meet him in 1631. About his background before he came to Rome in 1625 we know only that he was a poor youth from Tarano in the Sabine hills whose brother was a priest.[119] In Rome he started as a *novizio* in the Trastevere office of Marcello Cortellacci, where he lived with a *sostituto* named Marzio Mecci and another man.[120] Mecci, as his immediate superior, may well have had more to do with training him than the padrone; he later claimed to have supervised him closely during their two years together.[121] In 1627 Mecci left the Capitoline office to work for Marzio Nucula, a notary of the auditor of the Camera, but the two men remained friendly, and three years later Benedetti would arrange to have a will that he was writing for a wealthy client rogated in Nucula's office rather than by his own employer at the time. Meanwhile, in late 1627 Benedetti also departed from Cortellacci's employ and was hired by Angelo Canini in office 12, as a temporary replacement for another *giovane* who eventually returned. He worked for Canini for five or six months, but by Lent 1628 he was listed in Angelo Giustiniani's household. Benedetti formally became a notary on 9 June 1628 and continued to work for Giustiniani until he was fired in early May 1630.[122]

In a period of five years, Benedetti had passed from a novice to a *sostituto* with substantial responsibilities. In Giustiniani's office he served as the notary for the court of the *maestri giustizieri,* a tribunal with jurisdiction over crimes and disputes involving vineyards. Indeed, Giustiniani testified that he fired Benedetti by order of the pope's nephew, Cardinal Francesco Barberini, because the *sostituto* had helped release a youth imprisoned for stealing from a vineyard.[123] In those five years, Benedetti had become acquainted with three Capitoline notaries and their staff and clients and had grown familiar with the judicial and business world centered on notarial documents. One of the lessons he took from these five years in Rome was that he could not get rich as a sostituto, and, if the record of his trial for forging a will can be trusted, he seems to have longed desperately to escape his poverty.[124] Although we do not know the outcome of the trial, perhaps the Jesuits, who stood to benefit from the alleged forgery, were able to pull enough strings to obtain Benedetti's release. If this were the case, it would help to explain why the Archivio Urbano holds instruments rogated between 1636 and 1642 by a private notary named Bartolomeo Benedetti.[125]

Giacinto Gallucci from Montegiorgio in the Marche met Benedetti when they were both novices in different Capitoline offices, and their friendship deepened when he overlapped with him in Giustiniani's office for seven months between late summer 1629 and early spring 1630. Gallucci, the erstwhile student of logic in Macerata, came from a propertied family and relied on his father to supplement his notarial earnings, but his working life illustrates the mobility of labor among notarial employees. Gallucci arrived in Rome in the summer of 1626 and remained there until August 1630, when he went back to the Marche for half a year to recuperate from a serious illness. During this time, he worked for Tranquillo Scolocci in office 26 and briefly for Giustiniani. In April 1631 Gallucci again was back in Rome, employed by Cortellacci's office in Trastevere, but by October 1632 he had moved to a fourth Capitoline notary, office 9 at the Piazza della Pace.[126] We lose track of Gallucci after this, but we do know that he was still working as a notary in 1638 when he was nominated to the three-month post of notary of the syndics of the municipal officials.

When Ettore Alberti replaced Gallucci in Giustiniani's office in April 1630 it was his first job in Rome, though not the beginning of his career. Although he entered the Capitoline office as a twenty-one-year-old novizio, he had already worked as a notary since his mid-teens in his native Velletri and in the nearby towns of Frascati and Marino in the Alban hills. He spent just five months with Giustiniani. When we meet Alberti in March 1632, he had passed swiftly through three Capitoline notaries' offices and had made the switch from civil to criminal notarial work by taking a job at the prison of Tor di Nona.[127]

In 1632 this newly minted criminal notary was no stranger to penal justice himself. Called back in June 1632 to testify a second time about what he might know about Benedetti's alleged crime, Alberti was asked some routine questions pertinent to his own trustworthiness as a witness. Had he ever been imprisoned or prosecuted himself? Before arriving in Rome, he had been jailed for a debt in Velletri, Alberti admitted, and released when he paid off his creditor. He further confessed that in 1631 he had been accused in the senator's tribunal of altering a power of attorney issued in connection with a moneylending operation. Before his release on bail on those charges he spent time in the Roman prison of Corte Savella where Giustiniani had visited him to check on some money he was owed.[128] Not surprisingly, Alberti was silent about criminal proceedings initiated against him just ten days earlier in the governor's tribunal, and he was not asked about them. A grocer accused the notary from Tor di Nona of framing his wife on a trumped-up charge of slander and then taking a bribe to keep from jailing her.[129] None of this history seems to have affected Alberti's career adversely, however; in the late 1630s and early 1640s we find him on the other side of the interrogation table, working for the governor's tribunal.[130]

Unlike his migratory colleagues, Fulvio Benedetti, who was probably the youngest of the four, spent the first three years of his career in Giustiniani's office. He arrived in Rome from Stimigliano in Sabina in 1629 and, after a year's novitiate, moved up to the position of sostituto. Before May 1630, he shared a room with Bartolomeo Benedetti and was thought friendly to him, attempting to shield him when called to testify in the case of the disputed will.[131] But he profited from Bartolomeo's dismissal for Giustiniani assigned to Fulvio the job of registering the acts of the maestri giustizieri after his colleague's departure.[132] He apparently made a good impression on those civic judges: Fulvio Benedetti was destined for notarial posts at the highest levels of the municipal administration. He was elected notary of the syndics of the municipal officials in 1638, became coadjutor or assistant to the protonotary of the senator from 1651 to 1656, and again in the 1680s, and served as notary of the conservators from 1656 to 1688.[133]

While there was a great deal of mobility and even quick advancement for notarial employees at the beginning of their careers, the middle decades demanded patience, if not resignation. Before Sixtus V made the Capitoline notarial offices venal, this would not have been the case, for the open profession of those times would have allowed qualified notaries to matriculate. The 1586 legislation eliminated this option. By the seventeenth century, if the capital to purchase a notarial office could be accumulated, it was generally done, as we have seen, by the time a notary was in his mid-thirties. Because few sostituti could hope to come up with the several thousand scudi required, however, most settled down to long years of hired labor.[134] Sixty-year old Michele Picollo from Piemonte retired to tend his Roman vineyard in 1633 after twenty-five years in the office of Arsenio Mosca and his predecessor, notaries of the auditor of the Camera.[135] The sixty-one-year-old Ottaviano Nucci from Gubbio, with more than thirty years' service to the titleholders of office 11, was a lone symbol of continuity in Angelo Giustiniani's office with its constant ebb and flow of young clerks.[136] Eugenio Salvietti of Monte Santo (Spoleto diocese) had also spent twenty-five years in various Capitoline offices and in the office of a notary of the auditor of the Camera. Urban VIII's legislation of 1625 presented him with a new possibility, that of registering as a free-lance professional with the Archivio Urbano, and by 1631 Salvietti had shaken off the padroni and set up as a private notary.[137] The Capitoline titleholders would no longer be issuing orders to him.

The social relations of production in the notary's office were such that the bulk of scribal labor came from men who were both detached, mobile, professionally slippery figures and household intimates sharing a common table with their boss. While the workshop economy of early modern Europe would have found nothing exceptional in this paradox, the notary's banco put a higher premium on the manufacture of trust than did most businesses. Its products needed to be credible in order to sell. There was no intrinsic reason to believe that the post-1586 conditions of employment in the notarial profession undermined the production of authoritative documents, but it was certainly true that these texts were no longer the handiwork of the notary in whose name they circulated. Instead they were the work of hired, ill-paid, often temporary, hands with little investment in any particular office's prospects. Sostituti gossiped about their bosses when they met outside the judges' chambers on the Capitol, trading rumors about their finances.[138] Although employees regarded the padroni with fascination, their own networks may have been more compelling than ties with employers.

What happened around the common table, therefore, and more generally the interactions between Capitoline notaries and the men who wrote for them, could have an impact on the integrity of the final product. A court official asked Angelo Giustiniani if he had ever had occasion to reprove any of his scribes for their writing practices and instructed him to remind his giovani that they must tell the truth when called to testify in Bartolomeo Benedetti's trial.[139] Giustiniani, who had never questioned the young man when he saw him obsessively copying a client's name and who brushed aside his maid's revelation that she had found wax seals torn from a document under Bartolomeo's bed, claimed that he had reprimanded his staff only twice in twenty years.[140] Not all titleholders were indifferent employers; Ottaviani suggested that his heir give his giovani a special break if they wanted to purchase the office after his death, and Ascanio Barberino left his rights in office 10 to one of his sostituti.[141] But Capitoline notaries did not necessarily supervise their employees closely, as we see both from the repeated orders of papal officials that sostituti and giovani extend and bind instruments within the legal deadlines and from the clauses in the notarial statutes forbidding sostituti from signing public copies.[142] Much of the time, it seems, the titleholders were just not around. The fabrication of scriptura publica took place through mechanisms that owed a great deal to the padroni's faith that the staff was doing what it was supposed to be doing.

Servicing a Clientele
The Choices of Clients

Notaries needed customers just as much as hat makers or barbers did, and venal officeholders with payments hanging over their heads could ill afford to neglect the sale of their wares. Without clients all the legal authority and hired pens in the world would have borne no fruit; these were, after all, households set up to produce writing on demand. Yet the larger context for notarial production in baroque Rome was competition from other forms of evidence. The enormous quantity of surviving business acts can dazzle us into thinking that patronage of notaries was ubiquitous, but we know this was not the case, and, whether or not we can recover it, the choice always involved a client's calculation. Ginevra Bonincontro, for instance, the widow of Capitoline notary Lorenzo Bonincontro, kept detailed accounts of her income and expenses. The guardian of two children whose patrimony included her late husband's office, Ginevra was not likely to shy away from paying notaries their due. She filled her ledgers with receipts but rogated only a very few of them. What dictated her choice to use a notary was not necessarily the amount in question, but the transaction's relationship to other types of scriptura publica. When she paid the small sum of ten scudi to her maid Portia, she treated her account book as an insufficient record and turned to a notary because the payment was a bequest from her late husband's will.[143] She also preferred a notary's hand for documents serving as evidence in a civil action against a delinquent debtor.

With keen discrimination, therefore, large numbers of people did employ notaries. Generalizing all those individual calculations, we can identify the need for certification and for information as the two main desires driving notarial clients.[144] *Certification* describes Ginevra Bonincontro's motive. She sought documents with the authority to function as a form of proof in the Roman legal system—a goal that linked her choice directly or indirectly to the prospect of litigation. *Information*, on the other hand, refers to the client's use of the notary as a broker to find something she or he wanted—particularly, in the early modern context, money. Like attorneys in England in the same period, notaries on the continent played a key role in moneylending, bringing together those who needed loans and those who had capital to invest.[145]

Roman notaries vigorously participated in the credit market, parleying information into a wide variety of financial instruments for customers, all of which they had to rogate, archive and, when asked, turn into public copies. Providing certification and information to clients was not, therefore, necessarily two separate activities. It was often one linked business strategy, particularly for those professionals, like the thirty Capitoline notaries, attached to civil tribunals. When debtors and creditors fell out, they frequently sought out the notaries who could start their litigation proceedings for them. Contracting parties in Rome seemed to have viewed lawsuits not, as we might suppose, as their last resort, but rather as a way of renegotiating their agreements, the continuation of business by other means.[146] If civil proceedings were normal economic practice, the Capitoline notaries were nicely placed to provide clients with both records of their contracts and the documents needed to enforce them.

While in theory any notary could offer clients certification and information, in reality the venal officeholders had a decisive edge over the private notaries. Again Cardinal Giovanni Battista De Luca's comment from midcentury is pertinent. Romans prefer the public notaries, he contended, because they preserve their records better.[147] Being able to count on finding the documents they sought attracted customers. Equally compelling was the fact that, as court notaries, the venal officeholders also functioned as the gateway to the civil justice system. Yet there were quite a few tribunals in Rome, as we have seen, and much rivalry between courts—and their notaries—for judicial business, civil as well as criminal. While the Capitoline notaries had to concede the most lucrative civil cases to the notaries of the auditor of the Camera and the most aristocratic clients to the notaries of the Rota, they offered three distinctive enticements to consumers. The first was convenience. Thirty notaries, many more than for any other tribunal, dispersed around the city rather than concentrated in a particular street, were likely to be within easy reach of clients. Second, the prices of civil judicial acts in the tribunal of the senator were lower, sometimes much lower, than those of its biggest rival, the auditor of the Camera. Pope Paul V may have done the Capitoline notaries yet another service when his reform legislation of 1612 not only published fees for a greater number of judicial acts than ever before but divided them up by tribunal.[148] Nothing made comparison shopping for justice more efficient.

Finally, the kind of procedure employed by the civil judges of the Capitoline curia, rooted more firmly in ius commune than that used in the papal courts, produced speedier outcomes. This is somewhat counterintuitive, given that the labyrinthine methods of the senator's tribunal were notorious, at least among curial partisans, as far back as the seventeenth century. However, if its modus operandi is understood correctly, as Renata Ago has argued, we see that cases brought to the Capitoline curia did not necessarily take longer than elsewhere.[149] Although litigants might never obtain a final judgment, they seem to have pocketed as many judicial decrees as they could pay for, coming to terms with each other about the goods in dispute more rapidly than if they had had to await a judicial sentence. So for location, price, and speed, the thirty Capitoline notaries could compete handily with the notaries of rival civil jurisdictions for the city's business.

Can we discern any pattern to client preferences when it came to selecting among the thirty notaries who held the offices of the Capitoline curia or, indeed, choosing any particular notary in Rome? Although it happens all too rarely, we sometimes do hear the reasons for a customer's choice. Jacobus Landusgalli, shot near San Ambrogio on the Corso just before daybreak, shouted to a passing acquaintance to fetch Capitoline notary Girolamo Tranquillo "who is close by."[150] The ex-Capitoline notary Virgilio Lusanna said he occasionally used Angelo Giustiniani's office because his wife's dowry was invested there.[151] A courier who had first encountered the private notary Eugenio Salvietti at a house purchase three years earlier, and whose wife's relative was acquainted with him, asked Salvietti to rogate all his instruments.[152] Because the footman in the household of Princess Anna Maria Cesi Peretti had already met the sostituto Ottavio Franceschini when Franceschini was in office 22, he called on him again when Franceschini was working next door in office 20 at the Arco del Portogallo.[153] When Capitoline notary Flavio Paradisi was jailed in 1629 and his office 7 put under the care of administrators, his clients, the leaders of the vegetable sellers' guild, complained that it was being managed "by different people and in an irregular fashion." Although the guild officers were unable to convince their members to abandon Paradisi, they successfully executed a parliamentary maneuver to switch their business to Leonardo Bonanni, titleholder of office 2.[154]

More often, our evidence for clients' selections is circumstantial and ambiguous.[155] The master of horse (*cavallarizzo*) in the Peretti establishment also patronized Ottavio Franceschini while he was administering office 20 next door, and for two years Francescini had been handling all his investments in short-term loans. Had he chosen Franceschini because of his proximity, or because colleagues in the Palazzo Peretti had recommended him, or because, as it turned out, he and the notary had attended the same school?[156] Paolo Vespignani of office 28 in the Via dei Giubbonari did a good deal of business for the Spada family; was that because the Palazzo Spada was a block away or because Vespignani and the Spada both hailed from Brisighella in the Romagna? People from the same city often frequented a given notary, though not always because he was a compatriot.[157]

Sometimes customers and notaries had joint business interests. Lorenzo Bonincontro owned some cattle sheds in the Forum with one client and had loaned money in the form of censi to several others.[158] Sometimes the type of contract dictated the choice of notary. This was obviously the case in such moneylending operations as società d'ufficio loans because notaries brought investors and creditors together, but it also occurred for other reasons. A widow used the notary who rogated her husband's will for the instrument accepting the inheritance but went back to the notary who had drawn up her dowry agreement for the act that returned her dowry after her husband's death.[159] Similarly, a client might do a good deal of litigation in one office but opt for a different office when it came to rogating his will. In partnerships where one party put up the capital and the other pledged his labor, the choice of the rogating notary might be imposed by the investing partner.[160] Sometimes litigants preferred to use a familiar Capitoline process server (*mandatario*) who in turn habitually teamed up with a sostituto from a given notarial office.[161] For various reasons then, even when a patron showed particular attachment to a specific notary, he or she would occasionally rogate an instrument or obtain a judicial order with another. Cardinal Domenico Cecchini's loyalty to Capitoline office 1 survived the passage of the office from one Ricci to another over the course of several decades, but this did not prevent Cecchini's instruments from turning up in the protocols of other Capitoline notaries too.

Notwithstanding all this variety, however, proximity evidently meant a lot to a Capitoline notary's clientele. Giovanni Battista Ottaviani with his office near the Colonna palace on Piazza SS. Apostoli counted the Colonna among his clients over many years. He also rogated instruments for his colleague's wife, Ginevra Bonincontro, whose house on what is now Vicolo del Piombo was close by.[162] Torquato Ricci's office 1 next to S. Maria in Campo Marzio serviced the Borghese family, whose palace was not far away. Bernardino Velli of a patrician family based in Trastevere used office 17, which may have been the only Capitoline notarial office on the Tiber's west bank.[163] The clients of Carlo Constantini, titleholder of office 5 near the monastery of Tor de Specchi, included of course the nuns of Tor de Specchi, many Jews living in the nearby ghetto, and aristocratic neighbors like the Savelli and Capizucchi. Paolo Vespignani's location on the Via dei Giubbonari (near the Via dei Chiavari) put him within a convenient distance of not only the Spada but also the wealthy Sacchetti and Falconieri families, and such active institutional clients as the confraternity of the Trinità dei Pellegrini and the confraternity of the Conception at the Church of San Lorenzo in Damaso.

Vespignani's example points to a key ingredient in the success of a Capitoline office, the institutional client. The Capitoline notaries were generalists; their clientele ran the gamut from Jews to cardinals, from old-clothes sellers to bankers, and their business acts reflected a range of types of transactions.[164] This positioned them well to provide notarial services to Rome's numerous charitable institutions, churches, monasteries, religious brotherhoods, and artisan and trade guilds. Long Italian tradition had endowed the notary with a formative role not only in civic political associations but also in the pious and social organization of city dwellers. In Counter-Reformation Rome such sodalities flourished as never before, with new confraternities and hospitals or charitable foundations emerging every few years, each of which required the occasional or constant employment of a notary.[165]

Less formal or more ephemeral groups also hired notaries as a way to act collectively. Neighborhood gatherings of gentlemen did this, for instance, to choose the electors who would vet candidates for the election lists of the patrician-controlled municipal government of Rome. Faithful to the logic of proximity, the gentlemen of the rione of Pigna asked Angelo Giustiniani to take minutes at their gathering, while those of the Regola district turned to Leonardo Bonanni.[166] Lower down the social scale, the use of notaries was a vital resource for workingmen not yet organized into a guild or anxious to block a policy of the guild to which they belonged. Tensions in the new industry of carriage making brought the carriage makers to Ottaviano Saravezzio, notary for the carpenters, in the 1580s.[167] Masons protesting a dues increase imposed by their officers took the first steps to sue them by meeting in the presence of Leonardo Bonanni and then using him to collect supporting signatures from three hundred fellow masons.[168]

In these cases, Saravezzio, Giustiniani, and Bonanni were probably paid for the specific task they performed, but when Capitoline notaries worked regularly for an organization, they often received a retainer as the group's official secretary. As secretary of the hospital and confraternity of S. Maria della Consolazione, Lorenzo Bonincontro collected three scudi a month, and a little less from the hospital of the Mendicanti and from the confraternity and hospital of SS. Salvatore.[169] He was also notary for the confraternity of the Rosary and for at least three monasteries.[170] Other Capitoline notaries had large numbers of institutional clients too. Office 9 under several generations of the Gargario family had acquired the business of the chapter of St. Peter's Basilica as well as its confraternity of the Holy Sacrament, and the chapters of S. Maria in Via Lata and of S. Lorenzo in Damaso.[171] Vespignani in office 28 counted at least six monasteries and three confraternities among his clients, including, as we have seen, the city's largest confraternity catering to the needs of pilgrims.[172]

Although some notaries were elected to their posts, others purchased the right to be the secretary to an institutional client.[173] Giustiniani had paid to provide notarial services to Rome's hospice for the mentally ill (*pazzarelli*) as well as to the *convertite* (reformed prostitutes), and Bonanni had done the same for the confraternity and hospital for orphans (*orfanelli*).[174] Judging by the protocols of Giovanni Battista Ottaviani, notary for a confraternity that had used office 13 for decades for its specialization in dowry subsidies, such clients could keep an office quite busy.[175] The notary's relationship to a particular institution might well lead to a concentration of specific types of instruments, such as dowry agreements in the case of Ottaviani or apprenticeship contracts in that of Bonanni.

Rome's growing number of artisan and trade guilds also figured among the clients of the thirty Capitoline notaries. A sample of their protocols from the year 1630 revealed instruments or meeting minutes from more than two dozen trades-men's associations.[176] Perhaps not all of these collectivities had the funds or degree of formal organization necessary to put a notary on retainer or make him their official secretary, but some certainly did.[177] Moreover, until 1692 the more important guilds had their own tribunals for settling disputes, often competing with the Capitoline judges for the services of the Capitoline notaries and their staff.[178]

The majority of Capitoline notaries had guild clients, often with an obvious rationale for the connection. It made sense for the Roman fruit sellers to hire Giustiniani as their notary, for example, because he was also the notary for the tribunal where their disputes with vineyard owners were likely to be settled. Vespignani's office was close to the zone where the tanners had their workshops so it is not surprising that he became the notary of their guild. Similar thinking may have convinced the millers whose mills lined the banks near the Tiber island to use the office of Francesco Egidio. At times, of course, the motivation for the client's choice is obscure. Why did the painters and sculptors' academy switch from office 11 to office 15, for example, where they eventually shared Thomas Salvatori with the barbers' guild? The reason was a factional fight within the academy in 1609.[179] But why did the hotelkeepers pick Lorenzo Bonincontro, and why did the fishmongers whose market was so close to Bonanni's office drop him after only eight years? To these and similar questions we still have no answers.

A few Capitoline notaries attracted considerable business from tradesmen's orga-nizations, such as the very active office 25 near the market at Campo dei Fiori.[180] Under Giulio Raimondo (1586–1621) and later Taddeo Raimondo (1626–41), its staff routinely recorded meetings, rogated instruments, and staffed the guild tri-bunal for the masons, butchers, butchers' apprentices, pork butchers (*norcini*), and soap makers, and also served the butchers' confraternity of S. Maria della Quer-cia.[181] Even one guild client could be good for business, however, as we see in the case of Torquato Ricci's relationship with the tailors, who required their members to rogate their business acts in his office 1.[182] For this reason, Capitoline notaries must have tried hard to keep such clients from departing, and often, if the office passed to a new notary who had a personal tie with the preceding titleholder, institutional clients did remain loyal to a particular office. This is certainly the case for the masons and butchers with office 25, the tailors with office 1, and the tavern keepers (*osti*) with office 21. When the new notary did not inspire confidence, however, old clients might well make a change, as the hotelkeepers did after the death of their notary in 1634.

Institutional clients sometimes put up with a demanding notary. In a codicil to his will rogated a few days before his death, Lorenzo Bonincontro made quite explicit his wish that the business of the hospital of the SS. Salvatore remain with office 18 "at least until my heir has been entirely satisfied and paid the price of the value of the [secretaryship]." He added clauses that would have canceled all the bequests he had made to the SS. Salvatore should the officers fail in this regard.[183] The officers must have honored their notary's request because, after the early deaths of his children and his widow, all the Bonincontro property ended up with the hospital.

The Fabric of Trust

While governments dictated many details of their product line and also set their prices, notaries did contribute an intangible element to the hyperregulated texts that they wrote and sold to consumers. Clients understood this, and, although they expected the notary to turn their words into usable records, and perhaps intended to buy one or another of an array of special artifacts of that record, they knew that they wanted something more than mere writing from their purchase. They could obtain mere writing in other ways. That intangible something more, to which we could give the notaries' term *fides*, was trustworthiness. But what exactly was this quality and how did venal notarial offices produce it? The story of an unfortunate day in the career of Capitoline notary Erasto Spannocchia, titleholder of office 15 from 1615 to 1625, sheds light on these questions, so crucial to explaining the desirability of public writing.[184] The work of the pen alone, even within a notarial office, cannot explain the generation of these documents. The successful production of notarial acts rested on specific practices that kept clients and those in authority believing in their authenticity.

On a winter day in 1620, Erasto Spannocchia of San Polo in the Sabina had been titleholder of the office in Via di San Eustachio for five years when his young employee showed him the instrument with the holes in it. The eight-page document was a censo, a common type of long-term loan much favored by the Roman upper classes in which the borrower put up real estate as collateral for the sum advanced by the lender. The protagonists in this transaction were local scions of patrician stock going back several centuries. They knew each other well and almost certainly were related, at least distantly, for such families as the Del Bufalo and the Santacroce intermarried regularly. The agreement in which Elena Santacroce loaned one thousand scudi to Orazio del Bufalo, a regular Spannocchia client, had been rogated by the notary on 28 May 1618.[185] Following Roman custom, the clients would not have taken duplicates away with them but would have planned to use the one in the notary's protocol as an exemplar should they ever need copies. By city law, the censo of 28 May should have been extended in a full mundum version by the end of June and sent for binding with the other instruments from the second trimester of 1618 by 1 November. Spannocchia did not observe the letter of the law, however, but routinely waited until early the following year to take all the preceding year's instruments to his stationer, Matteo Franchi.[186] A veteran *cartolaio*, Franchi bound and stitched the documents together in four volumes, added blank sheets for a table of contents (*rubricella*) at the beginning, made covers of heavy parchment, and labeled them prominently with Spannocchia's name.[187] The protocol for April to June 1618 was probably back in the notary's office by early in 1619, when his staff would have "paginated" the entire volume and produced the alphabetical index of the first names of the contracting parties.[188]

Capitoline notaries counted on a regular income from the acts in their possession through the demand for public copies. On that day in 1620, when a scribe took this volume off the shelf, he was about to undertake this typical service for a client. A lawyer for Elena's husband, Valerio Santacroce, had asked for public copies of all the Santacroce censi in the holdings of office 15. Fees for public copies, those signed by the titleholder, were regulated, of course, just as were fees for rogating instruments in the first place, but they were a nice addition to the initial income from the transaction.[189] It was not difficult to find Valerio Santacroce's records in the index of first names at the beginning of each protocol, and soon the scribe, Giovanni Cepollini of Sarzana, had located the fully extended versions of several censi.

Before beginning to prepare the copies requested, however, Cepollini observed that the one involving Orazio del Bufalo and dated 28 May 1618 was in bad shape.[190] Franchi's needle would normally have made three separate perforations on the left margin of each document as it punctured the pile. Two of the three needle pricks on the censo of 28 May, however, had torn toward the margin, and these holes allowed the document to flap about almost freely. The first two pages were loose and the other six barely attached. Upon noticing this, Cepollini immediately brought the volume to his padrone. Although Spannocchia had never seen damage quite like this before, he quickly decided to have the giovane make a copy of the document. When the young man brought it to him later that day, the two checked to make sure that it was indeed a verbatim transcription of the original. This form of proofreading required one man to read the original aloud and the other to follow the text of the duplicate looking for any discrepancies.[191] When they had finished, Spannocchia tore up the instrument with the holes in it and stepped into a legal quagmire.

No one, not even the notary who had rogated it, was permitted to remove a contract from its protocol. If the local laws that had made this point since 1363 were insufficiently clear, there was the added word of the jurists that a notarial document without its protocol did not prove.[192] A loose instrument no longer bound in a dated sequence lost its status as judicial proof and was worthless from the client's perspective. But the notary who had duplicated the instrument potentially faced a worse fate than the client. Where was he going to put this fresh copy? And how was he going to explain the absence of its predecessor in the protocol? Criminal penalties threatened if he could not answer those two questions satisfactorily.

Although the notary's error had a certain logic to it, Spannocchia soon realized his predicament and did the only thing possible under the circumstances: nothing. That was how the matter stood five months later when his longtime client Orazio del Bufalo showed up at the office and asked a giovane to bring him the loan agreement from two years earlier. Handed the protocol of instruments for May 1618, Del Bufalo did what such gentlemen expected to do in Rome. He turned to the table of contents and looked under V for Valerio Santacroce and the page number of his censo. When he turned to the page, however, it was missing along with seven other pages. His instrument was gone.

Spannocchia was out. Clients were accustomed to treating the notary's office as an archive, and they did not assume their notary would necessarily always be present. The employee who was assisting him begged Del Bufalo to return the next day to get an explanation from the padrone. Del Bufalo did come back the following morning, and, when the notary still was not there, tried again after lunch. When he at last confronted Spannocchia, Del Bufalo was decidedly testy, exclaiming in wonderment that he "could have done such a thing" to someone who was his friend (*amico*).[193] Spannocchia defended himself by blaming the missing censo on the staff member who had copied and checked it, and asked why Del Bufalo wanted to see it. Because Del Bufalo had been cited by Santacroce to provide documentation that he did not think was required, the client replied that he had wanted to review the clauses in the censo. Spannocchia promised that he would bring the instrument to his house, but the next day when the impatient Del Bufalo returned again to the notary, Spannocchia told him the agreement was not in fact as Del Bufalo had remembered.[194] The angry client had had enough. On 20 May 1620 Del Bufalo swore out a complaint before the governor's criminal tribunal, charging that pages were missing from his notary's protocol.

Like many dossiers, this court case consists only of the accusation and a few interrogations of key figures like Spannocchia himself, his employees, and his stationer. It is unlikely that anything came of Del Bufalo's charges because the notary continued to run office 15 for another five years, which would have been unlikely if he had been convicted of a serious crime. Though he found Spannocchia's conduct puzzling and probably imprudent, the judge must ultimately have believed that the document was missing for reasons that were innocent, not malicious. He came to this conclusion, however, after incarcerating the notary for at least a week in Tor di Nona prison and questioning him in detail about the writing practices of his office. Spannocchia's answers shed light on the office's view of how documents were created, but they also reveal significant gaps between the practices of professionals and the notions of customers. Such gaps undermined the trust upon which notaries traded.

The judge took Spannocchia through the steps in the redaction of a valid record. In the first phase, the notary was supposed to make rough notes or *matrici* of the contract desired by his client. Spannocchia did not treat all transactions uniformly, however, and indicated that in the first phase his own practice varied, probably according to the degree of complexity in the agreement. He did not keep matrici for all instruments. Sometimes he wrote out a draft (*menuta*) of a contract before the clients formalized it, and he did keep these, but this was not routine practice. "When you are used to doing a hundred ordinary instruments you formalize them in a few words and, because you extend them immediately, you don't keep the original [*originale*]."[195] Whether the version was a detailed draft or just notes, however, the notary never put in the full legal clauses but simply indicated their presence with the abbreviation "etc."

The second phase in document production, extension, which we know had been legislated since 1580, was less subject to variation. Spannocchia filled out the abbreviated clauses completely when he (or more likely his staff) extended the instrument that would eventually be bound in the protocol. The judge did not ask him whether he extended Del Bufalo's censo within a month, as city law required (or three months under the more generous 1612 reforms), though Spannocchia certainly tried to give the impression that in his office little time elapsed between the two stages.

Spannocchia's footing was less sure when it came to the timing of binding the loose but fully extended instruments. His answer to the judge's direct question about how long the censo had lain unbound was that he did not remember.[196] Although he was supposed to bind every three months, Spannocchia seems to have accumulated all the instruments for a given year and then had the stationer make them up into the series of protocols that researchers find in the state archive today. As we have seen, he ended up with four volumes for 1618. Interestingly, the padrone was at pains to insist that he carefully kept the loose instruments, like the few matrici he saved, in his locked bedchamber rather than in the more public room (*sala*) where the office staff worked.[197]

Spannocchia's downfall, if such it was, was less the ordinary routines of handling documents than the crises, such as the unprecedented discovery of several sheets about to fall out of a volume. The court pressed repeatedly on his decision to destroy the original censo. Here a gap opened up between the expectations shared by the law and the client and the thinking of the notary. Spannocchia argued that it was his responsibility to see that no harm came to the records in his care. The contract that was clinging by one thread to the protocol seemed in imminent danger of disappearing. Moreover, he believed that he had the authority to make a new original of the act he had rogated. He asserted that the copy that he had directed Cepollini to make had become the real censo and denied that the earlier document was the original any longer. "The instrument that I had gone to the trouble of proofreading was the true and real one. . . . That other in the protocol was no longer necessary, and so I ripped it up."[198]

Another hole appeared in the fabric of trust when Spannocchia claimed to have set aside the new original until the time when the stationer would make his annual pickup of the office's unbound instruments. If, as he testified, the event had occurred six months earlier around January 1620, it would have been just the time when the business acts for 1619 would normally have gone out for binding. Mysteriously the notary did not follow through on this plan, in which the cartolaio would have rebound the second volume of 1618 acts with the new original censo in the place of the one Spannocchia had removed.[199] When Del Bufalo filed his charges with the governor's court in May 1620, the recopied "original" censo was still loose.

Spannocchia's predicament was not just that he had broken the law but also that his missteps had fatally undermined the credibility of the instrument in the client's own mind. The text was not as Del Bufalo had remembered it, and the original was not in the protocol. The fact that Spannocchia could produce a censo that he claimed was the true original just waiting to be replaced in the proper protocol could not restore Del Bufalo's confidence, although it must eventually have persuaded the court of the notary's innocence. It was not accurate, legally impeccable clauses written by notaries that proved. It was writing set in a specific sequence in a juridically privileged vessel, handled and labeled in authoritative ways. A Capitoline notary whose treatment of the matter of writing did not meet these specifications would not have customers for long.

Making It Pay

Poised between the clients who wanted trustworthy documents, the employees assigned to produce them, and the state that set their prices, the titleholder of a Capitoline office tried to take in more than he had to pay out. The costs added up. Heading the balance sheet for perhaps the majority of the thirty Capitoline notaries were payments to investors,[200] followed by monthly massa fees to the college (a minimum of 1.5 scudi), rent for the office's physical space,[201] supplies of paper and ink, binding services, and of course the board and salaries of the office staff. As we have seen, employees in the 1630s earned 1.5 to 2 scudi monthly, so a typical Capitoline notary with three or four scribes notched up another 5 to 8 scudi each month. While the padrone paid neither the college nor his staff on time, the moment to render accounts inevitably arrived.

Although Italy's notaries today have a reputation for prosperity, their financial condition in the Middle Ages and early modern period was far less secure. One scholar has argued that the only way a fourteenth-century Italian notary could make money was to hold public office or lease tax farms.[202] In baroque Rome, the few public offices open to notaries were not very remunerative, however, and tax farms were an option only for those, like Felice de Totis, a former notary of the Camera, who had already amassed a sizable capital.[203] Although the Capitoline notaries owned agricultural real estate like vineyards, meadows, and chestnut groves, we do not know much else about any extranotarial sources of income they might have enjoyed.[204] Venality did not necessarily lead to riches, and in their first century as venal officeholders more than one Capitoline notary ended up in debt and in jail.[205]

To make it pay, in addition to the material assets constituted by the protocols of the office's predecessors and the desks at which the giovani sat and wrote, the Capitoline notaries could hope to count on some immaterial assets. One of these was the trust of the office's former clients, especially noble families, institutions, and sodalities with their regular demand for documents, and another was the friendships they themselves had fostered as they made their way up to titleholder of one of the thirty Capitoline offices. There were more down-to-earth resources too, such as deposits put down by clients for court records or "credits" (*crediti*) left with the notary for various reasons, including the hope that he would be able to invest them for their owners.[206] One Capitoline notary in the 1630s seems also to have been buying up the rights of the heirs of the pre-1586 Capitoline notaries to fees for transunti of their ancestors' instruments.[207] Because of the value of the documents and deposits in the offices, everyone understood that they could never be left unattended, even if that meant saying no to a client who needed a will in a hurry.[208] But the key to the notaries' solvency lay not in the mere accumulation of records or clients, but in the capacity to turn their textual presence into cash or at least, given Roman payment practices, into promissory notes.

To understand from an economic perspective the unusual commodity the Capitoline notaries produced and sold, we must return to the distinction between act and artifact. A customer needed a notary to perform the act of rogating. Although it is tempting to think of this act as a physical document, we grasp its nature more accurately if we conceive of it as a service by the notary, the authorized rogating agent, which came at a specified price. Included in the rogation fee paid by the customer was some writing and document handling by the notary: rough notes metamorphosed into the extended original lodged in a protocol. The staff recorded payment for this service in the office's register of receipts (*liber receptorum*). Acts therefore generated fees. Allowing the client to view the original in the protocol earned a bit more for the notary, though, as we have seen, this income disappeared after Paul V's reforms in 1612.

Litigation drew money to the notary's coffers in a different way. As we saw in chapter 3, each of the legal steps required by a civil proceeding in the senator's court created a document of a specific type, usually a summons or one of dozens of different warrants (*mandata*).[209] When clients purchased such texts they were really paying for a juridical action, as they set in motion the delivery of the summons to an adversary, for example, or the seizure of property on which payment was owed. Nevertheless, as with rogation, judicial acts too necessitated some writing and document handling by the notary. The office staff had to write out the summons, to note them in the manuale, and to string them together in a stitched pile after they had been returned to the office by the process server charged with their delivery. Employees also marked down what fee the office had earned for each mandatum or summons in the *liber expeditionum*, the accounts of the office's judicial business.

In addition to acts, whether of a business or judicial nature, artifacts or subsequent copies of the original instrument or warrant also brought in revenue. Copying was a separate but important part of the notary's business. By the mid-seventeenth century the notary's product line had diversified to the extent of providing three levels of copies: public copies, *fedi* and simple copies. Writing practices distinguished these three types. Public copies included the titleholder's signature and the date and place of rogation; fedi bore a signature but lacked the defining formalities of publication;[210] and simple copies carried only the text of the agreement. Notaries, and copyists more generally in Rome, also charged customers a copy rate of one giulio per sheet of paper.[211]

Although Capitoline notaries depended economically on the sale of acts and artifacts of acts, the state, not the market, controlled what they could charge for their products. The rates for notarial instruments and judicial actions were fixed and, indeed, after 1562 had to be posted in the vernacular in public view in their workplaces.[212] Fixed rates did not mean flat rates, of course. The earliest evidence we have, the city statutes of 1363, assumed that notaries' fees would be based on the value of the contract they were rogating or on the amount in dispute between litigants.[213] The wealthier the clients or contending parties, presumably the more the notary earned.

Over time, the efforts of the municipality and the papacy to control the operations of the justice system at the notary's expense led them to differentiate between the pricing systems of business acts and judicial acts. By the fifteenth century, the principle of proportionality had disappeared from judicial rates, which became in essence flat rates by type of action. In addition, regulations guaranteed to litigants and customers that the copies they purchased from notaries would meet minimum standards as to number of pages and lines and words per page.[214] As early as 1521, city laws clamped down on another income stream when they made it plain that notaries could not charge litigants or judges to look at judicial acts.[215] The final development in judicial fees was the publication of the rates for all Roman tribunals in the 1612 reform legislation, which may have attracted budget-minded litigants to the Capitoline notaries.

The 1612 rates held fast through the seventeenth century. They advertise the Roman notary's enhanced array of wares, the proliferation since 1363 of various types of warrants and summons, and their low unit prices. A creditor hoping to put pressure on a debtor by seizing her goods, for instance, could pay three baiocchi (the price of three poor man's loaves of bread) for the act of distraint or ten baiocchi in a package deal that would include the distraint plus verifying his claim by either witnesses or a notary. To revoke the seizure would cost two more baiocchi.[216] By breaking civil process into minute fragments and charging for each piece, notaries both in the Capitoline tribunal and in other courts combated the flat rates for judicial acts that had been imposed on them. The price to begin a lawsuit was a modest two baiocchi, but notaries billed separately for every action from empowering an attorney to formulating questions for the witnesses to asking the questions of the same witnesses. This fee structure helps to explain why scholars have argued that civil justice in Rome was driven not by the state or the magistrates but by the contending parties.[217] They received exactly as much justice as they chose or were able to purchase.[218] While the state controlled the rates, therefore, notaries showed considerable ingenuity in determining what litigants would get for their money.

By contrast, the authorities tolerated the medieval rate structure for business acts in which notaries earned a fee proportional to the value of the contract they rogated. For the public instrument of a will involving an estate worth less than 25 scudi, for example, the Capitoline notaries collected 3 giulii (30 baiocchi or .3 scudo); for one worth 1,000 scudi, they earned twenty times that amount, 60 giulii or 6 scudi.[219] To obtain a copy of such an instrument, the client paid the standard copy rate plus one-fifth of the fee for the will (to a maximum of 10 scudi).[220] The proportional fee likewise governed rental agreements and even receipts.[221] Recent scholarship emphasizes the high cost of documenting business deals through notaries.[222] Yet there were good arguments for paying the price. The alternatives were not free either; popular new types of loans required scriptura publica, and consumers worried about leaving patrimonial transfers like wills and dowry agreements in scriptura privata. Institutions and many individuals in particular circumstances may have flinched, but in the end they purchased the extra force of notarial authority.

Despite their support for the key principle, the popes did cut into some of the notaries' time-honored income from business acts, as we have seen. Beginning in the 1560s and culminating in the 1612 reforms, legislation compelled Capitoline notaries to provide simple copies for all instrument types, except wills, at graduated rates that were lower than those for public copies. The public copy of a lease for a house renting at less than 100 scudi a year cost a flat 37.5 baiocchi; the simple copy cost from 10 to 30 baiocchi depending on the amount of the rent.[223] As mentioned, Paul V also made notarial records less remunerative by abolishing charges for merely looking at them.[224] We do not know how the Capitoline notaries, who criticized these changes in later years, reacted to them at the time, but they must have feared some pressure on their revenues from business acts. While fixed rates, competing modes of documentation, and lost sources of income may not have been enough to dry up the market for these offices, especially after they had become inheritable, they did nothing to lubricate it.

Help came from the judicial side of the Capitoline notary's business. The private notary Virgilio Lusanna shed light on the crucial connection between business acts and judicial acts when he recounted how he was lying sick in bed one day when some Genoese wood merchants he knew came knocking. His clients told him they urgently needed instruments in order to obtain warrants.[225] In other words, they wanted Lusanna to make public copies of contracts he had rogated for them so that they could hastily present them to a court notary in order to obtain distraint or arrest

warrants, presumably against other merchants. Because the archival series are separated, we only occasionally glimpse this everyday process at work in the Capitoline
offices, but it was vital to their income stream. Judicial acts spurred the production
of business acts, and business acts generated judicial acts. A warrant (*mandatum*)
issued by Taddeo Raimondo's office (25), for example, cleared the way for a payment, which gave rise to two business acts, a *quietantia* and a *cessio*, for the sum
received.[226] A procurator appeared at the daily judicial audience in Giacomo Attilio's
office (24), and, citing a dowry instrument rogated there twelve years earlier, requested an order from Attilio's judge protecting his client's dowry (presumably from
her husband's creditors) to the tune of 250 scudi.[227] Lorenzo Bonincontro's widow
purchased a simple copy of a censo to submit to Giulio Grappolini's office (18) in
order to force payment of the interest due from her debtor, the Marchese Olgiati, by
means of a warrant.[228] More generally, the practice of having notaries record decisions of the meetings of guilds, confraternities, and other corporate bodies may also
have been driven by the expectation of litigation.[229]

When customers sought out the arsenal of the senator's tribunal in their financial
dealings, they made money for the Capitoline notaries; when they went to the
Capitoline notaries to draw up their dowry and loan agreements, they bought
weapons to deploy in future litigation with creditors and debtors. The fact that the
notaries of the Capitoline curia and the notaries of the auditor of the Camera served
civil judges helps to explain why these two sets of notaries compass most of the
extant notarial protocols in Rome. While laws and writing practices distinguished
the notary's business acts and judicial acts, the early modern economy joined them
and, indeed, was inconceivable without both. Perhaps this practical fusion underlay
the convergence between the two kinds of documents that featured so prominently
in the 1612 reform legislation.

Grasping the nature of the Roman economy is key to understanding the ability of
the post-1586 Capitoline notaries to survive financially, despite the many obstacles
and competitors they faced. Among its salient features were the facts that demand
was weak, no one paid on time, and contracts had few institutional supports apart
from the courts.[230] If you were owed anything in baroque Rome, you were likely to
have frequent recourse to warrants. While it is true that a public instrument was not
the only way to pressure a debtor or creditor, alternative methods, like calling
witnesses before a judge, also required the services of Capitoline notaries. Citing a
witness to testify in such cases differed technically from rogating an instrument, but
it often involved the same setting and the same individuals; the witnesses in Paolo
Vespignani's judicial acts, for instance, show up as clients in his protocols.[231] The
neighborhood notary played a significant role in local business life, whatever the

type of writing he was paid to produce. The explosion of sophisticated money-lending techniques in Rome also assisted the solvency of many Capitoline notaries.

The business acts rogated by the thirty Capitoline notaries in the year 1645 have been sampled by a team of researchers, which helps to give an overall idea of the level and character of their output. The team did not count wills when they appeared in separate volumes, as they were supposed to do after 1612, but because seven of the offices had not obeyed this directive, some testaments slipped into the sample totals.[232] The thirty Capitoline notaries produced in all one hundred protocols in 1645, averaging about three per office for the year, a figure little changed from 1630.[233] Selecting fifteen of the offices for closer analysis, the researchers counted 8,453 instruments constituting 127 types of business acts between 19,556 customers.[234] The average Capitoline office rogated two or three instruments a day, or sixty to ninety per protocol, with volumes averaging 800 to 1,200 pages. Busy offices might have some that reached as many as 1,600 or even 2,000 pages in length.[235]

Things were not all that different in 1630. In the spring of that year, Giovanni Battista Ottaviani (office 13) rogated a little more than two hundred business acts, excluding wills, for the months of April through June. The types his clients favored corresponded generally to those found in 1645: obligationes (20), proxies (17), sales agreements (*emptiones* and *venditiones*) (15), rental agreements (*locationes, sublocationes, affictus*) (13), and nonspecific receipts (*quietationes*) (12).[236] As notary for the confraternity that dowered needy girls, however, Ottaviani's largest category was dowry instruments and their associated contracts (64), which helped to account for his large overall output. On the lower end, his office rogated just one *declaratio*, one *substitutio*, one *pomedium* (a fruit sharecropping contract), and one creation of a knight.

As the research team working on the protocols of 1645 discovered, and Ottaviani's output confirms, notaries classified their instruments juridically rather than by economic or social function. At the top left corner of the first page of each new document they wrote the *occhio*, the name of the type of instrument, and usually repeated these in the table of contents (*indice*) they later prepared for the bound protocol. Rarely, as when they recorded meetings of confraternities or artisan guilds, did they have no juridical conventions to which they needed to refer in order to shape the substance of the contract, though even with meeting minutes they tended to follow a set pattern.[237] More commonly they made the economic and social details fit a recognized category of act. Arranging a dowry, for example, might find expression in four different types of instruments;[238] borrowing money could appear as a *mutuum, recognitio debiti, fideiussio, censum, societas officium,* or *obligatio,* and these do not exhaust the possibilities.[239] While juridical labels are frustrating to scholars eager to use notarial records to find out about marriage and moneylending, to say nothing of commerce, agriculture, urban real estate, and personal property, they do highlight the kind of commodity that customers wanted from notaries. And occasionally, as we see with loans, they reveal the technical ingenuity of the profession, as practitioners squeezed new activities into traditional legal containers.

Although we do not have the detailed information available for 1645 for earlier years, we can make rough calculations about how well a particular office was doing over time by counting the annual number of protocols it produced.[240] Frequent turnover of titleholder was bad for business, as is shown by the example of office 27 between 1595 and 1704. In 1614, when Pietro Paolo Stella took it over, office 27 had had only one titleholder for nineteen years and produced three protocols a year. In 1616 the office's output dropped to two volumes; Stella divested himself of the business, and in 1618 Francesco Martanus stepped in. During his tenure the number of protocols rose briefly, then dropped to one volume a year. In 1627 Salvatore Melli became titleholder and output increased to two volumes a year, but after Melli resigned in 1630, it again fell to one a year under Ottavio Nardonio (1631–36). It grew back to two, albeit slim, volumes under Marino Contucci (1637–51), but never again reached the level of 1614.[241]

By contrast, Angelo Canini, titleholder and owner of office 12 (1623–49), had a salutary effect on an incoherent Capitoline notarial office. After seven years under Domenico Bardella (1604–11), it had fallen into the hands of a succession of administrators for ten or so years with production dipping to one protocol a year. Under Canini, the number of annual volumes rose to two and, after 1635, to three a year.[242] Studying the hands in the protocols shows that the office's growing business anticipated this increase by at least three years, however, for as early as May 1632 Canini had to hire a fourth employee to keep up with it. Although he turned out just two protocols in 1632, the one for January through June was a massive 2,200 pages with more than three hundred contracting parties.[243] Carlo Novio, Canini's successor, acquired a stable and prospering office in 1649, which he was lucky enough to be able to pass on in 1677 to a son who also became a Capitoline notary.[244]

Although the notaries willingly executed instruments of all kinds, they had several reasons to greet clients who wanted last wills and testaments or the short-term loans known as *società d'ufficio* with special warmth. Both these types of business acts offered out-of-the-ordinary ways to profit, though they did so in different ways. Together wills and società d'ufficio contracts illustrate well what notaries had to do in order to make their offices pay.

While wealthy noble families passed only a portion of their patrimonies through testaments, most Romans used their wills to distribute the bulk of their assets. A rate structure based on a percentage of the value of the transaction netted notaries larger sums when more property was involved, so naturally the transfer of all but the smallest estates brought welcome fees. One worth a modest two hundred scudi garnered two scudi (two hundred baiocchi) for the thirty Capitoline notaries, which equaled the monthly wage of a sostituto; by contrast, the power of attorney, one of their most common business acts, earned them only four giulii (forty baiocchi).[245] Depending on the size of the estate, Capitoline notaries could charge up to twenty-five scudi for a will, an amount equivalent to what office 26, for example, took in over an entire month in the 1650s.[246] Moreover, notaries were not required to provide simple copies of wills, so interested parties, heirs, and those who might want to dispute with heirs, had no choice but the higher priced public copies. Because wills were one of the few notarial documents of which most clients desired duplicates, testators sometimes deliberately left money to pay for these public copies.[247]

Wills were not an everyday item in a Capitoline notary's business. Early on in his long career, Leonardo Bonanni of office 2, for example, rogated ninety-six testaments over a seven-year period, which would average just over one a month.[248] Trial records often highlight notaries' competition to rogate the wills of the rich, and sometimes they reveal several notaries at the bedside of the dying, called by contending factions among potential heirs.[249] The stakes were high. When a will was challenged, the notary went to jail. But the stakes were worth the game not only because of the size of the fees but also because testaments paved the way for a whole series of subsequent notarial acts necessary for their execution.[250] Instruments might be needed to open and read the will, to accept or renounce an inheritance, to make an inventory, to take possession of individual properties, or to record receipt of a bequest. And, of course, anyone with a claim on the estate would want copies of these documents.

Testaments were windfalls. By contrast, loans accounted for a significant portion of the notaries' ordinary business.[251] As we saw in chapter 4, baroque Rome was one of Europe's most active capital markets, but it was not just big finance that demanded the services of notaries; it was also a myriad of small investors, both religious institutions and individuals of varied means. A well-articulated market for credit offered types of loans to fit almost any collateral from public bonds (*luoghi di monti*) to mortgages (*censi*) to partnerships (*società in accomandita* or more general *società*) to short-term instruments like the distinctive Roman *società d'ufficio*. Despite the vast domain of scriptura privata or oral debt that never showed up in notarial protocols, Roman notaries drew their sustenance from the spreading use of sophisticated lending mechanisms in which they did play a part—indeed, sometimes more than one part.

Clients of the Capitoline notaries exploited the whole array of credit offerings, but one that appealed especially to their need for short-term loans was the società d'ufficio.[252] This "really complicated and exotic contract" was a good example of notarial ingenuity in the face of new economic opportunities because technically it was not a loan at interest, which canon law prohibited, but a partnership to purchase an office.[253] In fact, it was indeed a loan, and one paying a dazzling 12 percent, in theory for six months, but in practice indefinitely.[254] The warning of a cultivated member of the Roman elite, Virgilio Spada, that these lucrative financial instruments were prey to defaults and that those who indulged had best keep a lawyer at the ready went unheeded.[255] Investors ranging from barely literate rope makers to well-born prelates routinely sought out notaries to find willing borrowers.[256] Giorgio Giorgi, just beginning what turned out to be a short-lived tenure as titleholder of office 6 in 1630, could hardly conceal his delight when he thought that Carlo Grationi, a wealthy gentleman he had met as a sostituto in Bonincontro's office several years earlier, wanted his help placing money in a società d'ufficio.[257] The padroni no doubt tended to the most prosperous customers, but their office staff also actively put together deals between lenders and borrowers. Ettore Alberti had been working in Capitoline notarial offices for less than a year when he was prosecuted for altering a power of attorney a client needed for a società d'ufficio.[258] A giovane in the office of one of the notaries of the auditor of the Camera casually stopped a client in the street to sound him out about his preferences in a società d'ufficio he was arranging for him.[259] Notarial employees developed their own information networks for these short-term, high-interest loans so desired by Romans of all classes.[260]

The società d'ufficio illustrates the range of loan products and services that clients expected of Capitoline notaries and their staff. In a relatively simple example, a student who had already found two willing borrowers approached the sostituto Bartolomeo Benedetti for help with a società d'ufficio for twenty-five scudi.[261] This client instructed Benedetti to obtain instruments of obligatio from the two parties, and then come back to him for the money. Benedetti would have tracked down the individuals, rogated the necessary acts, and distributed the sum, earning fees for at least five instruments (two obligatio acts, the società d'ufficio agreement, and two receipts). A slightly more complex case required a greater variety of notarial documents and functions. Capitoline notary Giorgio Giorgi thought Carlo Grationi wanted to back a three-hundred-scudi loan to Ventura Agatoni in the form of a società d'ufficio, and, because he knew what Grationi was worth, he gladly went in search of lenders.[262] Because Grationi could not come in person to execute the necessary obligatio, or so it seemed, Agatoni had to get a power of attorney to act for Grationi and then the obligatio in Grationi's name. Giorgi, having found the money, prepared to write out the order releasing the funds to Agatoni, asking him first to turn over the signed power of attorney and Grationi's surety and to execute his own obligatio. In addition, at Grationi's request, he paid him a visit to inform him of how the arrangements were progressing. Had the deal been concluded, Giorgio would have rogated the società d'ufficio, several receipts, and the payment order—all of which he would have extended and kept in his protocols; located the lender; kept in touch with the loan's backer; obtained the cash; and disbursed it to Agatoni. And, had all gone as planned, Giorgi would have become one of those unfortunate notaries undone by bad securities because Agatoni had committed Grationi without his consent, using a false power of attorney and fake obligatio.

If these were the lawful ways that moneylending via the società d'ufficio earned income for notaries, the lawful ways did not exhaust the possibilities, as the former Capitoline notary whom we met earlier in this chapter, Virgilio Lusanna, teaches us. According to the titleholders of office 8 who accused him in a 1616 trial, Lusanna specialized in fictitious società d'ufficio, and they deposited twenty-five examples with the court to prove their point.[263] Technically these contracts were not fictitious because they involved real money and real people, but they were drawn improperly and were legally invalid. His accusers explained why they thought Lusanna produced these dubious società d'ufficio. First, he earned fees for rogating the instruments, and quite good fees at that. A miller from his neighborhood testified that on every 25 scudi loan Lusanna charged 3 giulii, though he collected another 15 giulii for the theoretical holder of the office; because the loans had to be renewed every six months, the witness ended up paying him a hefty 3.6 scudi a year.[264] According to the plaintiffs, Lusanna also pocketed the broker's fee (*senzaria*) for arranging the loans, kept back some of his client's money for his own use, and made technical adjustments to dates and names on the contracts (i.e., forged them) to lessen the risk of losing the investment.[265] Under interrogation Lusanna admitted that he profited in yet another way, lending his own money for società d'ufficio while using the name of his illiterate brother-in-law.[266]

The judicial reforms of 1612 make it plain that Ettore Alberti and Virgilio Lusanna were not the only notaries who were exploiting the intricacies of moneylending contracts for illicit gain, and they tried to prevent this by better record keeping.[267] Of dubious efficacy, these measures paled by comparison to the even less effective ban on notaries serving as middlemen for loans, notwithstanding the threat of the galleys and loss of office.[268] The legislation specifically included sostituti and giovani in the prohibition, a clue as to how extensive their involvement must have been, and shows how uneasy the authorities felt about the role of notaries in the

Roman market for credit. It was all right for them to rogate the necessary business acts, but they were forbidden to receive any other payments.

If the 1612 regulations were manifestly unenforceable, Urban VIII's new archive of 1625 may indicate the state's more modest approach to controlling middlemen in moneylending operations. Although its main target was long-term loan contracts and testaments, and it did not explicitly name notaries, it did demand that powers of attorney be registered in the Archivio Urbano.[269] The use of such proxies, particularly but not exclusively those issued outside papal territory, enabled the movement of funds among debtors and creditors who did not know each other. As we saw in chapter 4, archive officials explicitly ordered cashiers, bankers, and employees of the public loan funds not to recognize unregistered foreign powers of attorney.[270] They did not order notaries and their staff to stop looking for money for their clients to borrow and lend.

If we turn from the Capitoline notaries' output of business acts, which exist today in such abundance, to exploring the economic impact of the judicial side of their business, we confront an immense void of documentation.[271] Gaps in the series of manuali had surfaced as early as 1704, but there was a hemorrhage over the next two centuries, and no global estimate of the number of litigants processed by the thirty Capitoline offices is possible.[272] Hints and fragments must serve to redress the imbalance of archival survival.

The price structure of lawsuits with their pay-per-action principle meant, as we have said, that Romans generally got the amount of justice they could afford, and they could generally afford more at the Capitoline court than at papal tribunals. Did Sixtus V signal the primacy of litigation in the economy of the Capitoline notaries when he ordered that their contributions to the common fund be computed mainly on the basis of their judicial acts? We do not have much evidence to confirm or negate such a hypothesis. Notaries owed massa payments on judicial records, sentences, and several common types of warrants.[273] Capitoline offices did keep track of the acts on which they owed massa, though these records have not come down to us.[274] The college's own massa accounts from the 1630s do not reveal the contours of the profits of justice, because they show that most notaries paid merely the statutory 1.5 scudi a month.[275] As we saw in chapter 2, only Raimondo of office 25 and Vespignani of office 28 exceeded the mandatory minimum. It was probably to swell an insufficient revenue source, therefore, that warrants (*mandata*) authorizing public bond transfers were added to massa obligations by midcentury.[276]

Yet massa amounts may not be a good indicator of the extent of judicial earnings or of their importance to the Capitoline notaries. Litigation drew a constant stream of customers to the office and spun off other sorts of business, as we have seen. In Giacomo Attilio's office 24, the manuale for 1630 shows that nine or ten clients might appear at the daily judicial audience, and sometimes as many as sixteen or seventeen.[277] While people might turn up just to consult the office's judicial records, which they could do for free, many were certainly paying fees. Each time a party called a witness, the notary collected one giulio (ten baiocchi) for the testimony; every time one of those legal summons arrived, another notarial document replied.[278] Though her demand for warrants fluctuated, Ginevra Bonincontro paid for as many as seven in 1639, and clients also purchased copies "for greater justification" of their claims in subsequent cases.[279]

Consumers of Capitoline judicial acts, as with business acts, often expected some services with their documents. What it took to make the notarial office pay was knowledge of the intricacies of civil procedure and Roman jurisdictions and skill in its deployment to benefit preferred clients. According to a witness at Bartolomeo Benedetti's trial for forgery, the judges of the vineyard court for which he was notary lamented his departure because the tribunal had been very profitable during his tenure.[280] We catch sight of the kind of activity that might please some judges—and clients—in a case involving Flavio Paradisi of office 7. According to the plaintiff Menica Pulita of Genzano, Paradisi promoted the interests of one of his customers by trying to beat her prior claim on the assets of a recently deceased debtor. She charged that the notary wrote out an order to move her case from the court of Ripetta to that of his own Capitoline judge, and then backdated an entry in the manuale so that his client's warrant appeared to be earlier than hers.[281] In an economy in which it was more important to prove that you had a debt than to collect it, Paradisi had rendered good service to his own client.[282]

Less skill but equal guile was shown by Giacomo Bernascone when he was a sostituto in office 5 in a case pitting a lowly cobbler against the patrician Pietro Antonio Muti.[283] The shoemaker rented his house on Piazza Giudea from Muti's mother, and after a dispute involving a pair of scissors, Muti told him that he had to move out and that he had registered an eviction order (*disdetta*) in Capitoline notary Constantini's office 5. When a month passed with no such order, the shoemaker sent friends to look for it in the office 5 manuale, and one of these friends brought Muti himself along. No eviction notice was to be found. Muti then asked the employee present, named Bernascone, what had happened to it. To the noble client, Bernascone replied that it had not been entered in the manuale because the process server had simply dropped it off, adding "but I will change it so that it says it was handed over to someone in the household."[284] Not long afterward an eviction notice did appear in the manuale, inserted quite obviously, according to witnesses, under a false date both in the chronological record and in the table of contents. Bernascone did not suffer for his sleight of hand and, indeed, five years later became titleholder of a Capitoline notarial office of his own, ironically that formerly headed by the upright Ottaviani.

Making it pay was a risky business. Jurisdictional disputes between tribunals might land both padroni and their employees in prison.[285] Notaries sometimes had to duck blows from litigants who punched each other out in the office.[286] Robbers broke into Tranquillo Pizzuti's office in 1628 and ran off with many documents, and a major fire almost consumed office 25 in 1654.[287] Debt was so common a condition in the early modern economy that it is scarcely worth mentioning, but notaries confronted the risks of debt in several different ways. Few owned their notarial offices free and clear, so they owed money to investors. Then, too, they were caught up in the same nets of deferred payment in which their fellow citizens flailed about. Years passed before the padroni gave sostituti and giovani their wages, and years passed before their clients paid them. Countess Virginia Mattei Spada delivered more than forty scudi owed to office 18 after Bonincontro's death, "for various public instruments, warrants, and other documents received from the office over the period that it was run by the late Signor Lorenzo," and several of the institutions he served also kept open accounts.[288] A notary in the papal territory of Avignon told the governor's court that "you don't sign, if you aren't paid," but clearly notaries in Rome did sign many an instrument and many a summons without following his advice.[289] Poor securities were also a danger, and the near miss of Giorgio Giorgi of office 6 highlights the risk of acting as middleman in moneylending operations.

Perhaps the gravest threat to solvency, however, was the inescapable result of the expanded size of venal offices and the Roman scribal labor market: ignorant, incompetent, or immoral employees. Of course, not all of them were bad, and even some of the young ones showed an alert sense of right and wrong. Stefano Bellini, who was employed in two Capitoline offices in 1632, knew when a rich man offered to tip him before his trial testimony that he should not take the money.[290] But the swindler Agatoni would not have come so close to success if he had not exploited a witless giovane in Tranquillo Pizzuti's office, not far from Giorgi's, who rogated a power of attorney for a man whose true identity he did not know. When the judge pressed the youth on this point, he replied "I put that he [Ventura Agatoni] was Carlo Grationi and that I knew him because he didn't say that he was called any other name."[291] Benedetti's suspicious scribbling in the corner of Giustiniani's office on the Via del Gesù turned into a nightmare for the padrone, not because he was implicated in the alleged forgery, which was rogated in a different office, but for another reason. According to his accusers, Benedetti had substituted the Jesuits in place of the Oratorians as heirs in the disputed will. Angelo Giustiniani's office was almost within sight of the Jesuit residence and church, and he stubbornly ignored four subpoenas before submitting to questioning in the case. Why, the court asked, was he so reluctant to testify? He did not want to damage his powerful neighbors, Giustiniani replied, by telling the truth about what he had seen Benedetti doing at his pulpito.[292]

Conclusion

Clearly employees or partners in notarial offices could undermine the fictions of trust production by their writing and document-handling practices. Just how much legal responsibility employers bore for the felonies of their sostituti had interested the jurists. Commenting in 1636, Giovanni Battista Fenzonio cited the opinion of Bartolus that the *dominus* of a notarial office was liable for his employees' crimes.[293] Bartolus doubtless could not conceive of a dominus who was not a notary himself, but the market in venal offices had overtaken his simpler world. Fenzonio hastened to elaborate, explaining that papal legislation had effectively undercut and limited the office owner's responsibility. How else would the popes have found buyers for the notarial posts they put up for sale? But the diminution of liability was more apparent than real, for while the titleholders might not face the same penalties as the culprit, they lost ground against their competitors if their office won a reputation for cheating clients or suffered bankruptcy because they were left holding worthless sureties.

Obviously the Capitoline notaries faced bigger risks both financially and legally after 1586. When, after enriching his treasury by selling the Capitoline offices, Sixtus V expressed the pious hope that the sale would result in better preservation of their records, he was gesturing to the titleholders' legal responsibilities as well as their financial interest.[294] His successors who disciplined so minutely the writing and keeping of notarial acts also increased the exposure of the padroni. They may not have been guilty of the crimes of their sostituti, but they were liable for their infractions of notarial legislation. In a 1616 trial, the titleholders of office 8 accused Virgilio Lusanna not only of drawing up fictitious loans but of failing to turn over the instruments he rogated in their office for binding as the 1612 reforms demanded.[295] In 1635 the new padrone of office 17 charged Mario Rangiani, partner of the ex-titleholder, of taking instruments with him when he left and thereby exposing him to damaging civil suits.[296] The Capitoline notaries who initiated these cases probably did not do so out of fear of visits by papal police inspecting their protocols, *pace* Cardinal Francesco Barberini. More likely they worried with good reason about the arrival of clients looking for the acts they had rogated and, upon failing to find them, accusing them of losing or destroying their instruments.[297] A system of checks and balances between customers and their notaries, resting upon the infrastructure of a court system, kept equilibrium in the market of public trust.

CHAPTER SIX

The State

Policing Notarial Practices

Public authority had always had a crucial, indeed a constitutive, relationship to *scriptura publica*, but the changing forms of what the twentieth century called *state power* over the period 1350 to 1650 had profoundly altered the ways public writing was made, consumed, and preserved in Rome. Whether through doubling jurisdictions, reforming writing practices, establishing archives, or selling notarial offices, the early modern papacy had reshaped the notarial profession and notarial documents in the course of its own consolidation as a state. We have seen what kind of working world these papal policies had created for the Capitoline notaries as they went from numerous self-employed individuals to a few privileged officeholders, but the relationship between the profession and the state was not all one way. The papacy had unquestionably extended its reach and tightened its grip on notaries, but by the late seventeenth century the venal notaries were squirming uncomfortably, and the popes were forced to look more closely at what they held in their grasp.

Against a backdrop of unprecedented questioning of nepotism and venality, the twin pillars of early modern papal government, what the notaries told the pontiffs in the course of the years 1670 to 1705, and what the pontiffs heard, led to several striking initiatives.[1] These climaxed in a series of investigations and decrees under Pope Clement XI (1700–1721). Although the new methods of notarial policing employed under Clement signaled the state's capacity to innovate, they also highlighted its enduring dilemmas, marking out the limits of what it was capable of changing. It is thus both for its boldness and for its timidity that we turn in this final chapter to the pontificate of Giovanni Francesco Albani.

Almost a century after Paul V, Roman notaries and notarial records found themselves again the target of a reforming state. Thanks to the pope's personal attention and to the industry of his officials, especially Cardinal Galeazzo Marescotti, an exhaustive dossier on the local notarial profession accumulated in the years 1702 to 1705. This remarkable collection of reports, inspections, correspondence, edicts, and inventories enables us to define much more precisely than at any previous moment who the city's notaries were, what documents they held, and how they treated them. Although as pope Clement XI failed miserably on the international scene, he was an industrious, hands-on ruler of the city of Rome and the Papal States, especially in the first decade of his pontificate. Rather than a narrow focus on justice, he and his advisers probed a vast array of administrative, economic, and religious problems of long standing.[2] Although they seldom resolved them, they crafted new tools of state and deployed them with a systematizing rigor that was notable in itself. Yet their shortcomings and failures are equally telling. Clement XI and his officials were undoubtedly innovators, but their unwillingness or inability to invest state resources, either legislative or pecuniary, in their vision meant that lasting solutions eluded them.

Notaries and the Papacy, 1670–1700

Although Clement's signature style and commitments are unmistakable, it is not surprising to find the papacy as an institution deeply engaged with notaries in 1700. The profession, and especially the venal officeholders, had preoccupied papal officials for several decades, beginning in the early 1670s under Clement X, again in the late 1670s under Innocent XI and his activist deputy Cardinal Giovanni Battista De Luca, and yet again in the early 1690s. The papal notaries serving the major tribunals with jurisdiction over clerical as well as lay subjects had emerged from these struggles fewer in number but with larger offices and brighter financial prospects. The thirty Capitoline notaries had fared less well. It will help us to understand the condition of the profession and the background of curial reformers at the time of Albani's election in 1700, if we look at the relations of the venal notaries and the papacy over the preceding thirty years.

In a sign that the system of venal offices was in trouble by the 1670s, notaries from two papal tribunals pleaded successfully with Clement X (1670–76) to reduce their numbers. In 1671 the pope permitted the forty-eight notaries of the Rota to reorganize as just four notarial offices, and in 1672 he agreed that the secretaries and chancellors of the Reverenda Camera Apostolica (known to contemporaries as the notaries of the Camera) could shrink their number from nine to four. Of course, fewer offices were always better for venal officeholders, because they meant less competition for business, but it must have taken serious arguments to convince the papacy to make these reductions. Because papal notarial offices were *vacabili*, unlike those of the Capitoline notaries, they returned to the Datary for resale when they were vacated, thus filling the state's coffers repeatedly over time. The more offices in circulation, the more the papal treasury had to gain. Only the notaries' complaints that their investment was not living up to expectations, and the hard evidence of falling prices for the offices, must have induced Clement X to make these dramatic cuts. He must also have believed that, by curtailing the number, his government would make these posts attractive to investors once again. Sufficiently concerned by these requests, the pope evidently wanted to learn more, for he invited the notaries of all the city's major tribunals to a meeting at the Quirinal Palace on 26 March 1673 to air their grievances.[3]

The pressures felt by venal notaries, though focused on the particular technicalities of each group's income sources, were not confined to the notaries of the Rota or the notaries of the Camera. In 1672, the same year that their colleagues had success, twelve Capitoline notaries also petitioned to eliminate more than half of their offices.[4] They proposed to cut their numbers from thirty to fourteen. Because the Capitoline offices were fully inheritable, only the investors, not the government, stood to profit when they were sold, and thus the pope could have granted their request without damage to his treasury. Yet Clement X did not agree to their proposal. Also unsuccessful, at least with Clement, was the request for a reduction from the ten notaries of the auditor of the Camera in 1675.[5] They persisted, however, and in 1693 Innocent XII halved their number to five offices. By the 1690s, therefore, of all the major groups of venal notaries, only those of the Capitoline curia were still dividing business among the same number that had been in existence before the election of Clement X. The gap between their resources and that of the papal notaries had widened. Not surprisingly, therefore, during Albani's pontificate it was the Capitoline notaries who complained most vociferously about threats to their income posed by changing documentary practices.[6]

In the last third of the seventeenth century at the same time that the participants in the market for venal notarial offices were complaining about its terms, venality drew criticism from other quarters. After captivating the architects of papal finances from at least the 1470s, the tide began to turn, very slowly, against the sale of curial offices. In 1680 one of the oldest venal colleges, that of the apostolic secretaries, was abolished, and in 1692 the sale of the high administrative post of clerk of the [Apostolic] Camera was prohibited, to be followed in 1698 by that of the cardinal chamberlain.[7] While this left all the venal notaries, and the vast majority of other venal officeholders, untouched, it did bespeak a new atmosphere in which calls to clean up papal administration arose within the very heart of this administration.[8]

The reform reputation of Clement X's successor Innocent XI (1676–89) rested in part on his high-profile adviser, the jurist Cardinal De Luca, who had led the charge against the apostolic secretaries, and in part on the most important judicial legislation since that of Paul V in 1612. Like the Borghese pope, Innocent XI directed his efforts at the courts, and thus to notaries insofar as they functioned in the judicial system. By making the iconoclast Cardinal De Luca his auditor or legal adviser and appointing him head of the standing curial committee on judicial reform that had limped along since Paul V's era, Innocent XI had given an outspoken critic the means to effect changes in the machinery of justice.[9]

Or so it seemed. De Luca, who published Italy's first vernacular legal handbook and once argued that notarial documents should be written in Italian so that clients could understand them, abhorred the fractured jurisdictions of the Papal States.[10] He believed strongly that it would be more rational to substitute uniform rules for all the privileged differences between one tribunal and another, and criticized, among other targets, what he considered the needlessly time-consuming procedures of the Capitoline court. Although resistance from his colleagues in the College of Cardinals meant that De Luca did not end up making the clean sweep that he might have wished under Innocent XI, the decrees of the late 1670s bear his distinctive imprint. They heap scorn on the "inanes circuitus" of the senator's tribunal, for example, and require that the senator act like other judges in handling appeals cases.[11] In an effort to streamline justice, he reinforced the role of the cardinal prefect of the Segnatura della Giustizia to terminate conflicts over jurisdiction among the Capitoline and other courts.[12] De Luca established a standard period of three hours for all witness interrogations, regardless of the court, and forced both papal and Capitoline notaries to charge identical fees for guardianship and inheritance instruments.[13] Furthermore, he protected all notarial records from creditors by forbidding their seizure for debt.

De Luca's commitment to uniformity meant that he did not differentiate among Rome's five major tribunals, especially when setting up new procedures and criteria for vetting would-be notaries. While acknowledging the rights of the various bodies holding the privilege of creating notaries, he instituted a standard mechanism for testing aspirants. The candidate must pass an examination before senior officials of whatever college had the power to authorize notaries or before the auditor of the Camera or cardinal chamberlain. Two curial "procurators of the college" [of the Sacred Apostolic Palace] and two notaries who were venal officeholders in the city should attend and certify that the candidate had been approved.[14] De Luca envisioned the participation of the Capitoline notaries alongside those of the four chief ecclesiastical courts; indeed, some twenty years later the Capitoline notaries' minutes show them deputizing four members to conduct exams at the invitation of a prelate who was an apostolic protonotary.[15] The 1679 decrees updated the old idea that notaries ought to be men of respectable family, personal probity, and professional expertise, found already in the fifteenth-century regulations, with a few nuances.[16] Aspirants ought to be at least twenty-five years old (up from twenty), of legitimate (not just reputable) birth, and in good legal standing. De Luca substituted more specific knowledge for the traditional language about knowing Latin and the city laws. Young men needed to master creating instruments, and to do this, they should work for six continuous months in Rome in one of the venal notarial offices before taking the test, which he hoped would be a "true, effective, and rigorous" examination.[17] These reforms, originally intended for Rome, were soon extended to the entire Papal States. De Luca articulated and perfected the logic of unifying notarial practices across competing jurisdictions that had been implicit in the reforms of Paul V and in the archive of Urban VIII, closing the circle that the popes had opened with the creation of separate tribunals for ecclesiastics three centuries earlier.

While Innocent XII (1691–1700) had no adviser of De Luca's stature, he kept the judicial reform commission alive and cleared away a vast thicket of Roman jurisdictions by abolishing all particular tribunals in 1692.[18] These were courts whose clients consisted only of members of a corporate group or institution, such as those of the guilds and the cardinal protectors. The pontiff also revived an old project of Julius II's to unite all the Roman tribunals in a single building, purchasing the palace of Montecitorio for the use of the notaries of the papal courts. Although several magistracies remained in their former locations, by 1695 the notaries of the auditor of the Camera (or the notaries AC, as contemporary sources referred to them), of the cardinal chamberlain, and of the treasurer general had moved to the new "Gran Curia Innocenziana," increasing the convenience and lowering the cost of justice for litigants.[19] Unlike Julius II, Innocent XII seems not to have envisioned including the Capitoline curia in this initiative. The Capitoline notaries arguably made what living they could precisely because of the access offered to clients by their dispersed offices. In any case, they did not catch the eye of the reformers in the 1690s and, as far as we know, did not speak about their festering grievances until after Clement XI's election in 1700.

Active in the Curia at De Luca's apogee and promoted to cardinal in 1690, Giovanni Francesco Albani (1649–1721) lent a helping hand to Innocent XII in his reform projects. He was not, however, so openly "zealous" that he frightened the moderate cardinals in the 1700 conclave, the way the more senior and more severe Cardinal Galeazzo Marescotti (1627–1726) did.[20] Ascending to the throne of St.

Peter, Albani showed his true inclinations by almost immediately reviving Innocent XI's committee to relieve food shortages, the Congregation of the Sollievo, and placing Marescotti at its head.[21]

Office Orders: The Investigation of 1702–1704

The initial purpose of the Congregation of the Sollievo was to redress failures in the agricultural economy, and neither the pope nor Cardinal Marescotti had intended to use it as a forum for notarial shortcomings. Indeed, it was not so much the congregation as the cardinal himself who seemed to attract an ever-widening array of projects—groups and customs to be investigated, critiqued, and fixed—all tucked under the mantle of the Sollievo simply because that was Marescotti's brief. Behind this proliferating portfolio, however, lay Clement XI who believed that the greatest evils never came to the ruler's attention and who showed immense curiosity about all facets of his realm.[22] He communicated frequently with Marescotti, and the two men shared a similar obsession with the minutiae of administration.

While it seems natural that preservation of documents would interest men of such tastes, in fact it may have been an accident that first brought notarial records to their attention. Just three months after Albani's election, the municipal government of Rome suddenly decided that it wanted to create a proper archive for its own papers in the Palace of the Conservators and would evict the Archivio Capitolino in order to do so. As we shall see, this action greatly upset the Capitoline notaries, and in February 1702, during the protracted aftermath of the debacle, they invited Cardinal Marescotti to visit their notarial archive. What he saw displeased him. At about the same time, reports about troubles in the Archivio Urbano may also have been circulating in curial circles.[23] By the summer of 1702 the city newssheets announced that the pope was showing a lively interest in historic documents, and wanted all archives put in good order.[24] His scrutiny of the Vatican's own holdings proved that he did not think it was just notarial archives that were deficient, but the glimpse he and Marescotti had had of the notaries' papers made them eager to see more.

In early October 1702 Marescotti dismounted at the palace of Montecitorio and began the first formal inspection ever of the venal notarial offices, visiting the five notaries AC and then the notaries of the other tribunals lodged in the palace or nearby.[25] Clement heard Marescotti's report and by the late fall had extended his commission to all the other notaries with public offices in Rome—that is, not to private notaries but exclusively to the venal officeholders connected to specific tribunals. By 1 December it was clear that the fiction that the investigation fell under the purview of the Sollievo was no longer useful, and six curial officials who gathered at Marescotti's palace debated by whose authority orders to remedy defects should be issued to the notaries. Marescotti argued that it would be faster and less public if the chief magistrate of each of the relevant tribunals should have this power, but Clement disagreed with him.[26] We can assume therefore that the sudden appearance of a "congregation for the inspection and reform of the city's notarial offices and archives" was the pope's preferred vehicle. It was under this title that the reform edict was published in March 1704, which listed the names of what was clearly an ad hoc congregation, the same men who had attended the December meeting in 1702 with the addition of only one Capitoline judge.[27] The impetus for this unprecedented investigation of the local notarial profession came directly from the pope and Marescotti, assisted by curial officials very close to the pontiff. They included his auditor Gian Domenico Paracciano and his secretary for memorials Curzio Origo, the secretary of the Sollievo Silvio de Cavalerijs, the clerk of the Camera Ferdinando Nuzzi, and two curial experts on notaries, Domenico Guelfio and Felice de Grandis, who were members of the legal staff (*collegio causarum*) of the Sacred Apostolic Palace.[28]

Although Sixtus V's archival legislation for the Papal States gave the contractor the right to scrutinize notarial protocols, the idea of a broad inspection dated back to 1637 when Cardinal Francesco Barberini threatened to send the Archivio Urbano staff to look for missing copies.[29] While they were at it, they should also check that notaries were complying with all of Paul V's directives. Nothing had come of this rather desperate effort to shore up the new archive, however. Though inspections were brandished again in 1643, there is no evidence that they occurred, and after the Barberini pontificate no state agency bore responsibility for policing the profession. As we saw in chapter 4, those in charge of the Archivio Urbano returned to tried and true medieval methods of enforcement—denunciations of wrongdoers enticed by monetary rewards.

Cardinal Marescotti's novel visit to the papal notarial offices at Montecitorio in October 1702 drew not on notarial models, therefore, but on the methods pioneered in episcopal visitations. Since the Council of Trent in the mid-sixteenth century, bishops had fine-tuned the procedures used to inspect their diocesan clergy and churches, including advance questionnaires to parish priests, personal visits, detailed reports on defects, and meticulous follow-up instructions. As bishop of Tivoli in 1681, Marescotti had undertaken just such a visitation. Notably thorough, he had not neglected even the episcopal archive and chancery, issuing orders that the judicial acts he found there should be signed and that lines should be put through the blank pages in the registers.[30] A nine-page questionnaire for the notaries of the

Camera before the inspection of their offices in 1702 must have drawn on precedents like these, as did the notion that Marescotti should undertake the visit in person.[31] Applying tools crafted for ecclesiastical purposes to secular institutions became one of the hallmarks of the *zelanti* program under Clement XI. After bruiting a traditional diocesan visitation in 1701, the pope extended its techniques to new categories of subjects, including the Roman notaries and the communities of the Papal States.[32]

The only questionnaires to come to light are those prepared for the notaries of the Camera and the notaries AC. The papal visitors wanted to know about the physical space in which the office was located, the name of the padrone of the office and the terms of his tenure, the different types of business and judicial acts that he held and how they were kept, and the number and mode of compensation of his employees. Detailed questions homed in on the writing practices of the sostituti and giovani. About those who produced instruments, for example, the inspectors asked how long they had been in this particular notarial office, and in which previous offices they had worked and for how long? Did the sostituti note in the office receipt book the instrument, the date, the name of the contracting parties, the title (type) of contract, and the amount paid on the same day that it was rogated? How long did it take them to extend the instruments "in a good hand without erasures?" Did they sign them and insert all the related documentation that had been submitted in scriptura privata? Within two months did they make a copy of those contracts governed by the Archivio Urbano regulations (*instrumenti perpetui*) and with their relevant insertions take these to the archive, and then note on the margin of the originals that they had been archived? The visitors interrogated the sostituti who wrote judicial acts too, asking whether they extended all the citations the same day that they received the judge's authorization (*decreto*)?[33] Somewhat mysteriously, a question about whether they were paid a testone for travel when they had to leave the office was crossed out, as was one asking if they were matriculated or had been examined. Descending the hierarchy of office skills the inspectors reached even the most junior staff, the novizi, wondering if they knew Latin well enough to be able to go on in their profession and whether they wrote legibly and correctly?[34]

The team investigating the papal notaries, Marescotti, the magistrate of the relevant tribunal, and the two curial legal experts Guelfio and De Grandis, did not confine themselves passively to collecting the written answers to their questions. They looked directly at the documents. The visitors requested to see a matrice, for example, and compared it to the final instrument to check whether it had been extended properly with the whole substance of the contract.[35] Yet, although such attention was unprecedented, they clearly believed that they were working within traditional parameters. The questionnaire repeatedly cited as authoritative not new directives but past legislation, in particular the 1612 reforms of Paul V and a 1681 edict on the Archivio Urbano, although several erroneous citations suggest that whoever drafted it had not yet thoroughly digested these texts. The vision of Albani and Marescotti was profoundly conservative; their predecessors had provided all the laws necessary to the proper functioning of the notariate. What was needed was simply to enforce those laws. Nothing less than meticulous research into the actual writing practices of the offices would reveal where the flaws lay, but when it did, it would be easy to see how to correct them. At the end of the vast multiyear effort, however, they discovered that some legal changes were in fact needed.

The Capitoline notaries were the first to open their doors to the papal visitors after the December decision to widen the investigation. A single notebook survives recording visits to sixteen of their thirty offices on 29, 30, and 31 December 1702 and 2 January 1703.[36] On 30 December the inspectors, probably without Marescotti and perhaps with one of the Capitoline judges, made their way down the Corso from Piazza Colonna to Trajan's Column with a short detour to the Trevi Fountain looking in at seven offices. The long-standing concentration of Capitoline notaries along the Corso promoted great efficiency that day; the other days they stopped in at no more than three offices. Although we lack the questionnaires that survive for the papal notaries, the inspectors made notes that indicate they were using a simplified version of the same template.

On 31 December they reached office 12 by the Arco dei Pantani near the Roman Forum, now held by Giovanni Giuseppe Novio, the son of Angelo Canini's employee-partner Carlo, who had purchased it at Angelo's death in 1649.[37] The visitors reported that the office "is in a very narrow space insufficient for keeping the documents and so they are kept in the room next to it." There was no inventory of its holdings, a deficiency they would find to be universal, but the two series of protocols, which began in 1523, and manuali were complete. They divided the records by their material form, first listing the contents of the bound volumes and then those in stitched piles (*filze*). Paul V's regulations echoed in their written comments. The instruments were indeed bound, at least through 1701, though most did not bear the signature of the sostituto who had rogated them; wills were preserved in their own series, at least from 1625; the entries in the office receipt books were properly dated. Urban VIII's legislation resounded in the notation that not all the instruments and wills had been "archiviati," that is, they lacked the indication that their copies had been delivered to the Archivio Urbano. The unbound documents kept in filze included many types that have since disappeared. Original sentences were filed in the general filze with all the supporting documents (*iura diversa*) submitted in the cases; original summons were put in long filze. The monetary instruments known as *cedole*, which resembled modern checks, were kept in separate filze depending on whether they were issued by private individuals or by the official loan bank, the Monte di Pietà, and finally 157 still-sealed wills, the oldest dating from 1606, remained tucked out of sight in more filze. In Novio's office, they failed to mention if or how witness depositions were kept.[38]

In general, the inspectors maintained the same intensity of scrutiny that they exhibited in the larger offices of the papal notaries. When visiting office 13, for example, they noted that the last two months of instruments had not yet been extended and that at least sixty instruments in office 2 still remained to be done. The specificity of these figures suggests that the general practice of the Capitoline notaries must have been to extend most of their business acts within a month, conforming to the regulation in the 1580 city statutes rather than the laxer three months permitted by Paul V's reforms.

A later hand annotated the visit to Novio's office, as well as to the other Capitoline offices, tersely highlighting in the broad left margin key information, like the number of protocols per year, and important deficiencies. These comments give us a good idea of what flaws most bothered the investigators. "Cramped office." Instruments "not all extended." "Not all delivered to the archive." Loose instruments, presumably rogated during 1702, "not all signed or extended." "No [separate] register for sentences."[39] Not surprisingly, these omissions often found their way into the congregation's reform measures in 1704.

It was not a faceless inquiry. When the visitors could not obtain all the data they sought from the Capitoline notaries, they extracted promises to bring it later to Cardinal Marescotti. In office 4, for example, the padrone could not tell them whether any protocols in a collection that dated back to 1479 were missing or when the documents in the series of filze began. They ordered him to find all this out and send word to His Eminence.[40] As numerous letters and petitions attest, the inspectors communicated successfully to the notaries the cardinal's direct engagement in the investigation.

This did not lessen the pressure, of course. As the offices of the notaries of the tribunals of Ripa, Ripetta, and agriculture followed upon those of the senator in January 1703, a sense of professional anxiety must have grown. At their meeting of 23 January, despite the disastrous earthquake that had just struck the city, the Capitoline notaries hired a lawyer and chose five representatives to consult with the notaries AC and other venal notaries about how best to defend their rights.[41] They did not confine themselves to legal action, however, but also tried persuasion. The notaries addressed an unnamed congregation with a series of "proposals" and drafted a separate memorandum complaining about the Archivio Urbano that may also date from this period.[42] The Capitoline notaries, under greater financial pressure than their papal colleagues, must have seen Marescotti's investigation as an occasion to bring long-standing grievances to the attention of the authorities.[43]

At the root of their complaints was declining demand for public copies of notarial documents. The Capitoline notaries blamed this on new legal and judicial practices that allowed clients and litigants to circumvent the high standard of proof that had been the notaries' stock in trade since the Middle Ages. "Before the reform of Paul V of holy memory, notaries kept the instruments they rogated locked in cabinets and whoever wanted to see them paid the visura, as is the custom today outside of Rome," they began.[44] The 1612 legislation had of course compelled them to show instruments for free. However, it had not envisioned the current abuse in which young attorneys "of sharp mind and sharper memory" repeatedly visit the office, memorize the instrument, and then make a summary of it for their clients. While abolishing the fees for looking at business acts, the reforms had assumed clients would purchase at least a simple copy from the notary, but that assumption was proving unfounded. Now, the notaries were losing out on making both public copies and simple copies of the records in their protocols, and they could not charge to view them.

Compounding the damage was a new laxity on the part of judges who instead of insisting that evidence arrive in public form allowed a simple copy—or, worse, a mere reference to it—to stand in for full proof. "Litigants or their procurators come to read and reread the instrument, learning its substance, confirming the facts, and [then] they summarize it, and the casebooks of the tribunal of the auditor of the Camera are full of these."[45] The notaries blamed the judges for encouraging the abuse by going even further and decreeing that a notation in the dossier would have the same legal value as the actual document. They begged "this congregation to consider the reasonable arguments of the Capitoline notaries [and] the observance of Paul V's legislation, to limit the excessive freedom to plunder the said instruments, and to prescribe a procedure that avoided prejudice to the said notaries against the intention of the reforms, and in addition to forbid judges to decree that a reference could substitute [for the public copy]."[46] In closing, they reminded their readers of the fundamental bargain struck in 1586 when the pope made their offices venal. After all, "Sixtus V of holy memory had promised to maintain the Capitoline notaries in their earnings when he established their college."

Their complaints about the officials of the Archivio Urbano pinpointed additional threats to the demand for their services.[47] In establishing this copy archive, Urban VIII had taken care to protect the interests of the venal notaries by forbidding archive staff from making copies of the notarial records in their custody. Anyone who consulted the Archivio Urbano and its helpful indexes would find the name of the notary and the date of the act he sought, but he had to return to that office in order to purchase the copy. Now, the Capitoline notaries charge, the archivist and his employees are ignoring these regulations and making duplicates for clients. They should confine themselves to discovering the document's location from the catalogs and then send customers back to the Capitoline offices.

Behind the lamentations about lost revenue lay two enduring structural realities. Alone of the major tribunals, as we have seen, the Capitoline court was still functioning with its original complement of thirty venal notaries. With no reduction in their numbers, they had not been able to offset shrinking income by consolidation into fewer offices. More profoundly, it was obvious that judicial reform as the popes understood it aimed to save litigants' money on notaries. While they doubtless also wanted to reduce the cost of lawyers, pontiffs at least since the time of Pius IV had striven to cut back on the quality and types of documentation that parties to lawsuits needed to produce in court. Simple copies were one such device, and so was the practice that the Capitoline notaries complained about in their petition, the judges' permission to litigants to substitute a citation for the document itself. That the auditor of the prefect of the Segnatura della Giustizia was one of the culprits specifically mentioned by the Capitoline notaries on an earlier occasion suggests that far from being an "abuse," it was yet another attempt at reform.[48] Perhaps this explains why Marescotti paid so little attention to their complaints about their falling income. While he responded parsimoniously to their pleas for help with the Archivio Capitolino, he ignored their invocation of Sixtus V and his promise to maintain them in their earnings. The stark fact was that, although their posts were venal, since 1612 the Capitoline notarial offices had lain outside the income stream of the papal treasury, and the state had little to gain from their sale.

In May 1703 Marescotti concluded his eight months of investigations with a visit to the notaries of the Rota. He was satisfied that the picture he had of the sixty or so venal notarial offices operating in Rome was complete.[49] By now the curial team must have been collating what it had gleaned and deciding on the specific failures to be remedied in its reform decrees, whose draft was ready by February 1704.[50] But the pope felt that one clamorous discovery had to be addressed immediately. The inspectors had found in city notarial offices six thousand unopened wills, more than four thousand of which were on the shelves of Capitoline notaries.[51] As we saw in chapter 3, ecclesiastical officials tended to believe that when no heir appeared to set testamentary formalities in motion, it was likely that the testator had left her or his property to the church. In June 1703 Clement XI ordered all notaries to go before their judges and open any sealed wills in their possession dating from before 1653 without charge.[52] Despite the fears of a frenzy of litigation, more than twenty-seven hundred sealed wills were opened in the next six months. The pope had delegated to the Archivio Urbano archivist the task of making an alphabetical index of the testators, and in the final edict he built in other safeguards to prevent such an "absurd" situation from recurring. Henceforth, notaries should open all sealed wills more than fifty years old annually in court and immediately give the names of the testators to the archivist to add to the master list in the Archivio Urbano.[53]

By the following February, the pope had approved the decrees "of the congregation to inspect and reform the venal notaries and archives in Rome," and they were published 13 March 1704.[54] Although much shorter than Paul V's legislation, like it they contained instructions common to all the notaries, twenty-six items in all, followed by special orders to the notaries of particular courts.[55] Not surprisingly, they repeated many past injunctions, including some, like the requirement that matrici record the names of the witnesses and the substance of the contract, with a fourteenth-century pedigree.[56] More frequently, the 1704 decrees echoed those of Paul V, as when they insisted that instruments and wills be bound every three months, that evidence submitted by the parties not be left lying in the desks of the staff, and that notaries and sostituti work for no more than one tribunal.[57] At times they gave a fresh twist to tradition, as when they revived the term *matriculation*, though not its substance, using it to mean having been created a notary by proper authority.[58] Only once did they acknowledge any shortcoming in Paul V's reforms, which were usually cited as authoritative, and in that case they created a new kind of judicial document to replace the lengthy extractus and registra used when litigating large sums.[59]

Nevertheless, Clement XI's reforms did innovate in small and in large. Some changes consisted of refinements to manage information more efficiently. The office receipt book ought to have an alphabetical table of contents, and a separate register (*liber accommodatorum*) should list the documents in active cases that had been loaned to judges or other notaries. The manuale with its global record of the office's judicial business must have a table of contents.[60] Insistence that instruments in all stages from matrici to full transcriptions could not under any circumstances leave the physical premises, and that the titleholder was responsible for his workers' negligence in this regard, reflected one of the major findings of the inspectors.[61] Delays in extending, binding, and archiving business acts arose from the fact that sostituti either left the office's employ without completing what they had started or took the raw materials with them to finish at home or at their next job. If the investigators had reread some of the old edicts of the Archivio Urbano, such practices would not have come as a surprise.

The 1704 decrees did not shrink from more-novel measures however. They put the final nail in the coffin of the private notaries when they prohibited venal officeholders from accepting their instruments in their protocols.[62] Another new feature was that for the first time the state demanded the production of inventories of the holdings in the venal offices and notarial archives. Not only did the decrees require that notaries list all their "protocols, broliardi, and certain volumes and filze of documents," but they set up a mechanism for ensuring that this was done at once.[63] Each week notaries had to demonstrate the progress they were making on the inventories to Cardinal Marescotti himself until they were complete. The edict also established a way to continue this practice by requiring that successors update the inventories and by designating a specific papal official to receive them and a specific body, the Congregation of the Sollievo, to punish infractions.

This unusual attention to enforcement worked, at least in 1704, and to it we owe the first collection of the inventories of the Capitoline notaries' papers.[64] While inventories for individual offices can sometimes be found in the notarial archives at the time when title changed hands, there was no previous government effort to view the totality of holdings.[65] The inventories offer a snapshot of scribal capital, showing not only what kinds of writing the venal offices produced and protected but also what records had survived up to 1704.[66] They prove that having their title free and clear made venal Capitoline notaries more diligent custodians of their patrimony than their pre-1586 predecessors, and perhaps even than their papal competitors.[67] The inventories also highlight the dramatically differing fate of business and judicial acts after 1704, which we have already noted. Series of judicial acts both in volumes and in filze abound in the inventories with only a few insignificant lacunae. The losses of civil litigation records have been particularly heavy since then.

As a crude measure of the varying fortunes of particular offices over time, the inventories are also useful. We can trace the impact on office 13 of the loss of the business of the confraternity of the Annunziata after Giovanni Battista Ottaviani's death in 1636, for the yearly output of protocols declines permanently.[68] On the other hand, we see very clearly the positive effects of longevity and generational continuity. As noted in chapter 5, Angelo Canini's tenure (1622–49) increased activity in office 12, and apart from a temporary setback when the plague struck in the 1650s, office 12 maintained its steady output under Carlo Novio and his son Giovanni Giuseppe Novio.[69]

While the state acquired a remarkable new source of information about notarial records from the global request for inventories, it is not clear what papal officials intended to do with it. Perhaps it reflected a style of governing under Clement XI that regarded the accumulation of data as inherently satisfying, or perhaps the pope and Marescotti thought of making inventories as performative, actions that would remind notaries of their responsibilities as curators of the papers in their offices. In any case, the policy caught on; for several decades in the eighteenth century, Clement's successors also ordered that notaries provide new inventories of their holdings.[70]

The 1704 decrees' detailed attention to the staff of the venal offices displayed a less ambiguously practical attitude. By comparison to the terse, grudging references to employees in Paul V's legislation, these reforms accept the fact that they did most of the work and discuss them more than any other single topic. Marescotti's text strikes a novel chord in declaring that notaries should treat their employees well, both in pay and in the conditions of their room and board, and in urging judges to make sure they did.[71] The subtext, of course, was that wrongdoers would find it easy to suborn penniless hungry scribes. While holding to the 1612 regulation that magistrates should approve the choice of sostituti in their notaries' offices, it allowed padroni to hire and fire lower-level staff without judicial interference. For the first time, notaries were encouraged to prefer subjects of the Papal States when they took on new workers. Family status was no longer mentioned, however, and there was a new emphasis on the quality of the employee's handwriting.[72] The 1704 decrees followed those of 1679 in requiring an examination by two curial specialists, men like the inspectors Guelfio and De Grandis, from the college of the Sacred Apostolic Palace.[73] With a bit more realism, however, they permitted failing candidates to retake the exam, especially on the formulary of instruments. Similarly, they anticipated what occurred in fact, that giovani and sostituti might depart without having extended all their instruments, and provided reimbursement to titleholders who went after them.[74] Marescotti's reform edict, mindful of the convenience of the notaries' customers, gave the employees more work to do by suggesting that if they had any spare time they might copy supporting evidence submitted by litigants into the manuale rather than merely filing it.[75] Finally, it smoothed the path of future inspectors by adding a rule that sostituti, giovani, and their bosses must show documents upon request.[76]

After the common orders followed brief specific instructions to the notaries of each of the six major tribunals, beginning with the notaries of the Camera and the notaries AC, who among other things, were reminded to wear the old fashioned *zimarra da notaro* both in the office and in court.[77] The Capitoline notaries did not have to don the professional garb of bygone days, but they did have to muster a total of six series of records, from protocols to registers of materials out on loan, on pain of fines or corporal punishment.[78] The decrees insisted that they track down any series that was missing, and promised that their judges and the Congregation of the Sollievo would help in this effort. The reform edict directed the Capitoline notaries to create a new manuale exclusively for judicial decrees and warrants and reminded them to treat witness depositions as Paul V's legislation had demanded.[79] It also reiterated the long-standing protection from eviction that Capitoline notaries were supposed to enjoy. The rough notes summarizing the inspectors' reports on the thirty offices had pinpointed fourteen items, eleven of which in the end found their way into either the general orders or these specific ones.[80]

While the content of the 1704 decrees was a mixture of old and new, entirely new was their instrumental character as a tool for policing the notarial profession. Unlike previous reform edicts, this initiated a process of compliance. Instead of merely laying out a lengthy list of dos and don'ts, Marescotti's team built in a series of short-term deadlines and demanded regular contact during the intervals. They set deadlines of one month to bring extended instruments and their copies to the Archivio Urbano; two months to extend all matrici of instruments; just short of three months to produce the inventories of office holdings; and four months to bind loose instruments. There was a new interactive quality between the reformers' text and the target audience of notaries; the decrees gave the notaries specific tasks to complete and set up a way to monitor each one.

Not surprisingly, the disciplinary persona of Cardinal Marescotti loomed large in this scheme. After turning in delinquent copies at the Archivio Urbano, notaries were to deliver the archivist's verification to Cardinal Marescotti. If an employee had left the office before extending all the instruments he had rogated, the titleholder should send his name and address to the cardinal.[81] Notaries were to report weekly to him on their progress with the inventories.[82] The message got through, at least to the Capitoline notaries. Petitions to the cardinal requesting extensions meant they were taking the deadlines seriously, and a list of venal notaries who had not yet delivered inventories contained no names of Capitoline titleholders.[83] By contrast, Marescotti was less successful with the notaries of the papal courts. In a pattern that would be repeated again with the Archivio Urbano, the notaries AC, the notaries of the vicario, and the notaries of the Rota failed to complete their inventories by the deadline. The techniques that Marescotti employed were most effective when directed at the most vulnerable venal officeholders.

Behind Marescotti's zeal lay that of his prince. Five months after the publication of the reform decrees, Clement XI's auditor Paracciani nudged the cardinal about follow-up.[84] Was it time for the head of each of the six tribunals to make a new inspection of his court's notaries to see whether they were complying with the orders? Although the pope had wanted more initial publicity for the reforms, he accepted Marescotti's reasoning that the judges should supervise mopping up operations. A draft request to the auditor of the Camera, the treasurer general, the vicegerent (for the vicario), the deacon of the Rota, and the senator was already prepared.[85] The cardinal himself would be responsible for those venal notaries who did not have a superior, the so-called *notari nullius.*[86] Clement had given the magistrates the option of reporting to him in person or in writing, and the absence of documentation suggests that most of them may have chosen the former. Marescotti characteristically did not spare himself, ignoring the pontiff's wish that he delegate the inspections to subordinates and submitting in October 1704 a final written report on the notari nullius.

Whatever the two-year investigation of practices in the venal offices taught the Roman notaries, it had an immediate impact on governmental officials at several levels. In December 1704 the municipality of Rome, proud feudal lord of four villages in the surrounding district, extended the Roman documentary regime to its fiefs. It ordered its local podestà to carry out yearly inspections of the notarial archives in his village and commanded village notaries to observe what were in effect the rules of the Archivio Urbano, bringing copies of specified instruments to the archive within two weeks of the contract.[87] The exemplary character of what had happened in Rome was also demonstrated the following spring on a much wider stage. The cardinal chamberlain of the Apostolic Camera, Giovanni Battista Spinola, announced that the prefect of the archives, a curial official with jurisdiction outside Rome and Bologna, would send agents to inspect notarial offices and archives throughout the whole Papal States.[88] Spinola emphasized too that state inspectors would be checking to see whether new notaries were properly examined, that is, according to the standards set by Cardinal De Luca's reforms of 1679. The tools that Clement XI and Marescotti had fashioned for Rome, modified only slightly by shifting duties to local governors, were a flexible new means of policing the notarial profession. Cheaply, that is, without setting up any new organ of state, the papal government now had a means to enforce those endlessly repeated orders of the past, at least for those who would listen to its officials.

What worked for notaries and their employees who were writing for living judges and clients, however, was not necessarily suited to institutions charged with preserving notarial documents. Even before inspecting the offices, Marescotti and Clement XI knew of flaws in the two key repositories of notarial records in Rome, the Archivio Capitolino and the Archivio Urbano. Their reforms logically embraced archives as well as offices, as the very title they gave their "congregation for the inspection and reform of the city's notarial offices and archives" indicated. To these efforts they brought their faith in improved methods of enforcement and their enormous energy and attention to detail. The silent volumes proved to be tougher subjects than the notaries, however. The means, or vision, at Clement's command could not quite match the material or political challenges posed by the city's notarial archives.

Archival Disorders
The Archivio Capitolino

The trouble in the Archivio Capitolino began in June 1701, although, if they had been alert, the Capitoline notaries would have seen it coming in March when the civic governing council decided to reorganize the city archive, the Archive of the Roman People, and began looking for some space in the Palace of the Conservators. It was not until 14 June, however, that the Roman People fixed on the chamber at the back of the courtyard that they had granted to the notaries in 1614 when the Archivio Capitolino required a second room.[89] Rights in the matter were simple enough. The civic authorities said they had given the space to the notarial archive on condition that they could reclaim it, if they wanted it for their own purposes.[90] The Capitoline notaries protested, arguing that the government did not have enough records to warrant such a move "because the room was large and the documents of the Roman People few."[91] They also pointed out that the civic secretary's office was better adapted to keeping documents from prying eyes than this room at the far end of the courtyard.

On 28 June, when the Roman People met in council, they learned that instead of handing over the keys, the notaries were planning to meet and would then give them their reply.[92] As far as the city government was concerned, the notaries had nothing to say in the matter, and the council vowed to open the room by force if the keys were not forthcoming. In the face of their intransigence, the Capitoline notaries turned to their recently elected pope. On 8 July they chose two delegates to take a petition to Clement XI, asking that they be allowed to retain the chamber so long assigned to them for use as an archive and where they held their meetings.[93]

The Roman People would not be put off. After a standoff of seven weeks, they gave the notarial college a week to move the contents of the courtyard room, which was filled completely with judicial records (*filze di scritture et atti*) of the pre-1586 Capitoline notaries. What happened next is obscure in its proceedings but not in its results. By mid-September the civic government had the keys back, but the notaries were beside themselves.[94] Writing again to the pope, they accused municipal officials of having "violently cleared the filze of documents and acts out of the archive and deposited them in the greatest confusion" in a small, dark hallway, "or better, rubbish heap" in the attic of the Palazzo Nuovo.[95] They besought him to force the conservators to return the documents or to make some other provision for them, not wishing, they said, to be liable for the damage that could arise nor to have to spend their own funds to repair it.

This final point was certainly not insignificant. It must have been especially galling to be told by the Roman People not only that the college had to move out and shift the old litigation records to the attic across the piazza but also that they had to pay to make the new space suitable.[96] Civic officials had offered no carrot, only the stick. More profoundly, they now treated a repository of documents that they themselves had established 140 years earlier as if it was worthless and its guardians a nuisance.

Clement XI's secretaries must have passed the notaries' complaints to Cardinal Marescotti as prefect of the Congregation of the Sollievo. In a move that undoubtedly startled papal subjects long used to dealing with subordinates, and that surely proved the old maxim "beware what you wish for," Marescotti promised to make a personal visit to the Archivio Capitolino.[97] And he charged the Capitoline notaries with putting the records that had been so unceremoniously dumped under the roof of the Palazzo Nuovo back in order. The notaries at once busied themselves purchasing new chests (*casse*) for the documents, and on orders from both the conservators and Cardinal Marescotti three months later, they voted more funds to bind loose instruments in the archive.[98] Meanwhile, in papal circles, whatever Marescotti had seen when he visited the Archivio Capitolino had spurred sharp questions about its deficiencies, as well as those of the city's younger but more ambitious notarial archive, the Archivio Urbano, and indeed about the preservation of old property and financial records more generally.

Laying out the problems and proposing limited solutions, a memorandum to the pope, possibly composed by Marescotti in spring 1702, defined the issues from the curial point of view.[99] It is a telling early witness of the Albani pontificate's distinctive preoccupation with well-kept archives, which was widely reported that summer.[100] Safekeeping of scriptura publica might not seem as important as military security, the memorandum warned, but it was in fact equally necessary to the defense (and indeed growth) of lineages, families, charitable entities, cities, and kingdoms. The author explained that he would describe a few archival "disorders," which, although they seemed slight on the surface, "are in reality of great consequence and for this reason, in [his] opinion, not to be dismissed, because it was well known from experience that neglecting a small spark can sometimes lead to a conflagration."[101]

The first "spark" attested to the thoroughness of Marescotti's inspection of the Archivio Capitolino because the author pointed out that in many protocols the tables of contents were inaccurate. Only someone who had opened the volumes and checked specific instruments against the indexes could have made such a statement. The second, more obvious defect, "a large number of loose sheets not bound in protocols but merely tied in bunches [*mazzi*]," was somewhat debatable.[102] Although no one mentioned it at the time, it had never been the policy of the Archivio Capitolino to bind the records given to its care. The initial regulations of 1562 imagined storing the protocols of deceased notaries in locked wooden drawers (*cassette*) inside large cupboards (*armarij*) but assumed they would arrive already bound.[103] Nor for that matter did they require the archive staff to make indexes for these protocols. They were silent too on how judicial acts were to be kept. These were particularly complex because they included not only the judicial logbook or manuale, required from 1446 to be bound, but also all kinds of written evidence (*iura*) submitted by the parties on loose sheets of paper. Even if these had once been stitched together as filze, they could easily have shaken out over time and, indeed, might have been intentionally preserved in the bundles disdained by Marescotti on his visit.

The final, more surprising, problem was that protocols of Capitoline notaries had not been delivered to the Archivio Capitolino at all but had ended up in ecclesiastical archives.[104] That this had happened was not news; before 1562 anyone could inherit Capitoline notarial records, including a confraternity or monastery, and papal authorities had long struggled to make religious bodies yield up their protocols.[105] What is startling is that by the early eighteenth century curial officials knew exactly which volumes were missing and where they were. They were also newly determined to get them back.

Not a mere catalog of complaints, the memo called for specific actions to remedy the problems it diagnosed. An odd reading of the 1562 edict of the conservators at the time the Archivio Capitolino was created produced the recommendation that the Capitoline notaries be forced to make tables of contents for the old protocols and bind all loose documents. Despite some confusion about which legislation actually made the notaries responsible for the Archivio Capitolino, the pope's adviser insisted that it was theirs and they would have to fix its deficiencies.[106] This curial logic spelled even more trouble for the Capitoline notaries than that initially caused by the municipal government.

Although the notarial college had invited Marescotti to intervene in February 1702 after half the archive was dispossessed of its quarters, they grew increasingly despondent as the scope and costs of the cardinal's orders broadened. In October, five months after they voted funds to bind loose contracts, they raised their own massa contributions to two scudi a month to cover expenses already incurred and also asked the cardinal for money.[107] We catch a glimpse of what they were using the money for when they empowered a paid archivist in December to set the salary of those to be hired to put the loose instruments in order before binding.[108] Hardly more than a month later, however, the true dimensions of the task must have revealed that this, too, would be insufficient so they decided to contribute the labor of their own giovani. By rotation in order of seniority, each office would send one employee each week to organize the unbound documents in the Archivio Capitolino.[109] Things were not going according to the plan imagined in the curial memorandum, which had suggested that, instead of opening the archive once a week, the notaries could open it twice a week with the archivist doing the organizing and indexing on the additional day.

Meanwhile, Cardinal Marescotti and his staff had been researching the history of the Archivio Capitolino and the notaries' own statutes in order to devise a fresh set of rules to govern its care in the future. On 18 December 1703 twenty Capitoline notaries listened as the eleven articles were read aloud and promptly voted to give up the archive and turn its documents over to Clement XI.[110] They were exasperated beyond measure by what they had been subjected to first from the conservators, who had confiscated their room and deposited its contents "in a huge heap," and then from Cardinal Marescotti, who had granted them only 130 scudi to do all the binding and indexing, which did not come close to covering their expenses. Because they had no wish, they said, to contradict the cardinal, they would simply surrender the Archivio Capitolino.

A petition that may well date from this period illuminates the reasons for their discontent in more detail.[111] The archival intervention had touched more than 1,000 volumes, 471 of which had been created (with indexes) from scratch and 570 of which had received new tables of contents when they were restored and rebound. New parchment covers, glue, and the labor of binding were costly, but what had really blown the budget was the price of hiring outside experts who could read the gothic script of the fourteenth- and fifteenth-century protocols, a necessity if they were to receive accurate indexes.[112] The notaries estimated that, even with the help of their own giovani, they had spent 364 scudi on the task, far more than Marescotti and the civic treasury had given them. They thought it unjust that they should have to fund this from their own revenues, especially because the Archivio Capitolino earned them very little.[113] However Marescotti rejected the suggestion that the pope, or more probably the Archivio Urbano, absorb the city's archive of pre-1586 notarial records. While insisting that it remain in the hands of the Capitoline notaries, he donated some additional funds to ease the pain.[114]

After completing a full inventory of the contents of the Archivio Capitolino and allowing their ailing archivist to retire, on 23 June 1705 the notaries rescinded their earlier action.[115] Proudly trumpeting their achievement in making new covers for all the protocols and manuali, binding the loose documents, and creating tables of contents for volumes where they were missing, they formally took the archive back. The notaries also agreed to the eleven distasteful regulations, although these had been modified somewhat in the interim. Instead of twice a week, they would have to open the archive only once a week on Thursdays while court was in session; it was in any case a much lighter burden than that envisioned in 1562 when the new archive was expected to be open every day.[116]

The upbeat mood of the 1705 meeting did not erase the traumas of the preceding four years, when the Capitoline notaries endured both archival troubles and the pressures of Marescotti's inspection and reform of office practices. Yet posterity has cause to regret deeply what the Capitoline notaries did to their oldest protocols between 1702 and 1705 and to question the wisdom of the papal government in forcing men with so little knowledge to do it. A recent scholarly examination of the fourteenth- and fifteenth-century protocols in the former Archivio Capitolino pointed out that they had been "artificially recombined at the beginning of the eighteenth century, paginated with arabic numerals, and supplied with tables of contents that do not reflect what had actually been put together."[117] The state of internal confusion in the volumes is striking. One "protocol" contains instruments scattered almost at random from various years for four different notaries, and it is far from the only one in such condition.[118] On the one hand, when we compare the curial description of the disorders in the Archivio Capitolino to the protocols in their current mixed-up state, the intervention of the Capitoline notaries appears very superficial. By their own admission, they could not read the documents, so they simply bound the loose ones previously fastened in bundles, paginated everything, and gave them all new covers and fresh-looking indexes. On the other hand, however superficial, a task for a trained archivist was performed by men who were either incompetent or hasty, so it is more than likely that they made matters worse.

Confirming such pessimism is the contrast with the intact protocols of Nardo Venettini (dating from 1382 to 1428), complete with the indexes that he himself prepared.[119] Venettini's records escaped the fate of those of his colleagues because they were not in the Archivio Capitolino between 1702 and 1705 but rather enjoyed the solicitude of the Benedictines of Santa Maria Nova. Papal officials did everything in their power to repossess Venettini's volumes, which finally entered the Archivio Urbano in 1712.[120] They were less successful with those of Antonio Scambi (dating from 1363 to 1409), supposedly stored at Sant'Angelo in Pescheria but in fact between 1706 and 1712 moved to the palace of Cardinal Carlo Colonna.[121] Like Venettini's, Scambi's twenty-two surviving protocols, which eventually found their way back to Sant'Angelo and stayed there until sometime between 1906 and 1919, are in good condition.[122] While we cannot lay all the blame for the mistreatment of documents in the Archivio Capitolino on one generation of Capitoline notaries, the fact is that notarial records left in ecclesiastical hands fared better.

In truth, it was a mistake to compel active professionals to take responsibility for what was by then a historical archive. The diffusion of the italic hand over the course of the sixteenth and seventeenth centuries had completely cut off the Capitoline notaries of 1702 no less than their customers from the writings of their pre-1500 forebears.[123] To their credit, they recognized that they lacked the skills needed to make proper indexes for the old protocols, but it is not clear that all the supposedly expert help they hired to read "gothic letters" had the requisites either. No doubt, time and money pressures played their parts too. As the scale and difficulty of the job gradually emerged during 1702, the notaries asked for more money to hire outside aid, but by January 1703 they had been forced back on their own limited paleographic resources and those of their unskilled employees. The hundreds of protocols needing indexes were simply divided up among the Capitoline notaries. Giovanni Battista Jacobelli of office 26, for example, received twelve, and went to the trouble of hiring someone who could read gothic script to whom he paid thirty baiocchi per protocol.[124] Because the handwriting was very difficult, however, he could not finish the tables of contents within the deadline set by Marescotti. The incentive to meet the deadline was that the notaries would be reimbursed for their expenses but would have to pay out of their own pockets if they delayed. The diligent Jacobelli did pay out of his own pocket, arguing that failing to hire someone who could understand the documents would have been a waste of time and would not have fulfilled the cardinal's orders. But faced with a similar choice between turning the protocols around quickly at no cost and buying more expert time at their own expense, how many of his colleagues likely followed suit?

The degree of Cardinal Marescotti's personal engagement with the notaries of the Capitoline curia and their archival problems between 1702 and 1705 was unprecedented but not unique. As we have seen, the cardinal was prodigiously diligent in all his undertakings, and his commitment was wholehearted. Clement XI and his right-hand man clearly thought that preserving notarial records, whether in archives or in the protocols of venal officeholders, was very important. What explains the well-intentioned mischief inflicted on the Archivio Capitolino?

In part the reformers made inappropriate assumptions about a historical archive. When it came to notarial documents, these representatives of an "improving" state defined order as neatness, regularity, and completeness. Aged covers on volumes should be replaced by fresh ones, loose contracts should be bound so that all looked alike, and stray medieval protocols should be reeled into the duly authorized archive. Neatness was not wholly irrelevant to documentary preservation, of course; Marescotti and the pope were rightly horrified that a valuable estate could disappear simply because of a loose document. Nor was accessibility insignificant to them. They wanted accurate tables of contents so it would be easy to find the names of contracting parties. What they did not grasp was that the thousand or so volumes cared for by the Capitoline notaries, containing mainly acts of the fourteenth to sixteenth centuries, had become a thing of the past.

In their callous fashion, the Roman People had understood this and had abandoned the archive that owed its existence to their forebears, the patrician landowning families of Rome, for that reason. They now treated the Archivio Capitolino as if it were a private fief of the Capitoline notaries, a trivial indulgence scarcely to be tolerated. The notaries also understood its loss of relevance, and even though they continued to draw small sums from people who came in search of specific documents, they perceived that the Archivio Capitolino no longer served their material interests.[125] The state's bargain with notaries had always been that public writing created private value, but when it no longer did so, when it turned out to have a shelf life, were they still bound to it? The illegibility of so much of the archive broke the spell. It was time to hand over its custody to those who could read gothic script and who made their living looking after old things, not those in the business of producing writing that still had commercial power.[126]

In part, the mischief arose from the limitations of the reformers' own vision and means. Guided by their views of what constituted order in a state as well as a notarial archive, Clement's officials mistakenly diagnosed a technical as a political problem.[127] They saw their job as determining from the edicts and legislation of the past who was responsible for a defined set of tasks, and forcing them to perform them. Having figured out that in 1562 the Roman People had laid down rules for the operation of the Archivio Capitolino, the state's job in 1702 was to make sure that those same rules were obeyed. In fact, the reformers permitted some changes in the regulations, alterations imposed by later laws emanating from pope or city or from the notarial statutes in the seventeenth century.[128] The principle, and the method of governing informed by the principle, remained the same: clarify responsibility and compel performance. Despite the evidence before them, Marescotti and his aides assumed that the tasks had not changed and that those to whom duties had once been given were still capable of executing them. Of course, this policy had the added advantage of not costing the state very much.

The Archivio Urbano

If the Archivio Capitolino posed material challenges that the reformers could not quite fathom, the failures of the Archivio Urbano were in fact political, and anyone zealous for reform should have foreseen them. Marescotti's barque ran aground on the same shoals on which Cardinal De Luca shipwrecked in the 1670s, the strength of elements within the ecclesiastical or papal bureaucracy that did not want to change their working practices. Of course, there had been some shifting about of the sands in the interval, and it may be significant that it was the papal notaries, not the monasteries, that succeeded best at resisting the cardinal's efforts. What is clear is that papal power was more than ample to obtain the obedience of the Capitoline notaries but not quite sufficient to compel that of its own bureaucracy.

During the citywide inspection of notarial offices in 1702–3, Marescotti's agents had found a great many instruments and wills that had not been archived—that is, copied, checked against the originals, and deposited in the Archivio Urbano.[129] The cardinal had broader concerns as well, if he was indeed the author of the memorandum that worried about the original notarial protocols still in the hands of Roman confraternities and monasteries.[130] He knew about loopholes that kept notarial documents generated within the Curia out of the Archivio Urbano and sought to cast the government's reform net widely enough to capture vital missing records for its shelves. The loopholes included the so-called notary of the Archive (i.e., Archivio of the Curia Romana) who after 1630 had never deposited any protocols in the Archivio Urbano and those notaries of the Apostolic Camera working for the Datary whose names were virtually impossible to discover.[131] In addition key documents that the state perhaps ought to preserve, but did not, were the books of the secretaries of the many public bond funds (*monti*) sold in Rome.[132] And the parish priests and hospital workers who rogated testaments for individuals who could not get to a notary in time all too readily forgot to bring these to the Archivio Urbano.

Institutionally and financially, the Archivio Urbano had settled into a stable if less prominent role than that envisioned for it by its founders. It was not a policing or even a certifying agency for the notarial profession. Policing was, and would remain, an extra-institutional task; the Albani pope had deputed his most meticulous associate to undertake it, and in the future it would wax and wane with papal interest.[133] On the certifying side, the 1679 reforms of Innocent XI had decisively reconfigured the procedures for authorizing new notaries, putting experienced professionals rather than bureaucrats in charge of examining aspirants. The profile of the Archivio Urbano was so low in fact that we lose track of its precise location in these years. Although some sources say that it was lodged in the Torre dei Venti within the Vatican Palace, the diarist Francesco Valesio records in November 1702 that a fire near the Piazza Colonna threatened the archive and that its contents were moved to safety.[134] Yet an architect's report from 1703 clearly indicates that the Archivio Urbano was among several archives housed in the Belvedere extension to the Vatican Palace.[135] Whenever the shift to the Vatican took place, the archive was still there in 1728, when a follow-up investigation ordered by Pope Benedict XIII highlighted the problem of access.[136]

The reform decrees of 1704 gave the Archivio Urbano, despite its diffidence, several general tasks that show that papal authorities still had no other official to whom to turn when they wanted to implement new notarial routines. The eighteenth-century reformers required the archivist to make an alphabetical list of the thousands of testators whose forgotten sealed wills the pope had ordered opened in summer 1703. Elaborating on the laconic notices of the founding legislation of 1625, the decrees of spring 1704 insist that he now keep a confidential volume in which to register all future sealed wills delivered to city notaries.[137] They supplemented this record-keeping task with others. Notaries, including administrators and lessors of notarial offices, must present documentation indicating that they have been made notaries by an authorized agent (i.e., someone with the power to create new notaries) to the archivist of the Archivio Urbano. The decrees charged him with keeping a special volume listing the name of the notary and the date each one received his privilege.[138] In Marescotti and Clement XI's vision, the archivist did not examine the candidates or judge their abilities, as did the first head of the Archivio Urbano in the 1620s, but exercised a purely bureaucratic function. Nevertheless, they also had a useful part for him to play in their innovative enforcement mechanisms. Marescotti had given notaries who were delinquent in making copies for the Archivio Urbano one month to complete them. To prove they had done so by the 13 April 1704 deadline, they must obtain a sworn statement from the archivist and present it to the cardinal.[139] A two-page "note of the documents in the General Archivio Urbano" attests to the fact that during Albani's pontificate the copy archive, or at least its archivist, had acquired a range of new secretarial duties.[140]

In part, the sense of stability in the archive arose from the lengthy tenure of its archivist Luca Antonelli, who ran the Archivio Urbano from 1696 until his death sometime after 1724. In later years, he remembered with pride that he had not only received the inspectors in 1702–3 but had also been honored by a visit from Clement XI himself in 1704.[141] The authors of the reform decrees knew, and must have had confidence in, Antonelli; if it was a secretary they wanted, they must have believed they had the right man.

Yet it was not clear that an efficient clerk was all that the Archivio Urbano needed. Critics lashed out at its failure to secure the copies that were its due. Some blamed the negligence of the permissive contractor and some that of the notaries themselves, but the most convincing explanation pinpointed the vulnerability introduced by the change in mode of payment in 1646, soon after Urban VIII's death.[142] Thenceforth, clients paid the archiving fees directly to the archivist, which satisfied the contractor's financial goals without necessarily producing the copy for which the fee was paid. And, of course, some papal agencies in one way or another managed to exempt themselves from the obligation.

An undated report, probably from after 1712, assessed the efforts to rectify the shortcomings of the Archivio Urbano in the preceding decade, announcing mixed results.[143] It registered the archiving of a staggering twenty-four-thousand copies, thanks largely to the obedience of the Capitoline notaries, and it also celebrated the acquisition of the early volumes of Lorenzo Bertonio and Nardo Venettini from their ecclesiastical owners.[144] On the debit side, however, was the fact that Antonio Scambi's fourteenth-century protocols continued to elude the archive, as they would for another two centuries.[145] More significantly, it lamented the fact that papal notaries had ignored repeated orders to bring copies to the copy archive. Chief delinquents were the busy offices of the notaries of the vicario and the notaries AC.[146] The report estimated that they might owe the archive as many thousands of documents as had the Capitoline notaries. Unlike the Capitoline notaries, however, these papal notaries had not complied with the deadlines set in 1704 or with subsequent edicts.

Perhaps Marescotti and the pope would have liked to stretch the original mandate of the Archivio Urbano beyond holding copies of wills and long-term mortgages, but consistent with their conservative vision they never wrote new legislation. Quite a few of the failings that emerged in the scrutiny of the period 1702 to 1704 were therefore never rectified. The notary of the Archive continued his errant ways and the public bond accounts remained dispersed. Although the state's efforts succeeded in prying loose a few medieval protocols from ecclesiastical hands and netted the Archivio Urbano an impressive number of missing copies, it could not obtain those it wanted from the notaries of its own tribunals.[147] As in Cardinal De Luca's era, the reformers never quite mustered the political will and resources necessary to force change among the personnel at the heart of the Curia.

Conclusion

The documentary regime that Clement XI's inspectors brought to light in the early eighteenth century receives high marks for its capacity to preserve notarial records of both business and judicial acts. Venality had proved a much better stimulus to their collection in neat bound volumes on the shelves of notarial offices than any other measure anyone had tried. Yet legislation had also played a positive role. Requiring that instruments be copied out in full, bound at regular intervals, and made easily retrievable through indexes helped to ensure that there would be neat bound volumes to be placed on those shelves. If we doubt its effects, we can take a look at the variety of formats and small number of the surviving fourteenth- and fifteenth-century protocols in Rome. So it made sense to send out personnel to find out what the relationship between the laws governing notarial writing and the actual practices of notaries was, though it would have been even smarter to do so on a regular basis. If, on the other hand, the copy archive was not an unqualified success, it was at least not essential. Clients and officials in need of a document could count on the protocols of the venal officeholders.

The report card on the state of the profession in 1705 seems more mixed. The papal notaries with their vacabile offices, fewer than they had been a half century earlier, appear to have enjoyed some independence and prosperity, though more research would be needed to verify this. They certainly complained less and were less compliant than their colleagues in the Capitoline tribunal. Evidently the fact that the state still profited from the sale of their offices put them in a better position to defend both their economic and political interests. The Capitoline notaries, enjoying the free disposal of their offices, accepted the new disciplines for the most part obediently. Nonetheless, they seemed to have very little leverage with papal officials and suffered, as they informed them, from past reforms the popes had imposed. The crisis over the Archivio Capitolino made abundantly clear that they had been totally abandoned by their old protectors, the civic government, yet they had not found new patrons. Their survival as a corporate professional group until the unification of Italy, however, suggests that, despite the strains, they had found an equilibrium within the papal ancien régime. Driven by their need for authoritative documents, clients continued to make their way to the offices of the Capitoline notaries until the Papal State itself came to an end.

Conclusion

The notary of modern Italy is a recent construction. Until the 1920s the profession was in disarray, rent by regional and economic inequalities, struggling to find its footing in the new conditions of a unified nation.[1] Loosed from their moorings in the duchies, republics, and ecclesiastical kingdoms that had depended on and nurtured them for half a millennium, Italian notaries in the late 1800s found they had very little in common. As we look back at the story of one city's notaries, we can appreciate the intensely local heritage that defined notaries from Italy's other early modern states as well.

It was not a timeless heritage of course, certainly not in the Roman case. Arriving back after three hundred years, a Roman from the fourteenth century would have been startled at much of what he saw and heard in the baroque capital. The city, quadrupled in size, teemed with visitors, migrants, and newcomers, and it had spread across the hilly areas so long abandoned to vineyards and gardens. Magnificent urban vistas cut open the knot of medieval streets and dozens of domed churches and high-topped palaces rose in homage to the faith, money, and taste that had poured into Rome since 1400. Renting a house or going into business with a partner or marrying off his daughter, however, would have entailed a familiar ritual. Our time traveler and his landlord, partner, or future in-laws would have sought out a notary to record their agreements.

He would have had to look a bit harder than before, because there were now only thirty Capitoline notaries plus the handful of whom he had never heard who worked for a papal civil tribunal. If he did not find himself on the Corso, he would also have had to walk further. It would have been easy for him to ask directions to the nearest notary, however, because now they had settled offices with addresses well known to city residents. They spent more time in those offices too, so he would have been well advised to go in person rather than expect a house call. The transaction itself would not have changed, or the language or the clauses granting and giving away particular rights; he or the other parties would have paid their fees as usual and left as usual without a record of their own. He might not have expected to find other employees working for his notary, jotting down what he had paid in a receipt book, perhaps even rogating the transaction themselves. Nor would he have ever seen shelves loaded with dozens of bound folio-sized volumes before. The notaries he was used to wrote in small notebooks, which were then whisked out of sight; one never knew where. It certainly would have surprised the trecento visitor to see the crowd at the notary's daily audience, waiting to give testimony or to complain that their suits were not moving ahead quickly enough. Back in the fourteenth century, if you litigated, you went to the judge's palace on the Capitoline Hill. Despite the changes, however, customers and notaries still seemed to be doing what they had done in his day.

Of course, much was familiar to him because the legal role played by notarial documents was the same in Rome in 1350 and 1650. He may not have studied law, but our traveler and the people with whom he negotiated had imbibed a set of behaviors and attitudes structured by the ius commune in all the areas where it prevailed. These could run deep. Spanish mercenaries who sacked Rome in 1527 hired notaries to document their depredations, while their German counterparts from the lands of customary law simply seized the booty and ran.[2] Another factor underpinning our Roman's experience of continuity was the particular contractual culture of an economy, which, in 1650, as in 1350, had few structural supports for borrowers and lenders apart from the public instrument.[3] Were private entrepreneurs selling publicly trustworthy documents? That a profession made a living simply from writing down his personal wishes and keeping a record of them did not strike the Roman as odd or illegitimate. That they were still doing so centuries after he had left did not surprise him, nor would it if he returned to Italy today.

Beneath the quiet surface of ordinary habits, however, we know that notaries and their documents in Rome had confronted many new demands in the course of the early modern period. We have solid material evidence of innovation in the thousands of uniformly sized, bound, paginated and indexed protocols that survive, starting mainly in the seventeenth century, as well as in the existence of a partial archive of duplicates. Other sources of dynamism affecting notarial writing have left subtler traces. Sometimes we can only glimpse them indirectly. A sixteenth-century Roman might have visited a notary to draw up an employment contract, which few people did any more in the seventeenth century. Renata Ago argues that informal agreements, relying on the word, the scriptura privata memo or witness testimony, were replacing notarial acts in certain kinds of transactions.[4] The ability to write was spreading. Because personal documents were also a form of legal evidence, some writers may have chosen to use their own new skills rather than paying for the service of authoritative certification.

Sometimes the evidence of change is clearer. Notaries had been compelled to diversify the products on offer, adding simple copies to the traditional public copies. To their chagrin, they had been made to dismantle profitable barriers they had erected between clients and their documents, allowing customers to consult their acts for free. But if some older uses no longer drew clients to notaries, new economic enticements partly filled the void. Novel credit instruments spawned in a city that was a leading European financial center in the late sixteenth and seventeenth centuries boosted the demand for notarial writing. Changing religious styles contributed too. The upsurge of piety that accompanied the Counter-Reformation in Rome stimulated new charitable foundations and strengthened many of the city's venerable ecclesiastical landowners. Institutions were among the notary's best clients in early modern Rome; their portfolios were growing, and their need for *scriptura publica* seemingly insatiable.

If our returning trecento Roman happened to be a notary, of course, he would have been much more shocked than an ordinary citizen by what had happened to his profession over three centuries. He may well have envied the thirty Capitoline notaries of 1650 their substantial staff, offices, and archives as well as their college, so much more richly endowed with rituals, rules, and income than his own. But where were the rest of the notaries? What had happened to that throng around the Capitol and the young men who dashed off contracts at the marketplace? Falling into conversation with an Angelo Giustiniani or a Giorgio Giorgi, our professional visitor would surely have been disabused of his illusions about the prosperity of a venal notarial officeholder in baroque Rome. Although their investment was greater than in the fourteenth century, notaries who owned their offices, or more likely owed on them, also faced a precarious existence.

If the medieval Roman notary had wondered about these changes, he would have needed to look no further for an explanation than the magnificent new basilica of St. Peter or the three papal palaces that had replaced the ruined one at the Lateran deserted by the pontiffs in the early 1300s. They embodied the renewed stature of the papacy. In our visitor's absence, the early modern popes had recouped the vigor of their age-old office. Through strategic religious, cultural, intellectual, and political policies, they had crushed all internal rivals and had successfully concentrated power in their own hands. Embracing the legal culture that placed notarial documents well up in its hierarchy of evidence, these rulers regulated and exploited their writers, counting on their continued willingness to put up with economic uncertainty in exchange for the right to sell that invaluable commodity, trust. They were not disappointed.

If we leave our fourteenth-century Roman notary to his astonishment and return to our own initial perplexity, we have gained some insight into how notarial documents in territories of the civil-law tradition acquired and maintained their mysterious power. The historical processes that produce a commodity whose distinguishing characteristic is its credibility may vary. In Rome, the notaries at work in the fourteenth century had very little in common with those living in the seventeenth, just as the ill-defined and ill-protected notarial profession of late medieval Rome shared hardly anything with the prestigious guilds of Bologna, Perugia, or Florence. Looking beyond the peninsula to the notaries of France, Mexico, or New Netherlands amplifies the diversity of Italian experiences. In early modern France, where they were excluded from the judicial system, Parisian notaries carved out a prosperous economic niche for themselves finding money for a young capitalist economy that lacked any other banking system.[5] In Mexico, Spanish colonizers encouraged the creation of Nahua notaries to serve indigenous local governments, though the prestige of record keepers in the preconquest era may have made this a less exotic import than we might think.[6] By contrast, in the former New Netherlands a Dutch notary's career was a dead end; British legal culture was supremely indifferent to the notion of public writing and the whole architecture of jurisprudence on which it rested.[7]

The story of the meaning and making of scriptura publica in Rome, while site specific, tells a larger tale. It teaches us that there is no single path to the creation of public writing just as there is no one set of conventions defining good and bad evidence. There are some essential elements, however: intellectuals who take an interest in problems of certainty, governments that believe in the process of certification but delegate it elsewhere, and writers happy to sell their time and skills so that they can earn their daily bread.

In our story, public authorities have been the most active agents in defining and redefining the meaning of notarial writing, which indeed could not exist without their support.[8] If we doubted this fact, we could listen to what the notaries themselves say when they have to rogate at times of contested political power. Because they must declare by whose title they write on every act, they are very sensitive to shifting masters. Who was in charge: pope, prefect, emperor? When faced with such questions, Roman notaries invoke them all.[9] But public authority is not immune from history either. Both as concept and as practice, it is subject to conflict, contradiction, and change, as we have seen in Rome between 1300 and 1700. The forces that impose on authoritative writing are at times incoherent, and their effects paradoxical, irrelevant, or counterproductive. We could hardly expect otherwise, because it is not only governments but also clients, judges, and notaries who hope words endowed with public trustworthiness will advance their goals. In Rome, the great transformation wrought by the sale of notarial offices set in motion legal, commercial, and political developments with profound, if unintended, consequences for documents. Power had imposed, but producers and consumers colonized the new regime and made of it something not quite foreseen by, and indeed rather frustrating to, rulers.

What this study has shown is how the words of specific writers acquired and maintained distinctive force. Legal documents became special not by magic but from the convergence of social, intellectual, economic, and political forces upon the act of writing and the artifact produced by that act. When we include notaries in a history of writing, we observe a cultural process at work that is not merely technological or expressive. The uniqueness of notarial records resulted from the deployment of writing within a setting defined by particular discourses, institutions, and practices. Notaries teach us that, while writing has a history, it is not a history of its own.

Study Sample of the Thirty Capitoline Notaries in 1630

The study sample was based on perusal of all the known volumes of the series (*fondo*) Thirty Capitoline Notaries in the Archivio di Stato di Roma (ASR) for the year 1630. This method resulted in a list of thirty-one notaries rather than thirty, because two notaries were apparently rogating in office 14. In fact, one of these two notaries, Francesco Egidio, was not formally admitted to the college of the notaries of the Capitoline Curia (the official title of the group labeled by later archivists "Thirty Capitoline Notaries") until 1638. Nevertheless, he is included in the sample because he has a single volume of acts in office 14 in 1630 (vol. 91). My information on the sample group and all notaries with offices in seventeenth-century Rome also depends heavily on the list of titleholders published by archivist Achille François in 1886. This invaluable list bears some comment, particularly with respect to names, dates, and office numbers of titleholders. François seems to have taken his spelling of the Latinized names of the titleholders from the spines of their protocols, obviously making a choice if there were variant spellings. While in my text and appendix I have used the Italian surnames of these notaries found in contemporary sources, I also list the Latin versions given by François. The years for which a specific notary was titleholder of an office provided by François are approximate. I have been able to confirm from research in other sources that they are not infrequently wrong, and the staff of the ASR was in the process of producing a more detailed inventory of the volumes in the fondo Thirty Capitoline Notaries as this book went to press. Because that more accurate inventory will be available to future researchers, I have not in this appendix made corrections to the dates given by François, but caution readers to treat them as, again, approximate. Regarding the identifying numbers of the notarial offices of the Thirty Capitoline Notaries, a word of explanation is in order. François assigned numbers to these offices, which were later changed by archivists at the Archivio Notarile Distrettuale, where the volumes were collected between the 1880s and the 1930s (Verdi 2005, 444–45). Inventory no. 1 in the ASR, an annotated copy of the François publication, provides the archival numbers by which these offices are currently identified and which I use in this book.

In addition to François, my study sample draws on a variety of contemporary sources, especially wills, other types of notarial documents, trial records, and annual parish censuses (*stati delle anime*). As mentioned in chapter 5, the information on date of birth taken from the annual parish censuses reflects the idiosyncrasies of the census taker, a parish priest, or his employee and is sometimes wildly inconsistent from one year to another within the same household. I have given office locations as of 1630, unless noted, as I have found them in various contemporary sources; this information therefore reflects a situation before the 1664 list of office locations published by Verdi (2005, 469–73). While some offices remained in stable locations, some (like offices 7, 8 and 20) were still quite mobile in the second quarter of the seventeenth century.

Name	Dates	Birthplace	Office	Titleholder	Location
Arrigone, Francesco Arrigonus	1598–1648	Milan diocese	21	1627–48	Fontana di Trevi
Attilio, Giacomo Attilius			24	1630–41	
Balducci, Lorenzo Balduccius			37	1619–42	
Balducci, Orazio Balduccius			23	1619–39	
Barberini, Ascanio Barbarino Barberinus	c. 1594–1650	Monte S. Vito Senigallia diocese	10	1627–49	Parish of SS. Vincenzo & Anastasia
Bonanni, Leonardo Bonannus	c. 1587–1667	Carrara	2	1622–67	Piazza dell'Olmo (Piazza Mattei)
Bonincontro, Lorenzo Bonincontrus	1581–1634	Rome	18	1605–33	Via del Corso, near SS. Apostoli
Camilli, Guido Guidus Camillus	d. 1636	Caseproda in Sabina	20	1626–36	West side of Corso at Arco di Portogallo
Canini, Angelo Caninus	c. 1583–1649	C. Fabri Orvieto diocese	12	1624–49	"Alla Pantani": 4th door on right after Sant'Adriano
Constantini, Carlo Constantinus			5	1624–58	Near Tor de Specchi
Cortellacci, Marcello Cortellaccius	d. 1631	Calvi	17	1616–30	At Ponte Sisto: "new houses going toward Farnese garden"
De Alexandriis, Felice Antonio Alexandri			8	1617–33	Near Piazza Rotonda
Dell'Huomo, Marco Tullio De Homine			16	1614–40	Piazza Montanara

Name	Dates	Birthplace	Office	Titleholder	Location
Egidio, Francesco Egidius (with Modio) Aegidus			14	1630, 1632, 1635–54	
Gargario, Gio. Fran. Garganus			9	1630–31	Piazza della Pace
Giorgi, Giorgio Georgeus		Avignon	6	1629–33	Under Borghese palace going toward Ripetta
Giustiniani, Angelo Justinianus	b. 1582 circa	Acquasparta	11	1611–44	Via del Gesù. Near palace of Cardinal Muti
Lucarelli, Angelo Lucarellus			29	1623–33	
Melli, Salvatore Mellius			27	1627–30	
Modio, Nicolo Angelo (with Egidio) Modius			14	1617–31	In parish of S. Maria in Campo Carleo
Ottaviani, Gio. Batt. Octavianus	c. 1552–1636	Villafranca Lunensis, Sarzana diocese	13	1595–1636	In parish of SS. Apostoli
Palladio, Alessandro Palladius	b. 1574 circa	Colleveteri in Sabina	22	1608–46	Piazza Colonna
Paradisi, Flavio Paradisus, Hilarius	b. 1594 circa	Città Castellana	7	1628–58	In 1634 in parish of SS. Vincenzo & Anastasia
Pizzuti, Tranquillo Pizzutus	d. 1641	Collescipoli	19	1612–41	Via del Corso, near S. Carlo
Raimondo, Taddeo Raymundus			25	1626–41	Campo dei Fiori
Ricci, Torquato Riccius		Collescipoli?	1	1616–41	"sotto Montecitorio"
Salvatore, Tommaso Salvatori		Spoleto	15	1626–47	Via di S. Eustachio
Saraceni, Michele Saracenus	d. 1634	Collescipoli	3	1591–1634	

Name	Dates	Birthplace	Office	Titleholder	Location
Scolocci, Tranquillo Scoloccius	d. 1652	Rocca Burga Terracina diocese	26	1594–1652	Piazza Madama
Tullio, [Gio.] Agostino Tullius			4	1607–34	Sant'Andrea della Valle
Vespignani, Paolo Vespignanus		Brisighella	28	1624–54	Via dei Giubbonari

The Proposals of the Capitoline Notaries

Proposte per parte de Notari Capitolini alla Sacra Congregazione della Nuova Riforma[1]

Prima della Riforma dell S. M. di Paolo V l'instromenti che si rogavano a Notari si tenevano serrati ne credenzoni, e chi voleva vedere qualche instrom[ento] pagava la visura, sicome si costuma hoggidi fuori di Roma.

In detta Riforma al cap[itol]o de Notarijs Tribunalium Urbis al no. 46 si ordinò sotto queste parole "alia cuiuscumq[ue] generis qualitatis quantitatis, contractus, acta, instrumenta, vel ab ipsis rogata, vel apud eos producta, teneantur partibus interesse habentibus ad earum bene-placitum gratis ostendere ipsisq[ue] copiam facere et tradere soluta solita mercede competenti sine tamen die, anno, mense, testibus, ita ut nullam in iudicio fidem facere possint."[2]

Onde in vigore di detta riforma li Notari sono solo tenuti mostrare l'instromenti gratis, e non altri [illegible] che le parti lo leghino, rilegghino, imparino à mente, sicome fanno li giovini procuratori di buon ingegno e meglio memoria, venendo spesso à vedere e rivedere detto instromento, e poi ne fanno il sommario.

Chiaro ità che la Riforma liga il Notaro à darle e liga la Parte che la piglia che non possi far fede in giuditio non ostante che la Parte litigante dichiari voler stare in giuditio alla copia semplice sapendosi che in giuditio deve esser scrittura publica, ne questo consenso puol pregiudicare al Notaro, che ha l'offitio titulo oneroso et è forzato di dare detta copia semplice come in detta Riforma sotto fede certa che in giuditio non deve far fede, e pure ogni giorno si vede quest'abuso.

Di più si pratica di stare all'indicatione, et in questo caso li litiganti ò loro Procuratori vengono à legere e rilegere l'instromento, imparano la sostanza, concordano il fatto, e lo danno in sommario, e di questo vi sono li broliardi pieni all'A[uditor] C[amerae].

Onde li Notari Capitolini vengono evidentemente pregiudicati si nelle copie publiche, che si doverebbero pigliare, come anche nelle copie semplici che per necessità doverebbero prodursi, sicome venendo il caso di qualche estratto andandosi in Rota, la medema suol giudicare con farsi portare le scritture indicate.

---

1. ASR, Cam. II, Notariato, b. 3. There are neither page numbers nor internal numbers in this volume. The document is undated, although an archivist has marked it "1704." For reasons discussed in chapter 6, I believe it dates from the period between the inspection of 2 January 1703 and the decrees of 11 February 1704.

2. See *Bullarium* 1857–72, 12:90, no. 46.

Si prega dunque questa congreg[azio]ne à riflettere le buone ragioni de Notari Capitolini, l'osservanza di detta Riforma, e limitare tanta licenza di spogliare detti instromenti, e prescrivere il modo, col quale non siano pregiudicati detti Notari contro la mente d'essa Riforma, et insieme ordinare alli Giudici che non decretino che si stia all'indicatione mentre le S. M. di Sisto V nell'erettione del Collegio de Notari Capitolini promise mantenerli li loro emolumenti.

The Creation of a Notary

Creatio notarij pro D. Bartholomeo de Benedictis[1]
Ill. & Rev.mus D. Alexander Abbas Mattheus Patritius Rom.s Protonotarius Apostolicus de
numero partecipantium decanus in vig. facultatum eisd. concessar. à S.mo D. Nró D. Sixto
Papa Quinto fel. rec. not.us et tabelliones creandi et alia faciendi prout latius in litteris
Apostolicis de super expeditis et eid. concessis sub datum Rome apud S.ti Petrus anno
incarnationis Domini 1586 nona februarij pontificatus sui anno p.o tenoris pro ut in eis habita
prius fide et optima informatione de probitate, integretate, sufficientia et idoneitate D.
Bartholomei filij D. Jóes de Bened.is de Tarano in Sabinis et quod est idoneus et sufficiens ad
illu. not.um publicum creandum sponte ac omni meliori modo d.is facultatibus utendo, ac in
vim motus proprij S. D. N. Pauli Divina Providentia Pape V fel. rec. super declaratione nove
reformationis Tribunalium Urbis sub datum Rome in Palatio Apostolico die XV [novem]bris
1612 quibus in hac parte fungitur. Creavit d.m D. Bartholomeum presentem in publicum et
authenticum not.um pennam et calamare eisd. Privilegium concedendo ac uti contractus
instrumenta actus quomodo. Iudicarios donationes inter vivos et causa mortis testamenta
codicillos et qualiter [?] alias ultimas voluntates et quacumq. alia inst. genera decreta et
authoritate pro ut latius in d.o privilegio conficere rogare stipulare et interponere resp. possit
authoritate tribuit pro ut id. D. Bartholomeus de Benedictis Notarius Creatus prestito prius
p. ipsu. solito iuramento in manibus d.i Ill.mi D. Alessandro Matthei genibus flexis facere et
adimplere promisit omni meliori modo. Super quibus.
Actum Rome in Reg.ni S. Angeli in domo solita habit.nis di Ill. et R.mi D. Matthei presenti-
bus Francesco Picino Romano et Ill. et Exc.s D. Nicolaus Jasco I. U. D. Florentin. testibus
Oct. Nucus stp.t

---

1. ASR, 30 NC, uff. 11 (Giustiniani) 1628, pt. 2, 214r–v (9 June 1628).

Abbreviations

All archives and libraries are in Rome.

b.	busta
AC	auditor of the Camera
ASC	Archivio Storico Capitolino
ASR	Archivio di Stato di Roma
ASV	Archivio Segreto Vaticano
ASVR	Archivio Storico del Vicariato di Roma
AU	Archivio Urbano
BAV	Biblioteca Apostolica Vaticana
CCN	Collegio dei Notai Capitolini
Code	*Codex* in *Corpus Iuris Civilis*
Cred.	credenzone
Digest	*The Digest of Justinian*
Notai AC	Notaries of the auditor of the Camera
reg.	registro
rub.	rubbrica
s. a.	stati delle anime
sez.	sezione
SPQR Statuta (1519–23)	*SPQR statuta et novae reformationes urbis Romae eiusdemq[ue] varia privilegia a diversis romanis pontificibus emanata in sex libros divisa novissime compilata.* Rome, 1519–23.
Statuta (Rome, 1831)	*Statuta venerabilis collegii DD. Notariorum Curiae Capitolinae eorumque facultates et privilegia.* Rome, 1831.
Statuta urbis (1580)	*Statuta almae urbis Romae.* Rome, 1580.
1363 statuti	Camillo Re, ed., *Statuti della città di Roma.* Rome, 1880.
30 NC	Trenta Notai Capitolini (Thirty Capitoline Notaries)
TCrG	Tribunale Criminale del Governatore
TCS	Tribunale Civile del Senatore
uff.	ufficio

Introduction

1. The tale of writing's history is particularly well told by Martin 1994, but see also the contrasting approaches of Harris 1986 and Goldberg 1990. For a recent global synthesis, see Christin 2002.

2. The *notarii* mentioned in ancient sources were actually scribes, not figures imbued with public authority as in the Middle Ages. Petrucci 1958, 3.

3. In the late thirteenth century, an Italian notary in the service of the archbishop of Canterbury noted the English reluctance to use notaries: "Italians, like cautious men, want to have a public instrument for practically every contract they enter into; but the English are just the opposite, and an instrument is very rarely asked for unless it is essential." Quoted in Cheney 1972, 135. Cheney's work helps to explain the legal reasons for this very different attitude toward the notarial document. The story of a seventeenth-century Dutch notary caught between the differing legal cultures of New Netherlands and New York has been poignantly told by Merwick 1999.

4. Some exemplary exceptions show us how mistaken we are to take the written record for granted: Clanchy 1993; Messick 1993; Kosto 2001; and K. Burns 2005.

5. For early modern Europe, see, among others, the classic studies of Darnton 1983; McKenzie 1986; Grafton 1997; and Johns 1998. See especially Chartier 1987, 1994, 1995.

6. See Bolzoni 2001. I thank Anthony Grafton for this reference.

7. For some examples of such an approach to the history of writing practices, see Chartier 1989 and Love 1993. In Italy, see especially Petrucci 1978a, 1978b, 1982, 1983, 1984, 1988, 1989, 1993. See also Marchesini 1992; Balestracci 1989; and Bartoli Langeli 2000.

8. In fact, the Roman notarial records began to be used as a source for writing family history as early as the seventeenth century; see the notes taken by Domenico Iacovacci, "Repertorii di famiglie romane," Rome, BAV, Ottoboni Lat., vols. 2548–54.

9. Earlier scholarship is summarized by Petrucci 1958, 3–44, to which we should add Barraclough 1934. For a representative later contribution, see Fasoli 1968. The series of historical studies sponsored by the Consiglio Nazionale del Notariato, inaugurated by Giorgio Costamagna's classic *Il notaio a Genova* (1970), consolidated this phase of research. These efforts received an interesting critique in Bartoli Langeli 1977; for an overview, see Pratesi 1983. See also the conference papers published under the title *Civiltà comunale* (1989), where the contributions of paleographers and diplomatists continued to predominate. The work of medievalist Bartoli Langeli is notable for connecting the histories of documentation and notaries in precisely the way I think most valuable; for a brief example, see Bartoli Langeli 1992 and, at greater length, Bartoli Langeli 2006. A medievalist who has made singular contributions to our knowledge of the earliest extant notarial documents in Rome in the course of preparing her magisterial study of trades and professions in the fourteenth century, *La Roma dei Romani* (2001), is Isa Lori Sanfilippo. Most recently she has published an edition of the 1446 statutes of Rome's notarial college (2008). For a sampling of the work of Roman scholars on fifteenth-century notarial acts, see Barbalarga et al. 1986.

10. Berengo led the way in Italian historical studies with his discussion of notaries in Lucca (1965), and in several subsequent essays (1976–77, 1981). A good sense of how the field

has developed may be gained from Pastore 1982; Bisazza 1993; the special issue of *Archivi per la storia* edited by Francesco Magistrale in 1993; D'Amico 1997; Dattero 1997; and Carrino 1998. In 1999 the École française de Rome organized a round table discussion on urban history and notarial records in early modern Italy. The papers were published in *Mélanges de l'école française de Rome, Moyen âge-temps modernes, Italie et Méditerranée*; see in particular the contributions of Ago 2000 and Groppi 2000.

In France, where historians associated with the journal *Annales: économies, sociétés, civilisations* made liberal use of notarial records for their massive exercises in "total history" from the 1950s onward, early modernists have been especially attentive to notaries. A pioneering figure in the field was former notary Jean-Paul Poisson, whose essays over the period 1951 to the 1990s have been published in three volumes (1985–90, 1996). Three monographs of the 1990s illustrate this important current in early modern French historiography: Limon 1992, Dolan 1998, and Hardwick 1998; for the earlier period, see Smail 1999. For especially original contributions, see also Davis 1987 and Fontaine 1993.

11. Fontaine 1993, 481; Bartoli Langeli 2006, 14.

12. The contemporary Italian notary retains this "hybrid" nature. Di Fabio 1978; Santoro 1998, 8.

13. See Meriggi's (1997) essay for an illuminating discussion of the terms *arte* and *professione*.

14. Santoro 1995, 139–44; see also his citation to the "late seventeenth-century model of the 'state profession,' " (118 n. 11).

15. Even in the more unified territory of ancien régime France, there was great diversity; see Fontaine 1993, 479–81. See, for example, the collection edited by Laffont 1991, as well as Limon 1992 and the bibliography she cites.

16. Martines 1968, 16; Pedani Fabris 1996, 33–35.

17. Pedani Fabris 1996, 1.

18. Two early assessments of the possibilities and problems of using notarial acts for social history are the conference papers assembled in *Les actes notariés* 1979 and Brezzi and Lee 1984. Although they, too, are documents by notaries, notarial records of meetings of government bodies and of judicial proceedings have tended to be of less interest to social historians.

19. *Il Cartolare di Giovanni Scriba* 1935. Editions of texts of notarial documents after 1300 are rarer; Berengo 1976–77, 149–50. However, in Rome, where there are no pre-1300 notarial volumes, see the published and online protocols edited by Mosti (1982, 1984) and Lori Sanfilippo (1986, 1989).

20. Fontaine 1993, 478; K. Burns 2005, 355–57.

21. To cite just two examples, through her close study of the eighty surviving notarial volumes from fourteenth-century Rome, Lori Sanfilippo (2001, 433–34) has discovered references to more than a hundred notaries c. 1365–72, although records from only seventeen survive. Although the matriculation book of the Roman notaries has disappeared, a notary's description of being registered in it in 1553 appears at the beginning of one of his volumes; Verdi 2005, 454.

22. Prodi 1982.

Chapter 1 • The Jurists: Writing Public Words

1. Here I use the term *jurists* broadly to mean authors of legal commentaries and treatises, some of whom were academic teachers of the law and others attorneys or judges.

2. Maclean 1992, 13–14; Stein 1999, 49.

3. The *ius commune* was the common law of continental Europe, but I will use the Latin term to avoid confusion with the quite different legal system that goes by the name of the common law in England.

4. Radding 1988, 10, 118; Grossi 1995, 154–59; Bellomo 1995, 53–54, 60–63; Stein 1999, 43–45.

5. The *Corpus iuris civilis* also included the *Institutes*, a textbook for law students, and the *Novels*, new materials added in the sixth century after the compilation of the other books. On the importance of the *Institutes* for training notaries in early modern Genoa, see L. Sinisi 1997, 340.

6. Radding 1988, 158–78; Bellomo 1995, 58; Stein 1999, 52–54.

7. The maxim went "Quidquid non agnoscit glossa, non agnoscit curia"; Watson 1981, 9. The jurists were not confined to their cathedras, and their opinions (*consilia*) in actual cases were much sought after; Kirshner 1999, 107–8; Kuehn 1999, 230–31.

8. In 1215 the Lateran Council outlawed trial by ordeal, a move long prepared by the opposition of churchmen to the practice; Lévy 1965b, 141. This is not to suggest that witnesses and documents had not functioned as evidence before this date; for a recent sensitive treatment of the judicial ordeal and competing modes of proof, see Bowman 2004, 119–82. See also Gualazzini 1964, 567–68; Smail 2003, 28.

9. *Digest* 22.4: De fide instrumentorum et de amissione eorum (Documentary evidence and the loss of documents). *Code* 4.21: De fide instrumentorum et amissione eorum et antapochis faciendis et de his quae sine scriptura fieri possunt. (Concerning the confidence to be reposed in written instruments, and their loss, and when receipts and counter-receipts should be given, and concerning what things can be done without their being committed to writing).

10. *Digest* 22.4.1.

11. Rogerius 1892, 111. Rogerius comments also on the *Digest* and, like other jurists, quotes it extensively without citation.

12. Ibid.

13. Petrucci 1958, 4.

14. It was understood that only the emperor or the pope could create notaries. However, because they often delegated this power, as Emperor Frederick I did in 1162 when he permitted the city of Genoa to name its own notaries, the notary's actual connection to their authority was nominal; Costamagna 1970, 20. For the manner of creating notaries in Rome, see chapter 2.

15. For an analysis of the public character of the notary's authority in an age before state institutions, see Montorzi 1984, 87–89. Cf. Bellomo 1995, 58.

16. The Muslim document gained its force from witnesses; Tyan 1959, 13–14.

17. Costamagna 1970, 7–32; Petrucci 1984a, 258; Folin 1990, 245. Cf. *Code* 4.21.17. By

contrast, the notary in France did not have this same autonomy, especially after 1554 when the client's signature was required for a valid notarial act; Fraenkel 1992, 9.

18. Rogerius 1892, III.

19. Costamagna 1970, 52; Petrucci 1984a, 258–59. See also Radding 1988, 113, and on the subject more generally, Genicot 1972. The process took until the thirteenth century in southern Italy, although it was dealt a slight setback in the kingdom of Naples. There, from 1231, the emperor required a "judge of contracts" to validate the notary's documents; Pratesi 1983, 770–71. This remained an isolated regional exception, however, confined to the mainland Regno.

20. Rolandino 1546c, 1:470r. For Rolandino's broader political contributions, see Giansante 1998, 37–47.

21. Rolandino 1546c, 1:470r.

22. Farinacci 1612, Q. 157 is devoted to this topic. Farinacci's multivolume handbook on criminal law, *Praxis et theorica criminalis,* came out under various titles between 1589 and 1616, and reappeared in many subsequent editions. *De falsitate* was first published in Venice in 1612.

23. Fenzonio 1636, 69. For what appears to be Roman custom in Fenzonio's day, see *Bullarium* 1857–72, 12:90, no. 46; this legislation is discussed in detail in chapter 3.

24. Rolandino 1546c, 1:407v.

25. Campitelli 1987, 95; Ascheri 1999, 355.

26. A fourteenth-century formulary used by the papal Curia illustrates the varieties of public act that were authored by notaries; Barraclough 1934, 22.

27. Campitelli 1987, 94–97.

28. Rogerius 1892, III.

29. "Most" but not all because the canon lawyers developed a new concept, *notorium,* for evidence that was so divinely obvious that it stood above all other types; Lévy 1965b, 160–65.

30. For an overview of the topic, see Salvioli 1925–27, 3.2:405–93; Lévy 1965a, 37–54; 1965b, 137–67.

31. Like spring blossoms, Mascardi opined, some modes of proof were perfect and brilliantly colored while others were pale and imperfect; Mascardi 1608, Q. 1, nos. 21–23. The three-volume work first appeared in Venice between 1584 and 1588 and had many subsequent editions. All citations are to the 1608 Turin edition. From his preface, we learn that Mascardi was from Sarzana (then part of the Genoese Republic) but pursued a varied career in ecclesiastical administration in Milan, Padua, Naples, and Piacenza, as well as serving as apostolic protonotary in the Roman Curia and finally bishop of Ajaccio (Corsica).

32. Mascardi 1608, Q. 16, no. 12. The definition is one he draws from Baldus, whom he also cites for a second definition, a thing "possible but not true" at no. 13. Mascardi treats the types of proof (*probationes*) in Qs. 4–16.

33. Mascardi 1608, Q. 4, nos. 1–5.

34. Mascardi 1608, Q. 4, nos. 15–18. *Fama's* classification was unstable, however, and Mascardi eventually relegated it, like notorium, to one of his detailed entries (*conclusiones*).

35. Mascardi 1608, Q. 4, nos. 6–10.

36. Lévy 1965b, 153–56.

37. For Innocent III, compare Lévy 1965b, 154, with Mascardi 1608, Q. 6, nos. 6 or 62; for Baldus, compare Mascardi, Q. 6, no. 1 and no. 15.

38. *Code* 4.21.15. Deuteronomy 19:15 and the Gospel of Matthew 18:16 say two or three witnesses; the Gospel of John 8:17 and *Digest* 22.5.12 both say two.

39. Mascardi 1608, Q. 6, no. 17.

40. Baldus 1599, 7:55v.

41. Baldus, 1586, 2:178v.

42. On Prospero Farinacci's career as a lawyer, state prosecutor, and writer on criminal law, see Del Re 1975 and Mazzacane 1995.

43. Farinacci 1612, Q. 156, no. 138.

44. Farinacci 1612, Q. 156, no. 146.

45. Gualazzini 1964, 568; Fenzonio 1636, 174, no. 2.

46. *Digest* 22.4.4.

47. Baldus 1599, 7:55v.

48. Baldus 1599, 7:60r.

49. Mascardi 1608, Q. 6, nos. 27, 28, 36–38.

50. Rogerius 1892, 111; Mascardi 1608, Q. 6, no. 32; Fenzonio 1636, 175. For examples, see Passeri 1615, 20, 52.

51. Farinacci 1612, Q. 158, gives the topic a full discussion; Nussdorfer 2003, 109–12.

52. Mascardi 1608, Q. 6, nos. 20–25.

53. We see this convergence in the formulation *scriptura et instrumenta* (writing and instruments), which the jurists so often employed. When they were talking generally about the legal efficacy of documents, they tended to ignore any distinction between those by private individuals and those by notaries. Cf. Fenzonio 1636, 174, no. 2.

54. Mascardi 1608, Q. 6, nos. 25, 30–31.

55. Kirshner 1999, 107–8; Kuehn 1999, 229.

56. Supino Martini 1995, 47.

57. We preserve this sense in our own usage where notarial act is a synonym for document.

58. Costamagna 1970, 71–72; see also Costamagna 1961.

59. The terminological confusion, remarked on by early modern theorists, is apparent in any perusal of the literature on notarial acts in the different Italian states or cities. See also L. Sinisi 1997, 347n.

60. Baldus 1599, 7:57r.

61. The *consilium* of Parisius was cited by Farinacci 1612, Q. 153, no. 129.

62. The abbreviation of the customary clauses consists of their opening words followed by "etc."; thus, the *clausulae ceteratae* are literally the "etcetera" phrases. To read them filled out, see Marta 1638. Cf. Farinacci 1612, Q. 153, no. 131; Q. 154, no. 28.

63. Mascardi 1608, Conc. 4.

64. Farinacci 1612, Q. 153, no. 142; Q. 153, nos. 133–45, are devoted to the notary's presumed guilt if the protocol was missing.

65. Fenzonio 1636, 69.

66. L. Sinisi 1997, 107, 121n. The style of the signature on what seventeenth-century Romans called a "public copy" varied from place to place but was highly formalized. In Rome, it included an affirmation of the act of rogating, signing, and publicizing as well as the notary's name. For an example of the publication signature of a notary of the auditor of the Camera,

see ASR, Notai AC, vol. 4526, 442v; for one by a Capitoline notary, see ASR, Ospedale del SS. Salvatore, reg. 209 (n.p., Giovanni Battista Ottaviani, 1632).

67. In Q. 6, nos. 99–129, Mascardi (1608) explains that the word *instrumentum* can refer broadly to anything used as a tool (no. 100) or, slightly more narrowly (as in *Digest* 22 .4. 1), to any kind of evidence (nos. 101–17). In its strictest sense, however, instrumentum is any document intended for future use in court (nos. 118–29). With this final functional definition, Mascardi does not discriminate between scriptura publica and scriptura privata, but he does capture a key cultural understanding underlying early modern thought about and use of notarial documents. For an illustration in real life, see ASR, TCrG, processi, 1631, vol. 264, 506v.

68. For interesting theoretical reflection on the notion of the copy, see Schwartz 1996, chap. 6.

69. This is the premise of the discussion by Farinacci 1612, Q. 154.

70. Farinacci 1612, Q. 154, no. 28. This, of course, was a frequent trope of legal commentators; see Mascardi 1608, Q. 6, nos. 108, 109; Fenzonio 1636, 167; Maclean 1992, 132.

71. Baldus is the first authority cited by Farinacci 1612, Q. 154.

72. In the interests of precision, it should be noted that this was not strictly speaking the case, because the imbreviatura included abbreviated versions of the technical clauses in the contract that were added after it was rogated with witnesses present.

73. Farinacci 1612, Q. 154, no. 28; Bartoli Langeli 2006, 13.

74. The brief "Tractatus de tabellionibus," long erroneously ascribed to Bartolus, was correctly identified in 1546 when republished by the Giunti firm in *Summa totius artis notariae*, 1:475v–78r, nos. 1–78, along with points by an earlier author (nos. 79–95). On the new practical tendency among late medieval jurists, beginning with Baldus's teacher Bartolus, see Stein 1999, 71–74, and Bellomo 1995, 211–14.

75. Baldus 1546, 1:477v–78r, nos. 62–65, 76. In a 1607 notarial handbook frequently cited by the Roman judge Fenzonio, Nicolaus Honthemius argued that the same exclusions that fell on the act of witnessing held for notaries, disqualifying the mentally unbalanced, Jews, and drunks; bk. 1, chaps. 10, 22. Honthemius did not exclude all *infames* but did ban the illiterate, not because they could not be witnesses, he said, but because the job of the notary was to write. See also Fenzonio 1636, 70.

76. Baldus 1599, 7:56r, rubrics 29–31.

77. For the notaries' view, expressed in their earliest extant corporate regulations, see ASC, Camera Capitolina, Cred. IV, vol. 88, 0147r–0148r.

78. Fenzonio 1636, 67, no. 113.

79. Baldus 1599, 7:56r.

80. Cited by Passeri 1615, 1. See also Baldus 1599, 7:57r.

81. Farinacci 1612, Q. 154, no. 99; Q. 155, no. 12, gives a more expansive interpretation, but Q. 157, no. 15, restricts it somewhat. See also Q. 156, no. 97. The jurists assume the language notaries will need to read and write is Latin.

82. Farinacci 1612, Q. 157, nos. 19–85; cf. Fenzonio 1636, 70, no. 34. Farinacci's discussion makes it clear that knowing the formulas is not considered intrinsic to the office of the notary, because it is a matter that pertains either to the nature of the contract, custom, the formu-

laries, or legal opinions (*consilia*). These four sources supply (and constrain) the contractual clauses that the notary ought to add in composing the imbreviatura.

83. Indeed, Giacomo Antonio Marta (1638, 1:166v) cites a series of judicial decisions holding that if the customary clauses were omitted by the notary, they were to be understood as expressed.

84. Farinacci 1612, Q. 157, no. 14.

85. Farinacci 1612, Q. 157, no. 17.

86. Farinacci 1612, Q. 157, no. 15. He also pointed out that presumptive evil intent deserved a milder punishment than proven malice; no. 18.

87. Mascardi 1608, Q. 4, nos. 2, 3. Montorzi 1984, 89, 90–93; Vallerani 2001, 682–83.

88. Mascardi 1608, Conc. 748–54. Waffling, Mascardi called fama both full proof and half proof in his introductory section (cf. Q. 4, no. 16 and Q. 11, no. 21) but chose not to discuss it with the other kinds of proof. Treating it in a series of ordinary entries (*conclusiones*) in his treatise, he indicated that at most it was a half proof in civil cases only.

89. Farinacci 1612, Q. 156, nos. 151, 154–56, 158.

90. Farinacci 1612, Q. 156, no. 155, citing Nevizzanus.

91. Farinacci 1612, Q. 154, no. 10; Q. 156, nos. 68, 74–75.

92. Baldus 1546, 1:477v, no. 57; Farinacci 1612, Q. 156, no. 97.

93. Mascardi 1608, Q. 6, nos. 63, 64.

94. Nussdorfer 2003, 105–9. Farinacci 1612, Q. 153, provides a thorough review of opinion on this topic to which he devotes an entire question.

95. Farinacci 1612, Q. 156, nos. 1–81. Interestingly, only at the end of this lengthy discussion does he report the opinions of some jurists who counsel the notary to make a new instrument rather than arouse suspicion by correcting an erroneous one (no. 81).

96. Baldus 1546, 1:477r–v, nos. 41, 42, 44, 46, 47, 49, 51–53, 55, 56, 58.

97. Mascardi 1608, Conc. 4, no. 16; Farinacci 1612, Q. 156, for example, nos. 7, 10, 16, 29, 66, 71, 80, 118. By this distinction, the formalities were deemed within the notary's sphere of action, while changes of substance were not.

98. Farinacci 1612, Q. 156, nos. 45, 56.

99. Farinacci 1612, Q. 156, nos. 38, 47, 69, 75, 76, 134, 135.

100. Mascardi among others cited in Farinacci 1612, Q. 156, no. 68; Fenzonio 1636, 73, no. 27.

101. Lori Sanfilippo 1987, 116n. Scambi could act as he did because, as we shall see in chapter 3, city law gave more latitude to notaries, and more privileges to public instruments, than did the jurists.

102. Nussdorfer 2003, 106. See, for example, Farinacci 1612, Q. 158, nos. 13, 153, 175.

103. Farinacci 1612, Q. 154, opening line; see also Q. 155, no. 73.

104. See the discussion of the *lex cornelia de falsis* in *Digest* 48.10.

105. Farinacci 1612, Q. 150, nos. 57, 114, 154, 239.

106. D'Amelia 2004, 231–65; Farinacci 1612, Qs. 150 to 164.

107. Farinacci 1612, Q. 155, no. 1.

108. Guicciardini 1970–81, 1:841, see also 762 (from his *Ricordi*). For this reason, he recommended keeping the *authenticum* of an instrument at home. I thank Thomas V. Cohen for this reference.

109. For some examples, see Feci 2004, 168–75.

110. Farinacci 1612, Q. 155.

111. Farinacci 1612, Q. 150, nos. 1–13.

112. Farinacci 1612, Q. 150, no. 5.

113. Mascardi 1608, Conc. 1097, no. 3.

114. The public quality of scriptura publica takes on yet another dimension when we learn that the notary could be compelled to show his clients' papers in an accusation of this kind; Farinacci 1612, Q. 150, no. 4.

115. Farinacci 1612, Q. 154, nos. 14, 28; Q. 157, no.1. Bartolus, however, thought the penalties for illicit contracts differed from those for falsum; Q. 154, nos. 15 and 16.

116. Farinacci 1612, Q. 154, nos. 92–103.

117. Farinacci 1612, Q. 154, nos. 52–91, especially nos. 54, 55, and 73. The discussion bleeds into another crime, that of simulating a contract, which Farinacci treats more fully in Q. 162. See also Abbiati 2000, 19.

118. Nussdorfer 1993, 109–10. Farinacci 1612, Q. 154, nos. 80–83, discusses the jurists' subtle views of the legal import of the notary's words "in my presence."

119. For some suggestions, see Farinacci 1612, Q. 154, no. 64. This precision and its ambivalence is mocked in the fourteenth-century tale by Franco Sacchetti in which guests confront an innkeeper who has given them dirty bed linen and demand white sheets. The innkeeper defends himself by saying that the sheets are not red or blue, and indeed they could not be any other color except white. His guests take his words in good spirit and agree, "[He] was right; he wasn't a notary writing that the sheets were a color other than white." Sacchetti 1996, 63–64, novella xix. I thank Thomas V. Cohen for this reference.

120. Farinacci 1612, Q. 150, nos. 19–51; Q. 155, nos. 1–16. His treatment is praised by Passeri 1615, bk. 1; see, for example, p. 51 where Farinacci is called the "king of jurists."

121. Farinacci 1612, Q. 150, no. 21. Farinacci recognized that ancient penalties also varied according to the status of the perpetrator; Q. 150, no. 19. Cf. *Digest* 48.10.1.13.

122. Farinacci 1612, Q. 150, no.24.

123. Farinacci 1612, Q. 155, no. 12.

124. Farinacci 1612, Q. 154, no. 113 (misprinted as 103).

125. *Statuta urbis* (1580), bk. 2, art. 48; Fenzonio 1636, 70. The procedure for *delicta publica* was *accusatio* by a public official. When therefore the 1580 municipal statutes authorize the chief justice (senator) to proceed by *inquisitio* in cases of false instruments, we see that the law kept open the possibility that the culprit was a private individual, which is confirmed by the penalties in art. 48; *Statuta urbis* (1580), bk. 2, art. 5.

126. 1363 statuti, bk. 2, art. 35.

127. *SPQR Statuta* (1519–23), bk. 2, arts. 35, 66 (1469); Rodocanachi 1901, 168n.

128. In ASR Inventory 282, which lists thousands of criminal cases in Rome's most extensive criminal jurisdiction, the Tribunale Criminale del Governatore (TCrG), I found about a dozen accusations of falsità against notaries between 1620 and 1638; there were at least as many against non-notaries. Of course, sometimes a close reading of trials will reveal notarial complicity even when the notary is not accused. Michele di Sivo is currently completing the inventory of the Tribunale Criminale del Senatore, which will add some cases to the

total, although by this period notaries were supposed to be tried in the governor's court (and its extension, the Curia di Borgo).

129. *Statuta urbis* (1580,) bk. 1, art. 29; Farinacci 1612, Q. 155, no. 15. A notary removed from a case who continued to interfere in it was also guilty of falsum; *Statuta urbis* (1580), bk. 1, art. 29.

130. ASR, TCrG, processi 1635, vol. 306, 301r; processi 1638, vol. 328, 1465r–v; processi 1640, vol. 361, 115r. I have focused here on notaries serving civil judges; for crimes notaries might commit in criminal proceedings, see Farinacci 1612, Q. 154, no. 107.

131. Born around 1594 in Civita Castellana, Paradisi was titleholder of Capitoline notarial office 7 from 1628 to 1658. For an incarceration (probably for debt) early in his tenure, see Nussdorfer 1993, 107.

132. Antonucci 1992, 297–303.

133. Antonucci 1992, 266–67. His words echo those of an earlier accuser; ASR, TCrG, processi, 1638, vol. 328, 1466r.

134. *Percosse* (blows), *ferita* (wounding), *truffa* (fraud), and even *adulterio* are some of the accusations leveled against notaries.

135. On two notable early modern Roman forgers, see Petrucci 1979 and D'Amelia 2007. On penalties, see also D'Amelia 2004, 256. For notaries who were fined, see ASR, TCrG, processi, 1624, vol. 190, 339r (150 scudi for fraudulent *società d'ufficio* contracts); TCrG, processi, 1631, vol. 264, 514v, 602r (200 scudi for altering the date on the copy [*fede*] of an instrument). For the law on women's contracts in Rome, see Feci 2004.

136. The opinions are reviewed by Passeri 1615, 30–51.

137. *Statuta urbis* 1580, bk. 2, art. 48.

138. *Digest* 1.3.37; Fenzonio 1636, 67.

139. Baldus 1599, 7:57r; Farinacci 1612, Q. 157, no. 73.

140. Mascardi 1608, Q. 14, no. 27.

141. Baldus 1599, 7:57r. Farinacci 1612, Q. 154, no. 68, reporting Baldus's opinion, added that a notary from Piacenza had used this defense.

142. Farinacci 1612, Q. 157, nos. 80–81 (for the more expansive formulation, nos. 19–20).

143. Farinacci 1612, Q. 157, no. 73.

144. Of course, notaries' fees were regulated.

145. Baldus 1546, 1:477r, no. 36. Fenzonio 1636, 72, no. 8, adds an approving citation to Honthemius's notarial handbook, which pointed out that the notary's right to his fee was stated in his sworn oath of office.

146. The legal premises in regard to venal Capitoline notarial offices are reviewed by Fenzonio, 1636, 55–56. As we shall see, from earliest times the notary's papers were considered his personal property and could be bequeathed to his heirs; Lori Sanfilippo 2008, 102–4.

147. Ascheri 1990, 66; Del Re 1993, 66. "[I]nter cives incolae et districtuales . . . servetur statutum urbis et ubi statutum non disponit servetur ius civile . . .," *SPQR Statuta* (1519–23), bk. 5, art. 37; cf. Fenzonio 1636, 173, no. 27. For a general view of the medieval period, see Sbriccoli 1969.

148. Farinacci 1612, Q. 157, no. 146.

149. Peto 1587; the first edition appeared in 1567. On the varieties of "execution" procedure in Italy, see Salvioli 1925–27, 3.2:626–736.

150. Fenzonio 1636, 168, nos. 22–23.

151. As Fenzonio 1636, 166–67, pointed out, municipal statutes pertained only to those who were subject to them, and in Rome, as we shall see in chapter 2, clerics were not. The Capitoline tribunal used inquisitional procedure; Di Sivo 1997, 284–85.

152. *Statuta urbis* (1580), bk. 1, art. 84. Technically, *recognitio* assumed an objection from the adverse party and was not necessary if no opposition was forthcoming, but according to Fenzonio 1636, 175, no. 8, the judge could require it even without an objection. Ago 1999b, 398.

153. *Statuta urbis* (1580), bk. 1, arts. 82, 83.

154. Fenzonio 1636, 168, nos. 19–20 (see also nos. 4, 13, 17).

155. Peto 1587, 132–33.

156. Fenzonio 1636, 168, nos. 22–23; 172, nos. 20–21 (misprinted 11).

157. Fenzonio 1636, 168–70; see, for example, "per quam minus laedatur ius commune," 170, no. 46.

158. Fenzonio 1636, 169, no. 43; 173, no. 23.

159. Fortunati 1996, 129; L. Sinisi 1997, 110n. On the importance of Rota decisions in the Papal States, see Ascheri 1989, 96.

160. Farinacci 1612, Q. 155, no. 43, Q. 158, no. 119; "Sacrae Rotae Romanae Decisiones quamplures quae vel ad materiam statutorum Urbis pertinent vel in Annot. alleganture," in Fenzonio 1636.

161. Feci 2004, 151, 214. For a look at the choice of evidence from the consumers' rather than the courts' perspective, see Ago 1999b.

Chapter 2 • *The Profession: Defining Urban Identities*

1. Noble 1984, 219; Frenz 1989, 63.

2. Petrucci 1958, 14; Carbonetti 1979; Lori Sanfilippo 2001, 6–7; Lori Sanfilippo 2008, 10–13, 101–3. In one of the miracles of Saint Francis narrated by Saint Bonaventure (d. 1274), the son of a notary in Rome was revived after jumping from a window; Saint Bonaventure 1941, 631–32.

3. Collins 2002, 204–40, discusses the significance of notaries in trecento Rome.

4. ASC, Camera Capitolina, Cred. IV, vol. 88, 0146v–0155r, now published by Lori Sanfilippo 2008. For surviving protocols (1344–1446) and their locations, see 2008, 143–48.

5. Lori Sanfilippo 2001b, 433–35. An organization of scribes in Rome dates back to the late twelfth century; Lori Sanfilippo 2008, 11–12. Collins (2002, 208) has found names of a thousand notaries from 1300 to 1400.

6. Lesellier 1933, 258. The situation is better for notaries serving the papal curia after 1507.

7. ASR, Biblioteca, Bandi, vol. 436 Campidoglio, edict of 16 December 1582; ASR, CCN, Registro delle congregazioni, vols. 1–13. I have not been able to substantiate Lori Sanfilippo's (2008, 7) claim of the existence of statutes from 1578; those published in the source she cites are a revision of statutes from 1618 and date from 1652; Statutes (1652) in *Statuta* (Rome, 1831), 40.

8. Biblioteca del Senato, Statuto ms. 517.

9. "On ne possède sur la commune romaine du XVe siècle ni les décisions du conseil

municipal, ni les listes des magistrats, ni les dossiers judiciares, ni les livres de dépenses et de recettes, bref tout ce qui a été conservé de manière presque naturelle dans les autres villes italiennes"; Esch 2000, 18, cited by Cherubini 2001, 159.

10. *The Life of Cola di Rienzo* 1975, 31. For population, see Rodocanachi 1901, 121; according to Brentano 1974, 13, this was down from perhaps 35,000 in the early 1200s.

11. Delumeau 1957–59, 1:280–81; Andrieux 1968, 11.

12. Sonnino 1994, 20; Canepari 2003, 36–47. See chapter 5 on the notarial work force in the seventeenth century.

13. Maire-Vigueur 1976; Stumpo 1985.

14. Delumeau 1961; Prodi 1982.

15. The 1363 statuti, which were published by Camillo Re, are the first to survive, though earlier versions seem to have existed; Collins 2002, 168n.

16. The phrase "notarios curiae Capitolii" appeared in legislation of 1521 that purported to reiterate measures dating from around 1508; *SPQR Statuta* (1519–23), bk. 5, art. 56.

17. Lesellier 1933, 258; San Martini Barrovecchio 1983, 3:850. Admittedly, these cases involved purchased offices, as we shall see later in this chapter.

18. For the fourteenth century, see the preface to the edition of the city statutes in Re 1880, and more recently, Maire-Vigueur 2001, Collins 2002, and Musto 2003. For the Renaissance and later periods, see Nussdorfer 1992.

19. Rodocanachi 1901, 110; Di Sivo 1998, 619.

20. Nussdorfer 1992, 95–105; for the fifteenth century, see Esposito 1994 and Modigliani 1994.

21. Collins 2002, 206, 211–12. See also Lori Sanfilippo 2001b, 434–35.

22. As we have noted, the late medieval sources on corporate life are extremely limited, but the fact that the only extant texts of regulations of Capitoline notaries that have come down to us before 1582 are attached to municipal legislation, in either manuscript or print, is suggestive. See ASC, Camera Capitolina, Cred. IV, vol. 88, 0146v–0155r and *SPQR Statuta* (1519–23), books 3, 4, and 5. Of course, the popes also made laws affecting Capitoline notaries, discussed in detail in chapter 3.

23. Collins 2002, 168; Pavan 1996, 322; Lori Sanfilippo 2001b, 450–52. By the seventeenth century their involvement was rare; Nussdorfer 1992, 76n, 80n.

24. Del Re 1954, 24–25; 1993, 39–40. The term *Camera* referred to the Apostolic Camera, the papacy's chief financial and economic bureau. For a survey of relevant papal institutions, see Nussdorfer 1992, 45–53.

25. For a helpful overview that carries the analysis into the seventeenth century, see Fosi 2007, 21–32.

26. Del Re 1993, 39–40.

27. Del Re 1972, 11.

28. Del Re 1954, 27.

29. According to Camerano 1997, 44–47, this was the effect of Pope Sixtus IV's important jurisdictional legislation of 1473. Sixtus IV also gave the governor of Rome jurisdiction over notaries of all criminal courts, which laid the foundation for his power eventually to decide criminal cases brought against most notaries (apart from those serving the auditor of the Camera).

30. De Luca 1673, bk. 15, pt. 3, ch. 40. Fosi 1989, 62; see also the series in ASR, Notai del Consolato dei Fiorentini.

31. Lori Sanfilippo 2001b, 442; 2008, 28. To be sure, elsewhere in Italy there was considerable variation in a notary's training, ranging from apprenticing to attending several years of university lectures; Martines 1980, 280.

32. *SPQR Statuta* (1519–23), bk. 5, art. 43.

33. *Statuta urbis* (1580), bk. 1, art. 32.

34. Orlandelli (1965) traces the evolution of the genre, which culminated in Rolandino dei Passeggeri's version of c. 1250, still authoritative in the early modern period.

35. Barraclough 1934, 20–24. The first printed *Formularium instrumentorum ad usum Romanae Curiae* came out under Sixtus IV in 1474; L. Sinisi 1997, 23–27.

36. L. Sinisi 1997, 445–58.

37. Luca Peto [Lucas Paetus], *De iudiciaria formula Capitolini Fori,* was published in Rome in 1567 and 1578 and in a revised version in 1587, 1610, and 1625. As mentioned, Peto was also largely responsible for revising the text of the city statutes of 1580; Del Re 1986, 319–22. For more on his work, see chapter 3.

38. L. Sinisi (1997) provides a good deal of information about manuscript formularies in early modern Genoa. The 1494 inventory of a Roman notary's library includes a tantalizing reference to a "Pratica"; Spotti Tantillo 1975, 90, cited by Feci 2004, 125. Prospero Farinacci cited a manuscript notarial formulary in his treatise, *De falsitate* 1612, Q. 156, nos. 33, 37. A six-page manuscript of the formulas used in judicial acts by the notaries of the tribunal of the Rota is found in ASR, Camerale II, Notariato, b. 3 (n.p. but document dated 22 May 1703).

39. Lori Sanfilippo 2001b, 439. Usage could be quite alert to changing political conditions; Lori Sanfilippo 2008, 25.

40. Lori Sanfilippo 2001b, 439–40.

41. Admitting that this was an unusual practice, Corbo (1984, 52–53) points out that in general in the fourteenth and fifteenth centuries Capitoline notaries derived their powers from the emperor, not the pope.

42. San Martini Barrovecchio 1983, 3:851n.

43. ASV, Misc. Arm. IV–V, vol. 84, no. 178, edict of 12 September 1588. A formulary widely used in the papal Curia includes the creation of notaries by counts or viscounts palatine; *Formularium instrumentorum* 1589, 196–201. On this text, see L. Sinisi 1997, 26–27. For cases of investiture of Capitoline notaries by counts palatine in 1542 and 1567, see Verdi 2005, 460n.

44. For an example, see appendix C. For other examples, see ASR, 30 NC, uff. 11 (Saravezzio) 1610, pt. 2, 92 r–v, 343 r–v, 795 r–v. In these cases the official is also a *referendarius,* so highly placed in curial service.

45. Petrucci 1958, doc. no. 82; San Martini Barrovecchio 1983, 3:858.

46. *Decreta* 1679, 9. See also chapter 6.

47. The act, "datio penne et calamari [calamaio]," is discussed by Corbo 1984, 52–53.

48. Rub. 34, ASC, Camera Capitolina, Cred. IV, vol. 88, 0148v: "examinetur et repertus fuerit bonus grammaticus et sequutus fuerit aliquem procuratem [*sic*] vel praticam tabellionatus habuerit per unum annum ad minus ac aliam artem mechanicam non exercuerit." Rub.

37 clarifies that they must have abandoned manual labor for four years (0149r). The text, discussed in the next note, dates to 1446, although it may have earlier roots.

49. 1363 statuti, bk. 3, art. 112 (110). The description is contained in a manuscript of revisions (*reformationes*) to an earlier (lost) set of statutes for the college of notaries in ASC, Camera Capitolina, Cred. IV, vol. 88, 0146v–0155r, now published by Lori Sanfilippo 2008.

50. Rubb. 37, 42, ASC, Camera Capitolina, Cred. IV, vol. 88, 0149r, 0150v. Notaries were not allowed to enter taverns or gamble (rub. 46, 0151v). They could not matriculate if they were infamis (rub. 61, 0155r).

51. Rub. 36, ASC, Camera Capitolina, Cred. IV, vol. 88, 0149r.

52. Rubb. 34, 35, ASC, Camera Capitolina, Cred. IV, vol. 88, 0148v.

53. Lesellier 1933, 263n; Pavan 1991; see also *Statuta urbis* (1580), bk. 3, art. 57.

54. Barraclough (1934, 13–19, 24–27) describes the rising importance of notaries in the Curia while the papacy was still in Avignon. They were needed not only for the disposition of ecclesiastical benefices but also for the full range of instruments used by individual officials and churchmen.

55. Lori Sanfilippo 1990, 32. On the general phenomenon, see Partner 1990. For the career of a German-born Capitoline notary active from 1467 to 1494, see Esch 2001.

56. Lesellier 1933, 252; Barraclough 1934, 24. According to Barraclough (1934, 19), earlier in Sixtus's pontificate the notaries of the Rota, the highest papal appeals court, were the first to be organized along these lines in 1477. Within the Curia, the introduction of venality was a subtle process that built, for example, on the practice by judges of selling the office of their *attuarius* and sharing the fees the court notary subsequently collected (ibid., 18–19).

57. Lesellier 1933, 253–55; Barraclough 1934, 25; Grisar 1964, 267–71. The founding legislation, *Sicut prudens*, appeared on 1 and 13 December 1507; *Bullarium* 1857–72, 5:458–66.

58. *Bullarium* 1857–72, 5:462, no. 10: "Possitque collegium ipsum per eorum correctores et clericos deputandos per eum, creare notarios undecumque venientes, cuiuscumque nationis, et creatos per alios, exceptis officialibus perpetuis, volentes tabellionatus officium in Urbe et districtu eius exercere, examinare; et repertos insufficientes ab exercitio dicti officii perpetuo vel ad tempus suspendere vel privare; et idoneos approbare et in matricula et archivio describere, . . ." On the Archive of the Roman Curia, see chapter 4.

59. The price of 1 of the 101 offices in the College of Scriptors ranged between 1,125 and 1,500 scudi during the sixteenth century, while a corrector's office cost somewhat more; San Martini Barrovecchio 1983, 3:847n. For an example of terminological conflation in 1619, see Verdi 2005, 460n.

60. For the act of investiture and oath of a curial notary from Metz in 1532, see San Martini Barrovecchio 1983, 3:868–69.

61. Lesellier 1933, 260; San Martini Barrovecchio 1983, 3:857.

62. Lesellier 1933, 260. According to Lesellier, the four extant matriculation registers for the sixteenth century cover the following years: 1507–19, 1539–49, 1549–61, 1577–87. At least four others are missing.

63. Lesellier 1933, 263–64.

64. One way to find out would be to do the painstaking kind of work carried out by Lori Sanfilippo (2001b) on the fourteenth century on the much larger body of sources available for

the sixteenth century. Suggestive in this connection is research on notarial protocols during the aftermath of the Sack of Rome (May 1527–February 1528), which identified approximately fifty notaries still working in the city; Esposito and Vaquero Piñeiro 2005, 129.

65. *Bullarium* 1857–72, 5:540. The archival regulations are discussed in chapter 4.

66. A senator's order from around 1508 refers to the "matricula Conservatorum Camer[a] Urbis;" *SPQR Statuta* (1519–23), bk. 5, art. 56. For the matriculation of Luca Antonio Butii in 1553, see Verdi 2005, 454; this evidence indicates that matriculation carried an attachment to a particular rione of Rome. The edict of 23 December 1562 giving the archivist the duty of keeping the "matricula Capitolij" implies that the secretary of the conservators was already doing this. The fee to be registered in the book was three giulii; ASR, Biblioteca, Bandi, vol. 2, no. 164. In the 1580 edition of the city statutes, the secretary of the conservators alone had the responsibility for entering newly approved notaries in the "matricula notariorum urbis"; *Statuta urbis* (1580), bk. 1, art. 32. If a notary needed proof of his matriculation, the secretary was to provide it for no more than one giulio; *Statuta urbis* (1580), bk. 3, art. 103.

67. *Statuta urbis* (1580), bk. 1, art. 32.

68. Berengo and Diaz 1975, 162.

69. *Statuta urbis* (1580), bk. 1, art. 32. There is evidence from 1562, however, that the Capitoline notaries did not acknowledge the monopoly over foreign notaries implied by the papal matriculation process. We find this statement in the edict establishing the Archivio Capitolino: "considerato anco & visto che di essi notai capitolini & d'altri ne sono stati, e sono di molti forastieri." ASR, Biblioteca, Bandi, vol. 2, no. 164.

70. *Statuta urbis* (1580), bk. 3, art. 57. Pavan (1991, 39) says that judges and notaries frequently sought this status.

71. He petitioned in 1587; Pavan 1991, 39.

72. The names of the notaries, active from the fourteenth to the early seventeenth century, whose protocols were deposited in the archive, are listed in François 1886, 36–79. In addition, protocols of pre-1586 Capitoline notaries may sometimes be found in the holdings of the post-1586 ASR series called Thirty Capitoline Notaries (30 NC), as is revealed by the new inventories of each office; Verdi 2005, 443.

73. Lori Sanfilippo 2001b, 435–36. As mentioned previously, there are twelfth-century references to a prior and camerarius of the "scrinarium urbis," professional scribes from whom the notaries may have descended (ibid., 436).

74. 1363 statuti, bk. 1, art. 127 (1).

75. 1363 statuti, bk. 1, art. 114.

76. 1363 statuti, bk. 1, art. 37. In Roman law, a legal contract had to be entered freely, not coerced.

77. ASC, Camera Capitolina, Cred. IV, vol. 88, 0146v–0155r; Lanconelli 1983, 315–16; Pavan 1996, 326–27. The city statutes of 1469 were reprinted as book 3 of a six-volume edition issued between 1519 and 1523; *SPQR Statuta* (1519–23). Within book 3, arts. 282 to 317 are regulations concerning notaries. These thirty-five articles consist entirely of material drawn from the 1363 city statutes and the 1446 revisions to the notarial college statutes; they contain nothing later than the 1446 text.

78. *Statuta urbis* (1580), bk. 1, art. 35.

79. A papal official ordered that the notaries' revisions be inserted in the municipal

statutes in 1446, and in 1469 civic officials attempted to assure their wider distribution among notaries of the rioni; Lori Sanfilippo 2008, 18, 60.

80. Martines 1968, 18; Costamagna 1970, ch. 5; Liva 1979, ch. 5; *La società dei notai di Bologna* 1988; Feci 2004, 42.

81. Rub. 29, ASC, Camera Capitolina, Cred. IV, vol. 88, 0147r–0148r. On Andrea Santacroce, who held many civic offices, see Esposito 1981.

82. ASC, Camera Capitolina, Cred. IV, vol. 88, 0148r: "ad componendum mores dicti officii tabellionatus."

83. D'Addario 1984, 307.

84. I use the term senator's palace because that is the name by which the building is best known today, but contemporary sources always refer to it as the "Capitoline palace."

85. Rub. 31, ASC, Camera Capitolina, Cred. IV, vol. 88, 0148r.

86. Rub. 63, ASC, Camera Capitolina, Cred. IV, vol. 88, 0155r.

87. Rubb. 32 and 33, ASC, Camera Capitolina, Cred. IV, vol. 88, 0148v.

88. Rub. 34, ASC, Camera Capitolina, Cred. IV, vol. 88, 0148v.

89. Rub. 36, ASC, Camera Capitolina, Cred. IV, vol. 88, 0149r. In addition to those named here, there was also a *scriptor* and perhaps other officials.

90. Rub. 43, ASC, Camera Capitolina, Cred. IV, vol. 88, 0151r. From rub. 44 we also learn that the actuary notaries attached much importance to the observation by judges of a prescribed order in the assignment of cases. See chapter 3, section on judicial acts.

91. Rub. 53, ASC, Camera Capitolina, Cred. IV, vol. 88, 0152v. See chapter 3, section on business acts.

92. Rub. 62, ASC, Camera Capitolina, Cred. IV, vol. 88, 0155r. The fine was fifty ducats. Heirs who were notaries could keep the locked chests at home; the others were supposed to go to the sacristy of the Aracoeli. See chapter 4.

93. It is to be hoped that research in the notarial protocols themselves, which has been so useful for shedding light on the civic administration of Rome during the period when it left few other records, will eventually turn up more information on the activities of the pre-1586 Capitoline notaries and their college. Evidence that the gentlemen of the Colonna rione chose Melchiorre Vola, who would become titleholder of Capitoline office 13 after 1586, as their notary in 1585 is a promising case in point; Verdi (2005), 453. The relationship between Capitoline notaries and particular districts is attested in sixteenth-century sources, but we know very little about its mechanisms and meanings.

94. In 1521 Francisco Maccio and Hieronymo Riccio are named as correctors, Jacobo Lyrico as *prefectus*, and Antonio Leonio simply as consistorial advocate, which indicated membership in Rome's college of judges but who may also have been proconsul; *SPQR Statuta* (1519–23), bk. 5, 2r. On the edict of the proconsuls and correctors of 16 December 1582, Pietrus Sanctus Butius and Galdinus Burlaschinus are named as correctors, Giovanni Battista Bovius as *advocatus* and proconsul, and Cesar Marsilius as *advocatus concistorialis* and proconsul; ASR, Biblioteca, Bandi, Campidoglio, vol. 436. Compare these chance discoveries with the officials of Bologna's notarial college who were recorded by Giovanni Niccolò Pasquali Alidosi in a publication of 1616.

95. *SPQR Statuta* (1519–23), bk. 5, art. 56.

96. *Bullarium* 1857–72, vol. 7, p. 222, no. 67. Actuary notaries may have had to put down

a deposit, which was collected by the correctors, before taking their seats at the bench. The legislation, *Cum ab ipso*, dated 30 June 1562, is discussed in chapter 3 in the section on judicial acts.

97. ASR, Biblioteca, Bandi, vol. 2, no. 164, arts. 1, 5, 6, 11. See also chapter 4.

98. *SPQR Statuta* (1519–23), bk. 4, I, art. 32.

99. "Et quia multi impetraverunt privilegia de exe[m]plandis et transumptandis instrumentis maxime ex prothocollis et abbreviaturis notariorum mortu[or]um non observata solemnitate requisita ac matura cognitione ex forma statutorum urbis unde multa inconvenientia nascuntur maxime multa auctenticantur qu. non merentur auctenticari." *SPQR Statuta* (1519–23), bk. 5, art. 39.

100. ASV, Misc. Arm. IV–V, vol. 45, 82r, undated motu proprio of Julius III (1550–55).

101. Heirs were to have "integra la tassa ordinaria"; ASR, Biblioteca, Bandi, vol. 2, no. 164 (23 December 1562). See chapter 4 for a possible explanation of this policy.

102. The 1580 legislation is discussed in chapters 3 and 4. See also ASR, Biblioteca, Bandi, Campidoglio, vol. 436, edict of 16 December 1582, art. 5.

103. *Statuta urbis* (1580), bk. 1, art. 36 (and art. 35 for the distribution of fees).

104. The senator continued as chief magistrate with both civil and criminal jurisdiction, but the six judges who worked under him were now reduced to four. Those who remained were one criminal judge, one appeals judge, and two civil judges called collaterali. *Statuta urbis* (1580), bk. 1, arts. 3, 4, 5, 6, 10.

105. *Statuta urbis* (1580), bk. 1, art. 23.

106. *Statuta urbis* (1580), bk. 1, art. 37. Although the statutes did not give figures, an edict of 16 December 1582 named two proconsuls and two correctors; ASR, Biblioteca, Bandi, Campidoglio, vol. 436.

107. Rubb. 32 and 33, ASC, Camera Capitolina, Cred. IV, vol. 88, 0148v; *Statuta urbis* (1580), bk. 1, arts. 37 and 38. Even in 1446 the proconsuls' jurisdiction had not extended to serious crimes, however, such as the charge of falsum; the maximum penalty they could impose was a fine of five gold ducats, raised to twenty-five gold ducats in 1580.

108. *Statuta urbis* (1580), bk. 1, art. 26.

109. *Statuta urbis* (1580), bk. 1, art. 21.

110. *Statuta urbis* (1580), bk. 1, art. 35. See chapter 4, section on Archivio Capitolino.

111. ASR, Biblioteca, Bandi, Campidoglio, vol. 436.

112. To my knowledge, this is the first reference to an external mechanism for determining the qualifications of sostituti, who were formally invested notaries working as employees in a notarial office. Both city and papal legislation had long forbidden notaries in the Capitoline courts from using sostituti to perform their judicial duties, most recently in the *Statuta urbis* (1580), bk. 1, art. 22. Four of the sixteen articles in the 1582 edict mention the sostituti in court contexts, however, and the decision to have the correctors examine "the quality of their persons" seems a concession to the fact that they were indeed performing such duties.

113. *Statuta urbis* (1580), bk. 1, art. 31.

114. For the elaborate stamped symbol, see ASR, 30 NC, uff. 11 (Saravezzio) 1584, n.p. (penciled pagination f. 30r).

115. *Erectio* (1586) in *Statuta* (Rome, 1831), 41–53. For additional locations, see Comune di Roma 1920–58, 1:83, no. 511.

116. Matriculation in the Capitoline list ended, but it remained possible to matriculate as a curial notary in the Archive of the Roman Curia.

117. For the rumors, see Rodocanachi 1901, 315–16; for the discussion in several meetings of the civic councils, see ASC, Camera Capitolina, Cred. I, vol. 29, 0015r, 0016v, 0019r, 0039v, 0048r, 0064r. See also M. Franceschini 1991; San Martini Barrovecchio 1992.

118. Piola Caselli 1991, 121. The office of scriptor of apostolic letters had been sold since the time of Martin V, but curial venality spread very rapidly between 1470 and 1490; Partner 1990, 12, 16. See also Delumeau 1957–59, 2:777. Sixtus V stood out among the popes for the zeal with which he laid hands on any and all assets that could be sold to benefit the Apostolic Camera; Feci 2004, 110.

119. Rodocanachi 1901, 202, 212–13.

120. Grisar 1964, 276. "Criminal notaries" were those who kept the records of criminal proceedings. This legislation excluded Rome and Bologna, as was customary; ASV, Misc, Arm. IV–V, vol. 45, 26v–27r. It is worth noting that in contrast to the popes, French monarchs from the sixteenth century on sought to separate notaries and court officials, although both sets of offices were sold; Dolan 1998, 183.

121. For this legislation *Cum ab ipso*, dated 30 June 1562, see *Bullarium* 1857–72, 7:222, especially no. 64.

122. Del Re 1970. The literature on the pontificate of Sixtus V is vast; for an orientation, see the references in Spezzaferro and Tittoni 1991 and Fosi 1993.

123. ASV, Misc. Arm. IV–V, vol. 84, edict of 12 September 1588. Scoccianti 1992, 187–99. See chapter 4. On 1 August 1588 Sixtus had created the post of prefect of the archives, to be held by a high curial prelate (one of the Chierici di Camera), with the task of overseeing the new public archives of the Papal States; *Enchiridion* 1966, 22–23.

124. Erectio (1586) in *Statuta* (Rome, 1831), 42–43. There is evidence that notaries were assigned to specific judges (collaterali) before 1586; see the preface to the inventory quoted by Trasselli 1936b, 94. The carpenters' confraternity records of 2 February 1584 describe Capitoline notary Ottaviano Saravezzio as "notaro del 2.o coll. di Campidoglio"; Paul Anderson, art historian, electronic communication to Peter Lukehart, art historian, 19 December 2005.

125. *Statuta urbis* (1580), bk. 1, art. 9.

126. Erectio (1586) in *Statuta* (Rome, 1831), 42–44.

127. Erectio (1586) in *Statuta* (Rome, 1831), 45; Guasco 1919a, 99–101. See also chapter 4.

128. This probably explains the consignment of papers to the archive in 1587 and 1613, quoted by Trasselli 1936b, 94; see also Verdi 2005, 427, 442, 450.

129. Erectio (1586) in *Statuta* (Rome, 1831), 44–45. Transunti of judicial acts had not figured in previous legislation, and it is unclear what sort of demand there was for these documents. In theory, clients might have wanted copies of judicial sentences from the manuali of deceased notaries, though, if extant records are any indicator, sentences seem rarely to have been preserved and may have been infrequently issued.

130. In reality, the college was not able to gain possession of this office until 1728; Guasco 1919a, 99.

131. Erectio (1586) in *Statuta* (Rome, 1831), 47–48. See chapter 3, section on judicial acts.

132. Erectio (1586) in *Statuta* (Rome, 1831), 43, 48. For a clear definition of these terms, see Rietbergen 1983, 336.

133. Guasco 1919a, 99.

134. ASC, Camera Capitolina, Cred. VI, vol. 59, 310r–11v. The 1591 petition to the conservators from the Guerrini family gives an unusual insight into the way Capitoline notarial offices were transferred before and after the onset of venality. Capitoline notary Alexander Guerrini was active between 1553 and 1578. After his death in 1578 Pope Gregory XIII granted his office to his son Carlo, who intended to use it as a dowry for Carlo's sister. Carlo died in 1585. When Sixtus sold the thirty Capitoline offices the following year, this one was purchased by Carlo's brother Giovanni Martino Guerrini for the set price of five hundred scudi. In their petition, his heirs, none of whom were apparently notaries, seek the conservators' consent to retain the vacabile part of the office, which they argue is still being used to support their aunt. It was this office, number 18 in the modern archival numeration, that would eventually become the property of Lorenzo Bonincontro, whose career is discussed in chapter 5.

135. "Reductio ad perpetuitatem officiorum DD. Notariorum Collegii Curiae Capitolii," in *Statuta* (Rome, 1831), 54–62.

136. The "regaliis" in this case was a payment of five scudi d'oro; ASV, Fondo Confalonieri, vol. 6, 142 r.

137. "Sacrae Rotae Romanae Decisiones" in Fenzonio 1636, 18 (Decision XIV). For the notaries' possible role in this decision, see ASR, CCN, Registro delle congregazioni, Libro della massa, vol. 10, n.p. (December 1619).

138. Guasco 1919a, 106.

139. "Reductio" in *Statuta* (Rome, 1831), 56. The pope seems to have thought it would be useful to the municipality to have an "annual, certain, and perpetual" fund for building repairs, and indeed civic officials complained bitterly when payments finally ceased in 1847; Guasco 1919a, 106.

140. This is an inference based on the massa records between 1589 and 1607. After years of pronounced variation in December 1604, thirteen of the thirty Capitoline notaries paid in 1.50 scudi and the rest paid a higher amount. The stable pattern continued; in October 1606 the entry for a massa payment by "successor [to] Cardine" of 44.5 baiocchi (rather than 150) is accompanied by the notation "more antiqua." ASR, CCN, Registro delle congregazioni, Libro della massa, vol. 9, n.p.

141. "Reductio" in *Statuta* (Rome, 1831), 59. We recall that the college had the right to collect from individual members one-fourth of the fees from their judicial acts and from transunti of instruments held in their offices.

142. "Super expeditione titulorum" in *Statuta* (Rome, 1831), 62–66.

143. ASR, CCN, Registro delle congregazioni, Libro della massa, vol. 10 (November 1617).

144. "Super expeditione titulorum" in *Statuta* (Rome, 1831), 64.

145. San Martini Barrovecchio 1983, 3:850.

146. *Bullarium* 1857–72, 12:86, no. 2. Citing this passage, the college later claimed the right to investigate the moral and technical qualifications of administrators or lessors of offices and decide on their suitability; Statutes (1652) in *Statuta* (Rome, 1831), 21–22.

147. This was just the distinction underlined by Fenzonio (1636, 56) when citing the Rota's decision—"officij titulus potest esse penes unum & dominium penes alium." Undoubt-

edly, this is why it is to this day much easier to find out which notary headed a Capitoline office than who owned it.

148. Senato, Statuto ms. 517, 18r. The admission fee was divided up and distributed by seniority to those attending the meeting, as we see from a sheet at the end of vol. 8 (1588–98) of ASR, CCN, Registro delle congregazioni, Libro della massa, n.p.

149. Nonetheless there is evidence that owners did apply to the Capitoline judges for approval to lease these offices or transfer them by sale or resignation. See, for example, the transfer of office 37 to Lorenzo Balducci after a *mandato* from the second collaterale, dated 12 February 1618, in ASR, CCN, Registro delle congregazioni, Libro della massa, vol. 10, copy inserted after expenses for September 1618. Another example is found in ASC, Protonotaro del Senatore, sez. I, Atti del notaro dei Conservatori, vol. 1, 4r–5v.

150. Senato, Statuto ms. 517, 17v. Possibly motivated by Paul V's warning of the previous year, these are a revision of a lost text.

151. Statutes (1652) in *Statuta* (Rome, 1831), 39.

152. Statutes (1652) in *Statuta* (Rome, 1831), 29.

153. See the series of letters patent in ASC, Camera Capitolina, Cred. XI, vols. 19 and 20; see also the description of the documentation submitted by Protogine Delfino as he sought office 2 in ASR, CCN, Registro delle congregazioni, Libro della massa, vol. 10 (November and December 1618).

154. For some examples, see ASR, CCN, Registro delle congregazioni, Libro della massa, vol. 11 (1635–38), 92v, 95v.

155. Statutes (1652) in *Statuta* (Rome, 1831), 36.

156. The 1618 notarial statutes are in Biblioteca del Senato, Statuti, ms. 517. Payments for formal copies of the statutes were recorded in 1618, but otherwise we have no information about the timing and process of drafting them; ASR, CCN, Registro delle congregazioni, Libro della massa, vol. 10, n.p. (August and October 1618). The first printed edition, which has no publication information but must be after 1711, is entitled *Statuta venerabilis Collegii D.D. Notariorum Curiae Capitolii eorumque facultates et privilegia* [1711?]; Biblioteca del Senato, Statuti, no. 1221. In 1831 the Apostolic Camera republished the earlier text under the same title. The only changes were adding a new dedication and replacing p. 71 (the order to be observed by the thirty Capitoline notaries in performing certain duties for the auditor of the Segnatura di Giustizia, as of 1710) with a nine-page listing of the locations of the thirty notarial offices and the names of their titleholders from 1585 (*sic*) to 1831.

157. The citation is ASR, CCN, Registro delle congregazioni. The series consists of three types of record: vol. 1 sindici (1667–1730); vols. 2–7 meetings (1667–1749, 1814–33); vols. 8–13 massa accounts (1588–1681 with lacunae).

158. ASR, CCN, Registro delle congregazioni, Libro della massa, vol. 8 (1588–98), vol. 9 (1598–1607), vol. 10 (1615–20), vol. 11 (1635–38), vol. 12 (1642–44), vol. 13 (1667–81).

159. This was a statutory requirement in both 1618 and 1652; see also the payment of one scudo to Giovanni de Amici, secretary of the college in February 1638, "for a volume in which to write the decisions of the meetings." ASR, CCN, Registro delle congregazioni, Libro della massa, vol. 11, 96r.

160. Erectio (1586) in *Statuta* (Rome, 1831), 44.

161. In July 1591 there is an entry of five scudi "p[er] li statuti p[er] il Bovio"; ASR, CCN,

Registro delle congregazioni, Libro della massa, vol. 8, 49r. I have been unable to identify either il Bovio or the *statuti* in question. In August 1618 the accounts record a payment for parchment given "a quello che rescrisse [copied] li statuti del Collegio"; it is just possible, therefore, that they had been composed earlier. ASR, CCN, Registro delle congregazioni, Libro della massa, vol. 10, n.p. (August 1618).

162. ASR, CCN, Registro delle congregazioni, Libro della massa, vol. 8, 38r–v (January 1591). Gregory XIV was elected in December 1590.

163. Guasco 1919a, 100.

164. In May 1593 the notaries had appealed to a papal official, perhaps the prefect of the archives, in connection with the archive; ASR, CCN, Registro delle congregazioni, Libro della massa, vol. 8, n.p. (under date). ASR, CCN, Registro delle congregazioni, Libro della massa, vol. 9, n.p. (under May and June 1602). Guasco 1919a, 100–101. These reduced rates, for so-called simple copies, are discussed in more detail in chapter 3.

165. Nussdorfer 1992, 117.

166. ASR, CCN, Registro delle congregazioni, Libro della massa, vol. 8, 16v, 29r, 35r, and after 1592 when pagination ceases under the following dates, January and April 1596; ibid., vol. 9, under May, July, September, and October 1606; July and December 1607.

167. On the office of protonotary of the senator, see *Statuta urbis* (1580), bk. 1, art. 20. In rare detail, the massa accounts record payment of 2.60 scudi for a forty-two-page extractus in the lawsuit with the protonotary; ASR, CCN, Registro delle congregazioni, Libro della massa, vol. 9, n.p. (under October 1606).

168. ASR, CCN, Registro delle congregazioni, Libro della massa, vol. 8, 16v, 18v, 54v (later in volume under January and April 1596); vol. 9, n.p. (under December 1602, March 1604, December 1606, June and July 1607).

169. ASR, CCN, Registro delle congregazioni, Libro della massa, vol. 8, n.p. (under April 1596); vol. 9, n.p. (under December 1606, January and April 1607).

170. ASR, CCN, Registro delle congregazioni, Libro della massa, vol. 8, n.p. (under February 1596).

171. ASR, CCN, Registro delle congregazioni, Libro della massa, vol. 8, n.p. (under October 1594, October 1595, October 1596). The existence of a secretary's office is especially significant because it implies that the fledgling organization held meetings and kept records of those meetings (now lost). An entry in the massa accounts indicates that transunti fees were processed by the secretary (under October 1594).

172. ASR, CCN, Registro delle congregazioni, Libro della massa, vol. 9, n.p. (under May and June 1602).

173. On the compulsory minimum contribution, see the previous section of this chapter.

174. Indeed, they had paid in thirty-nine scudi in August 1604, though in September the much higher figure of seventy scudi (including some transunti) just before the new policy seems to have been implemented; ASR, CCN, Registro delle congregazioni, Libro della massa, vol. 9, n.p., sub datam. Massa were not always entered monthly. Because they were collected and recorded by a different mensario virtually every month, recording practices varied considerably, and it is difficult to get a consistent body of massa income data. In the five-year period 1589 to 1593, there are two entries for 1589, six for 1590, five for 1591, two for 1592, and seven for 1593. ASR, CCN, Registro delle congregazioni, Libro della massa, vol. 8,

n.p., sub datam. However, they do reveal that while average intake ranged from fifteen to forty-five scudi a month, an intake of thirty-three to thirty-six scudi was not uncommon. Thus, setting a minimum of forty-five scudi a month meant new sacrifices, at least for some Capitoline notaries.

175. ASR, CCN, Registro delle congregazioni, Libro della massa, vol. 9, n.p. (under November 1604; June, October, and December 1605).

176. ASR, CCN, Registro delle congregazioni, Libro della massa, vol. 9, n.p. (under February, March, and June 1606).

177. Vol. 9 of the "libro della massa" ends in 1607 and vol. 10 begins in 1615. In the summer of 1605 the Capitoline notaries appear to have bought the vacabile portion of office 17 for six hundred scudi from his heirs after the death of the titleholder, Camillo Argenti. References to an instrument of *donatio*, however, slightly obscure the nature of the transaction, which took some time to complete. ASR, CCN, Registro delle congregazioni, Libro della massa, vol. 9, n.p. (under February, July, August, September 1605, and February 1607).

178. This is the first recorded payment for such masses, which would have been celebrated during the annual observance of the feast of their patron Saint Luke; ASR, CCN, Registro delle congregazioni, Libro della massa, vol. 9, n.p. (under October 1606).

179. ASR, CCN, Registro delle congregazioni, Libro della massa, vol. 10 (1615–20), n.p. (under August and October 1618). The massa accounts mention at least three copies; ibid., n.p. (under November 1618 and March 1619).

180. Senato, Statuto ms. 517, 26r. The first collaterale was Marco Antonio Gozzadini, perhaps the same man who would become cardinal in 1621, and the second, Federico Monaldensi.

181. The decano sat at the head of the table with the mensario on his right and the secretary on his left, while the rest of the notaries sat by order of their admission into the college; Senato, Statuto ms. 517, 16rv. Statutes (1652) in *Statuta* (Rome, 1831), 6, 8. As mentioned, no contemporary manuscript or edition of the 1652 statutes, the final version emanating from the Capitoline notaries, exists.

182. As we recall, massa were levied on specific judicial acts, not business acts, produced by the Capitoline notaries. The *liber expeditionum* or *libro delle spedizioni* was the designated registry of payments for these documents. While evidence of actual practice is scarce, it does support the notion that notaries kept a record of the acts for which they owed massa; ASR, TCrG, processi, 1624, vol. 190, 373v (testimony of 1616). It also indicates that the mensario routinely reviewed these volumes; see his entry for November 1605, "D. Cardinus [office 18] detulit librum sine massa." ASR, CCN, Registro delle congregazioni, Libro della massa, vol. 9, n.p. (November 1605).

183. ASR, CCN, Registro delle congregazioni, Libro della massa, vol. 11 (1635–38). (We recall that no meeting minutes survive before 1667.) The amount they received in the 1630s ranged from thirty to fifty baiocchi. The fifteen-scudi admission fee paid by new notaries was also shared exclusively by those at the meeting in which it was delivered.

184. ASR, CCN, Registro delle congregazioni, Libro della massa, vol. 10, n.p. (March 1619). The 1652 statutes defined a quorum for general meetings as fifteen; for "private meetings," which are referred to in accounts and statutes but not otherwise described, six notaries constituted a quorum; Statutes (1652) in *Statuta* (Rome, 1831), 24.

185. The lawsuits can be followed through payments to legal counsel (*procuratori*) and from the defendants in the account books, ASR, CCN, Registro delle congregazioni, Libro della massa, vol. 11 (1635–38) 29, 93v, 113r, 123r.

186. Senato, Statuto ms. 517, 15v–17r.

187. Statutes (1652) in *Statuta* (Rome, 1831), 35–36. They stipulate speaking and voting, though not sitting, by seniority, 6.

188. Statutes (1652) in *Statuta* (Rome, 1831), 3, 5–7. Cf. Senato, Statuto ms. 517, 5r. Girolamo Tranquillo was decano at the time the 1618 statutes were approved and held the office until 1628; he was likely succeeded by Michele Saraceni, who was probably succeeded by Scolocci in 1634 (Scolocci can be documented as decano from 1635). Bonanni served as decano until his death in 1667. For his notarial motto, see Verdi 2005, 451.

189. Senato, Statuto ms. 517, 15r; Statutes (1652) in *Statuta* (Rome, 1831), 4, 35–36.

190. Statutes (1652) in *Statuta* (Rome, 1831), 4.

191. Senato, Statuto ms. 517, 23r–v. Statutes (1652) in *Statuta* (Rome, 1831), 7–8. The mensario's role in settling such disputes remained in both sets of statutes notwithstanding the explicit prohibition in Paul V's 1612 judicial reform legislation; *Bullarium* 1857–72, 12:90, no. 52.

192. Signs of the depositario's enhanced powers included the fact that it was he rather than the decano who supervised the expenditures of the mensario and the fact that he had to sign a formally notarized *obligatio* to perform his office properly. (Such a document would have eased the college's path were it to pursue litigation against the depositario.) Statutes (1652) in *Statuta* (Rome, 1831), 8–9.

193. ASR, CCN, Registro delle congregazioni, Libro della massa, vol. 11 (1635–38). The octogenarian Ottaviani served until the year before he died; he was succeeded in 1635 by Paolo Vespignani of office 28. A new member, Antonio Bardi of office 8 (1641–45), kept the books from 1642 to 1644.

194. Statutes (1652) in *Statuta* (Rome, 1831), 4.

195. Statutes (1652) in *Statuta* (Rome, 1831), 4–5. This bussola provided for an elaborate balance between the fifteen notaries attached to the first collaterale judge and those attached to the second judge, which had its roots in a clause in Sixtus's founding legislation of 1586; Erectio (1586) in *Statuta* (Rome, 1831), 45.

196. Senato, Statuto ms. 517, 6v–9r, 14v; Statutes (1652) in *Statuta* (Rome, 1831), 9–12.

197. Senato, Statuto ms. 517, 9r–12v. The massa accounts show that all activities that the 1618 statutes describe as being done by two members elected to the post of archivist (*archivista*) were in fact being performed by a hired archivist (*custode dell'archivio*) at the time. This reality was finally acknowledged in the 1652 statutes; Statutes (1652) in *Statuta* (Rome, 1831), 10–11, 13. See also Fenzonio 1636, 74, no. 6.

198. The signatures documenting these payments offer intriguing evidence of writing literacy in early modern Rome, as well as hints about the early careers of men who became Capitoline notaries much later in life. ASR, CCN, Registro delle congregazioni, Libro della massa, vol. 8, n.p. (under September 1594, March 1595, and April 1595).

199. ASR, CCN, Registro delle congregazioni, Libro della massa, vol. 10 (1615–20), n.p. (August 1618).

200. Statutes (1652) in *Statuta* (Rome, 1831), 6.

201. Chellini 1647, 10.

202. Statutes (1652) in *Statuta* (Rome, 1831), 2. The annual costs of the festivities are recorded in greater or lesser detail from October 1591; see, for example, ASR, CCN, Registro delle congregazioni, Libro della massa, vol. 8, 53v; vol. 9, n.p. (under October 1602); vol. 11, 97r. In case members did not fully perceive the benefits of civic patronage, however, the statutes threatened fines if they did not show up for mass or failed to close their businesses "at least in the morning" of Saint Luke's feast day; Statutes (1652) in *Statuta* (Rome, 1831), 37–38. The only other ceremony in which the notaries regularly participated was the Corpus Christi procession to Saint Peter's for which the college provided candles; ASR, CCN, Registro delle congregazioni, Libro della massa, vol. 11 (1635–38), 11.

203. The holiday gifts are found throughout the "libri della massa," vols. 8–12.

204. ASC, Cred. IV, vol. 106, 116v (1641). See also ASR, CCN, Registro delle congregazioni, Libro della massa, vol. 11, 92r, where these gifts are valued at forty baiocchi per notary. The notaries also had the right to payments from the city government during each vacant see or papal interregnum.

205. The dispute involved the protocols of one Francesco Lilla; in any such case, it was the archivist who received the legal summons; Fenzonio 1636, 74. ASR, CCN, Registro delle congregazioni, Libro della massa, vol. 10, 2v–3r. Cardinal Fabrizio Veralli, protector of new converts to Catholicism, received holiday gifts from the college twice that year; ibid., vol. 10, 16r, 26r. For other instances of support from the Roman People, see Feci 1997, 133n; ASC, Cred. I, vol. 31, 0239v (16 July 1608); ASC, Cred. I, vol. 32, 0238r (1 March 1622).

206. Twice in 1616 the notaries paid for a carriage to take the first collaterale to see the governor of Rome on matters of concern to the college; ASR, CCN, Registro delle congregazioni, Libro della massa, vols. 10, 28v.

207. ASR, CCN, Registro delle congregazioni, Libro della massa, vol. 8, n.p. (under December 1601).

208. Guasco 1919a, 100; Senato, Statuto ms. 517, 10v; Statutes (1652) in *Statuta* (Rome, 1831), 13, 37. ASC, Camera Capitolina, Cred. VI, vol. 59, 319r. The contested subject of cheap ("simple") copies is discussed in chapters 3 and 6.

209. The case involved Virgilio Lusanna, who left Capitoline office 8 in 1607; ASR, TCrG, processi, 1624, vol. 190, 319r. If the evidence that the thirty Capitoline notaries rented a deposit box at the "cassa dei cursori" indicates that they collected the judges' fees as well as their own, this would give the magistrates another reason to watch out for malefactors; ASR, CCN, Registro delle congregazioni, Libro della massa, vol. 10, n.p. (July and October 1617); vol. 11, 72 (1636).

210. Erectio (1586) in *Statuta* (Rome, 1831), 47–48; Clement X's chirograph of 1674 in *Statuta* (Rome, 1831), 70.

211. ASR, CCN, Registro delle congregazioni, Libro della massa, vol. 8, n.p. (April 1596). He is described as protector in this volume under the date October 1597.

212. ASR, CCN, Registro delle congregazioni, Libro della massa, vol. 9, n.p. (November 1605); ibid., vol. 10, 26r. See Bortolotti 2001.

213. ASR, CCN, Registro delle congregazioni, Libro della massa, vol. 10, n.p. (October 1618).

214. ASR, CCN, Registro delle congregazioni, Libro della massa, vol. 10, n.p. (July 1620 [sic]).

215. Peretti, who was elevated to the cardinalate in 1641, was described as protector in the 1652 statutes; Statutes (1652) in *Statuta* (Rome, 1831), 1.

216. Statutes (1652) in *Statuta* (Rome, 1831), 1.

217. For example, ASR, CCN, Registro delle congregazioni, Libro della massa, vol. 10, 26r (also December 1617).

218. Erectio (1586) in *Statuta* (Rome, 1831), 46. Despite his efforts, competition for these cases proved a source of strain within the college; see Statutes (1652) in *Statuta* (Rome, 1831), 26.

219. ASR, CCN, Registro delle congregazioni, Verbali, vol. 4, n.p. (18 September 1710, 3 October 1711, 18 October 1711). The need for an orderly rotation in reading summonses may have been the stimulus for printing the first edition of the 1652 statutes of the Capitoline notaries. The *ordo* as of 1710 is found in the first printed edition, *Statuta venerabilis Collegii D.D. Notariorum Curiae Capitolii eorumque facultates et privilegia* [1711?], which can be consulted at the Biblioteca del Senato, Statuti no. 1221, p. 71.

220. In 1622 the councils of the Roman People had decreed that caporioni had to use Capitoline notaries as their notaries; ASC, Cred. I, vol. 32, 0238r (1 March 1622). By the 1630s the notaries decided that to enforce this monopoly they needed the added strength of a papal chirograph; Urban VIII chirograph of 1639 in *Statuta* (Rome, 1831), 66–67.

221. On the gift to Pietro Colangelo, Capitoline *fiscale*, see ASR, CCN, Registro delle congregazioni, Libro della massa, vol. 11, 95v (December 1637); see also Nussdorfer 1992, 85.

222. Payments for the War of Castro are among the receipts dated January and February 1644 stuck into the depositario's accounts for 1642–44; ASR, CCN, Registro delle congregazioni, Libro della massa, vol. 12 n.p. (following 100r).

223. The sentence in the case was printed on 12 September 1636; ASV, Arm. IV–V, vol. 45, 91r. For fees paid by the college to the judge, his notary, and the college's attorney, see ASR, CCN, Registro delle congregazioni, Libro della massa, vol. 11 (1635–38), 75, 77–78.

224. Senato, Statuto ms. 517, 9v.

225. ASR, CCN, Registro delle congregazioni, Libro della massa, vol. 8, n.p. (June and July 1598).

226. ASR, CCN, Registro delle congregazioni, Libro della massa, vol. 10 (1615–20).

227. In 1599 the massa accounts also record unspecified expenses for the archive; ASR, CCN, Registro delle congregazioni, Libro della massa, vol. 9, n.p. (under December 1599).

228. After 1586 what the thirty Capitoline notaries produced did not pass to the Archivio Capitolino, or any other archive, but remained with their successors. Yet the archive continued to expand modestly after 1586 as the papers of deceased city notaries who were not venal officeholders arrived there; Trasselli 1936b, 92, 94. The depositario included a complete record of the transunti made from the Archivio Capitolino between 1642 and 1644 in his massa accounts; ASR, CCN, Registro delle congregazioni, Libro della massa, vol. 12, 91r–93v. This list shows that the documents of notaries active as late as 1623 and 1627 were deposited after their deaths. As we shall see in chapter 4, this small stream of new volumes gradually dried up after the pope established the Archivio Urbano in 1625.

229. Guasco 1919a, 101; ASR, CCN, Registro delle congregazioni, Libro della massa,

vol. 10 (1615–20), 2r. The condition was that if the Roman People should need it in the future, the notaries would have to give it back.

230. ASC, Camera Capitolina, Cred. VI, vol. 59, 319r.

231. ASR, CCN, Registro delle congregazioni, Libro della massa, vol. 10 (1615–20), vol. 11 (1635–38).

232. Statutes (1652) in *Statuta* (Rome, 1831), 13–15.

233. Berengo 1976–77, 155.

234. Of the thirty-four copies delivered between 1642 and 1644, only six originals were earlier than 1543 (and three of these were for a single request); ASR, CCN, Registro delle congregazioni, Libro della massa, vol. 12 (1642–44), 91r–v; vol. 13 (1667–81), 91r–, 114r, 134v.

235. ASR, CCN, Registro delle congregazioni, Libro della massa, vol. 13 (1667–81), 91r–, 114r; ASR, CCN, Registro delle congregazioni, Libro della massa, Verbali, vol. 4, n.p. (18 October 1709; 18 October 1711). See chapter 6.

236. We recall that the college had the right to one-quarter of the fees the thirty Capitoline notaries were paid for judicial acts and one-quarter of the transunti fees from instruments they held in their offices (not to be confused with its share of the transunti fees from the Archivio Capitolino).

237. They were to list the payer, purpose, and fee; Senato, Statuti, ms. 517, 19r–v.

238. Over twenty-eight months Vespignani paid massa of 55.28 scudi, 13.28 scudi more than the mandatory minimum; ASR, CCN, Registro delle congregazioni, Libro della massa, vol. 11 (1635–38), 20, 26, 40.

239. ASR, CCN, Registro delle congregazioni, Libro della massa vol. 10 (1615–20), 39v.

240. ASR, CCN, Registro delle congregazioni, Libro della massa vol. 11 (1635–38), 72; Statutes (1652) in *Statuta* (Rome, 1831), 22.

241. ASR, CCN, Registro delle congregazioni, Libro della massa, vol. 11 (1635–38), 29, 93v, 113r, 123r.

242. ASR, CCN, Registro delle congregazioni, Libro della massa, vol. 12 (1642–44), 4–85, 94v. The total massa collected over two years was 1,029 scudi; if all had paid the required minimum, it should have been 1,080 scudi.

243. Statutes (1652) in *Statuta* (Rome, 1831), 38. Of course, we lack massa records between 1652 and 1667, so it is possible that they did levy these higher fines.

244. Statutes (1652) in *Statuta* (Rome, 1831), 18.

245. Statutes (1652) in *Statuta* (Rome, 1831), 9.

246. Statutes (1652) in *Statuta* (Rome, 1831), 18–19.

247. Statutes (1652) in *Statuta* (Rome, 1831), 20–21.

248. Statutes (1652) in *Statuta* (Rome, 1831), 27–28.

249. A former Capitoline titleholder described himself as "franco nell'offitij di Campidoglio"; ASR, TCrG, processi, 1624, vol. 190, 368r, 372v (testimony of 1616).

250. Statutes (1652) in *Statuta* (Rome, 1831), 23; ASR, CCN, Registro delle congregazioni, Libro della massa, vol. 10, n.p. (October 1618, September 1619).

251. Statutes (1652) in *Statuta* (Rome, 1831), 35.

252. *Bullarium* 1857–72, 12:143, no. 208. The reforms are discussed in detail in chapter 3.

253. Statutes (1652) in *Statuta* (Rome, 1831), 35. For the litigiousness of French notaries, see Fontaine 1993, 481.

254. Statutes (1652) in *Statuta* (Rome, 1831), 6.

255. Suggesting a minimum of five scudi, they nonetheless left the amount up to the meeting to decide; Statutes (1652) in *Statuta* (Rome, 1831), 39.

256. Statutes (1652) in *Statuta* (Rome, 1831), 32.

257. Statutes (1652) in *Statuta* (Rome, 1831), 33. Indeed, because of the difference in social status between most Capitoline notaries and most gentlemen caporioni, this seems like a formidable challenge. The duties of a notary of the caporione are still rather obscure, though further research in the notarial archives may eventually shed more light on them.

258. Fenzonio 1636, 64. For the Sistine privilege, see Erectio (1586) in *Statuta* (Rome, 1831), 47.

259. Senato, Statuti, ms. 517, 24v.

260. Statutes (1652) in *Statuta* (Rome, 1831), 30–31.

261. Statutes (1652) in *Statuta* (Rome, 1831), 26–27.

262. Statutes (1652) in *Statuta* (Rome, 1831), 31–32.

263. They make it plain that they imagine conflicts only over the notaries' judicial documentation; Statutes (1652) in *Statuta* (Rome, 1831), 34–35. Cf. Senato, Statuti, ms. 517, 23r–v. On competition for court business in Rome, see Di Sivo 1997, 280.

264. Statutes (1652) in *Statuta* (Rome, 1831), 7, 21–22, 29–30, 32–34.

265. Statutes (1652) in *Statuta* (Rome, 1831), 37–40.

266. ASR, CCN, Registro delle congregazioni, Libro della massa, vol. 13 (1667–81), 91r, 92r, 114r. Notaries did not necessarily pay the requisite amount each month, but the yearly totals were achieved.

267. ASR, CCN, Registro delle congregazioni, Verbali, vol. 2, n.p., meeting of 24 July 1670.

268. ASV, Fondo Carpegna, vol. 29, 146r–v (copy of a letter dated 9 February 1672); Donati 1994, 177. See chapter 6.

269. ASR, CCN, Registro delle congregazioni, Verbali, vol. 2, n.p., meeting of 19 September 1672.

270. ASR, Congregazioni particolari deputati 43/2, 441–42, 741. See chapter 6.

271. ASR, CCN, Registro delle congregazioni, Verbali, vol. 2, n.p., meeting of 2 April 1674.

272. Clement X's chirograph of 1674 in *Statuta* (Rome, 1831), 68–69.

273. Ibid.

274. Ibid.

275. Clement X's chirograph of 1674 in *Statuta* (Rome, 1831), 69–70.

276. ASR, CCN, Registro delle congregazioni, Verbali, vol. 2, n.p., meeting of 20 July 1674.

277. ASR, CCN, Registro delle congregazioni, Libro della massa, vol. 13 (1667–81), 137v.

Chapter 3 • *The Laws: Shaping Notarial Pages*

1. Milan (Liva 1979, 94); Venice (Pedani Fabris 1996, 114); Bologna and Modena (Berengo 1976–77, 156–57); Florence (Panella 1934, 165).

2. This is demonstrated clearly in a model study by Simona Feci (2004) focused on a single clause of the 1494 Roman statutes; see especially 100, 105.

3. See the nuanced historiographical survey of Ago 2002a.

4. Collins 2002, 191–202.

5. 1363 statuti, edited by Re (1880). For references to earlier versions dating from at least 1279, see Collins 2002, 168n; Lori Sanfilippo 2001b, 9 nn. 28–29, 433. See also Re 1880, xxxv–xxxvii. Although we have no copies of the 1363 statutes that predate the reign of Pope Martin V (1417–31), I nevertheless follow Collins in regarding the text as reflecting Rome's fourteenth-century political realities rather than subsequent changes in power relations between the city and the popes.

6. 1363 statuti, bk. 3, art. 1; Cherubini 2001, 159; Camerano 1997, 46–47.

7. Judicial acts are further divided between criminal and civil proceedings; Di Sivo 1998, 625. These are modern terms. Fifteenth- and sixteenth-century Roman sources generally referred to business acts as *instrumenta* or occasionally *contractus*; judicial acts were termed *actus iudiciales* (or *iuditiarii*); see, for example, rubb. 44–46 of the 1446 revisions to the statutes of the notarial college in ASC, Camera Capitolina, Cred. IV, vol. 88, 0152v–0153v.

8. Business acts of the Capitoline notaries from the fourteenth to the nineteenth century are found in two series in the ASR, Collegio dei Notai Capitolini (CCN) and Trenta Notai Capitolini (30 NC), as well as in a series in the ASC, Archivio Urbano, Sezione I. Judicial acts of the Capitoline notaries are located in the ASR series, Tribunale Civile del Senatore.

9. For the entire period before 1880, more than thirty thousand volumes of business acts are extant in three archival series, while fewer than four thousand volumes and folders of judicial acts survive; Verdi 2005, 438, 442, 445.

10. Ascheri 1990, 66. Kuehn (1989, 525–26) also warns against an overly rigid distinction between "business" and judicial motives in seeking out a notary.

11. This supports the reading of the 1363 statutes as a political victory of the well-to-do over the less well-off *popolo*; Collins 2002, 197.

12. 1363 statuti, bk. 1, art. 41, 46. But see art. 40 for the legal advantages given the instrument.

13. 1363 statuti, bk. 1, art. 40.

14. See chapter 1.

15. 1363 statuti, bk. 1, art. 115. If proved, the crime was harshly punished, though it was not a capital offense; bk. 2, art. 35.

16. 1363 statuti, bk. 1, art. 35.

17. 1363 statuti, bk. 1, art. 41.

18. For Milan, see Liva 1979, 112; for Piemonte, see Berengo 1976–77, 154–55.

19. 1363 statuti, bk. 1, art. 102.

20. 1363 statuti, bk. 1, art. 114. The term *transumptum* (and its vernacular equivalent *transunto*), which came into use in the sixteenth century to designate such copies, is not used in the 1363 statutes. For the process of making authorized copies before the fourteenth century as well as for evidence of actual practice in the trecento, see Lori Sanfilippo 2008, 36–37.

21. 1363 statuti, bk. 1, art. 34. Art. 114 extended these procedures to the imbreviature of notaries who were still alive but absent from the city.

22. 1363 statuti, bk. 1, art. 102.

23. 1363 statuti, bk. 2, art. 35. A 1469 statute revision added public humiliation of the convicted notary; *SPQR Statuta* (1519–23), bk. 2, art. 66.

24. 1363 statuti, bk. 1, art. 36. The 1363 statutes do not comment on how an imbreviatura should be marked to indicate that it had been extended and/or emitted as a public copy, which was the subject of Venetian legislation as early as 1242; Pedani Fabris 1996, 114. This was not mandated in Rome until 1580.

25. 1363 statuti, bk. 1, art. 38. See also bk. 2, art. 35. By contrast, judicial acts of notaries who had been excommunicated or were *diffidati* were considered valid; bk. 3, art. 113 [111].

26. 1363 statuti, bk. 1, art. 37. Documents might deceive in other ways too, and the statutes were alert to simulated agreements, especially pretended sales of property by clerics to lay kinsmen. They did not punish the notary for these deceptions but simply declared the contracts null and void, relying heavily on the oral testimony of witnesses to establish the facts of the situation. 1363 statuti, bk. 1, art. 39.

27. 1363 statuti, bk. 1, art. 113: "in the notebook of his protocols."

28. Lori Sanfilippo 2001b, 7.

29. *Quaternario* and *quaternucolo*, 1363 statuti, bk. 1, art. 113n.; a fifth manuscript was unknown to Re (Pavan 1996), 319n. *Caterni* is also found in notarial sources; Lori Sanfilippo 1987, 119.

30. The usual format measures 11 by 15 centimeters, though there is some variation among the extant protocols of the fourteenth-century Roman notaries for whom we have documents (16 by 23.5 centimeters for the volumes of Nardo Venettini, for example). Very few of these volumes retain their original covers, made from reused parchment documents; Lori Sanfilippo 1987, 105–6. Early fifteenth-century protocols show more variety of format; Lori Sanfilippo 1992, 441–53 (appendix with description). The 1705 inventory of the contents of the Archivio Capitolino indicates that this diversity continued in the later fifteenth- and early sixteenth-century protocols, with examples of ottavo-, quarto-, and folio-sized volumes; ASC, Camera Capitolina, Cred. IV, vol. 61, 39r.

31. Lori Sanfilippo 1992, 420–22. The author stresses, however, the variety in practice evident even in the small number of extant Roman protocols from the 1340s to the 1420s, and the difficulty of ascertaining precisely what phase of redaction some of their contents represent.

32. Lori Sanfilippo 1992, 420–22, 413.

33. L. Sinisi 1997, 105–13, 120n. In Tuscany, too, notaries abandoned the protocol toward the end of the fourteenth century, preferring to write imbreviature on loose sheets collected in filze; Catoni and Fineschi 1975, 34. For an exceptional Roman use of the filza, see Lori Sanfilippo 1992, 422.

34. 1363 statuti, bk. 1, art. 113.

35. Costamagna 1970, 74–75; Scoccianti 1992, 198.

36. In the exceptional case, when two notaries were drawing up a contract, they ought to sign the instrument in their own protocol and in that of their colleague, and both should sign any later public versions made for clients; 1363 statuti, bk. 1, art. 113. Lori Sanfilippo (1987, 118–19) has found no evidence of compliance with this requirement in the surviving protocols.

37. On government registries in Italian cities, see Berengo 1976–77, 156–58, and Pedani Fabris 1996, 114.

38. See also 1363 statuti, bk. 3, art. 112 [110]; Collins 2002, ch. 6.

39. Pavan (1996, 319) gives a plausible account of why the revived papal monarchy in the fifteenth century might have prompted more written records on the part of Roman citizens and institutions.

40. ASC, Camera Capitolina, Cred. IV, vol. 88, 0146v–0155r, now published by Lori Sanfilippo 2008. The revisions refer to an earlier statute (0154r) now lost. They bear the internal date of 1446 (0147v), but also claim to contain twenty-six rubrics (0146v) when in fact there are thirty-four, raising the possibility that this version might incorporate later material. In the manuscript they follow directly after the revised city statutes of 1469. Several rubrics include identical language to the 1363 city statutes.

41. Pavan 1996, 326–27; Lanconelli 1983, 315–16; Lori Sanfilippo 2008. When the 1469 city statutes were printed as books 1–3 of the edition of 1519–23, they preceded thirty-five articles concerning notaries; these thirty-five articles represented a fusion of relevant articles from the 1363 statutes together with the college's revisions of 1446; *SPQR Statuta* (1519–23), bk. 3, arts. 282–317. See also the introduction to the 1363 statuti; Re 1880, cxiii.

42. Rub. 38, ASC, Camera Capitolina, Cred. IV, vol. 88, 0149r. Earlier they were subject only to civil liability; 1363 statuti, bk. 1, art. 113.

43. "Cum numero cartarum" carries the implication that the sheets within the protocol would be numbered, though this is not explicit; Rub. 52, ASC, Camera Capitolina, Cred. IV, vol. 88, 0152r–v.

44. Rub. 53, ASC, Camera Capitolina, Cred. IV, vol. 88, 0152v: "qui liber debeat stampari collegii stampa notariorum."

45. Rub. 57, ASC, Camera Capitolina, Cred. IV, vol. 88, 0154r–v. The text notes that "similarly any copy of an instrument or document of which copies are sought is to be made and extended in the same way"; it refers to the sheets as "folii" and the written pages as "carte scripte." Similar rules appear in Milan in 1498, though the number of lines and letters differ; Liva 1979, 196.

46. Rub. 49, ASC, Camera Capitolina, Cred. IV, vol. 88, 0152r; rub. 58, 0154v. Comparing this added detail to the 1363 city laws, which simply demanded mutual signatures, suggests that such disagreements had probably occurred.

47. Rub. 62, ASC, Camera Capitolina, Cred. IV, vol. 88, 0155r; the 1363 provisions reappeared in rub. 41 (0150r–v).

48. Rub. 39, ASC, Camera Capitolina, Cred. IV, vol. 88, 0150r.

49. The municipality had a similar notion at this same date; Scano 1988, 381–82.

50. *SPQR Statuta* (1519–23), bk. 4, "primus liber," art. 32; see also *SPQR Statuta* (1519–23), bk. 5, art. 56.

51. *Statuta urbis* (1580); Rodocanachi 1901, 286–308; Del Re 1986, 319–22; Nussdorfer 1992, 64–66.

52. This had included reworking changes to the statutes made in 1494 and 1521 that were included as books 4 (1521) and 5 (1521) of an earlier edition. On the complex printing history of this earlier edition, see Re's introduction to the 1363 statuti (1880, cxiii); Rodocanachi 1901, 218–31; Pavan 1996, 328–29.

53. *Statuta urbis* (1580), bk. 1, art. 33.

54. *Statuta urbis* (1580), bk. 1, art. 33: "Singuli Notarij, annis singulis, suu[m] conficiant

Protocollum, quod consistat ex chartis numeratis, bene compactis, & ligatis, quotquot ipse Notarius voluerit, in quo instrumenta, de quibus rogatus fuerit, salte[m] substantialiter in mundum infra mensem à die rogitus omnino redigat, & describat."

55. Although this was the general practice, medieval notaries did sometimes keep full transcriptions; Lori Sanfilippo 1992, 423.

56. Of course, the three steps did not include the final phase of making a public copy, which remained subject to the client's wish to pay the extra fee. The 1580 statutes did not mention the number of lines and letters per page required for copies of instruments, as had the 1446 statutes.

57. For rare survivals, see Verdi 2005, 447, 451.

58. *Statuta urbis* (1580), bk. 1, art. 34: "& si duo fuerint Notarij de uno instrumento aut testamento rogati, si non in solidum, (quod in dubio praesumatur) quilibet notulae alterius incontinenti, & antequam ex loco recedat, se subscribat; quod & in protocollis & instrumentorum ipsorum publicatione facere omnino teneantur & si in breviatura fuerint partium aut testium subscriptiones, eam diligenter conservent, eoque casu in protocollis de subscriptione, ita ut est in matrice, faliant mentionem, & clausulas in matrice ceteratas, secundum suum stylum, in protocollo & publico instrumento extendere possint."

59. *Statuta urbis* (1580), bk. 1, art. 34.

60. L. Sinisi 1997, 21–27. See also chapter 1. *Style* was a term employed also to designate the form of a valid notarial signature; examples of this usage by Capitoline notaries appear in the college statutes of 1618 and 1652; Biblioteca del Senato, Statuto ms. 517, 26r; statutes (1652) in *Statuta* (Rome, 1831), 25.

61. *Statuta urbis* (1580), bk. 1, art. 34; cf. 1363 statuti, bk. 1, art. 36.

62. *Statuta urbis* (1580), bk. 3, art. 93; Corbo 1984, 56; Verdi 2005, 451–52.

63. *Statuta urbis* (1580), bk. 1, art. 33.

64. This was up from three days in 1363. *Statuta urbis* (1580), bk. 1, art. 34; cf. 1363 statutes, bk. 1, art. 113 and 1446 revisions, ASC, Camera Capitolina, Cred. IV, vol. 88, 0149r.

65. *Statuta urbis* (1580), bk. 1, art. 36. Cf. 1363 statuti, bk. 1, arts. 34, 102, 114; 1446 revisions, rub. 39, 0150r. Evidence that these procedures were being ignored by heirs can be found in the 1521 statutes and in papal legislation from the 1550s: *Statuta SPQR* (1519–23), bk. 5, art. 39; ASV, Misc. Arm. IV–V, vol. 45, 82r.

66. *Statuta urbis* (1580), bk. 1, arts. 35 and 36. The insistence on copying even the crossed-out letters and words added between the lines on the original continued in the transunti legislation of the notarial college; see statutes (1652) in *Statuta* (Rome, 1831), 14.

67. See chapter 2 for this important innovation of 1494.

68. The reform commission's secretary was Prospero Farinacci, then fiscal procurator for the pope; in addition to papal and curial officials, one of the two Capitoline collaterali, Prospero Turriziani, also took part; Feci 1997, 126–27. Turriziani would have had intimate knowledge of the methods of work of the Capitoline notaries. Although all court personnel, including judges, were regulated in Paul V's legislation, notaries took up the largest amount of space. See also Fosi 1997, 27–30.

69. *Universi agri dominici, Bullarium* 1857–72, 12:58–111. Chapter 19, "De notariis tribunalium Urbis," contains seventy provisions directed to all notaries working in Roman

courts, and fifty-seven aimed at specific groups of notaries (nos. 116–18, for example, were addressed to the Capitoline notaries). Chapter 20 regulated judicial records. Notarial fees for business and judicial acts are found on pp. 111–60.

70. *Bullarium* 1857–72, 12:86–90, nos. 2, 7, 42. See also 85, no. 10.

71. *Bullarium* 1857–72, 12:89, no. 40.

72. *Bullarium* 1857–72, 12:89, no. 36. Some years later, a sostituto in Capitoline office 19 received a stern lecture from a judge for rogating a power of attorney for a client whom he did not know; ASR, TCrG, processi, 1630, vol. 253, 301r–302r.

73. *Bullarium* 1857–72, 12:87. no. 17. For their use in criminal investigations, see chapter 5.

74. The legislation is somewhat ambiguous on the deadline for fully extending instruments: compare *Bullarium* 1857–72, 12:90, no. 43 (daily) and no. 44 (within three months). Fenzonio 1636, 70. The commission had originally thought binding every six months, as they ordered for judicial acts, would be sufficient, but the chief judge of the Rota proposed three months, which was accepted instead; ASV, Arm. XI, vol. 90, 63v. The new inventories of the ASR, 30 NC offices show that few offices bound four volumes of business acts per year. In one of the few concessions to the new college, its officers kept their authority to inspect the protocols of Capitoline notaries yearly; *Bullarium* 1857–72, 12:143, no. 208.

75. Corbo 1984, 56; Berengo 1976–77, 160. The loss of initial pages in some of the oldest extant protocols makes it difficult to chronicle the early history of this practice; Lori Sanfilippo 1987, 110, 118. At the beginning of a 1609 protocol of Alessandro Saravezzio is a loose set of narrow folded sheets that were made a draft of the index for the volume; ASR, 30 NC, uff. 11 (Saravezzio) 1609, pt. 3 (vol. 82).

76. *Bullarium* 1857–72, 12:90, no. 45. The legislation did not address the problem of sealed wills that were overlooked at the time of the testator's death.

77. *Bullarium* 1857–72, 12:96, no. 116; 89, no. 34. Cf. *Statuta urbis* (1580), bk. 1, art. 22.

78. *Bullarium* 1857–72, 12:86, no. 7; 90, no. 42.

79. *Bullarium* 1857–72, 7:179. It also included a third category, the "signed copy" or *fede* at a price between those of the simple copy and the public copy. To my knowledge, the 1562 list is the first to charge lower rates for simple copies.

80. *Statuta urbis* (1580), bk. 3, art. 93.

81. *Bullarium* 1857–72, 12:90, no. 46; 137, nos. 40–45. The chief judge of the tribunal of the Rota, Orazio Savelli, had lobbied the commission specifically on this point; ASV, Misc. Arm. XI, vol. 90, 63v. Guasco records an inscription from 1600 purportedly ordering the Capitoline notaries to provide simple copies of records from their archive, which their own statutes stoutly prohibited, but his evidence is ambiguous and may refer to a different archive; Guasco 1919a, 100. Cf. statutes (1652) in *Statuta* (Rome, 1831), 13.

82. *Bullarium* 1857–72, 12:90, no. 46. Cf. 1363 statuti, bk. 1, art. 102.

83. "Proposte per parte de Notari Capitolini," ASR, Cam. II, Notariato, b. 3 (n.p.) (for the text, see appendix B). See chapter 6 on the dating of this document. There is evidence from as early as 1634 that simple copies were in fact being used to initiate lawsuits; ASR, Ospedale del SS. Salvatore, reg. 216, 87v.

84. *SPQR Statuta* (1519–23), bk. 5, art. 12; *Statuta urbis* (1580), bk. 1, art. 28. Compare, too, the identical description of copies of judicial evidence in Fenzonio 1636, 59, no. 2 B.

85. Collins 2002, 197, see also 199.

86. The urgent political pressures of the period somewhat obscure the fact that, because litigants paid all the costs, they presumably also controlled the pace of civil proceedings. One scholar has recently highlighted the paradoxical nature of legislation on the duration of lawsuits; Ascheri 1999, 362.

87. 1363 statuti, bk. 1, arts. 3, 4, 40, 41, 46. Some early fifteenth-century formulas for summons (*citationes*) are published in the 1363 statutes edited by Re, 287–88. For the first archival survivals, see Trasselli 1936b, 95–96. For a comparison with civil procedure in fourteenth-century Marseilles, see Smail 2003, 35–72.

88. Complaints also had to be submitted in writing; Campitelli 1987.

89. The situation may have been similar for notaries assigned to criminal cases (*notarii malleficiorum*), although their procedures, and thus their documents, were different. There were four such notaries, who, like the senator, the chief judge of the Capitoline tribunal, were required to be foreigners. Book 2 of the statutes describes criminal procedures. On criminal notaries, see bk. 2, art. 174; bk. 3, arts. 1, 62–64, 115.

90. 1363 statuti, bk. 1, art. 5, 21, 40.

91. 1363 statuti, bk. 1, art. 115: "Additum est quod Notarius qui in curia Capitolii fuerit ad aliquod officium seu banchum alicuius iudicis deputatus ad illud banchum tantummodo ad quod deputatus est non possit pro aliquo officium procurationis exercere durante tempore sui offitii." As we shall see, this prohibition was elaborated in the notaries' statutes of 1446 and repeated in papal legislation of 1562 and 1612; *Bullarium* 1857–72, 7:222, no. 71; 12:87, no. 10.

92. 1363 statuti, bk. 1, art. 113. Should a question arise about the fees for other types of judicial acts, the judge at whose bench those acts were made should establish the payment owed to the notary.

93. 1363 statuti, bk. 1, art 115.

94. 1363 statuti, bk. 1, arts. 40, 46, 102.

95. 1363 statuti, bk. 1, art. 32: "Notarius qui dicta testium examinatorum scribit teneatur substantialiter et explicite scribere dictum testis et non dicat talis dixit ut talis, et si explicite non dixerit capitulum sive articulum verum esse queratur ab eo de causa scientie quam notarius diligenter scibere teneatur aliter non valeat dictum eius." See also the rules for civic scribes, ibid., bk. 3, art. 18 (2). Unlike criminal cases, it was expected in civil cases in Rome that notaries, not judges, would conduct interrogations, often at their own or the deponent's home. Mascardi 1608, Q. 5, nos. 99–102, summarizes a range of juridical opinion on whether, in addition to taking testimony, the notary could also administer the oath to the witnesses or whether this had to be done by a judge.

96. Rodocanachi 1901, 165–74; Di Sivo 1998, 619; Fosi 2007, 19–20. The number and functions of the judges in the senator's tribunal were largely unchanged in the 1469 statutes, as was the bulk of book 1 on civil procedure. From the point of view of civil justice, the most important innovation was the codification of the limitations on who was subject to the senator's tribunal, a limit that the popes had been extending since the 1390s.

97. See, for example, D. Sinisi 1996.

98. Rub. 43, ASC, Camera Capitolina, Cred. IV, v. 88, 0151r. There were six judges in all, with four covering civil matters in the Capitoline court in this period; Rodocanachi 1901, 110; Di Sivo 1998, 619.

99. Rubb. 35, 45, 61, ASC, Camera Capitolina, Cred. IV, v. 88, 0148v, 0151v, 0154v.

100. See chapter 1.

101. Rub. 44, ASC, Camera Capitolina, Cred. IV, v. 88, 0151r.

102. Rub. 47, ASC, Camera Capitolina, Cred. IV, v. 88, 0151v.

103. Rub. 43, ASC, Camera Capitolina, Cred. IV, v. 88, 0151r: "et quilibet debeat tenere librum manualem in quo debeat omnia acta conscribere anteq[uam] de bancho recedat et demum in registrum reducere cum omnium originalium iurium instrumentorum testium et aliorum productorum."

104. An inventory of the possessions of a Capitoline notary in 1494 includes twenty-seven manuali along with eighteen protocols; Spotti Tantilo 1975, 89–91. A manuale from 1496 began with a list of the various types of judicial acts it contained: "Hic est liber manualis sive bastardellus in se continens omnes et singulos actus iudiciarios, protestationes petitiones comparitiones responsiones contradictiones relationes et terminos iudiciarios inter infra-scriptas partes factas et factos ac receptos nec non fideiussiones iudicialiter prestitas." Trasselli 1936b, 100, and more generally 95–100. For their registers, criminal notaries on the Capitol used the notebook format (*quaternus*) like that used for business acts, as well as filze; Cherubini 2001, 159, 162 n. 46.

105. Rubb. 43, 57, ASC, Camera Capitolina, Cred. IV, v. 88, 0151r, 0154r.

106. Rub. 51, ASC, Camera Capitolina, Cred. IV, v. 88, 0152r.

107. Rub. 48, ASC, Camera Capitolina, Cred. IV, v. 88, 0151v. Although the senator's palace was the implied judicial setting, the nearby church and convent of Santa Maria in Aracoeli was actually used during much of the fifteenth century; Del Re 1954, 26.

108. Rub. 44, ASC, Camera Capitolina, Cred. IV, v. 88, 0151r. See also Trasselli 1936b, 99.

109. Rubb. 40, 43, 50, ASC, Camera Capitolina, Cred. IV, v. 88, 0150r, 0151r, 0152r. Cf. 1363 statuti, bk. 1, art. 115.

110. Lori Sanfilippo 2001, 441.

111. Rub. 51, ASC, Camera Capitolina, Cred. IV, v. 88, 0152r.

112. *Statuta urbis* (1580), bk. 1, art. 24.

113. For one example that could surely be multiplied, see Cherubini 2001, 160.

114. Rodocanachi 1901, 231; Lori Sanfilippo 1990, 31.

115. Rub. 57, ASC, Camera Capitolina, Cred. IV, v. 88, 0154r–v.

116. Rubb. 44, 45, ASC, Camera Capitolina, Cred. IV, v. 88, 0152v–0153v.

117. Rub. 60, ASC, Camera Capitolina, Cred. IV, v. 88, 0154v.

118. Rub. 38, ASC, Camera Capitolina, Cred. IV, v. 88, 0149r. Fees for instruments were similarly perplexing; some were listed in this text, others were to be set by the college officers, and "the former statutes should be followed" in case of conflicts between notaries and contracting parties; Rub. 56, ASC, Camera Capitolina, Cred. IV, v. 88, 0154r.

119. Pompeo 1991, 46; Camerano 1997, 52, 66.

120. Fosi 1997, 29; 2007, vi–vii.

121. Verdi 2005, 443. Only a few volumes of Capitoline litigation records survive from the fifteenth century, while no more than 155 complete volumes and some fragments are extant from the sixteenth century. On the archive of the Tribunale Civile del Senatore, which consists of close to 4,000 volumes, see in addition to Traselli's two articles (1936a, 1936b), ASR,

Inventory 286 I. Renata Ago utilized these sources in *Economia barocca* (1998, viii), but no one, to my knowledge, has studied those before the seventeenth century, perhaps because of the difficulties she discusses.

122. *SPQR Statuta* (1519–23), bk. 4. The revisions to the city statutes under Alexander VI were divided into two "books"; the first consisted of thirty-five articles regarding civil cases and the second of thirty-nine on criminal cases. On their publication history, see Re 1880, cxi. One 1494 change of considerable import was the restriction on women's rights to make contracts; Feci 2004, 83.

123. *SPQR Statuta* (1519–23), bk. 4, art. 14. The 1363 statutes may well have intended witness examinations to be conducted within ten days, but this is largely left to inference; see bk. 1, arts. 40, 46.

124. *SPQR Statuta* (1519–23), bk. 4, art. 14: "Omnis autem utilitas et lucrum tam examinis quam copiarum sit ipsius notarii examinantis."

125. Feci 2004, 85–87.

126. ASC, Camera Capitolina, Cred. I, vol. 15, 71v.

127. *SPQR Statuta* (1519–23), bk. 5.

128. *SPQR Statuta* (1519–23), bk. 5, art. 56. Article 56 was prefaced with the comment that the authors were reviving "certain statutes, orders, and constitutions concerning the notaries of the Capitoline tribunal, which had been made or published during the tenure of Senator Egidio Angelo de Archa of Narnia," because these had been ignored. Arca served as senator in 1508, but I have not found these statutes or other references to them.

129. Rub. 43, ASC, Camera Capitolina, Cred. IV, v. 88, 0151r.

130. Notaries who had been forcibly taken off a case three times automatically lost their right to work in the Capitoline tribunal; *SPQR Statuta* (1519–23), bk. 5, art. 8.

131. *SPQR Statuta* (1519–23), bk. 5, art. 10.

132. *SPQR Statuta* (1519–23), bk. 5, art. 56: "Itaq[ue] quilibet notarius Romanus contractus et alia acta publica scribens sit intentus sua prothocolla et scripturas bene ornate et composite scribere ut ab omnibus perpetuo laudari et com[m]endari possit et valeat."

133. *SPQR Statuta* (1519–23), bk. 5, art. 56: "debeat de actis iuribus et scripturis omnibusque fierent et dabuntur in causis ipsis facere solemnem et ordinatum extractum." The omission of witness testimony here implies that attorneys did not see this; later we read how it was made available to the judge.

134. It was assumed that litigants in a dispute over such an amount would have attorneys. The notary was forbidden from showing the extractus to the parties themselves.

135. Feci 1997, 131 n. 73, lists seven separate pieces of legislation each directed at a different set of court officials. Additional laws will be cited below. For Pius IV's purposes, the ordinary tribunals were, in addition to the Capitoline court, those of the governor, conservators, Maestri di Strada, Savelli, Borgo, Tor di Nona, Ripa, Ripetta, and the guild tribunals (*consolati*). See chapter 2 on these jurisdictions.

136. What Grisar (1964, 276) calls the papacy's first major law reforming the notaries of the Papal States (1 September 1556) was in fact the sale of notarial offices in all criminal jurisdictions; ASV, Misc. Arm. IV–V, vol. 45, 26v–27v.

137. *Bullarium* 1857–72, 7:214–24. *Cum ab ipso* had a total of eighty-four provisions; nos.

58–74 were devoted to notaries, of which nos. 64–68 concerned particularly the Capitoline notaries. See also Camerano 1997, 55.

138. As mentioned in chapter 2, I have not thus far found evidence that this reduction was implemented. Capitoline notaries did sometimes work for other judges; Verdi 2005, 447.

139. *Bullarium* 1857–72, 7:177–80 (civil); 180–84 (criminal). These included rates for instruments as well as judicial acts for the court notaries of the governor, vicar, Borgo, and Maestri di Strada, and rates for criminal acts for the court notaries of the governor, senator, vicar, Borgo, and the auditor of the Camera.

140. Feci 1997, 124, n. 33.

141. See Rurale 2000.

142. Del Re 1993, 53. See also Camerano 1997, 52. In reality, the parties themselves played the key role in determining how expensive a lawsuit was, because they paid at each point to advance the proceedings.

143. Nussdorfer 1992, 65. This is the context also for jurist Luca Peto's formulary on judicial procedure in the Capitoline courts, which he began shortly after 1560 and published in 1567; Del Re 1986, 312, 320–25.

144. Camerano 1997, 54, 65–66.

145. There is evidence of this concern in the 1363 statutes, but it is obliquely and indirectly expressed. It had earlier precedents in medieval Italy; Ascheri 1999, 363.

146. ASV, Misc. Arm. IV–V, vol. 45, under date 22 November 1561, "Reformatio registrorum per notarios quorumcumque iudicum et tribunalium Romanae Curiae." The extractus, we recall, was available for disputes over smaller amounts, down to a minimum of twenty-five ducati. By 1580 the minimum for the extractus in gold ducati was 27.5 scudi; *Statuta urbis* (1580), bk. 1, arts. 26, 195.

147. *Bullarium* 1857–72, 7:221–22, no. 62.

148. *Bullarium* 1857–72, 7:216, no. 14; 221, no. 61.

149. *Bullarium* 1857–72, 7:180.

150. *Bullarium* 1857–72, 7:179.

151. *Statuta urbis* (Rome, 1580); Del Re 1954, 40–45. The new statutes followed the traditional division into three books, with the first devoted to civil procedure, the second to criminal, and the third to all the other provisions for municipal government, including notarial fees.

152. There was polemical comment on these differences in the seventeenth century, which has begun to be subjected to critical scrutiny in recent studies. De Luca 1673, bk. 15, pt. 3, art. 34; Pompeo 1991, 46; Di Sivo 1997, 283; Ago 1999b, 396.

153. On the chronology of composition, see Del Re 1986, 319–22. From 1555 until his death in 1581, Luca Peto served in the Capitoline tribunal. His formulary for use in the court, *De iudiciaria formula Capitolini Fori*, went through five editions between 1567 and 1625.

154. *Statuta urbis* (1580), bk. 1, art. 29. See also *Cum ab ipso*, *Bullarium* 1857–72, 7:222, no. 67. The 1494 sortition method is described in *SPQR Statuta* (1519–23), bk. 4, art. 14.

155. *Statuta urbis* (1580), bk. 1, art. 21. The 1521 requirement that they work for a procurator for three years had disappeared.

156. Peto 1587, 6: "praefinitum numerum non habent: siquidem modo plures, modo pauciores sunt."

157. Del Re 1954, 42–43.

158. *Statuta urbis* (1580), bk. 1, art. 22. The penalty was invalidating the records. See also *SPQR Statuta* (1519–23), bk. 5, art. 43.

159. *Statuta urbis* (1580), bk. 1, art. 24; cf. rub. 51, ASC, Camera Capitolina, Cred. IV, v. 88, 0152r. They were to sit before their judge's tribunal during the two hours each morning in which the court was in session; Peto 1587, 5–6.

160. Peto 1587, 6: "licet qui primo aditus fuerit ab actore causae notarius esse debeat." See also Erectio (1586) in *Statuta* (Rome, 1831), 46. Cf. 1446 notarial regulations in ASC, Camera Capitolina, Cred. IV, vol. 88, 0151r, rub. 44.

161. *Statuta urbis* (1580), bk. 1, art. 29. "Ante litem contestatam" referred to the stage following presentation of the charges when the defendant formally responded to them. After converting the Capitoline notaries into venal officeholders, Sixtus made it more difficult to remove them from a case on unproven suspicion; Erectio (1586) in *Statuta* (Rome, 1831), 47.

162. Peto's (1587, 6–7) handbook suggests a somewhat milder regime operated in practice; notaries removed as "suspicious" from witness interrogations, for example, were not to be penalized.

163. *Statuta urbis* (1580), bk. 1, art. 25. *Manuale actorum* or *manuale* rather than *bastardello* was now the official term for this volume. As in 1446 the manuale was to begin with the name of the notary and his judge, the year, the pope, and the number of sheets.

164. *Statuta urbis* (1580), bk. 3, arts. 94 and 95.

165. *Statuta urbis* (1580), bk. 1, art. 28: "Debeantque quoties legitime fuerint requisiti, Iudici & partibus acta ostendere, nulla recepta mercede; nihilque omnino pro ostendendis actis, scripturis & iuribus productis, neque pro portandis ipsis actis, iuribus, scripturis, vel extractu Iudici, a' partibus etiam sponte dantibus, recipiant." See also *SPQR Statuta* (1519–23), bk. 5, art. 12.

166. *Statuta urbis* (1580), bk. 1, art. 26: "de actis, iuribus & scripturis omnibus, quae in causis ipsis fient, & producentur, solemnem & ordinatum Extractum conficere, in quo omnia acta de verbo ad verbum, & ut in Manuali sunt descripta, nihil addito vel extenso adnotare debeat." This passage reminds us that the court record contained abbreviations, which were to be copied exactly in the extractus.

167. The rate per folio was three baiocchi; *Statuta urbis* (1580), bk. 1, art. 26.

168. Peto 1587, 129–33. Cf. 1363 statuti, bk. 1, art. 40.

169. *Statuta urbis* (1580), bk. 1, art. 75. The fees for judicial testimony were the same whether taken in the courtroom or in the notary's house, but higher if he had to leave his house; *Statuta urbis* (1580), bk. 3, art. 95. For a model study of these sources, see Ago 1998a. On witness examination in criminal cases, see *Statuta urbis* (1580), bk. 2, art. 9.

170. *SPQR Statuta* (1519–23), bk. 4, art. 14; bk. 5, arts. 6, 7, 56.

171. *Statuta urbis* (1580), bk. 1, art. 27. Although the 1580 statutes do not demand this, at least one Capitoline notary in the 1580s collected interrogations in a separate volume; Trasselli 1936b, 94. This was required after Paul V's judicial reforms; *Bullarium* 1857–72, 12:87–88, no. 20.

172. The statutes recognized that sometimes witnesses were away or could not appear for questioning without putting their lives in danger, in which case the judge could delegate a more conveniently located notary to take testimony; *Statuta urbis* (1580), bk. 1, art. 27. This article also repeated the 1508 provision that gave wide powers to the notary to conduct an examination about the facts in the case even in the absence of the *interrogatoria* from the accused; cf. *SPQR Statuta* (1519–23), bk. 5, art. 56.

173. ASR, Biblioteca, Bandi, vol. 436, Campidoglio, edict of proconsuls and correctors, 16 December 1582.

174. This regulation bore immediate fruit. A 1587 inventory of the documents of Capitoline notary Vespasiano de Bonis listed five *manuali* of judicial acts, as well as one volume of witness testimony, covering the years 1581 to 1586; Trasselli 1936b, 94.

175. Erectio (1586) in *Statuta* (Rome, 1831). See chapter 2.

176. *Bullarium* 1857–72, 12:58–111, with supplementary legislation 111–62.

177. Donati 1994, 171–72; Feci 1997. The tribunal reform commission would continue intermittently throughout the seventeenth century with a second important burst of energy in the 1670s under Cardinal Giovanni Battista De Luca.

178. Feci 1997, 121.

179. Fosi 2007, 20.

180. Donati 1994, 171; Fosi 1997, 34–35.

181. *Bullarium* 1857–72, 12:97–100. The structure of the legislation stressed both vertical and horizontal vectors in that it began with nine articles devoted to specific tribunals, including that of the senator, but then went on to address categories of judicial personnel (like judges, lawyers, or notaries) that cut across the different jurisdictions.

182. *Bullarium* 1857–72, 11:470–73, but also 12:91–92, nos. 62–65. One of the two Capitoline judges for whom the thirty Capitoline notaries worked participated in the papal tribunal reform commission; Feci 1997, 126–27. Notaries were permitted to speak to the commission on 10 October 1608 and later were informed about the new rules on judicial acts "and acquiesced"; Feci 1997, 133n.

183. *Bullarium* 1857–72, 12:89, no. 36. See also nos. 44, 114, 117.

184. *Bullarium* 1857–72, 12:86, no. 5.

185. *Bullarium* 1857–72, 12:98, no. 15. Capitoline notaries furnish our only point of comparison here, of course; in 1446, reiterated in 1580, they were expected to make court registra with twenty lines per page, and eight words and thirty-two letters per line. Rubb. 43, 57, ASC, Camera Capitolina, Cred. IV, vol. 88, 0151r, 0154r. According to *Cum ab ipso* 1562, registra could only be made for cases involving two hundred scudi or more; *Bullarium* 1857–72, 7:221, no. 62.

186. See, for example, *Bullarium* 1857–72, 12:99, no. 17.

187. This and other numbered citations in this paragraph are found in *Bullarium* 1857–72, 12:97–100.

188. *Bullarium* 1857–72, 12:99, no. 16.

189. *Bullarium* 1857–72, 12:87–88, nos. 20, 25.

190. *Bullarium* 1857–72, 12:87–88, no. 20. It should be recorded in the *manuale* "even when the submission was noted on the bottom of the summons."

191. *Bullarium* 1857–72, 12:98, no. 15.

192. *Bullarium* 1857–72, 12:87, no. 16.

193. All citations in this paragraph are to *Bullarium* 1857–72, 12:87–89. In addition, see nos. 11, 12, and 23.

194. Particularly in the case of a *mandatum exequtivum*, a warrant to execute a distraint of goods or property.

195. *Bullarium* 1857–72, 12:99, no. 21.

196. In addition to this procedure, a litigant could pay half price for judicial fees by obtaining from a judge a *mandatum in forma pauperum*; *Bullarium* 1857–72, 12:92, no. 66.

197. *Bullarium* 1857–72, 12:100, no. 27.

198. *Bullarium* 1857–72, 12:143.

199. *Bullarium* 1857–72, 12:90, no. 52; cf. *Statuta urbis* (1580), bk. 1, art. 38.

200. *Bullarium* 1857–72, 12:143. The 1612 reforms gave them a two-month grace period to present them.

201. *Bullarium* 1857–72, 12:87, no. 19.

202. A client uses it in just this way in an altercation with Capitoline notary Erasto Spannocchia in 1620; ASR, TCrG, processi, 1620, vol. 163, 1124v.

203. See, for example, the case of a disputed will in ASR, TCrG, processi, 1640, vol. 358, 2nd fasc., 194v–95v.

204. Fosi 1997, 26, 30–31.

205. *Bullarium* 1857–72, 12:86, no. 1. Cf. *Cum ab ipso*, ibid., 7:221, no. 58.

206. *Bullarium* 1857–72, 12:85, no. 10.

207. *Bullarium* 1857–72, 12:89, no. 34: "substituti, scribae, iuvenes vel alii quicumque." Cf. *Cum ab ipso*, ibid., 7:221, no. 60.

208. *Bullarium* 1857–72, 12:96, no. 116; cf. *Cum ab ipso*, ibid., 7:222, no. 64. The 1580 city statutes were even more restrictive: "Notarii actuarii omnes, coram quocumque Iudice, scribant per se ipsos; . . . nulloque modo (etiam extra tribunal iuris) eorum officium per substitutum exercere possint"; *Statuta urbis* (1580), bk. 1, art. 22.

209. ASR, Biblioteca, Bandi, vol. 436, Campidoglio, edict of proconsuls and correctors, 16 December 1582, arts. 10, 11, 12, 13. Erectio (1586) in *Statuta* (Rome, 1831), 43.

210. *Bullarium* 1857–72, 12:88, nos. 21, 31.

211. *Bullarium* 1857–72, 12:88, no. 27.

212. *Bullarium* 1857–72, 12:88, no. 25.

213. *Bullarium* 1857–72, 12:92, no. 67.

214. *Bullarium* 1857–72, 12:99, no. 22. To enforce this, the legislation ordered that a judge's written permission was needed before the notary made an extractus; *Bullarium* 1857–72, 12:97, no. 2.

215. *Bullarium* 1857–72, 12:91, nos. 56, 57.

216. Di Sivo 1997, 285–87; Fosi 2007, 22, 158–72.

217. Feci 1997, 125n.

218. Quoted in Fosi 1997, 34–35.

219. See the grocer's complaint in a 1632 trial; ASR, TCrG, processi, 1632, vol. 278, 815r–v; Fenzonio 1636, 59; CCN, Registro delle congregazioni, Verbali, vol. 3, n.p. (5 June 1702); Fosi 2002a, 349–50.

220. De Luca 1673, bk. 15, pt. 3, ch. 43.

Chapter 4 • *The Archives: Creating Documentary Spaces*

1. Cesarini-Sforza 1914, 308; Cencetti 1943, 301.

2. This rather oversimplifies the various modes of control created in thirteenth- and fourteenth-century Italy. For an overview, see Berengo 1976–77 and the more specific studies he cites.

3. Lori Sanfilippo 2001b, 445n, 447.

4. Liva 1979, 120–21, 185–86; Cammisa 1989, 57–149; Bitossi 1995, 553–60.

5. Panella 1934, 174–77; Catoni and Fineschi 1975, 19.

6. ASC, Camera Capitolina, Cred. IV, vol. 88, 0155r, rub. 62.

7. Lesellier 1933, 252.

8. *Bullarium* 1857–72, 5:458–66. The legislation appeared in two parts on 1 and 13 December 1507. See also Lesellier 1933, 253; Grisar 1964, 267–71; Marquis 1979, 467–71. As we saw in chapter 2, some Capitoline notaries also purchased offices in the College of Scriptors; San Martini Barrovecchio 1983, 3:850n.

9. *Notae* is the term used in the 1507 bull, but a close reading shows that it is synonymous with *imbreviatura* or *matrice*, that is, the witnessed transaction with the crucial formalities of date and place; *Bullarium* 1857–72, 5:460–61, no. 6. In contrast to Capitoline rules, the bull required the notary's signature on the notes.

10. *Bullarium* 1857–72, 5:461, no. 8. Specifically, he named the tribunals of the Apostolic Camera, governor, vicar, and the papal palace. For a 1608 archival edict regarding judicial acts, see *Enchiridion* 1966, 33–34.

11. He exempted heirs of venal notarial offices from this decree, however; *Bullarium* 1857–72, 5:461.

12. *Bullarium* 1857–72, 5:460, no. 5; Lesellier 1933, 270, cites Leo X's legislation, *Bullarium* 1857–72, 5:540, no. 6.

13. San Martini Barrovecchio 1983, 3:849, 852. Nevertheless, certain kinds of acts of these privileged exemptions, such as wills and gifts between the living, were to be submitted for registration in the archive and then restored to the owners of the offices; *Bullarium* 1857–72, 5:460.

14. For Julius II's specific instructions on checking transunti orally for accuracy, see *Bullarium* 1857–72, 5:462, no. 9.

15. The Archivio Urbano is located today in Rome's municipal archive, the Archivio Storico Capitolino; three series cover instruments, warrants (*mandati*), and wills brought in to be registered between 1507 and 1550. To these should be added a volume in a misnamed *fondo* in Rome's Archivio di Stato, Miscellanea dei Notai Capitolini, which holds more notes from curial notaries from the same period; see also San Martini Barrovecchio 1983, 3:852n.

16. San Martini Barrovecchio 1983, 3:850.

17. Ibid.

18. Lesellier 1933, 265–73.

19. Lesellier 1933, 272; San Martini Barrovecchio 1983, 3:852, 870–71. Some of these must belong to the 143 seventeenth-century notaries listed by Guasco 1946, 51–58.

20. The stamp can be seen, for example, on the frontispiece of the volume covering Campora's instruments for 1622 under the following inscription: "Hic est liber instrumen-

torum de quibus ego Antonius Campora Ro[manus] pub[licus] Apostolica auctor[itat]e not[arius] in Archivio Ro[manae] Cur[iae] descriptus rog[atu]s fui. Coep[tus] die 29 Xbris [December] 1621 et finiend[us] die 21 Xbris [December] 1622. Ad gloriam omnipotenti Dei cuius nomen sit benedictum." in ASC, AU, sez. 1, vol. 213. It is possible that close inspection of the original protocols in sections 1 and 2 of the Archivio Urbano would reveal more clues about the operations of the Archivio di Curia in its waning days.

21. Edicts of 14 October 1561, 11 March 1572, 10 November 1604, and 22 November 1608. ASV, Misc. Arm. IV–V, vol. 84, nos. 173, 176, 180. 1572 edict cited by San Martini Barrovecchio 1983, 3:851n. See also Comune di Roma 1920–58, 2:102, no. 812.

22. Rub. 62, ASC, Camera Capitolina, Cred. IV, vol. 88, 0155r. See chapter 3. For at least one Capitoline notary who obeyed, see Esch 2001, 180.

23. 1363 statuti, bk. 1, arts. 102, 114.

24. *SPQR Statuta* (1519–23), bk. 4, I, art. 32. According to Camillo Re (1880, cxi), editor of the 1363 statuti, the 1494 revisions may not have received their first printing until this edition; book 4 was published in 1521. They were divided into two libri of several dozen articles each, the first concerned with civil procedure and the second with criminal procedure.

25. *SPQR Statuta* (1519–23), bk. 4, I, art. 32: "Et in potestate heredum libere omnia consignentur."

26. *SPQR Statuta* (1519–23), bk. 4, I, art. 32. There is some ambiguity as to whether the passage refers to municipal or notarial officials. One other practical innovation was the requirement that city process servers (*mandatari*) attend the funerals of notaries and that their officers inform the officers of the notarial college when a notary had died.

27. Lori Sanfilippo 1990, 30.

28. *SPQR Statuta* (1519–23), bk. 5, art. 56: "Item est decretum et ordinatum q[uod] statutum sub rubrica De prothocollis in libris notariorum defunctorum quod est in novis reformationibus editis t[em]p[or]e felicis recordationis Alexandri PP.VI in usu ponantur et in omnibus et per omnia prout in eo continetur . . . observetur."

29. Civic officials tried to create an archive for their own records in these same years; this was known as the Archive of the Roman People; Guasco 1919a, 9–14; Del Re 1986, 312–13; Scano 1988, 382–84. Although the Archive of the Roman People scarcely functioned before the eighteenth century, contemporary sources sometimes did not distinguish the two archives carefully. Paul V's reform legislation offers a case in point; *Bullarium* 1857–72, 7:90, no. 50; 97, no. 118.

30. Guasco 1919a, 108. It is now a series within Rome's Archivio di Stato known as the Archivio del Collegio dei Notai Capitolini; Lori Sanfilippo 1987, 103. In light of the overlapping authorities involved in its long history, it is not surprising to learn that disputes among city, professional, and state officials broke out over control of this archive again in the aftermath of Italian unification; Verdi 2005, 440.

31. It is unclear what relation these developments had to the order of the papal auditor of the Camera in October 1561 demanding delivery to the Archivio di Curia of the documents of deceased notaries on its matriculation list; the order was addressed to city and curial notaries. ASV, Misc., Arm. IV–V, vol. 84, no. 180.

32. Guasco 1919a, 94–95. Lesellier (1933, 270n) disputes Guasco's view that there was an earlier Capitoline notarial archive. A fairly accurate account of this foundation, composed in

the early eighteenth century, can be found in ASR, Camerale II, Notariato, b. 16, fascicle 36 (n.p.) See also Grisar 1964, 259–67.

33. *Cum ab ipso, Bullarium* 1857–72, 7:222, no. 68.

34. ASR, Biblioteca, Bandi, vol. 2, no. 164. Lesellier 1933, 270n; the correct date for the bando of the senator and conservators is 23 December. For additional papal support for the new archive, see the 12 February 1566 edict of the apostolic protonotary cited in Lori Sanfilippo 1990, 35.

35. ASR, Biblioteca, Bandi, vol. 2, no. 164: "considerato anco & visto che di essi notai capitolini & d'altri ne sono stati, e sono di molti forastieri."

36. ASR, Biblioteca, Bandi, vol. 2, no. 164.

37. The notarial college officers were to keep a record of fees paid for transunti in the archive; the archivist was to make a second volume listing transunti fees collected each month; and the notary of the notarial college was also to record transunti and their fees; ASR, Biblioteca, Bandi, vol. 2, no. 164.

38. 1363 statuti, bk. 1, art. 34; *SPQR Statuta* (1519–23), bk. 4, I, art. 32; bk. 5, art. 39. This silence is all the more surprising in light of a papal edict of the early 1550s specifically disciplining heirs of Capitoline notaries who provided transunti without the necessary signatures from the authorities; ASV, Misc., Arm. IV–V, vol. 45, 82r.

39. ASC, Camera Capitolina, Cred. IV, vol. 61.

40. ASR, Biblioteca, Bandi, vol. 2, no. 164: "I conservatori siano soprintendenti & patroni di detto officio d'Archivio in l'administratione d'esso & provedino à ogni bisogno necessario."

41. In the early years there were many complaints about archive personnel; Guasco 1919a, 95–96. Some of these complaints were made by notarial college officials; ASC, Camera Capitolina, Cred. I, vol. 23, 72r–v (3 July 1567).

42. ASR, Biblioteca, Bandi, vol. 2, no. 164. Such a volume was in use in 1553; Verdi 2005, 454.

43. Piccialuti 1999, 96.

44. Guasco 1919a, 96.

45. The governor of Rome's order was dated 26 August 1568; Piccialuti 1999, 64, 78.

46. *Statuta Urbis* (1580), bk. 1, art. 35. The 1446 notarial regulations had used the term *cassa*, chest, rather than *capsa*, which in antiquity referred particularly to a case for scrolls and later to a bookcase.

47. See chapter 3, section on business acts.

48. *Statuta Urbis* (1580), bk. 1, art. 36, (referring to art. 35): "Merces autem erit eadem quae pro instrumentis Notariis viventibus & publicantibus instrumenta debetur: quae merces distribuetur prout in supra proximo Capite est dispositum." Heirs were entitled to two-thirds of the transunto fee, and the officials to one-third. As we saw in chapter 2, art. 35 established specific amounts for the officials: 15 bolenenos (baiocchi) to the judge and archivist/scribe, 7.5 bolenenos to the notary of the college, and the remainder to the college.

49. Edict of the proconsuls and correctors, 16 December 1582, ASR, Biblioteca, Bandi, Campidoglio, vol. 436. Six of the sixteen subheadings in the edict related to the Archivio Capitolino.

50. According to the 1507 legislation all notes (i.e., *matrici*) of wills and instruments were

to be registered in the Archivio di Curia "nisi partes contrahentes vel alias disponentes contractus, testamenta aut instrumenta alia publicari noluerint, sed secreta teneri; quo casu fieri debeat per dictos correctores liber secretus, in quo tales notae registrentur . . .; dictusque liber remaneat penes unum ex dictis correctoribus totius collegii iudicio approbatum, vel, si magis parti videbitur, deferatur ad archivium nota vel instrumentum clausum et signatum per dictos scriptores, inviolabiter conservandum usque ad tempus quo illius publication fieri debebit." *Bullarium* 1857–72, 5:460–61, no. 6.

51. They specifically included simple copies, public copies, and *fedi* in this prohibition; edict of 16 December 1582, ASR, Biblioteca, Bandi, Campidoglio, vol. 436.

52. Erectio (1586) in *Statuta* (Rome, 1831), 45.

53. See chapter 2. Guasco 1919a, 101. After the problems of the 1560s, the notaries seemed especially keen to make the hiring decisions on archivists (*custodi*).

54. Lori Sanfilippo 1992, 417. The inventory of 1704 is in ASC, Camera Capitolina, Cred. IV, vol. 61.

55. Domenico Iacovacci produced his genealogical manuscripts between 1621 and 1642; his citations are discussed by Lori Sanfilippo, who points out that Iacovacci conducted his labors on a body of pre-1620 notarial sources that is virtually the same as our own; Lori Sanfilippo 1987, 118n.

56. Statutes (1652) in *Statuta* (Rome, 1831), 13.

57. Erectio (1586) in *Statuta* (Rome, 1831), 47. Because the legislation did not assume that the notary who had died was the owner of the documents ("dominus scripturarum"), it stipulated that the inventory go to the notary's successor not the owner.

58. *Bullarium* 1857–72, 12:96–97, no. 118. Here the pope calls it the "Archive of the Roman People." Such a consignment in 1613 is quoted in Verdi 2005, 427.

59. *Enchiridion* 1966, 20.

60. Panella 1934, 174–82; Delumeau 1957–59, 2:808. For fiscal motives, see also the interesting undated memo to a pontiff in BAV, Vat. lat. 7023, 306r–309v, cited by Feci 1998, 276n. Sixtus V's decision to lease out the archives rather than run them as an organ of the central government, however, sharply distinguished his policy from that of the Medici ruler; Scoccianti 1992, 200.

61. Edict of 12 September 1588, ASV, Misc. Arm. IV–V, vol. 84, no. 178.

62. *Pastoralis officii* in *Enchiridion* 1966, 38–47. The first announcement seems to have been the vernacular edict of the Cardinal Sant'Onofrio on 1 September 1625 giving details about how the archive was to operate; ASV, Misc. Arm. IV–V, vol. 84, no. 172. The newsletters reported on 24 September that the cupboards (*credenzoni*) were already under construction; BAV, Urb. lat. 1095, 577r.

63. 6 June 1566 in *Enchiridion* 1966, 1–4; Lori Sanfilippo 1990, 33; Burke 2002, 256.

64. Edict of the cardinal vicar, 25 January 1585; ASV, Misc. IV–V, vol. 45, 32r. He asked specifically for notes of bequests and donations made in the preceding decade. See also for 1568 orders, Comune di Roma 1920–58, 2:89, nos. 706, 707, and edict of 21 January 1576; ASV, Misc. IV–V, vol. 45, 31r.

65. *Enchiridion* 1966, 11–18. The plan for a central Roman archive for all religious institutions was withdrawn.

66. *Enchiridion* 1966, 31–36. His 1614 chirograph sought to prevent the notaries of the

Apostolic Camera from going into the archive "looking for bulls and other documents" (36). See also Ruggiero 1993, 159.

67. *Enchiridion* 1966, 47–58.

68. Panella 1934, 186–91; Scoccianti 1992, 200.

69. *Pastoralis officii* in *Enchiridion* 1966, 39.

70. *Pastoralis officii* in *Enchiridion* 1966, 38–47. This papal constitution focused primarily on the powers to be wielded by Perini as conservator of the Archivio Urbano.

71. In 1588 the *appalto* or lease of the income from the Papal State archives for nine years had been granted to the Florentine banker Paolo Falconieri; ASV, Misc. Arm. IV–V, vol. 84, no. 178. Panella 1934, 189.

72. *Avviso* of 24 September 1625; BAV, Urb. lat. 1095, 577r. "Conservator" was also the title used earlier in Cosimo I's notarial archive; Panella 1934, 189.

73. BAV, Urb. lat. 1095, 577r, 599r.

74. These edicts are all found in ASV, Misc. Arm. IV–V, vol. 84. An additional edict from 1625 (without day or month) is in ASC, Camera Capitolina, Cred. XIII, vol. 30, 255r, "Instrumenti da rimettersi in Archivio da Notari che hanno offitio e Tasse."

75. BAV, Urb. lat. 1095, 599r (4 October 1625).

76. ASV, Misc. Arm. IV–V, vol. 84, no. 172: "Provisioni et ordini sopra il nuovo archivio," art. 20. "Ogni sorte di vendite, resolutioni di vendite, cessioni, renuncie, transattioni, divisioni, dationi in solutum, permutationi tutte di cose immobili e stabili solamente. Item censi e loro estensioni, quando saranno fatte per instromento separato, tanto delli passati, quanto in avenire, feudi, enfiteusi, livelli, contratti censuali, donationi inter vivos, insinuationi, instromenti dotali sopra scudi cento, aditioni e repudiationi d'heredità con la copia dell'inventarij che fanno gl'heredi e li fideicommissarij e l'usufruttuarij, emancipationi, adottioni, e arrogationi, iuspatronati, mandati di procura irrevocabili & ad vendendum & donandum solamente, fideiussioni perpetue per instromento separato, quietanze d'obblighi perpetui overo dependenti da stabili & immobili solamente." Julius also included judicial acts, and Sixtus placed no restrictions on the types of contracts he wanted brought to the notarial archives of the Papal States.

77. Almost a quarter of the thirty-six regulations for the Archivio Urbano were devoted to wills; see especially arts. 17 to 25. See also the clarifications in "Dichiarationi e tasse sopra le provisioni dell'Archivio," 14 November 1625, ASV, Misc. Arm. IV–V, vol. 84, no. 171.

78. The fee was one grosso (five baiocchi or one-twentieth of a scudo) per one hundred scudi of value; for direct heirs this was capped at two scudi. In the Archivio Urbano this was the standard archiving rate, such that it came to be called the "gabella del grosso per cento."

79. ASV, Misc. Arm. IV–V, vol. 84, no. 172. Art. 20 spoke of durable powers of attorney when employed for sales and gifts of property, but art. 34 stated all powers of attorney, except for those used to begin lawsuits in Rome.

80. ASV, Misc. Arm. IV–V, vol. 84, no. 170. The fee for archiving a foreign power of attorney was one giulio; ASC, Camera Capitolina, Cred. XIII, vol. 30, 255r.

81. ASV, Misc. Arm. IV–V, vol. 84, no. 172. Art. 31: "Le polize o scritture private de contratti perpetui di sopra espressi fatti in Roma, non habbino esecutione alcuna se non saranno archiviate." The parties were to pay the archive fees, which were the same as for notarial documents, and leave a copy there. See also art. 34.

82. Edict of 12 September 1588, ASV, Misc. Arm. IV–V, vol. 84, no. 178. Rome and Bologna were, of course, excluded from this legislation.

83. One hopes that researchers will one day investigate the character and quantity of scriptura privata deposited in the Archivio Urbano.

84. Passeri 1615, 27–28.

85. This alteration was confirmed in the follow up edict of 14 November 1625; ASV, Misc. Arm. IV–V, vol. 84, no. 171.

86. ASV, Misc. Arm. IV–V, vol. 84, no. 172, arts. 27 and 28.

87. A few apparent concessions may have sweetened the deal. An edict published by the Apostolic Camera in 1625 (no other date) promised two legal privileges to the cooperative notary: (1) if his clients had not paid him the archiving fees, he could sue them using the judicial fast track of summary justice, and (2) his own account books would constitute sufficient evidence to take execution on the delinquent's property. ASC, Camera Capitolina, Cred. XIII, vol. 30, 255r.

88. That matriculation in the Archivio di Curia (or College of Scriptors) continued can be seen in the oath taken in 1619 by Bernardino Gargarius, titleholder of Capitoline notarial office 9 from 1618 to 1628, cited in Verdi, 460n.

89. ASV, Misc. Arm. IV–V, vol. 84, no. 172, art. 13. As we saw in chapter 2, however, the College of Scriptors did not concede its right to examine and approve notarial employees and continued to keep matriculation lists of notaries without offices.

90. *Pastoralis officii* in *Enchiridion* 1966, 40–44.

91. ASV, Misc. Arm. IV–V, vol. 84, no. 172, art. 3. The *mensario* was the officer specified.

92. The best documented of the four groups of notaries is the Capitoline notaries, and neither their account books nor their statutes (1652) mention the mensario's service in the Archivio Urbano. Because their other records are missing, however, we cannot know for certain whether trial was ever made of the structure envisioned by the founders.

93. ASV, Misc. Arm. IV–V, vol. 84, no. 172, art. 8.

94. ASV, Misc. Arm. IV–V, vol. 84, no. 172, art. 9. Art. 10 extends this to *donationes inter vivos*. These catalogs, highly prized by scholars, are themselves the subject of a recent inventory in the Archivio Storico Capitolino.

95. ASV, Misc. Arm. IV–V, vol. 84, no. 172, arts. 22, 34, 35. The fee provisions of 1 September 1625 were repeated in an edict of 14 November 1625; ASV, Misc. Arm. IV–V, vol. 84, no. 171; see also the edict in ASC, Camera Capitolina, Cred. XIII, vol. 30, 255r. The copy rate was one giulio (ten baiocchi) per sheet of the original document.

96. Lesellier 1933, 274n. On the contents of the Archivio Urbano, see, in addition to the studies of Lesellier and San Martini Barrovecchio, also Guasco, 1919b. Guasco lists the notaries from the fifteenth to the seventeenth century whose original protocols are located in sections I and II of the Archivio Urbano. For a different view as to why they are there, see Lori Sanfilippo 1987, 102, and 1990, 37.

97. Edict of 30 June 1626, ASV, Misc. Arm. IV–V, vol. 84, no. 169.

98. Guasco 1919b, 239. The only copies of this edict known to me are in the booklet *Archivio Urbani Erectio* 1629, 34–36, which is found in many Roman libraries, including BAV, Editti, 1624–27.

99. *Archivio Urbani Erectio* 1629, 37–39.

100. Lori Sanfilippo 1987, 103.

101. Ago 1998b, 244; 1999a, 198. The *società in accomandita* was not new to Italy; it was used in Florence in the mid sixteenth century and in Milan by the end of the century.

102. Ago 1998a, 190–95; on the general topic, see Stumpo 1985 and for recent bibliography, Colzi 1999.

103. Cf. Hardwick 1998, 43.

104. ASV, Misc. Arm. IV–V, vol. 84, no. 167.

105. ASV, Misc. Arm. IV–V, vol. 84, no. 167: "Volendo la Santità di N. Sig. provedere a gl'inconvenienti che nascano fra Mercanti per non sapere lo stato con chi negotiano, e renderli in qualche parte certi, ha comandato."

106. *Archivio Urbani Erectio* 1629.

107. ASR, Ospedale di SS. Salvatore, reg. 216 (under dates 10 June 1634 and 7 September 1639).

108. Palmerino Speranza's will of 30 March 1627 bears a notation by an archive official dated 7 April; ASR, 30 NC, uff. 11 (Giustiniani), Testamenti (1616–27), 879v. The will of Hortentia Vola rogated by Leonardo Bonanni on 2 November 1629 was not presented until 6 December, well after the ten-day deadline; ASR, 30 NC, uff. 2 (Bonanni), Testamenti (1627–34), 274r. We should recall that these wills were returned to the offices of the Capitoline notaries after archive officials noted them and collected their fees.

109. ASC, AU, sez. 10, vols. 1–10, sez. 14, vols. 1–23.

110. No evidence has yet come to light, for example, of the "brief summaries" of all instruments that the Capitoline and other notaries with offices were supposed to make or of the claim that they kept their perpetual instruments in distinct volumes. Wills were often separate, but that was required by the 1612 reforms.

111. ASR, TCrG, processi, 1631, vol. 264, 513v, 514v. The bond posted by another private notary, Giovanni Battista Siconcellus of Rome, is recorded in an obligatio of 13 January 1628 in favor of the Archivio Urbano; ASR, 30 NC, uff. 2 (Bonanni) 1628, pt. 1, 74r–v.

112. More research is needed to verify the size of this component, which is judged to be quite low by Lesellier (1933, 273n). For the names of such notaries, see Guasco 1919b, 240–50. In addition to Antonio Campora, discussed earlier, see the examples of Angelo Carosio, as cited in San Martini Barrovecchio 1983, 3:853, and Giulio Nini, whose protocols in the Archivio Urbano are described after his death in court testimony; ASR, TCrG, processi, 1635, vol. 306, 532v, 549r.

113. ASR, TCrG, processi, 1635, vol. 306, 527r–v.

114. Permission was granted in a letter dated 16 February 1629; ASR, Camerale II, Notariato, b. 16, fasc. 36. The will of Antwerp painter Paul Brill was among the pilfered documents.

115. Edict of 22 August 1628, ASV, Misc. Arm. IV–V, vol. 76, 244.

116. See the testimony of Capitoline notary Angelo Canini in ASR, TCrG, processi, 1630, vol. 244, 264r.

117. ASV, Misc. Arm. IV–V, vol. 76, 244.

118. ASR, Camerale II, Notariato, b. 22, fasc. 56.

119. As we shall see, this reality was finally registered in a 16 January 1643 edict in which the title conservator disappeared and was replaced by that of archivista; ASR, Bibli-

oteca, Bandi, vol. 18. On Donati, see Visceglia 1995, 48, and ASV, Misc. Arm. IV–V, vol. 84, no. 162.

120. Edict of 16 January 1643, ASR, Biblioteca, Bandi, vol. 18.

121. Edict of 16 February 1639, ASV, Misc. Arm. IV–V, vol. 84, 161. Earlier, the College of Scriptors had argued successfully that the Archivio Urbano would undercut the income of the Archivio della Curia Romana, and Urban VIII had allowed it a yearly payment of fifty scudi from the new archive; this seems to have been cut to twenty-five scudi in the course of the seventeenth century; ASR, Camerale II, Notariato, b. 22, n.p.

122. ASR, Camerale II, Notariato, b. 22, fasc. 56. This is the source for all information on the Archivio Urbano leases.

123. Rodomonte de Nobili from Fermo is recorded as a sostituto under the notary responsible for the criminal proceedings of the governor's court in the 1620s and as the head notary for the Borgo tribunal from 1632 to 1646. ASR, Inventory 278 II, pt. 1, 99–108.

124. On fees, see the treasurer general's edict of 31 October 1646, ASV, Misc. Arm. IV–V, vol. 84, 159.

125. ASR, Camerale II, Notariato, b. 22.

126. Edict of 19 September 1637, ASV, Misc. Arm. IV–V, vol. 84, 162.

127. The passage hinted at some of the recalcitrants: "even if [such gifts] were made to children, college, guild, [or] religious and charitable institution." Notaries were not to execute any instruments based on such documents.

128. Perini received papal permission, documented along with the wills in ASR, 30 NC, uff. 13 (Ottaviani) Testamenti (1628–1634), 83r.

129. ASV, Misc. Arm. IV–V, vol. 84, 162, art. 9: "Havendo la. fel. mem. di Paolo V nella Riforma de' Tribunali di Roma fatta l'anno 1612 ordinato santamente, che i Notari riduchino in libro e leghino in protocollo tutti l'instrumenti che tra certo tempo haveranno rogato. Noi in essecutione di cosi buono ordine e per interesse dell'archivio comandiamo a tutti li notari come sopra che in termine di tre mesi da computarsi dal giorno della stipulatione dell'instrumenti faccino legare tutti l'instrumenti che haveranno rogato cosi essi, come i loro giovani e cosi continuare respettivamente sotto le pene e censure contenute in detta Riforma, e d'altre maggiori a nostro arbitrio e del Conservatore. Dando facultà alli ministri dell'Archivio di rivedere e far rivedere l'offitij a tal effetto, accio trovando alcuno transgressore si proceda contro esso a dette & altre pene irremissibilmente."

130. Edict of 16 January 1643, ASR, Biblioteca, Bandi, vol. 18.

131. The notion and the word *visitatore* had appeared in a curial document possibly prepared in connection with Sixtus V's 1588 law establishing notarial archives in the Papal States (except in Rome and Bologna); BAV, Vat. lat. 7023, 308r.

132. Edict of 16 January 1643, ASR, Biblioteca, Bandi, vol. 18. "ne si possa retardare l'essecutione de mandati dal detto nostro Auditore relassati per virtù di qualsivoglia inhibitione, non gravetur, ò altro sutterfugio [*sic*]."

133. He approved them, that is, after they were also created notary by proper authority and matriculated in the list of the College of Scriptors.

134. "In oltre ordiniamo alli sudetti, che in termine di un mese dal giorno della stipulatione debbiano haver stesi in forma polita da legarsi l'instrumenti, de quali si saranno rogati;

& anco debbiano ritenere appresso di loro la prima minuta, ò matrice per un'anno dal giorno del rogito, havendoci l'esperienza dimostrato il tardare ad estenderli, causare scordanze, e delle circostanze, e qualità, e tali quali alcune volte mutano il contratto con gran danno de contrahenti." Edict of 16 January 1643, ASR, Biblioteca, Bandi, vol. 18.

135. Nussdorfer 1992, ch. 13.

136. ASV, Misc. Arm. IV–V, vol. 84, 159.

137. Interestingly, the note (*nota*) was to include essentially the same information as the old imbreviatura: the date and place of the transaction, the names, birthplaces (*patrie*), and residences of the contracting parties, the names of the witnesses, and the signature of the rogating notary.

138. ASR, Camerale II, Notariato, b. 22, fasc. 56.

139. Their dates were 31 October 1646, 18 December 1659, 31 December 1681, and 30 September 1696; all were emitted by the treasurer general. Guasco 1919a, 73.

140. Edict of 18 December 1659, ASR, Biblioteca, Bandi, vol. 23. With the exception of one passage in which the language was streamlined, the text is a word-for-word copy of that of 1646.

141. According to Lesellier 1933, 274n, the Archivio Urbano remained in the Palazzo Alicorni near St. Peter's until around 1665. Its next location was the Palazzo Salviati just outside Porta Santo Spirito; San Martini Barrovecchio 1983, 3:847. The guidebook to rione Colonna locates the Archivio Urbano in the Palazzo Wedekind (then the seat of the Vicegerente of Rome) on Piazza Colonna in the 1690s; Pietrangeli 1980, pt. 1, 36. See chapter 6 for the knotty problem of dating its transfer to the Vatican.

142. Ago 1999b, 403.

143. Scoccianti 1992, 201.

144. Ago 1998a, 104.

145. BAV, Vat. lat. 7023, 306r–309v.

Chapter 5 • The Office: Building Scribal Lives

1. For two such examples, see a coach maker's receipt, ASR, Ospedale di SS. Salvatore, reg. 214, 19r, and a power of attorney included in ASR, 30 NC, uff. 7 (Paradisi), 1635, pt. 1, 583r.

2. Feci 2004, 150; Ago 2000, 42; 1999a, 200. Cf. Corbo 1984, 60.

3. Ago 1999b, 403–4; 1999a, 202.

4. Passeri 1615, 8–9. See also Ago 1998a, 133; Feci 2004, 151, and on the general topic Fortunati 1996.

5. Petrucci 1978b, 1989.

6. Ago 1998a, 75.

7. ASR, Camerale II, Notariato, b. 3, "Notari che hanno offitio public . . .," (1703), n.p. Some offices operating during the seventeenth century had been suppressed by the time this document was prepared. To clarify the terminology used here, *offices* refer to purchased or leased notarial posts that had some judicial duties. Over time the city and papal governments had also created purely honorific notarial offices that were bought and sold in Rome along with many other honorific posts, such as Capitoline bell ringer, which had no links whatsoever to actual duties of any sort. On this type of office, see De Gregori 1942, 268; Nussdorfer

1992, 92. Many of the "notaries" who received Christmas gifts from the city government in 1641, therefore, were not actual notaries; ASC, Camera Capitolina, Cred. IV, vol. 106, 122v–123v.

8. The number had been cut to five in 1693; *Archivio di Stato di Roma* 1986, 3:1129. In a 1621 list of office prices in Rome, these were the most costly notarial offices, averaging 8,400 scudi each; by contrast, the offices of the thirty Capitoline notaries averaged 1,000 scudi each; Dinarelli 1621, 16, 18. For a comparison of the tribunal of the auditor of the Camera and the Capitoline curia, see Ago 1999b, 397–98.

9. Initially *non vacabile* the offices had become *vacabile* in 1594; ASR, Congregazioni particolari deputate, 43/2, 482–83.

10. The notaries of the Camera are known as the secretaries and chancellors of the Reverenda Camera Apostolica in today's ASR inventories.

11. *Summarium* 1700 explained that they had become venal offices under Alexander VI (1491–1503) and that Sixtus V had added the fourth office. This pamphlet can be consulted in ASR, Camerale II, Notariato, b. 1. For a 1673 survey of notaries attached to Rome's tribunals that varies slightly from these figures, see De Luca 1673, bk. 15, pt. 3, ch. 43.

12. This is not to suggest that the notaries in the other three tribunals did not occasionally act collectively, but there is increased evidence of such activity in the later seventeenth century, as we shall see in chapter 6. For a reference to a *mensario* of the notaries of the Camera in 1621, see Dinarelli 1621, 6.

13. Rome's upstream river port, Ripetta, seems to have had several offices; see ASR inventory no. 368 (II). Before its abolition in 1652, the Curia Savelli had two notaries; Del Re 1957, 394.

14. San Martini Barrovecchio 1983, 3:861. In the early eighteenth century, he was known simply as the notary "of the Archive."

15. Hoberg 1994, 54. ASR, Camerale II, Notariato, b. 3, n.p. (22 May 1703). Scattered references to notaries of the Rota in the 1620s and 1630s confirm the picture of a fluid and ill-defined group. Rota notaries sometimes lacked surnames in the parish registers; ASVR, S. Celso, s. a., 1629, n.p.

16. Bologna, with a population about half that of Rome, had 324 active notaries in 1630; Pastore 1982, 263.

17. Lesellier counted several thousand foreign curial notaries in Rome over the course of the sixteenth century; there is no reason to think the number declined subsequently.

18. On the Jewish notaries, active between 1536 and 1640, see Stow 2001, 8–13. Just as their Christian counterparts wrote in Latin rather than in romanesco or Italian, Jewish notaries used Hebrew in their documents rather than the Italian dialect spoken by their Jewish clients. Clearly a similar conception of a language appropriate for expressing law was operating in both communities.

19. Trasselli 1937, 232. These notarial offices had disappeared by 1700, but the tasks of the notary of the neofiti, who has left a massive archive, had been taken over by one of the Capitoline notaries; Rocciolo 1998, 554. The ASC has an inventory of the notaries of the neofiti.

20. The candidate lists (*bussole*) are in BAV, Barb. lat. 2211, 2213–16, 2218, 2221–23. Missing are the years 1630–31. See Nussdorfer 1992, 74–76.

21. As mentioned in chapter 4, the Archivio Urbano houses the original business acts of eighty-one private notaries active between 1627 and 1699; Guasco 1919b, 240–50. Trial records provide additional names and career details; see, for example, Michele Picollo, born in the 1570s in the diocese of Alba in Piemonte and living in Trastevere in 1633; ASR, TCrG, processi, 1630, vol. 244, 568v–76v (testimony of 9–10 June 1633). The best source, of course, is the parish census records; see, for example, Ludovico, a notary living with his sister and niece in the parish of S. Maria del Popolo in 1631, or Giovanni Felice, a notary residing in the household of Sig. Giovanni Battista Gottifredi in the parish of S. Maria della Rotonda in 1624 and 1625, or Lorenzo Legnini, a notary living with his wife and three other men next to the Giustiniani palace in the parish of Sant'Eustachio in 1629. For these men and others like them, see ASVR, *stati delle anime,* for the relevant parishes and years.

22. François 1886. See appendix A for a discussion of this source; although François' work is an essential research tool for use of notarial records in the ASR, his dates are not necessarily accurate, and his spelling of names often arbitrary. The ASR project of inventorying each of the thirty Capitoline notaries' offices begun in 2005 should provide more-secure dates and identifications.

23. For the list of notaries in the 1630 sample, see appendix A. The series is ASR, 30 Notai Capitolini (30 NC). The numbers of the notarial offices that I use in this book are those currently employed in the Archivio di Stato; for the original office numbers, see table 1 in Ago et al. 1998.

24. The norm was three or four volumes a year, but the exceptions are instructive. Giovanni Francesco Gargario had just begun to exercise office 9 in 1630, yet had six volumes, a number attained by only a handful of colleagues. However, two predecessors surnamed Gargario had been operating office 9 since the 1560s, so he had probably inherited a long-standing client base. At the other extreme, Orazio Balducci's office 23 had been in his name since 1619 but was in the hands of administrators and had only one volume of instruments for the year. More typical is what we see in office 12, where Angelo Canini began to work in 1621; for the first two years he had only one volume of instruments per annum, but in 1623 that had grown to two; following a period of transition, the trajectory of activity was upward. ASR, Camerale II, Notariato, b. 25, inventory of Gaudenzio Antonio de Galassiis in 1704.

25. ASR, 30 NC, uff. 2 (Bonanni), Testamenti, 1627–34, 423v: "So that it is not handled and administered by unworthy individuals of bad character who would tarnish the documents and the good name of the testator."

26. Nor, indeed, were their clients. In 1645 in the seven offices still headed by Capitoline notaries from my 1630 sample, between 31 and 45 percent of contracting parties were from outside Rome; Ago et al. 1998, table 5.

27. Erectio (1586) in *Statuta* (Rome, 1831), 44.

28. Arrigone will in ASC, AU, sez. 34, vol. 28 n.p. (16 June 1648); Canini will in ASC, AU, sez. 34, vol. 28 (15 April 1649); Ottaviani will in ASR, 30 NC, uff. 2 (Bonanni), Testamenti, 1627–34, 421r. On acquiring citizenship, see *Statuta urbis* (1580), bk. 3, art. 57.

29. Cavallo (2007, 136) has recently suggested that occupational transmission from father to son may be dwarfed by transmission among a more broadly defined kin network. On the predominance of male immigrants, see Sonnino 1994, 19–29.

30. Donati 1994, 282–83.

31. Fenzonio 1636, 55.

32. On this general topic, see Nussdorfer 1992, 95–114.

33. Nussdorfer 1992, 76. For a notary's record of one such meeting in the rione of Regola, see ASR, 30 NC, uff. 2 (Bonanni) 1631, pt. 3, 882v.

34. Indeed, nine of the thirty-one notaries in the 1630 sample did not even make it onto the lists of nominees for civic notarial offices between 1623 and 1643.

35. ASC, Camera Capitolina, Cred. I, vol. 33.

36. ASC, Camera Capitolina, Cred. IV, vol. 96, 30v–31v (lease 1616–21), 46v–47v (lease 1622–25); ASC, Camera Capitolina, Cred. I, vol. 32.

37. For the late fifteenth century, by contrast, we are aided by references to books belonging to Roman notaries; Spotti Tantillo 1975, 89–91, and Modigliani 2001, 2:475, 481–83, cited by Feci 2004, 101n; Esch 2001, 178.

38. Bonincontro will, ASR, 30 NC, uff. 18 (Grappolini), Testamenti, vol. 7 (1634–39), 17v. The notary left many pious bequests, but the chapel was begun before his death in 1634; he seems to have served as business manager (*economo*) for the friars of Sant'Isidoro; ASR, Ospedale del SS. Salvatore, reg. 216, 4r.

39. ASR, 30 NC, uff. 2 (Bonanni), Testamenti, 1627–34, 421r–23v, 426r–28r.

40. ASR, TCrG, processi, 1630, vol. 244, 336r. This is not to imply that in Rome impatience with the clergy necessarily meant lack of piety.

41. ASVR, S. Lorenzo in Lucina, s. a., 1632, 51r. ASR, CCN, Registro delle congregazioni, Libro della massa, vol. 11 (1635–38), 38.

42. ASR, TCrG, processi, 1630, vol. 244, 488r–v.

43. ASR, Camerale II, Notariato, b. 16, fascicle 36, n.p. The information comes from litigation connected to Plautilla Scolocci's claims in the 1650s.

44. ASR, 30 NC, uff. 15 (Tigrinus), 1626, pt. 2, 190v (De Fabijs); ASR, CCN, Registro delle congregazioni, Libro della massa, vol. 11, 84r (Muti); 93v, 113r (Barisiani). Vitelleschi ownership of this Trastevere office is attested in ASR, TCrG, processi, 1635, vol. 308, 1019r–v. Barisiani had to be sued for delinquent massa payments; on Barisiani, see also Feci 2004, 227.

45. ASR, 30 NC, uff. 7 (Paradisi), 1628, pt. 1, 374r–75v, 395r–99v.

46. ASR, 30 NC, uff. 7 (Paradisi), 1628, pt. 1, 374r–v; ASVR, S. Eustachio, s. a., 1625, 50r; s. a., 1626, 93v; S. Lorenzo in Lucina, s. a., 1630, 54v; s. a., 1632, 51r.

47. The owners exhorted Camilli to "conduct himself well and maintain the office as a good, true, faithful, and diligent leaseholder and father of a family." ASR, 30 NC, uff. 7 (Paradisi), 1628, pt. 1, 398v.

48. This was a not uncommon amount. In 1626 the annual payment to the owner of office 8 was also fifteen scudi; ASR, 30 NC, uff. 15 (Tigrinus), 1626, pt. 2, 190r–v, 201 r–v.

49. The contract refers enigmatically to judicial acts "of the other office," ASC, Protonotaro del Senatore. Conservatori. vol. 1, 4r–5v. The owner was Maria Provida, daughter of a Neapolitan official, who had received the office as part of her dowry.

50. Mandrico Ayola had been a *sostituto* for Capitoline notary Giovanni Battista Angeletti in 1588 and a year later described himself as *affittuario*. Agostino Amatucci leased office 24 in 1589 and, according to François 1886, became its titleholder in 1592. ASR, CCN, Registro delle congregazioni, Libro della massa, vol. 8, 6r, 17r, 18v, plus unnumbered sheet between f. 21 and f. 22.

51. For office 16, see ASR, CCN, Registro delle congregazioni, Libro della massa, vol. 10, n.p. (October 1619); for Franceschini, see ASR, TCrG, processi, 1640, vol. 358, 196v.

52. Gironimo Arconio and Ludovico Facentino in ASVR, S. Maria in Campo Carleo, s. a., 1622, 40v; François 1886, 95. The succession of short-term administrators lasted for twelve years in office 12 before Angelo Canini acquired it in 1624.

53. Ironically the college's account books are the best testimony of the presence of *affittuari*, for example, in offices 16, 22, and 27 in 1637; ASR, CCN, Registro delle congregazioni, Libro della massa, vol. 11, 82r, 83r, 85v, 92r.

54. ASR, 30 NC, uff. 25 (Raymundus), 1628, pt. 3, 391r–98v.

55. ASR, TCrG, processi, 1630 [sic], vol. 244, 410v.

56. ASC, Protonotaro del Senatore. Conservatori, vol. 1, 4r–5v; ASR, 30 NC, uff. 25 (Raymundus), 1628, pt. 3, 392r; the sale to Pacichelli is described on a sheet inserted between f. 86 and f. 87 in ASR, Ospedale del SS. Salvatore, reg. 216. It is interesting to compare this information to that furnished in a list of Roman office prices and income published in 1621; here the Capitoline notarial offices as a group were valued at thirty thousand scudi or one thousand scudi apiece; Dinarelli 1621, 18. It is to be hoped that further research in the notarial archives will reveal in more detail how the prices of Capitoline notarial offices changed over time.

57. ASR, 30 NC, uff. 25 (Raymundus), 1628, pt. 3, 392r.

58. Biblioteca del Senato, Statuto ms. 517, 20r–v.

59. For Grappolini's rental, installment, and interest payments, see ASR, Ospedale del SS. Salvatore, reg. 216, 6r–v, 10r. See also unpaginated insert between f. 86 and f. 87. The Bonincontro properties included housing for the new notary and his family.

60. Ago (1998a, 57–60) argues that this was not due to a shortage of coin but to other factors.

61. Ago 2000, 37–39. A partnership was called a *societas* or in the vernacular, *compagnia*, so a partner would be known as a *socio* or *compagno*.

62. For office 8, ASR, TCrG, processi, 1624, vol. 190, 347r; for office 17, ASR, TCrG, processi, 1635, vol. 308, 1019r.

63. On Arrigone and Grillo, ASR, 30 NC, uff. 25 (Raymundus), 1631, pt. 1, 87r; on Canini and Novio, ASC, AU, sez. 34, vol. 28, n.p. (15 April 1649).

64. For example, the dowry of Tranquillo Scolocci's wife, which was invested in office 26; ASR, Camerale II, Notariato, b. 16, fascicle 36, n.p.

65. ASR, 30 NC, uff. 25 (Raymundus), 1628, pt. 3, 391r–98v. Guido Camilli's lease of office 20, ASR, 30 NC, uff. 7 (Paradisi), 1628, pt. 1, mentions *scripturae* and *pulpiti* (374v); his office furniture also included stools, benches, and cupboards (396v).

66. Inventory of scripturae in office 20, exercised by Palmerino Speranza from 1616 to 1626, ASR, 30 NC, uff. 7 (Paradisi), 1628, pt. 1, 395r–97r.

67. ASR, Camerale II, Notariato, b. 25, has inventories of the documents of the Capitoline notaries in 1704.

68. Petrucci 1993a, 553.

69. In addition to information gleaned from specific references to the 1630 sample of notaries, I have used three general sources on office locations. The earliest is a list drawn up in 1664 in ASR, Camerale II, Notariato, b. 25; next is an official visitation of sixteen Capi-

toline offices conducted between 29 December 1702 and 2 January 1703 found in ASR, Camerale II, Notariato, b. 3; the last is the locations of Capitoline notaries in 1831 published with their statutes, *Statuta* (Rome, 1831), 71–79. See also Ago et al. 1998, table 2; Verdi 2005, 457, 469–73.

70. Ago et al. 1998, 381; Verdi 2005, 469–73. When in 1673 Cardinal De Luca described the Capitoline notaries as spread throughout the city, he was no doubt comparing them to curial notaries who concentrated heavily in specific streets; 1673, bk. 15, pt. 3, ch. 43.

71. Camilli was in his new location by 1630, ASVR, S. Lorenzo in Lucina, s. a., 1630, 54v.

72. For Tullio's address, ASR, 30 NC, uff. 15 (Spannocchia) 1624, pt. 3, 28r. De Alexandriis must have moved again because he was no longer at this location in 1629; ASR, 30 NC, uff. 2 (Bonanni) 1629, pt. 3, 185r–v, 214 r–v. The competition between the offices on Piazza Mattei emerges from trial documents of 1616, ASR, TCrG, processi, 1624, vol. 190, 353r. "All'olmo" was office 2, Leonardo Bonanni's office from 1622 to 1667 (Nolli, no. 887).

73. Angelo Giustiniani was thought to have this kind of tenure at his Via del Gesù office, ASR, TCrG, processi, 1630, vol. 244, 410r. In Via dei Giubbonari, Paolo Vespignani rented a "domus in qua dictus D. Paulus inhabitat et exercet offitium notariatus Cur. Cap."; ASR, 30 NC, uff. 2 (Bonanni) 1624, pt. 2, 548r. Office 28 was still located in that street in 1886. The way that a given piece of real estate circulated exclusively among notaries is illustrated in the 1629 rental contract for an office near Piazza Rotonda. This was originally rented to the titleholder of office 24 and subsequently sublet to two other notaries who were not attached to the Capitoline curia; it was described as "apothecam cum domo . . . ubi exercet dictum officium." ASR, 30 NC, uff. 2 (Bonanni) 1629, pt. 3, 185r–v, 214 r–v.

74. Statutes (1652) in *Statuta* (Rome, 1831), 32.

75. Ago et al. 1998, 381.

76. The parish priest of S. Lorenzo in Lucina used Guido Camilli's *banco del notaro* as a point of reference in the parish census of 1632. ASVR, S. Lorenzo in Lucina, s. a. 1632, 51r. However, his counterparts in other parishes tended to prefer the term *officio* when enumerating inhabitants. *Studio* is not Roman usage in this period.

77. Although household composition can be traced in the *stati delle anime*, annual censuses executed by parish priests to determine who was eligible to take communion, searching systematically for specific names in the yearly records of more than eighty parishes over a period of several decades is not a feasible task. I have found information on about a third of the Capitoline notaries in the 1630 sample; in addition, I also have household data on several notaries of the auditor of the Camera, for which I thank Patrizia Cavazzini.

78. ASVR, S. Lorenzo in Lucina, s. a., 1630, 54v. Though not mentioned in the 1630 census, the son Cesare is described in the 1632 census as six years old; ASVR, S. Lorenzo in Lucina, s. a., 1632, 51r.

79. The prevalence of males over females in the Roman population is a long noted phenomenon. "The abnormal sex composition of the Roman population in the seventeenth century can be attributed to the large presence in households of males who were not kin and were there for other reasons." Sonnino 1997, 65–66. Sonnino's computerized study of the 1645 parish census data showed that 10 percent of Roman households (9.5% of individuals) were composed of unrelated persons in a startling sex ratio of 420 men to 100 women. This compared to a sex ratio of 167 men to 100 women in the 24 percent of households (34.5% of

individuals) composed of kin and unrelated inhabitants, and 97 men to 100 women in the 66 percent of solely kin-related households (56% of individuals).

80. ASVR, S. Stefano del Cacco, s. a., 1626–30, 91r. Detailed information on Giustiniani's staff and household in 1630 is also found in ASR, TCrG, processi, 1630, vol. 244.

81. For Cortellacci, see ASVR, S. Giovanni della Malva, s. a., 1610–33, (1627, n.p.). For Canini's household, see ASVR, S. Maria in Campo Carleo, s. a., 1620–50, 76r, 110v, 350r, 593r, 790v, 840r–v, 935r. The office is listed separately: 74v, 109v, 350r, 745v, 791r; these young men's names can often be found on notarial acts for the pertinent years. The age range of cohabitants indicates that the living patterns of notarial employees were closer to those of merchants' employees than of artisans' employees; Ago 1998a, 93.

82. ASVR, SS. Apostoli, s. a. 1620–30, 197v. One of the two children was an infant in 1629 who did not appear in the census until 1631 when he was listed as three years old; ASVR, SS. Apostoli, s. a. 1631–37, 8r.

83. Domenico Amadei headed a household of twenty-seven in 1617 and twenty-four in 1629, ASVR, SS. Celso and Giuliano, s. a., 1617–18, 28r, 136r–v, and s. a. 1629 (n.p.). Domenico Fontia lived with sixteen other people in 1629, including a wife and two children; ASVR, SS. Celso and Giuliano, s. a., 1629 (n.p.).

84. While François (1886) gives the beginning of his tenure as 1595, Ottaviani was not admitted to the college until October 1596; ASR, CCN, Registro delle congregazioni, Libro della massa, vol. 8, n.p. (October 1596).

85. ASVR, SS. Apostoli, s. a., 1620–30, 120v, 193v, 209v; s. a. 1631–37, 13r, 138v. Comparing ages over several years in the parish censuses reveals that these must always be regarded as approximate figures; Hortensia Vola's age goes from sixty-six in 1623 to eighty-one in 1630. Hortensia Vola, who seems to have died between the parish censuses of 1630 and 1631, made a will on 2 November 1629 in which she left bequests of ten scudi to her two daughters and to her sister Prudentia [Patritia] Vola, a nun in nearby S. Giacomo delle Moratte; ASR, 30 NC, uff. 2 (Bonanni), Testamenti, 1627–34, 274r–v, 295r–v. Her father, Giovanni Battista Vola, was a Capitoline notary from 1515 to 1575 and her brother Melchiorre, who must have purchased office 13 after 1586, was active from 1575 to 1595; François 1886, 105; Verdi 2005, 453. Giovanni Battista Ottaviani's will drawn up on 5 April 1631 made his daughter Girolama his heir, which would have been unlikely had his son still been alive; ASR, 30 NC, uff. 2 (Bonanni), Testamenti, 1627–34, 421r–23v, 426r–28r. He left fifty scudi a year to his daughter Sister Maria Angelica, who had already received her monastic dowry. Ottaviani exhorted the two to comport themselves affectionately "as good sisters," instructing Girolama to visit her sister monthly. He also asked her to visit and be generous to her elderly aunt (423v) because "the poor thing will have lost the companionship and kindness of this testator and every other human support."

86. ASR, TCrG, processi, 1630, vol. 244, 262r (testimony of 14 April 1632). The *pantani* or swamps had formed in the area of the imperial fora in the Middle Ages and were drained in the late sixteenth century after which the zone was a scene of rapid urban development; Salvagni forthcoming. Canini's house seems to have been located in the block between Strada Bonella and Strada di Croce Bianca (Nolli map, nos. 93 and 98) close to the vanished church of the weaver's guild (Nolli, no. 92). For the location and household information, see ASVR,

S. Maria in Campo Carleo, s. a., 1620–50, 76r, 110v, 350v, 593r, 745v, 790v, 840r–v, 935r (missing 1624–30, 1633).

87. In addition to the parish census data cited in the previous note, see Canini's will in ASC, AU, sez. 34, vol. 28, 15 April 1649, n.p. While the will mentioned Canini's partnership with Novio, the parish census showed Novio in residence at Canini's nearby notarial office in 1646 and 1647; ASVR, S. Maria in Campo Carleo, s. a., 1620–50, 745v, 791r. Much later Novio's grandson reported that his grandfather had purchased the notarial office in 1649; ASR, Camerale II, Notariato, b. 3, n.p., 31 December 1702.

88. ASR, 30 NC, uff. 11 (Saravezzius) 1611, pt. 2, 452r.

89. ASVR, S. Stefano del Cacco, s. a., 1626–30, 12v, 28v, 44v, 64r, 91r. In 1630 Giustiniani was described as guardian for the children of the late Giustiniano Giustiniani, but we do not know what their relationship was; ASR, 30 NC, uff. 17 (Cortellacci) 1630, pt. 3, 5r–v. Most of this information comes from Giustiniani, his servants, and several employees during interrogations in a trial that lasted from 1630 to 1633 and occupies an entire volume of ASR, TCrG, processi, 1630, vol. 244; see especially 247r–61r, 265v–74r, 773r. For Vittorio Giustiniani's formal designation as a notary, see ASR, 30 NC, uff. 11 (Saravezzius) 1610, pt. 2, 795 r–v.

90. ASR, TCrG, processi, 1630, vol. 244, 658v, 773r, 794r, 796r, 798r, 800v.

91. ASVR, S. Stefano del Cacco, s. a., 1639–41, 14v, 43v.

92. While François (1886) gives the beginning of his tenure as 1605, Bonincontro was admitted to the college only in July 1607; ASR, CCN, Registro delle congregazioni, Libro della massa, vol. 9, n.p. (July 1607). Remarkably, he doubled the number of volumes produced by office 18 in just three years; ASR, Camerale II, Notariato, b. 25, inventory of office of Giuseppe Maria Pacichelli.

93. ASR, Ospedale del SS. Salvatore, regg. 214–16. As noted, Ginevra Zeloni Bonincontro was guardian for the couple's two young children and these account books are the *libri tutelari* recording financial transactions relating to their inheritance from their father. Like many Roman family papers, they seem to have ended up in the hospital's possession when the family died out and made the hospital a beneficiary. In addition to these volumes, reg. 209 records separate transactions Ginevra made from her own income before her husband's death.

94. ASR, 30 NC, uff. 18 (Grappolini), Testamenti, 1634–39, 16v. ASVR, SS. Apostoli, s. a., 1620–30, 197v, and 1631–37, 8r, 23r, 41v. François (1886, 47) lists a Marc'Antonio Bonincontro in office 18 in 1586. A Lorenzo Bonincontro, possibly Marc'Antonio's father, seems to have registered acts from the 1540s; see ASR, Camerale II, Notariato, b. 25, n.p. (inventory for office of Giuseppe Maria Pacichelli). Camillo Bonincontro was one of four officials known as "reformers of the university"; Renazzi 1803–6, 2:251. The 1629 agreement between the brothers required that Lorenzo repay the debts that Camillo had contracted between 1625 and 1628 in order to pursue the suit. Lorenzo was to furnish Camillo, who may have had a separate apartment in the Bonincontro mansion, with an annual income of 180 scudi plus linens and household utensils in an amount to be decided by two arbitrators; Lorenzo was to pay the costs of expediting Francesco's benefice, to continue to pay his living expenses, and to give him a yearly income of 80 scudi; ASR, 30 NC, uff. 2 (Bonanni), Testamenti, 1627–34, 171r–74v, 224r–v (9 February 1629). Camillo and Francesco are referred to as deceased in an instrument of 8 August 1631; ASR, 30 NC, uff. 13 (Ottaviani), Testamenti, 1628–34, 656r.

95. The ages of members of the Bonincontro family are more than usually approximate, because data in the parish census of 1629, when they first appear, vary considerably from that given in 1631–33; ASVR, SS. Apostoli, s. a., 1620–30, 197v, and 1631–37, 8r, 23r, 41v. Ginevra Zeloni's year of birth ranges between 1595 and 1601. ASR, Ospedale di SS. Salvatore, reg. 209, indicates that her father's will was notarized in 1626, at which time her brother Vangelista must already have been dead. Zelone Zeloni (also Zenone Zenoni) was originally from Castro San Marcello in the diocese of Pistoia; becoming a Roman citizen, he had been the agent (*fattore*) and procurator for the Roman convent of Tor de Specchi for thirty-seven years. Ginevra disbursed a bequest of seven hundred scudi from her father's estate, including land in their village, to relatives remaining in Castro San Marcello; ibid., n.p. The continuing ties with her father's family in Tuscany are also suggested by the presence in her household in the 1630s of her nephew Matteo Zeloni (born c. 1610). The Capogalli notaries are listed in François 1886, 41. Indeed, they were long settled in the parish of SS. Apostoli where Ginevra lived; Isa Lori Sanfilippo 1992, 426, and 2001b, 443–44. Lorenzo Bonincontro's will and codicil were made 11 and 25 January 1634; he died 1 February; ASR, 30 NC, uff. 18 (Grappolini), Testamenti, 1634–39, 15r, 16r–18v, 19r–v, 22v, 23r–26v. In his will, Bonincontro noted gratefully that his wife did not require support from his estate, commenting that "by the grace of God she has so much of her own property in addition to her dowry that she has no need of what I leave to my and her [*sic*] children, so beloved by her" (18v). Making his son his principal heir, Bonincontro left a dowry of seven thousand scudi to his daughter (23r). Ginevra's guardianship was approved by judicial decree 6 February 1634; ASR, Ospedale di SS. Salvatore, reg. 216, 80r.

96. ASR, Ospedale del SS. Salvatore, reg. 214, 216. The Bonincontro children's income in the first eleven months after their father's death was 1,491 scudi; ibid., reg. 216, 6v. Reg. 209 includes copies of notarial instruments and expenditures related to Ginevra's purchase and renovation of the second house, next to the vanished Church of Santo Spirito (Nolli map, no. 114), in 1632 and 1633. She was no longer listed in the parish census of SS. Apostoli in 1634, though she continued to pay pavement taxes and repairs on the Corso mansion (reg. 214, 137v; reg. 216, 111r). Her daughter died around 1644 (reg. 214, 3r), and her son also predeceased his mother; indirect evidence suggests Ginevra herself died around 1658, at which time the confraternity responsible for managing the hospital of the SS. Salvatore, for which Lorenzo had been notary for many years, was one of the couple's beneficiaries.

97. On Giorgi, see his testimony in ASR, TCrG, processi, 1630, vol. 253, 254v–56r.

98. Because curial posts were venal, the key factor in this ascent was undoubtedly the profits of tax farming. De Totis's story is illuminated by the case of an even more successful family, the Spada of Brisighella, who parleyed tax farming contracts in the Romagna into a cardinalate; Ferraro 1994, 1:299–314. De Totis's will and codicil, rogated by notary of the camera, Rufino Plebani, were opened at his home on the Via dei Coronari on 6 May 1648; ASC, AU, sez. 48, vol. 14, 253r, 254r–61v, 280r–86v. His wife, Caterina Zeccadori, was also denied any voice in family decisions and was instructed to sell the jewels she had been given by her husband and to give the proceeds to the monsignor to invest for the other heirs (254r). It is unclear how many of De Totis's children were also Caterina's, but she also had children from an earlier marriage. De Totis's lease of the city wine tax was meant to run for nine years from 1637; see Nussdorfer 1992, 90; ASC, Camera Capitolina, Cred. IV, vol. 106, 131v. On the Roman ecclesiastical family, see Ago 1997, 87; Pellegrini 1994, 564.

99. Lusanna's history and career are detailed in a copy of his 1616 trial in the Borgo tribunal inserted in the dossier of his 1624 trial in the governor's tribunal, ASR, TCrG, processi, 1624, vol. 190, 338r–77v. After the creation of the Archivio Urbano, Lusanna may have registered as a private notary, for his notarial acts from 1608 to 1629 are in its collection; Guasco 1919b, 246. Office 8 was located at this time just off the Piazza Mattei on the small street leading to the convent of S. Ambrogio. His involvement with office 8 continued after the trials; ASR, 30 NC, uff. 15 (Tigrinus) 1626, pt. 2, 190v.

100. ASR, TCrG, processi, 1624, vol. 190, 353r–54v, 359r, 370v.

101. ASR, TCrG, processi, 1624, vol. 190, 347r–50v, 356r–57v, 360r–61r.

102. ASR, TCrG, processi, 1630, vol. 244, 248r. On labor mobility more generally in Rome, see Ago 1998a, 20–23.

103. *Bullarium* 1857–72, 12:89, nos. 35, 38; Nussdorfer 2008, 124. In Rome the word *giovane*, which literally meant "young man," held the more specific sense of a male worker in a shop or office. In notarial settings, therefore, giovani were not necessarily young. Cavallo (2007, 138) defines the age range of surgeons' giovani in Turin as 17 to 33. For additional references to employees of notarial offices in the reform legislation, see *Bullarium* 1857–72, 12:89–90, nos. 34, 35, 37, 40, 42. Cf. Ago 1998a, 43–45.

104. Later evidence suggests that novices paid titleholders for a one-year training period; this may also have been the case in the 1620s and 1630s. ASR, CCN, Registro delle congregazioni, Verbali, vol. 2, n.p. (meeting of 2 April 1674).

105. For an example of the act of creating a new sostituto, see appendix C.

106. In an edict of 16 February 1639, for example, papal officials reminded employees to sign their names on the instruments they rogated; ASV, Misc. Arm. IV–V, vol. 84, 161. This had been mandated by Paul V's reforms.

107. The confraternity of the orfanelli was one of the contracting parties in both of the apprenticeship contracts I have seen, and the brotherhood clearly wanted formal instruments to record its placement of charges around the city. Interestingly, it was private notaries, not notaries with offices, who made use of this particular labor pool. For Demofonte Ferrini's contract, see ASR, 30 NC, uff. 2 (Bonanni) 1633, pt. 3, 462r–v. Ferrini, who was the confraternity's own notary, agreed that if the boy ran away during his service, he would try to find and return him to the orphanage. For Alexander Prezzatus's contract, see ASR, 30 NC, uff. 2 (Bonanni) 1634, pt. 2, 527r–v.

108. ASR, TCrG, processi, 1630, vol. 244, 262r. Marzio Mecci, a sostituto in the office of a notary of the auditor of the Camera in 1630, also studied with the Jesuits; ibid., 397r.

109. ASR, TCrG, processi, 1630, vol. 244, 408r.

110. Testimony of Ettore Alberti, a giovane in Capitoline offices 10 and 11 between 1630 and 1632; ASR, TCrG, processi, 1630, vol. 244, 326r–v. Giacinto Gallucci, working in office 9 in 1632, said he earned between fifteen and twenty giulii (1.5–2 scudi) a month plus room and board; ASR, TCrG, processi, 1630, vol. 244, 407r.

111. Francesco Oddo earned two scudi (twenty giulii) a month as sostituto in office 21 in 1628, receiving it, as was common, only at the end of twenty-one months; ASR, 30 NC, uff. 25 (Raymundus), 1628, pt. 3, 982r–83v.

112. ASR, TCrG, processi, 1630, vol. 244. Six current or former notarial employees were questioned or submitted statements: Ettore Alberti (twice), the defendant Bartolomeo Bene-

detti (six times), Fulvio Benedetti (no relation), Angelo Falcidio (d. 1633), Giacinto Gallucci, and Horatio Martagna (hired Dec. 1631). Ottaviano Nucci died in May 1631 before he could be interrogated.

113. ASR, TCrG, processi, 1630, vol. 244, 407r, 326r.

114. ASR, TCrG, processi, 1630, vol. 244, 248r, 532r.

115. ASR, TCrG, processi, 1630, vol. 244, 407r.

116. D'Amico 1994, 91.

117. See, for example, Angelo Canini's comments, ASR, TCrG, processi, 1630, vol. 244, 262v.

118. ASR, TCrG, processi, 1630, vol. 244, 248r.

119. ASR, TCrG, processi, 1630, vol. 244, 248r, 398v–99r.

120. ASR, TCrG, processi, 1630, vol. 244, 397v, 408r; ASVR, S. Giovanni della Malva, s. a. 1627, n.p.

121. Mecci, a defense witness, explained, "as sostituto everything passed through my hands. . . . I saw to everything." He said that Benedetti frequently asked him how to do things and "was always afraid of making mistakes." ASR, TCrG, processi, 1630, vol. 244, 397v–398r.

122. ASR, TCrG, processi, 1630, vol. 244, 397r, 262v, 273v; ASVR, S. Stefano del Cacco, s. a. 1628, 44v. The act registering Benedetti's elevation to sostituto, rogated by his older colleague Ottaviano Nucci, is reproduced in appendix C.

123. Giustiniani was aware that his staff thought he had let Benedetti go because of the will he registered in Nucula's acts, but he insisted the real reason was Barberini's instructions; ASR, TCrG, processi, 1630, vol. 244, 270r–v, 23r–v; cf. 63r.

124. In two trials that lasted three years and amassed more than 1,500 pages of documentation, opinions for and against Benedetti were offered by dozens of witnesses; defense witnesses did not mention the theme of his poverty. ASR, TCrG, processi, 1630, vol. 244, 215r–v, 254v.

125. Guasco 1919b, 242.

126. Gallucci was one of the witnesses called to testify on Benedetti's behalf; ASR, TCrG, processi, vol. 244, 406v–15r. In his testimony of 12 and 14 October 1632, Gallucci said that he worked for Giovanni Francesco Gargario, titleholder of office 9. Although François (1886) places this office in the hands of Gargario's successor, Giovanni Francesco Abinante, by 1632, financial records indicate that Abinante was not admitted to the Capitoline college until 1637; CCN, Registro delle congregazioni, Libro della massa, vol. 11, 92v. Nevertheless, the same source showed Abinante owing massa from May 1635 (ibid., 39). For Gallucci's presence in Cortellacci's office, see ASVR, S. Giovanni della Malva, s. a. 1631, n.p.

127. ASR, TCrG, processi, vol. 244, 251v–54v.

128. ASR, TCrG, processi, vol. 244, 324r–28v, 330v–31r. Alberti was interrogated on 15 March and 26 June 1632.

129. ASR, TCrG, processi, 1632, vol. 278, 815r–817v. The brief dossier consists of the complaint of the plaintiff and a statement from a witness, which vividly describe the shakedown by the notary and a constable from his prison.

130. ASR, Inv. 278 II, pt. 1, 99–108.

131. ASR, TCrG, processi, 1630, vol. 244, 27r–v, 60r–v, 64r–v, 247v, 254v.

132. ASR, TCrG, processi, 1630, vol. 244, 60v–61v.

133. Except for the elected position, Fulvio Benedetti would have leased the other offices. Of Giustiniani's other giovani from this period, we know that Horatio Martagna, who worked as his sostituto from December 1631 to Lent 1633, later became a papal notary "di Camera," leasing office 8 of the secretaries and chancellors of the Reverenda Camera Apostolica from 1655 to 1658. Giovanni Matteo Massari of Velletri, who joined the office around December 1631, was Giustiniani's eventual successor in 1645.

134. Although close inspection of Capitoline protocols would certainly add more examples, I have found four cases of sostituti who eventually became titleholders, only one of whom was in the same office. Agabito Ricci, sostituto in office 22 in 1588, became titleholder of office 1 in 1590; Joseph Frosciantes, a sostituto in office 9 in 1597, became titleholder of office 37 in 1601; Alessandro Palladio, sostituto in office 21 in 1598, became titleholder of office 22 in 1608; Angelo Giustiniani, sostituto in office 11, became its titleholder in 1611.

135. ASR, TCrG, processi, 1630, vol. 244, 569r.

136. Nucci had his own bedroom above Giustiniani's office, but the mix of generations in the house seems not to have been without tensions. Irritated by the teasing of the giovani, Nucci occasionally chased them around the room with a club; ASR, TCrG, processi, 1630, vol. 244, 401v. Nucci was involved with office 11 as early as 1596; he served briefly as sostituto in office 25 in 1597, but was back in office 11 by 1599; ASR, CCN, Registro delle congregazioni, Libro della massa, vol. 8, n.p. (April 1596, June 1597), vol. 9, n.p. (August 1599, September 1600).

137. ASR, TCrG, processi, 1631, vol. 264, 513v; he supplemented this with work in the chancery of Tor di Nona prison.

138. "Io ho inteso dire più volte mentre stavo in Campidoglio con l'occas[io]ne de discorsi fatti tra noi altri sosti[tut]i sopra li n[ost]ri p[ad]roni," said Marzio Mecci, sostituto in the office of the notary of the auditor of the Camera Marzio Nucula, commenting on one of them; ASR, TCrG, processi, 1630, vol. 244, 400v.

139. ASR, TCrG, processi, 1630, vol. 244, 330r–v, 334r–v.

140. ASR, TCrG, processi, 1630, vol. 244, 267r–68r, 334r–v.

141. ASR, 30 NC, uff. 2 (Bonanni), Testamenti, 1627–34, 426r; ASC, AU, sez. 31, vol. 19, 575v. Angelo Falcidio, a former giovane in Giustiniani's office, accompanied his new boss, Antonio Lucatelli, notary of the Vicariato, to St. Peter's to make his annual Easter communion; ASR, TCrG, processi, 1630, vol. 244, 533r.

142. Edict of 25 September 1634, ASV, Misc. Arm. IV–V, vol. 45, 66r; edict of 19 September 1637, ASV, Misc. Arm. IV–V, vol. 84, 162, no. 2; edict of 16 February 1639, ASV, Misc. Arm. IV–V, vol. 84, 161; edict of 16 January 1643, ASR, Biblioteca, Bandi, vol. 18; edict of 31 October 1646, ASV, Misc. Arm. IV–V, vol. 84, 159. Statutes (1652) in *Statuta* (Rome, 1831), 25; the college permitted sostituti to sign certain types of mandati.

143. The bequest was rogated with other sums owed Portia, perhaps back wages; ASR, Ospedale del SS. Salvatore, reg. 214, 35v. For a similar case, see Cavallo 2007, 140.

144. Groppi 2000, 77; Hoffman, Postal-Vinay, and Rosenthal 2000, 117–26.

145. Fontaine (1993, 478) claims that credit was at the core of all notarial transactions. See also Brooks 1986, 196–97; Hardwick 1998, ch. 2; Hoffman, Postal-Vinay, and Rosenthal 1999.

146. According to Ago (1999a, 192), "Litigation occurred as a way of establishing the terms of transactions." While acknowledging the dominance of debt in litigation, Smail (2003, 27) makes a different argument for motivation in lawsuits.

147. De Luca 1673, bk. 15, pt. 3, ch. 43. As Capitoline notary Erasto Spannocchia said in 1620, "The protocols are kept in the offices so that anyone can see them when they wish"; ASR, TCrG, processi, 1620, vol. 163, 1167v.

148. *Bullarium* 1857–72, 12:111–53; Ago 1999b, 400.

149. Ago 1999b, 400–1. She has found that even papal kinsmen and highly placed prelates, who of course had access to curial tribunals, sometimes chose the Capitoline court.

150. ASR, TCrG, processi, 1600, vol. 23, 4r–v. I am grateful to Elizabeth S. Cohen for this reference. Under a successor, Tranquillo's office 6 was located near the Palazzo Borghese in 1630, which was very close to the site where these events took place in 1602.

151. ASR, TCrG, processi, 1616, vol. 190, 370v. An instrument of 23 July 1628 shows that Lusanna had at least four hundred scudi invested in a società d'ufficio; ASR, 30 NC, uff. 11 (Giustiniani) 1628, pt. 2, 393r–v.

152. ASR, TCrG, processi, 1631, vol. 264, 601r.

153. ASR, TCrG, processi, 1640, vol. 358, 141v–45v. Palazzo Peretti is now known as Palazzo Fiano. Relations with sostituti were not inconsequential in the choice of notarial office; Feci 2004, 147.

154. ASR, 30 NC, uff. 25 (Raymundus) 1630, pt. 1, 277r; Nussdorfer 1993, 107.

155. Ago 1998a, 75–77.

156. ASR, TCrG, processi, 1640, vol. 358, 234r.

157. Ago 1998a, 77. For the pre-1586 world, Esch 2001, 176.

158. ASR, Ospedale del SS. Salvatore, reg. 214, 100r–01r; *censi* noted in reg. 216, 1r, 2r, 4v, 5r–v, 8r–v; Countess Virginia Mattei Spada's payment to the notary's estate for notarial documents, reg. 216, 9v.

159. Caterina di Corsi, widow of former Capitoline notary Adolfo Ruberteschi: *adhibitio hereditatis*, ASR, 30 NC, uff. 1 (Ricci) 1630, pt. 3, 476r; *fidantia*, 30 NC, uff. 14 (Modio) 1630, pt. 1, 597r–98v, 625r–26r; *restitutio dotis*, uff. 14 (Modio) 1631, pt. 1, 577r–80v, 600r–03v.

160. Ago 1998a, 40.

161. Ago 1999b, 406.

162. ASR, 30 NC, uff. 13 (Ottaviani) 1630, pt. 2, 577r–v, 580r.

163. As mentioned, office 17 was located on the Trastevere side of the river near Ponte Sisto. I know of no other Capitoline office in Trastevere; although there were certainly notaries further upstream in the Vatican Borgo area, they were not Capitoline notaries.

164. See Ago et al. 1998, 382, table 8, though some did more of certain types. By contrast, one notary of the auditor of the Camera did only società d'ufficio loans; Ago 1999a, 197. See also Verdi 2005, 454, 456.

165. To give an idea of the scale of their business, a topic that deserves more research, the charity that looked after new converts (*neofiti*) produced enough business acts in six years in the 1690s to fill a volume of 1,200 pages; Rocciolo 1998, 554.

166. ASR, 30 NC, uff. 11 (Giustiniani) 1631, pt. 3; uff. 2 (Bonanni) 1631, pt. 3.

167. ASR, 30 NC, uff. 11 (Saravezzius) 1584, 555r–56r. They appeared with a list of rules

they wanted him to record; their plan was to take a public copy to the conservatori for confirmation, which would make the rules enforceable.

168. Nussdorfer 1993, 112. They pointedly chose Bonanni over their guild's usual notary Taddeo Raimondo.

169. ASR, Ospedale del SS. Salvatore, reg. 216, 4v, 2r, 7r. Notaries valued the regular income from this kind of relationship; D'Amico 1994, 92.

170. ASR, 30 NC, uff. 18 (Bonincontro) 1630, pts. 1–6.

171. ASR, 30 NC, uff. 9 (Garganus) 1630, pts. 1–3; Verdi 2005, 458.

172. ASR, 30 NC, uff. 28 (Vespignani) 1630, pts. 1–4.

173. Although the 1608 statutes of the hospital of the SS. Sacramento do not mention it, evidence that the secretary's post was purchased appears in ASR, 30 NC, uff. 18 (Bonincontro), Testamenti, vol. 7, 19v. The confraternity of the Genoese nation in Rome elected Sancti Floridi to the job in 1630; ASR, Notai AC, vol. 2991, 45r–v.

174. ASR, TCrG, processi, 1630, vol. 244, 488v; ASR, 30 NC, uff. 11 (Giustiniani) 1630, pt. 1; 1631, pt. 3; ASR, 30 NC, uff. 2 (Bonanni) 1630, pt. 2; 1635, pt. 3. Office 11 had served another charity, the Domus Pia, since 1595 and the guild of fruit sellers since 1606, but Giustiniani added substantially to the business with these new clients in the 1620s; ASR, Camerale II, Notariato, b. 25, n.p. (inventory of Domenico Orsini's office). Bonanni was notary for the orfanelli for almost forty years; Romani 1983, 3:807. In both cases, the institutions remained with these offices long after Giustiniani's and Bonanni's deaths.

175. The confraternity of the Annunziata had turned to his father-in-law long before venality and remained with the same office until Ottaviani's death; ASR, Camerale II, Notariato, b. 25, n.p. (inventory of Francesco Maria Octaviani). See also ASR, 30 NC, uff. 13 (Ottaviani) 1625, pt. 1; 1630, pt. 1; Verdi 2005, 453.

176. Nussdorfer 1993, 105.

177. Groppi 2000, 64; Nussdorfer 1993, 106. For example, the carpenters' guild paid its notary five scudi a year; statuti (1617), 32v, in ASR, Biblioteca, Statuti, 377/5. The Accademia di San Luca, an organization of painters and sculptors, decided to pay its notary three scudi a year in 1623; ASR, 30 NC, uff. 15 (Spannocchia) 1623, pt. 1, 326r–v.

178. The carpenters addressed the issue directly. Saying that they did not want to have to hold up their decisions waiting for the notary's giovane, they insisted that he "stay in our tribunal for at least two hours, and not [leave to] read summons in the Capitoline curia." Quoted in Groppi 2000, 74. The guild tribunals were in the Palace of the Conservators next door to the Senator's palace where the civil judges sat.

179. Nussdorfer forthcoming.

180. The evidence for its location at the corner is from 1645, but it may well have been there earlier; Ago et al. 1998, table 2.

181. As mentioned previously, the masons' guild was another Raimondo client. See also Ago 1998a, 20.

182. Groppi 2000, 64.

183. ASR, 30 NC, uff. 18 (Bonincontro), Testamenti, vol. 7, 19v (codicil dated 25 January 1634).

184. ASR, TCrG, processi, 1620, vol. 163, 1123r–75r.

185. The cénso is copied into the court record, ASR, TCrG, processi, 1620, vol. 163, 1128r–35r. See also Ferraro 1994, 2:958. Ferraro shows that Orazio del Bufalo also made loans (censi) worth many thousands of scudi; ibid., 887, 891. I am grateful to Patricia Waddy for information on Orazio del Bufalo and the property he used as collateral for this loan.

186. Erasto Spannocchia was understandably reluctant to reveal this information to the court, but it is clearly implied by his comments in ASR, TCrG, processi, 1620, vol. 163, 1149r, 1150r.

187. ASR, TCrG, processi, 1620, vol. 163, 1142v–43r.

188. ASR, TCrG, processi, 1620, vol. 163, 1139r. Each sheet was numbered once on the recto, so these are not strictly speaking paginated but foliated. The Roman notaries' verb for this numbering procedure was *cartalare* from the noun *carta*, meaning in this context a sheet of paper. The numbered sheets were said to be *cartalatine*.

189. Capitoline notaries were permitted to charge five scudi to make a public copy of a censo worth one thousand scudi; *Bullarium* 1857–72, 12:135, no. 6.

190. ASR, TCrG, processi, 1620, vol. 163, 1151v.

191. ASR, TCrG, processi, 1620, vol. 163, 1147r–48r, 1151v–52r. At his boss's request, Cepollini made a public copy at the same time (1152r).

192. According to Baldus, a notary should not rewrite an instrument without a court order from the parties; Baldus 1599, 7:55v (ru. 48). On the notary's tearing an instrument by accident, see Fenzonio 1636, 73.

193. ASR, TCrG, processi, 1620, vol. 163, 1125r.

194. ASR, TCrG, processi, 1620, vol. 163, 1126r.

195. ASR, TCrG, processi, 1620, vol. 163, 1148v.

196. ASR, TCrG, processi, 1620, vol. 163, 1149r.

197. ASR, TCrG, processi, 1620, vol. 163, 1148v, 1150r, 1163r.

198. ASR, TCrG, processi, 1620, vol. 163, 1147v, 1168r.

199. ASR, TCrG, processi, 1620, vol. 163, 1138r–v, 1164r. It should be noted that protocols sometimes do include out of sequence instruments inserted at the end of the volume; Ago et al. 1998, 377.

200. The evidence is scanty, but, as we have seen, sums of 11 to 15 scudi a month have been documented. Again, it is interesting to compare them to the figures published in 1621; the Capitoline notarial offices were supposed to provide an average annual profit of 150 scudi each; Dinarelli 1621, 15.

201. Paolo Vespignani (office 28) paid one hundred scudi a year in six-month installments to rent the house on Via dei Giubbonari where his office was located; ASR, 30 NC, uff. 2 (Bonanni) 1624, pt. 2, 548r; Felice Antonio de Alexandriis (office 8) paid the same amount for his space near the Pantheon; ibid., 1629, pt. 3, 185r–v, 214 r–v.

202. Larner 1965, 147–52.

203. As mentioned, there were two civic offices for notaries, notary of the syndics of the officials [of the municipality] and notary of the *paciere*, who earned 7.5 scudi a year; Nussdorfer 1992, 93n.

204. Lorenzo Bonincontro is the exception in this as in so much else. Further research would undoubtedly bring to light more evidence on the other business interests of the Capitoline notaries. Francesco Arrigone of office 21, notary for the tavern keepers' guild,

seems to have been part owner of an *osteria* in Piazza Monte Giordano; ASC, Protonotaro del Senatore, Conservatori, vol. 1, 428r–v. The titleholder of office 15 invested in a partnership with a secondhand goods dealer in 1616; ASR, 30 NC, uff. 15 (Moschinus), 1618, pt. 1, 191r–v. I thank Eleonora Canepari for this reference.

205. For example, the titleholder of office 16, Marco Tullio dell'Huomo in 1618, discussed earlier in this chapter, and that of office 29, Biagio Cigni in 1622, described by Ago 1998a, 149.

206. See reference to this practice in *Bullarium* 1857–72, 12:140, no. 136.

207. Flavio Paradisi (office 7) did this in several instances, including paying thirty-five scudi to Livio Prati's heiress for the right to collect the fees due on transunti of her grandfather's instruments; ASR, 30 NC, uff. 21 (Arrigone) 1635, pt. 3, 120v.

208. ASR, TCrG, processi, 1640, vol. 358, 238r; ASR, TCrG, processi, 1630, vol. 244, 396v. As we saw earlier in this chapter, some leases carried this stipulation. Titleholders also expected to provide constant access to clients coming to see business acts archived in the office's protocols.

209. The jurist Cardinal De Luca likened civil proceedings to the four ages of man: infancy, when the suit was introduced, followed by adolescence, when evidence was gathered, then adulthood, when arguments and counter arguments were made, and finally old age, when the judge pronounced sentence; 1673, bk. 15, pt. 1, ch. 12. See also Salvioli 1925–27, 3.2:232–326, 503–36.

210. One of the definitions of the term *fede* in modern Italian is document or certificate. In early modern usage, the term denoted a signed copy that was not "public"; it was used in reference to both business instruments and judicial warrants (*mandata*).

211. In addition to previously cited sources on the copy rate, see the testimony of Angelo Giustiniani and numerous references in the 1612 reform legislation; ASR, TCrG, processi, 1630, vol. 244, 336r; *Bullarium* 1857–72, 12:126, no. 102; 135, no. 7; 136, no. 34.

212. *Bullarium* 1857–72, 7:221, no. 58. The city statutes explicitly imposed this rule on Capitoline notaries in 1580; *Statuta urbis* (1580), bk. 3, ch. 113.

213. 1363 statuti, bk. 1, art. 113.

214. As we saw in chapter 3, the earliest evidence for this is from 1446, and judicial acts led the way.

215. *SPQR Statuta* (1519–23), bk. 5, art. 12; see chapter 3.

216. *Bullarium* 1857–72, 12:137, no. 54.

217. Ago 1999b, 396. The role judges played in defining the types of warrant or summons on offer needs further research.

218. It has been argued elsewhere that even the poor knew how to use the courts to block a seizure of property; Kagan 1981, 85. In Rome, as we saw in chapter 3, the popes did not abandon the poor. In 1562 they banned written evidence in disputes involving two scudi or less, meaning that judges should hear oral arguments, and they raised this ceiling to five scudi in 1612; *Bullarium* 1857–72, 7:221, no. 61; 12:86, no. 5.

219. *Bullarium* 1857–72, 12:135, nos. 1–6. The ceiling was set at twenty-five scudi.

220. *Bullarium* 1857–72, 12:135, no. 7.

221. *Bullarium* 1857–72, 12:136, nos. 21–23, 35–38.

222. This is a central theme of Ago 1998a, chs. 5 and 6; 1999b; and 2000, but see also Ago 1996, 131.

223. *Bullarium* 1857–72, 12:136–37, nos. 21, 41–43.

224. The 1612 legislation also did away with the rate differential for house calls found in the 1580 statutes; *Statuta urbis* (1580), bk. 3, ch. 93. Clients paid the same fee regardless of whether the notary came to their home or shop, or they visited him in the courtroom or office. However, notaries were still allowed to charge for their travel expenses when examining witnesses outside the office; *Bullarium* 1857–72, 12:139, nos. 92, 93.

225. ASR, TCrG, processi, 1624, vol. 190, 371r. Lusanna's testimony is from a 1616 trial inserted here.

226. This is pieced together from references in ASR, 30 NC, uff. 25 (Raymundus) 1631, pt. 1, 87r–v, 90r, but almost any contract would reveal a similar intersection of document types.

227. ASR, 30 NC, uff. 24 (Attilio) vol. 10, 587r.

228. ASR, Ospedale del SS. Salvatore, reg. 216, 87. Admittedly, she was not supposed to have been able to obtain a warrant with a simple copy.

229. For an example of a meeting explicitly authorizing litigation, see the painters' confraternity in ASR, 30 NC, uff. 11 (Saravezzius) 1593, pt. 3, 168r–69v. I thank Peter Lukehart for this reference.

230. Ago 1998a, 38, 108–9, 155–57.

231. ASR, TCS, b. 2083; Ago 1998a, 76.

232. Ago et al. 1998, 376n, 380.

233. Ago et al. 1998, 377. They uniformly ignored the 1612 mandate that they bind their business acts every three months.

234. Ago et al. 1998, 376. This is the total number of contracting parties, not the total number of individuals.

235. Ago et al. 1998, 377, 379.

236. ASR, 30 NC, uff. 13 (Ottaviani) 1630, pt. 2.

237. Roman notarial acts exhibited a high degree of formal stability from the fourteenth century onward; Verdi 2005, 450. Meetings (designated as *adunantia* or *congregatio*) usually began with the time and place of the assembly followed by the names of those in attendance; Nussdorfer 1993, 108.

238. Ago et al. 1998, 382.

239. Ago et al. 1998, table 8; Ago 1999a, 195.

240. This is admittedly a very crude indicator because it does not take into consideration the size of the protocols or the value of the transactions they record.

241. ASR, Camerale II, Notariato, b. 25, inventory of Giovanni Antonio Cimarroni in 1704. This is a more accurate source for the titleholders than the list in François 1886, though the recent inventories of the fondo 30 Notai Capitolini should be even more precise. In 1645 under Contucci, office 27 produced a total of 383 business acts, well below the average of 563; in the sample of fifteen offices, only offices 4 and 6 had a lower number (347); Ago et al. 1998, table 3. Although we have only limited information on ownership of office 27 over the whole period, the patrician Lelio Barisiani owned it in the 1630s.

242. ASR, Camerale II, Notariato, b. 25, inventory of Gaudenzio Antonio de Galassiis in 1704.

243. ASR, 30 NC, uff. 12 (Canini) 1632, pt. 1.

244. ASR, Camerale II, Notariato, b. 3, n.p., 31 December 1702.

245. *Bullarium* 1857–72, 12:135, no. 4. Despite the lengthy lists of fees in the 1612 regulations, the profession's standard for the rest of the century, it is actually very difficult to find out how much any specific transaction earned a Capitoline notary. The series of mandatory office receipt books (*libri receptorum*) that contained this information has almost completely disappeared; the only extant seventeenth-century example covers the years 1673–78; ASR, Inventory 286 I, appendix D (office 37). The price of the Capitoline power of attorney (*mandato di procura*) comes from part of office 20's receipt book that was copied into trial testimony; ASR, TCrG, processi, 1640, vol. 358, misnumbered folio between 195 and 196.

246. *Bullarium* 1857–72, 12:135, no. 6; ASR, Camerale II, Notariato, b. 16, fascicle 36, n.p. The fee for the disputed will of Scipione Muratore for which Angelo Giustiniani's sostituto was arrested was to be fifty scudi, but fifty scudi d'oro if the notary would give the heirs a public copy of the document; ASR, TCrG, processi, 1630, vol. 244, 29v. Muratore's will was rogated by Marzio Nucula, a notary of the auditor of the Camera; in this tribunal, notarial fees for wills were capped at one hundred scudi; *Bullarium* 1857–72, 12:125, no. 95.

247. It was not uncommon for testators to specify in their wills the amount the notary should be paid by heirs.

248. ASR, 30 NC, uff. 2 (Bonanni) Testamenti (1627–34). Despite its title, the volume includes a range of other instruments, though usually they are closely related to a will.

249. ASR, TCrG, processi, 1640, vol. 358, 135r–36v. The fact that Giustiniani's sostituto worked extensively on a will that was rogated in a different notary's office received much comment during the young man's trial; ASR, TCrG, processi, 1630, vol. 244.

250. This point emerges in Giustiniani's testimony; ASR, TCrG, processi, 1630, vol. 244, 335v–36r.

251. Ago estimates that they made up 12 percent of all contracts, while pointing out that more are hidden in nonspecific types like obligationes; Ago 1998a, 191. The involvement of Roman notaries in the commerce in money is documented from the fourteenth century; Lori Sanfilippo 2001b, 448.

252. Ago 1998a, 191.

253. Ago 1999a, 195n. For their origin in the fifteenth-century papal curia, see Partner 1990, 63. The locus classicus on the società d'ufficio (also known as *compagnia d'ufficio*) is De Luca's 1673 treatment in *Il Dottor Volgare*, bk. 5, pt. 4. Another source, which I have not been able to consult, is Silvester Zacchias, *De modo validè contrahendi societates super officijs Rom. Cur. Sive Ad formulam instrumenti societatis officij* (Rome: Reverenda Camera Apostolica, 1619).

254. Ago 1999a, 195–96. My description oversimplifies for, in fact, the way that these short-term loans were turned into de facto long-term loans involved some risk to the parties involved, which justified their elevated rate of return. Ago's is the best technical discussion of the società d'ufficio available in English.

255. Ferraro 1994, 1:354–55.

256. Romans seemed to have been fairly promiscuous in their choice of notaries for società d'ufficio loans, as is illustrated by the list of nine società d'ufficio owned by Lorenzo Bonincontro's brother Camillo. Although he favored his neighbor Giovanni Battista Ottaviani, he also used the services of other Roman notaries; ASR, 30 NC, uff. 2 (Bonanni)

Testamenti (1627–34), 382r–v. This contrasts with the findings of researchers studying the role of notaries in the Parisian market for long-term loans, where clients definitely stuck to a preferred notary; Hoffman, Postal-Vinay, and Rosenthal 1999, 84.

257. ASR, TCrG, processi, 1630, vol. 253, 255r.

258. ASR, TCrG, processi, 1630, vol. 244, 324v.

259. ASR, TCrG, processi, 1630, vol. 253, 252v.

260. Nussdorfer 2008, 132–34.

261. ASR, TCrG, processi, 1630, vol. 244, 263r–v.

262. The case is found in ASR, TCrG, processi, 1630, vol. 253, 251r–318v.

263. ASR, TCrG, processi, 1624, vol. 190, 350r.

264. ASR, TCrG, processi, 1624, vol. 190, 357v.

265. ASR, TCrG, processi, 1624, vol. 190, 350r. For similar *truffe* in Vicenza in this period, see Lavarda 2002, 38.

266. ASR, TCrG, processi, 1624, vol. 190, 357v, 358v, 367v–68r.

267. *Bullarium* 1857–72, 12:89, nos. 38, 39.

268. *Bullarium* 1857–72, 12:89, no. 40.

269. ASV, Misc. Arm. IV–V, vol. 84, no. 172, arts. 11, 20, 34. See chapter 4.

270. ASV, Misc. Arm. IV–V, vol. 84, no. 170.

271. As noted in chapter 3, more than thirty thousand volumes of business acts survive compared to fewer than four thousand volumes and folders of judicial acts; *Archivio di Stato di Roma* 1986, 3:1131, 1196, 1213; Verdi 2005, 438, 442, 445. Because the yearly output of protocols was roughly double that of manuali, at least in the seventeenth century, these figures give a rough sense of the disproportionate losses of judicial acts.

272. For the extant holdings, see ASR, TCS, Inv. 286 I. For the losses since 1704, cf. ASR, Camerale II, Notariato, b. 25, inventories. In 1704, for example, Canini's successor (G. A. de Galassijs) still retained all seventeen manuali originally produced in office 12 between 1640 and 1648; now only five exist. The same story could be repeated for other offices. Although many more manuali for the seventeenth century survive than for the sixteenth century, the series is spotty for the notaries in my 1630 sample: Bonincontro has none, for instance, while Scolocci has one a year for forty years of his more than fifty-year tenure. While useful for some purposes, another fragmentary series, *testes* (witness testimony), gives only a limited picture of the volume of Capitoline notaries' judicial business. For more on this source, see Ago 1999b, 397–98.

273. In Sixtus V's legislation, this was one-quarter of the fees for "registris, extractibus, instrumentis sententiarum, mandatis executivis, ac de immittendo, seu manutenendo in possessionem . . .," Erectio (1586) in *Statuta* (Rome, 1831), 44.

274. ASR, TCrG, processi, 1624, vol. 190, 373r.

275. ASR, CCN, Registro delle congregazioni, Libro della massa, vol. 11 (1635–38).

276. The 1652 notarial college statutes added one-quarter of the fees from the following mandata related to public bonds (*loca montium*) "de transferendo loca montium; de delendo quaecumque vincula in dictis locis montium, vel eorum partitis descripta, atque apposita; quaecumque alia mandata secretariis locorum montium directa; de consignando, gratiosa et rigorosa, loco tamen mandatorum executivorum," Statutes (1652) in *Statuta* (Rome, 1831), 18.

277. ASR, 30 NC, uff. 24 (Attilio) vol. 10. This *manuale actorum*, missing the first 286 folios, covers April through December 1630.

278. See, for example, ASR, TCrG, costituti, vol. 600 (1605), 88v; my thanks to Elizabeth S. Cohen for this reference. See also Ago 1999b, 406; Di Sivo 2001, 15. On costs of witness testimony: *Bullarium* 1857–72, 12:138–39, nos. 86–94. Although not mentioned among Capitoline fees, "summary testimony" in which witnesses did not answer questions but simply made a statement was available in the curia di Ripa for an economical three baiocchi; *Bullarium* 1857–72, 12:146, no. 3.

279. Ospedale di SS. Salvatore, reg. 216, unnumbered folio (loose) between 86 and 87. The quotation is from the plaintiff in the case against Capitoline notary Flavio Paradisi, discussed below; ASR, TCrG, processi, 1638, vol. 328, 1465v.

280. ASR, TCrG, processi, 1630, vol. 244, 491v. He was referring to the *maestri giustizieri*.

281. ASR, TCrG, processi, 1638, vol. 328, 1463r–66r. The plaintiff charged both Paradisi and his unnamed sostituto with forgery and added that they "were accustomed to doing such crimes and had been accused in several tribunals and in particular before the Capitoline court" (1466r). Although these cases have not yet come to light, Paradisi does figure in a bizarre slander case in 1646. Paradisi accused Lorenzo Lazzonio, who allegedly owed him money, of writing a defamatory libel calling him a cuckold (*becco*). Handwriting experts proved that Lazzonio was innocent, and the real author of the libels was Paradisi himself. Lazzonio added in his own defense that if he had wanted to injure Paradisi, he would have called him a forger (*falsario*), not a cuckold; Antonucci 1992, 266–67, 300–301.

282. Ago 1998a, 104.

283. ASR, TCrG, processi, 1635, vol. 306, 298r–306v. Muti held the Roman People's most prestigious office, conservator, in 1631, after having been twice on the eligibility list (*bussola*) for civic offices. In 1643 he married a niece of Cardinal Jules Mazarin; Dethan 1968, 35–36.

284. ASR, TCrG, processi, 1635, vol. 306, 300r–01r. It is not clear that the plaintiff knew of Bernascone's role, for he was not named in the original accusation.

285. ASR, TCrG, processi, 1630, vol. 244, 329r.

286. ASR, TCrG, processi, 1640, vol. 361, 1151r–v.

287. ASV, Misc. Arm. IV–V, vol. 76, 244; Gigli 1994, 2:708.

288. ASR, Ospedale del SS. Salvatore, reg. 216, 9v.

289. ASR, TCrG, processi, 1603, vol. 44, 1056v.

290. ASR, TCrG, processi, 1630, vol. 244, 423v–24r, 784r, 786r. This is a small contribution to the provocative question historians have recently posed of whether judicial corruption was perceived as misconduct or simply as one of a number of ways to make the early modern state function. The presence of so much private enterprise at the heart of what Fosi terms the "state apparatus of the ancien régime" makes the problem especially challenging; Fosi 1997, 28.

291. ASR, TCrG, processi, 1630, vol. 253, 301r–v.

292. ASR, TCrG, processi, 1630, vol. 244, 265v–66r.

293. Fenzonio 1636, 57.

294. Erectio (1586) in *Statuta* (Rome, 1831), 41.

295. ASR, TCrG, processi, 1624, vol. 190, 350v.

296. ASR, TCrG, processi, 1635, vol. 308, 1019v.

297. Evidence of litigation between a client and Giovanni Felice Iuvenale, the titleholder of office 24 from 1615 to 1629, can be found in his successor's manuale for July 1630; ASR, 30 NC, uff. 24 (Attilio) vol. 10, 529v–30r, 536v–37r, 582r, 605r. Of course, they might also lodge criminal charges, as in Spannocchia's case.

Chapter 6 • The State: Policing Notarial Practices

1. While not directly relevant to notaries, the suppression of nepotism was urged in the same circles that criticized venality; see Pellegrino 1994. It should be noted that the debates were frequently more daring than the ensuing policies.

2. Pastor 1928–41, 33:11; Andretta 1982–; 2000; Tabacchi 1997, 174; Visceglia 2004, 268.

3. The Capitoline notaries learned of the invitation the preceding December; ASR, CCN, Registro delle congregazioni, Verbali, vol. 2, n.p., meeting of 1 December 1672. At the Quirinal meeting, they made two main complaints. Asking for enforcement of the 1580 city statutes that mandated the use of the senator's tribunal by all citizens and residents (*incolae*) of Rome, they claimed that the public was going elsewhere, especially for their supporting documents (*informationibus*). They also objected to the fact that soldiers cited to appear in their court were evading their creditors by going to the judge of the Castel Sant'Angelo. ASR, Congregazioni particolari deputati 43/2, 441–42, 741.

4. ASV, Fondo Carpegna, vol. 29, 146r–v (copy of a letter dated 9 February 1672); Donati 1994, 177. Twelve Capitoline notaries signed the petition. Their proposal was to borrow ninety thousand scudi via a *monte camerale*, pay off about thirteen thousand in debts and charges, and purchase the sixteen offices that would be suppressed. They would then repay the loan at the rate of thirty-six hundred scudi a year. The sixteen suppressed notaries would go to work for the fourteen remaining titleholders, who would be authorized to add on to their residences or lease more space without an increase in the rent.

5. ASR, Congregazioni particolari deputati, 43/2, 718–19, 731.

6. See appendix B, discussed later in this chapter. Adding to the strain might be a decline in the use of notaries, as Ago (2000, 42) suggests. Further research would be needed to confirm this hypothesis. I have tried to verify it using the crude index of the number of protocols produced by a sample of the thirty Capitoline offices, as revealed by their early eighteenth-century inventories, but have been unable to discern a consistent pattern.

7. Donati 1994, 168–70, 173.

8. Most venal curial offices lasted until the nineteenth century; Frenz 1989, 68.

9. Prodi 1982, 156n; Donati 1994, 171–72; Lauro 1991, 296–98.

10. Lauro 1991, 298–300; Donati 1994, 172; Di Sivo 1997, 280; L. Sinisi 1997, 117n.

11. *Decreta* 1679, 1.

12. *Decreta* 1679, 1; Lauro 1991, 298–99. As we saw in chapter 2, Sixtus V had introduced a role for the cardinal prefect of the Segnatura della Giustizia in his 1586 legislation making the Capitoline notarial offices venal. Later records refer to the Capitoline notaries' regular custom of reading summons before the cardinal prefect's auditor; ASR, CCN, Registro delle congregazioni, Verbali, vol. 4, n.p. (18 September 1710, 3 October 1711, 18 October 1711).

13. *Decreta* 1679, 8. Interestingly, he chose as the standard rate the fees authorized by the 1580 civic statutes for use in the Capitoline court.

14. *Decreta* 1679, 9. The system outlined in the 1679 decrees does not conform in all details with the description given by San Martini Barrovecchio 1983, 3:858–59.

15. ASR, CCN, Registro delle congregazioni, Verbali, vol. 3, n.p., 5 October 1702.

16. Rubb. 36, 37, 42, 46, 61, ASC, Camera Capitolina, Cred. IV, vol. 88, 0149r–0151v, 0155r. By 1679 it was no longer necessary to specify that would-be notaries should not have performed manual labor for four years.

17. As we saw in chapter 2, a one-year apprenticeship with an attorney or notary had been mandated in the 1446 statutes of the Capitoline notarial college. This was raised to three years in the 1521 city statutes, only to be dropped altogether in the final redaction of the city statutes of 1580.

18. Donati 1994, 169, 174–75. It was said that ninety-seven courts were suppressed by this legislation (165).

19. Donati 1994, 165–66. The tribunals of the governor of Rome and the cardinal vicar with their notaries did not move to Montecitorio. The notaries of the Camera had offices nearby in Piazza Colonna.

20. Pastor 1928–41, 33:4; Donati 1994, 176; Andretta 1982–. *Zelanti* was the contemporary term applied to the reformers in the Curia who asserted strict ecclesiastical principles at the expense of such long-standing customs as nepotism and venality.

21. Valesio 1977–79, 1:286. Clement XI was elected in November 1700, and the Sollievo was reestablished in February 1701. For its initial establishment, see Lauro 1991, 528.

22. Lafitau 1752, 1:64, 66–67, 247–48.

23. ASV, Fondo Albani, vol. 14, 40r–v. While the document is undated, I believe on the basis of internal evidence that it was composed in early 1702. See the discussion of the Archivio Capitolino later in this chapter.

24. Pastor 1928–41, 33:503n.

25. Valesio 1977–79, 2:295. ASR, Camerale II, Notariato, b. 3, n.p. (October 1702).

26. ASR, Camerale II, Notariato, b. 3, n.p., dated Friday, 1 December 1702.

27. The ex post facto quality of this congregation is evident also in the fact that many affected petitioners seemed unaware of its existence, addressing themselves to Cardinal Marescotti, prefect of the Congregation of the Sollievo. (See also ASR, CCN, Registro delle congregazioni, Verbali, vol. 4, 2v.) Its ad hoc nature also helps to explain why it has no archival series of its own; cf. Blouin 1998, 279.

28. ASR, Camerale II, Notariato, b. 3, n.p., dated Friday, 1 December 1702. One of the judges for whom the thirty Capitoline notaries worked, the first *collaterale* Giovanni dei Gambis, later joined them; ASV, Misc. Arm. IV–V, vol. 45, 42r. Pastor 1928–41, 33:12.

29. Edict of 12 September 1588, ASV, Misc. Arm. IV–V, vol. 84, no. 178; Edict of 19 September 1637, ASV, Misc. Arm. IV–V, vol. 84, 162; see also the edict of 16 January 1643, ASR, Biblioteca, Bandi, vol. 18. In the Kingdom of Naples from at least the late sixteenth century inspectors were sent to provincial notaries to ensure compliance with regulations about how protocols were to be made; Nardella 1993, 288–89.

30. Cola, lxxiii–lxix. I thank Dott.ssa Lucilla Cola for kindly allowing me to consult her thesis. This last instruction is found also in the 1704 decrees; ASV, Misc. Arm. IV–V, vol. 45, 44r.

31. ASR, Camerale II, Notariato, b. 3, n. p., questionnaire addressed to the secretaries and chancellors of the Reverenda Camera Apostolica (i.e., notaries of the Camera).

32. Pagano 1980, 326; Tabacchi 1997, 169; Santoncini 1998, 361n, 380–82; Castiglione 2005, 95.

33. Because this tribunal had both civil and criminal jurisdiction, there were also particular questions for the sostituto who did the criminal cases. Did he extend the criminal judge's decreto under the pertinent warrant on the same day? Did he register criminal warrants and decrees in a separate manuale or in the same one used for civil cases? Did he make public copies of the criminal sentences and record them with the rest of the case and bind them in a separate volume or with the office's civil sentences? Each year did he bind criminal cases that had been concluded? ASR, Camerale II, Notariato, b. 3, questionnaire addressed to the secretaries and chancellors of the Reverenda Camera Apostolica; n.p.

34. Ibid., "Se habia carattere intelligibile e scritto corretto."

35. It is likely that Guelfio and De Grandis did this part, because they routinely set the examinations for novizi and sostituti and were intimately familiar with notarial practices.

36. This is included in the unpaginated file, ASR, Camerale II, Notariato, b. 3.

37. ASR, Camerale II, Notariato, b. 3, n.p., visitation of the office of Giovanni Giuseppe Novio, titleholder and owner of office 12 from 1678 to 1703.

38. Depositions (*testes*) were supposed to be bound in their own volumes, but the inspectors instead found a great variety of practices in evidence. Sometimes they were recorded in loose notebooks, sometimes bound in the *broliardo* of judicial acts, and sometimes just stacked, as for example in office 24 where several years' worth of testimony accumulated because there was not enough yet "to make a protocol"; ASR, Camerale II, Notariato, b. 3. This helps to explain the spotty survival of these valuable documents.

39. ASR, Camerale II, Notariato, b. 3, visitation of the office of Giovanni Giuseppe Novio. Paul V's reforms had mandated three separately bound series for judicial acts: the manuale, witness depositions, and sentences.

40. ASR, Camerale II, Notariato, b. 3, n.p. All details are drawn from the notebook recording the visitation of sixteen Capitoline notaries in this file.

41. ASR, CCN, Registro delle congregazioni, Verbali, vol. 4, 2v. The earthquake hit on 14 January 1703. Interestingly, they refer to their persecutors as the Congregation of the Sollievo.

42. See appendix B ("Proposte") from ASR, Camerale II, Notariato, b. 3, n.p., n.d. While some issues raised in the "proposte" are referred to in meetings of the Capitoline notaries held before the inspection, its references to "questa congregazione" lead me to believe that it was written at some point after the decision was taken to launch the full investigation of the notaries in December 1702 and before completion of the final draft of the reform decrees in February 1704. The petition regarding the Archivio Urbano is found in ASR, Camerale II, Notariato, b. 16, fascicle 36. Although it too is undated, it is addressed to Cardinal Marescotti.

43. Cf. ASR, CCN, Registro delle congregazioni, Verbali, vol. 3, n.p., 23 May 1701, 2 June 1702.

44. See appendix B.

45. Ibid.

46. Ibid. In fact, Paul V's legislation may have fostered a version of this disdained judicial practice; see *Bullarium* 1857–72, 12:97, no. 9.

47. ASR, Camerale II, Notariato, b. 16, fascicle 36.

48. ASR, CCN, Registro delle congregazioni, Verbali, vol. 3, n. p., 23 May 1701.

49. ASR, Camerale II, Notariato, b. 3, n.p. These "public notaries" are listed with their locations in a document dated 1703; the list seems to have been drawn up in order to ascertain which had made inventories of their holdings.

50. In ASR, Camerale II, Notariato, b. 3, there is a page of notes headed "in the Capitoline notaries' offices" that begins "in addition to the failings common to the other notaries" and lists fourteen items. These range from the general, "missing tables of contents in many volumes," to the quite specific, "in Pasquarucci's office [8] the instruments are torn in many protocols" or in office 6 "some instruments have not been extended according to the tenor of the matrici." This document must represent a preliminary processing of the notes on the thirty visitation reports.

51. ASR, Camerale II, Notariato, b. 3.

52. Valesio 1977–79, 2:640. Valesio worried that "an infinite number of lawsuits" would ensue.

53. ASV, Misc. Arm. IV–V, vol. 45, 43v. It proved impossible to prevent all future absurdity: a cache of several hundred sealed wills dating from 1598 to 1798, which were deposited in the Archivio Urbano, recently came to light; Scano 1989.

54. Drafts of the decrees are included in ASR, Camerale II, Notariato, b. 3, n. p. My source for the published decrees is ASV, Misc. Arm. IV–V, vol. 45, 41r–50r. The decrees addressed specifically the notaries of the Camera, the vicar, the auditor of the Camera (AC), the Rota, and the Capitoline curia plus, representing the College of Scriptors, the notary of the Archive.

55. The most important common orders regarding judicial acts in 1704 were those requiring that notaries copy the judge's decree on the back of the relevant warrant the day it was handed down, and that they keep a separate manuale for each judge with the decree and warrant, written out in full; ASV, Misc. Arm. IV–V, vol. 45, 44r.

56. ASV, Misc. Arm. IV–V, vol. 45, 42v.

57. ASV, Misc. Arm. IV–V, vol. 45, 43r, 44r. Cf. *Bullarium* 1857–72, 12:87, 90, 96, nos. 9, 20, 44, 116.

58. ASV, Misc. Arm. IV–V, vol. 45, 42v. See also the discussion of the Archivio Urbano in this chapter.

59. ASV, Misc. Arm. IV–V, vol. 45, 44r.

60. ASV, Misc. Arm. IV–V, vol. 45, 44r. The inspectors must have tried to read some of the old judicial manuali for the decrees specified for the first time that they be written clearly and on good-quality paper.

61. ASV, Misc. Arm. IV–V, vol. 45, 43r.

62. ASV, Misc. Arm. IV–V, vol. 45, 43r.

63. ASV, Misc. Arm. IV–V, vol. 45, 45r. Other evidence indicates that the deadline was 7 June 1704.

64. ASR, Camerale II, Notariato, b. 25 contains the inventories.

65. As discussed in chapter 4, a more limited procedure had been envisioned in the sixteenth century when civic legislation required heirs or the staff of the Archivio Capitolino to prepare inventories of the protocols of deceased Capitoline notaries.

66. The offices of the thirty Capitoline notaries held a total of fifteen thousand volumes in 1704; Verdi 2005, 443.

67. Although it would take detailed analysis of all the 1704 notarial inventories to verify the claim, the notaries AC, who were unsuccessfully attempting to obtain inheritability of their vacabili offices in the 1650s, did make the point that "l'esempi delli notai capitolini ridotti da Papa Paolo V da vacabili à non vacabili, che questo sia motivo di poter meglio conservare le scritture con magg[iore] amore mentre siano perpetui in una casa." ASR, Congregazioni particolari deputati 43/2, 482r.

68. ASR, Camerale II, Notariato, b. 25, inventory by Francesco Maria Octaviani, n.d. [1704].

69. ASR, Camerale II, Notariato, b. 25, inventory by Gaudenzio Antonio de Galassijs, n.d. [1704].

70. ASR, Congregazioni particolari deputati 43/2, 144–214, includes inventories from the 1730s from nine Capitoline notarial offices.

71. ASV, Misc. Arm. IV–V, vol. 45, 42v.

72. They should have "decent habits and be well taught in fluent, correctly spelled Latin and clear, legible script"; ASV, Misc. Arm. IV–V, vol. 45, 42v.

73. Although the involvement of the notaries with venal offices was not mentioned, the Capitoline notaries had continued to participate in the examinations as late as 1702; ASR, CCN, Verbali, vol. 3, n.p., 5 October 1702.

74. ASV, Misc. Arm. IV–V, vol. 45, 43r.

75. ASV, Misc. Arm. IV–V, vol. 45, 43v.

76. ASV, Misc. Arm. IV–V, vol. 45, 45v.

77. ASV, Misc. Arm. IV–V, vol. 45, 45v–46r.

78. ASV, Misc. Arm. IV–V, vol. 45, 46v.

79. Depositions were to be recorded in bound volumes, not loose sheets. The new manuale for summons had already been described in the section of common instructions for all notaries; ASV, Misc. Arm. IV–V, vol. 45, 44r.

80. ASR, Camerale II, Notariato, b. 3, n.p., n.d., manuscript sheet headed "in the Capitoline notaries' offices."

81. ASV, Misc. Arm. IV–V, vol. 45, 43r.

82. ASV, Misc. Arm. IV–V, vol. 45, 45r.

83. ASR, Camerale II, Notariato, b. 3., n.p., n.d., contains the requests for extensions from a half-dozen Capitoline notaries, which usually bear in another hand notations like "fifteen days" or "one month" indicating the outcome. The same file includes the list of those who had and had not yet turned in their inventories (dated 7 June 1704).

84. ASR, Camerale II, Notariato, b. 3., n.p., 21 August 1704. The tone of the letter is solicitous. While warmly appreciative of the efforts the seventy-seven-year-old Marescotti had made in personally visiting the offices, the pope bids him not to do it again "since you have already suffered enough."

85. ASR, Camerale II, Notariato, b. 3., n.p., 10 August 1704.

86. ASR, Camerale II, Notariato, b. 3., n.p., 28 October 1704. These were single officials, the notary of the Archive (Archivio della Curia Romana), the Borgo, agriculture, Ripa, and Ripetta. Of course, their courts did have judges, but not of the same rank as the major tribunals.

87. ASV, Misc. Arm. IV–V, vol. 45, 96r, edict of SPQR, 20 December 1704.

88. ASV, Misc. Arm. IV–V, vol. 45, 13r, edict of cardinal chamberlain, 29 May 1705. One

of the findings of this investigation was that local archives were in desperate need of dry rooms; ASV, Fondo Albani, vol. 14, 36r–38r.

89. Guasco 1919a, 14, 101–2. Three years later on 4 March 1704 civic authorities voted that an inscription to read "Archive of the Roman People" be placed over the entrance of the room they had confiscated; ibid., 16.

90. While the notaries did not dispute this, they could not be accused of lack of foresight. Their petition to the conservators in November 1614 asking for a decree that the room be granted to them in perpetuity had been ignored; ASC, Camera Capitolina, Cred. VI, vol. 59, 319r.

91. ASR, Camerale II, Notariato, b. 3, "gl'espone che nella bolla della Sa. me. di Papa Sixto V." The contents of the folders in this series are not paginated, and many are without dates. Because salutations of petitions to the pope are conventional, opening phrases often do not distinguish different documents. Here I have identified sources by quoting the first line after the salutation.

92. ASC, Camera Capitolina, Cred. I, vol. 41, 100v.

93. ASR, CCN, Registro delle congregazioni, Verbali, vol. 3, n.p. (under date).

94. ASR, Camerale II, Notariato, b. 3, "gl'espone che nella bolla della Sa. me. di Papa Sixto V," which is the notaries' account, contradicts the version based on civic records in many details; cf. ASC, Camera Capitolina, Cred. I, vol. 41, 103r, 106r; Guasco 1919a, 14–15.

95. ASR, Camerale II, Notariato, b. 3, "gl'espone che nella bolla della Sa. me. di Papa Sixto V." The Palazzo Nuovo faced the Palace of the Conservators across the piazza. I would date this petition tentatively to January or early February 1702.

96. ASC, Camera Capitolina, Cred. I, vol. 41, 103r.

97. This was reported to a meeting of the Capitoline notaries on 14 February 1702; ASR, CCN, Registro delle congregazioni, Verbali, vol. 3, under date.

98. ASR, CCN, Registro delle congregazioni, Verbali, vol. 3, 22 May 1702.

99. ASV, Fondo Albani, vol. 14, 39r–44r. Because the college's meeting of 22 May 1702 refers to orders to undertake specific tasks that are proposed in this memorandum, it appears to predate that meeting. The specific knowledge and assured tone of the writer point to the cardinal's authorship.

100. Pastor 1928–41, 33:503 n. 3.

101. ASV, Fondo Albani, vol. 14, 39r.

102. ASV, Fondo Albani, vol. 14, 39r.

103. ASR, Biblioteca, Bandi, vol. 2, no. 164, art. 1.

104. ASV, Fondo Albani, vol. 14, 39v, 41v–42r.

105. See, for example, the July 1626 edict in *Archivio Urbani Erectio* 1629, 37–39.

106. ASV, Fondo Albani, vol. 14, 39v–40r. It was Sixtus V's 1586 legislation making the Capitoline offices venal that gave the college authority over the Archivio Capitolino, although not without oversight from the civic magistrates. The memorandum wrongly identifies the 1562 edict as emanating from Pius IV; this misunderstanding was corrected in later papal directives to the college, to the advantage of the papal treasury.

107. ASR, CCN, Registro delle congregazioni, Verbali, vol. 3, n.p. (18 October 1702).

108. ASR, CCN, Registro delle congregazioni, Verbali, vol. 4, 1r (4 December 1702).

109. ASR, CCN, Registro delle congregazioni, Verbali, vol. 4, 2r (12 January 1703).

110. ASR, CCN, Registro delle congregazioni, Verbali, vol. 4, 10r–12v (18 December 1703).

111. ASR, Camerale II, Notariato, b. 3, "gl'espongano che p[er] ridurre in protocolli."

112. We recall that the 1521 city statutes mandated the use of italic script by notaries for court records; *SPQR Statuta* (1519–23), bk. 5, art. 10. The process of forgetting how to read the gothic hand was already well underway in Rome by the sixteenth century.

113. Income from transunti never exceeded thirty scudi a year, and was sometimes considerably less; ASR, CCN, Registro delle congregazioni, Libro della massa, vol. 13 (1667–81), 91r–94r, 114r; ibid., Verbali, vol. 4, n.p. (18 October 1709; 18 October 1711).

114. The conservators were induced to shift eighty scudi from the budget for their 1704 carnival banquet to the Capitoline notaries for archive expenses; Guasco 1919a, 103; ASC, Camera Capitolina, Cred. VI, vol. 57, 127r.

115. ASC, Camera Capitolina, Cred. IV, vol. 61, 106v–108r. The inventory, which is in the same volume, is a document that merits further study. It is 104 folios long and organized by drawer (*cassetta*), each of which apparently contained up to ten volumes. Business acts were separated from judicial acts; there were 207 drawers of protocolli and 177 drawers of judicial acts (mainly manuali and witness depositions). The notaries claimed that the inventory had been checked by one of their judges, by someone deputed by Marescotti and by the two members who held the office of archivist that year (107r). See also ASR, CCN, Registro delle congregazioni, Verbali, vol. 4, 23r–24v.

116. ASC, Camera Capitolina, Cred. IV, vol. 61, 107r. It was not as light as it had been in the notarial statutes of 1652, however, when it was the job of the paid *custos*, not one of the Capitoline notaries themselves, to be in attendance during the archive's opening hours; Statutes (1652) in *Statuta* (Rome, 1831), 10. I have been unable to determine whether the exiled judicial acts remained in the attic of the Palazzo Nuovo.

117. Lori Sanfilippo 1987, 110.

118. Lori Sanfilippo 1987, 112–13nn. The codex is ASR, CCN, vol. 1163.

119. Lori Sanfilippo 1987, 114n.

120. ASV, Fondo Albani, vol. 14, 45r. At Santa Maria Nova, Lori Sanfilippo (1987, 103 n. 17) found a record of the deposit of Venettini's protocols dated 20 October 1712.

121. ASV, Fondo Albani, vol. 14, 45r. The cardinal chamberlain could not apparently force another cardinal to turn in an overdue book.

122. Lori Sanfilippo 1987, 103, 117n; Verdi 2005, 438.

123. Petrucci 1983, 242.

124. ASR, Camerale II, Notariato, b. 3, request to Cardinal Marescotti for reimbursement from Giovanni Battista Jacobelli, n.p., n.d. I would date this to 1703 or 1704. Jacobelli was one of the two college officials who signed off on the archive inventory before the meeting of 23 June 1705.

125. At the meeting of 18 October 1709 the total earned from archive fees the preceding year was just over seven scudi; at that of 18 October 1711 the total was just over thirty scudi; ASR, CCN, Registro delle congregazioni, Verbali, vol. 4, n. p. (under date).

126. That the notion of a historical archive was not unthinkable is evidenced by the civic government's decision in 1722 to find a qualified archivist for Rome's municipal archive; Romani 1983, 3:783–85.

127. ASV, Fondo Albani, vol. 14, 39v–40r.

128. ASC, Camera Capitolina, Cred. IV, vol. 61, 107r–108r. For example, the transunti procedure and the manner of choosing college officials who would be responsible for the archive each year reflect the notarial statutes of 1652.

129. We recall that original documents in the notary's protocols would have borne the mark (*l'archiviatione*) of an official of the Archivio Urbano, if the proper procedure had been completed, and also that the brief of the Archivio Urbano was copies of wills and long-term loans secured on land (*instrumenti perpetui*).

130. ASV, Fondo Albani, vol. 14, 39r–44r. As mentioned in the preceding section, I believe that he was the author and that on the basis of internal evidence it dates to the early months of 1702.

131. ASR, Camerale II, Notariato, b. 3, n.p., report dated 28 October 1704. See also San Martini Barrovecchio 1983, 3:861, 866. The comments on the Datary notaries are found in ASR, Camerale II, Notariato, b. 22, in an undated memorandum, n.p. The pope ultimately permitted exemptions from the rules of the Archivio Urbano to continue for the notaries of the vicario and the Reverenda Fabbrica of St. Peter's; ASV, Misc. Arm. IV–V, vol. 45, 43v. See the related letter from the notary of the Fabbrica reminding Cardinal Marescotti of this privilege, which dated back to 1642, in ASV, Camerale II, Notariato, b. 3, n.p., n.d.

132. ASV, Fondo Albani, vol. 14, 41r–v.

133. Benedict XIII (1724–30) attempted to redress this inevitable inconsistency in 1728 by ordering that a cardinal visitor be appointed to undertake an inspection every ten years and that its records be kept in a special volume in the acts of the notary AC Giuseppe Perugini; *Constitutio* 1728, 3–6. Although this may have happened in the 1730s, I have been unable to find later traces. See also Verdi 2005, 444. On Benedict XIII's archival interests, see Loevinson 1916. For additional papal archival legislation (1712, 1721, 1748), see *Enchiridion* 1966, 68–150.

134. Valesio 1977–79, 2:325. Even papal sources are contradictory. In the packet of undated, unpaginated documents grouped together as ASR, Camerale II, Notariato, b. 22, one indicates that the Archivio Urbano was in Piazza Colonna and needed more space, while another claims it was moved from "stanze del cortile" in the Vatican palace to the Torre dei Venti in 1698. The reason for the move may have been dampness.

135. By 1703 a Vatican location is securely documented. A cluster of preliminary investigations into converting space in the palace for the use of archives is found in ASR, Camerale II, Notariato, b. 3, n.p. The Archivio Urbano is described in one as "in luogo detto Tor de Venti" and in another as above the gallery on the garden (west) side. The architect Carlo Fontana, who was charged with assessing whether the attics (*tetti*) above the gallery were suitable for archives, completed his report, included in this volume, by 23 July 1703; n.p. See also Courtright 2003, 3.

136. *Constitutio* 1728, 45–46. The custodian was ordered to keep it open Saturday mornings from November to June. The editor of the Valesio diaries details the later travels of the Archivio Urbano; Valesio 1977–79, 2:789n.

137. ASV, Misc. Arm. IV–V, vol. 45, 43v.

138. ASV, Misc. Arm. IV–V, vol. 45, 42v. Interestingly, listing in this record is referred to as matriculation, reviving the letter, if not the spirit, of the city's late medieval notarial profession.

139. ASV, Misc. Arm. IV–V, vol. 45, 43r.

140. This document, without date or page, is inserted into a bundle of papers related to the 1702 inspection of the offices of the secretaries and chancellors of the Reverenda Camera Apostolica (identified on the reverse as "Secretarij di Camera"); ASR, Camerale II, Notariato, b. 3.

141. Benedict XIII actually confirmed Antonelli in the job for nine more years in 1724; ASR, Camerale II, Notariato, b. 22, n.p., n.d.

142. For a range of views, see ASR, Camerale II, Notariato, b. 22, fascicle 56 (where the date of the edict is erroneously given as 1659) and the job application of Domenico Carbone, also in b. 22, n.p., n.d., as well as the memorandum that I attribute to Cardinal Marescotti, ASV, Fondo Albani, vol. 14, 40r–v.

143. ASV, Fondo Albani, vol. 14, 45r. Because the report mentions the recovery of Venettini's protocols, it must postdate their delivery by the prior of Santa Maria Nova in October 1712; Lori Sanfilippo 1987, 103n.

144. For Laurentius de Bertonibus, active 1469–1503, see Guasco 1919b, 242.

145. In fact, these would never arrive at the Archivio Urbano. They entered the Vatican Library in the early twentieth century; Lori Sanfilippo 1987, 103, 117n.

146. The notaries of the vicario could well have defended themselves by recourse to their exemption in the 1704 decrees; ASV, Misc. Arm. IV–V, vol. 45, 43v.

147. ASV, Fondo Albani, vol. 14, 45r.

Conclusion

1. Santoro 1995, 139–44.

2. Esposito and Vaquero Piñeiro 2005, 131.

3. Of course, civil tribunals functioned as a support of last resort; Ago 1998a, 156–57. For the antiquity of this contractual culture, see Pomata 1998, 26–30.

4. Ago 1999a, 200.

5. Hoffman, Postel-Vinay, and Rosenthal 1999.

6. Lockhart 1992, 40.

7. Merwick 1999.

8. Two examples remind us of the effects authority can have on writing practices and documentation even in the contemporary world. On 1 October 2000 the federal law of the United States gave the electronic signature the same legal status as the manual signature. In 2001 a decree of the Italian government of Prime Minister Silvio Berlusconi withdrew evidentiary status from photocopies; applying this legislation retroactively to current trials meant that foreign documents could no longer be admitted in court.

9. For examples of the notaries' responsiveness to changing political power in Rome in two moments of transition, one enduring (the papal return from Avignon) and one temporary (the sack of 1527), see Lori Sanfilippo 2008, 24–25, and Esposito and Vaquero Piñeiro 2005, 136.

actuary: Notary serving in a judicial capacity in a civil tribunal

Apostolic Camera (Reverenda Camera Apostolica): Papal administrative organ responsible for the temporal government of the Papal States, especially its financial aspects

archiviatione: After 1625 a symbol placed on a notarial document to indicate that the required copy had been made and submitted to the Archivio Urbano with payment of fee

ars notariae: Medieval genre of instructions for preparing notarial documents

articuli: Plaintiff's questions for witnesses

auditor of the Camera: Prelate-judge who headed the most important papal civil tribunal in Rome

avvisi: Handwritten newssheets that functioned as a periodical press before the appearance of printed newspapers

bastardello: A term for the material support of the matrice (loose sheet or booklet)

business acts (atti negozianti): Notarial instruments for private clients, contracts

cartalare: To place numbers on recto of sheets of paper sequentially

cedola: A document functioning as a form of money, like a check or banknote

censo: Annuities backed by real estate

ceterare: To abbreviate (as in the use of "etcetera")

chirograph (papal): Letter with autograph signature of the pope

citatio: Court summons

clausulae caeteratae: Standard clauses in a notarial instrument that were normally abbreviated

clausulae consuetae: The clauses customarily included in a notarial instrument of a specified type

collaterale: Civil judge of the Capitoline tribunal. After 1580 there were two, known as the "first collaterale" and the "second collaterale."

compagnia d'ufficio: See società d'ufficio.

Curia: A general term for the papal administrative staff responsible for the ecclesiastical and temporal needs of the Catholic Church

curia: A court of law or tribunal

decano: The most senior member of a corporate body

decreto: Judicial order or decree

donatio: Legal action of making a gift of something

extend: To fill out all the abbreviations in a notarial transaction (Lat. complere)

extractus (plur. extracta): Copy of all the written evidence submitted and actions taken in a court case where the value of property in question is between twenty-five and two hundred scudi

falsum: The Roman crime of falsification, including but not limited to forgery

fede: General term for document in early modern Italy; specific meaning must be established by local usage. In Rome it was usually a signed copy that was not "published" by a notary; used both for business instruments and warrants (mandata).

fideicommessa: Legal mechanisms restricting alienation of estates; entail

fides: Trust, credibility

filze: Loose sheets stitched together in bunches using a string equipped with a metal point

fondo: Archival series

giovani: Literally "young men." The term designates young to middle-aged male employees in workshops and other enterprises. In notarial offices, giovani, unlike sostituti, were not certified notaries and could neither rogate business acts nor write judicial acts.

governor: Rome's ecclesiastical chief magistrate with civil and criminal jurisdiction over all Romans, lay and clerical (except those connected to the papal Curia)

imbreviatura: Valid but abbreviated form of a notarial act (also abbreviatura)

indice: Table of contents (also called rubricella) of a notarial protocol

instrument (Lat. instrumentum): General term referring to most types of notarial documents except wills

interrogatoria: Defendant's questions for witnesses

invacabile: Office that could be transferred by its owner via sale or bequest (also non vacabile)

ius commune: The legal system of continental Europe from c. 1200 to 1700

judicial acts (atti giudiziari): Court orders or records of various sorts written by notaries

liber accomodatorum: Volume in a notarial office listing documents that have been loaned to other offices or courts for use in court cases

liber expeditionum: Volume recording the judicial acts expedited by a notarial office

liber receptorum: Volume recording daily income of a notarial office (also called liber memorialium)

libro delle spedizioni: See liber expeditionum.

mandatario (Lat. mandatarius): Process server

mandato (Lat. mandatum): Warrant authorizing an officer of the court to take a designated action, such as a seizure, search, or arrest

mandato di procura: A power of attorney

manuale: Log of all the judicial business conducted by a notary for his judge or in his office

massa: Periodic deposits into a common fund required of a given group of venal officeholders

matrice (Lat. matrix): Notary's rough draft of a legal transaction

mensario: Official of a venal college of notaries in seventeenth-century Rome

monti: Public bonds (individual units were luoghi di monti)

mundum: Fully extended notarial instrument (with minimal use of abbreviations)

neofiti: Converts to Christianity

non vacabile: See invacabile.

notai AC: Notaries of the auditor of the Camera

notaries of the Camera: Secretaries and chancellors of the Reverenda Camera Apostolica

notarii curiae capitolinae: Notaries attached to the tribunal of the senator; after 1586 numbering thirty

notarii urbis: Notaries of the city of Rome (pre-1586)

novizio: Holder of an entry-level position in a notarial office, usually lasting one year .

obligatio: A specific type of notarial instrument binding someone to do something; often used in loan transactions

procura: Power of attorney. See also mandato di procura.

procuratori: Procurators, attorneys; lower-level legal professionals corresponding to solicitors in the British system where there is a distinction between solicitors who do the legal paperwork on cases and barristers who make the arguments. The equivalent distinction in Rome was between procuratori and avvocati.

protocol (Lat. protocollum): In Rome a volume of instruments of a particular notary, normally arranged chronologically (called a cartularium in Genoa)

public copy: A document prepared by a notary in public form, that is, with the formalities of date, place, names of witnesses, and his style of signature

publish: In notarial contexts to render a document in public form

quinterno: Quarto-sized notebook; material units from which Roman protocol was composed

registrum (plur. registra): Copy of the record file for a single case, including evidence submitted, legal opinions solicited, and entries copied from the official court manuale for cases involving two hundred scudi or more

repertorij: Originally lists of instruments in a given protocol indicating contracting parties, type of contract, and date, which were kept separately from the protocol. Later catalogs to the holdings of a notarial archive; in the Archivio Urbano organized by client's name (usually baptismal name)

rione: One of fourteen urban districts into which the city of Rome was divided

rogate: Technical term for the notary's action in certifying the truth of a given transaction in writing

Rota: Highest civil court of appeal in the Papal States

rubricella: Table of contents (also called an indice)

scriptura privata: Documents by individuals in their private or unofficial capacity

scriptura publica: Documents by writers who hold some kind of public authority

senator: Chief magistrate judging civil and criminal cases for lay Romans

signum: Individual notary's identifying symbol; stamped on notarial acts in sixteenth- and seventeenth-century Rome

simple copy: In contrast to a public instrument, lacked the formalities of the date and place of the transaction, the names of witnesses and notary and the notary's signature; explicitly prohibited from serving as judicial evidence

società d'ufficio: A way to borrow small amounts of money in Rome that took the form of a purchase of shares in an office (also called compagnia d'ufficio)

società in accomandita: A new type of financial transaction in late sixteenth-century Italy in which the partners carry unequal amounts of risk

sostituto: An officially certified notary who acts in the name of another notary. Used in early modern Rome to refer to employees in the offices of public notaries who were entitled to rogate acts but not to publish them.

style: The way the notary signs a public copy

termini: Judicial deadlines, as established by the type of civil action sought

testes: Witness depositions

transunto (Lat. transumptum): Legal copy of a notarial instrument made from the protocol of a deceased notary

vacabile: Office that reverted to its originating authority after the death or resignation of its owner. See also invacabile.

vicario: Cardinal delegated to oversee the religious life of the diocese of Rome who headed his own tribunal

visura: Fee charged by notaries for consulting documents

Abbiati, Antonia. 2000. "Fonte giudiziaria e fonte notarile: Metodi, problemi, sollecitazioni." *Mélanges de l'École française de Rome: Italie et Méditerranée* 112, pt. 1: 15–30.

Les actes notariés: Source de l'histoire sociale XVIe–XIXe siècles. 1979. Strasbourg: Librairie Istra.

Adorni, Giuliana. 1995. "Statuti del collegio degli avvocati concistoriali e statuti dello Studio Romano." *Rivista internazionale di diritto commune* 6: 293–355.

Ago, Renata. 1996. "Di cosa si può fare commercio: Mercato e norme sociali nella Roma barocca." *Quaderni storici* 91: 113–34.

———. 1997. "The Family in Rome: Structure and Relationships." In *Rome-Amsterdam: Two Growing Cities in Seventeenth-Century Europe*, edited by Peter van Kessel and Elisja Schulte, 85–91. Amsterdam: Amsterdam University Press.

———. 1998a. *Economia barocca. Mercato e istituzioni nella Roma del Seicento.* Rome: Donzelli.

———. 1998b. "Politica economica e credito nella Roma del Seicento." In *La Corte di Roma tra Cinque e Seicento: 'teatro' della politica europea*, edited by Gianvittorio Signorotto and Maria Antonietta Visceglia, 243–61. Rome: Bulzone.

———. 1999a. "Enforcing Agreements: Notaries and Courts in Early Modern Rome." *Continuity and Change* 14: 191–206.

———. 1999b. "Una giustizia personalizzata. I tribunali civili di Roma nel XVII secolo." *Quaderni storici* 101: 389–412.

———. 2000. "Le fonti notarili del XVII secolo: Alcune istruzioni per l'uso." *Mélanges de l'École française de Rome: Italie et Méditerranée* 112, no. 1: 31–44.

———. 2002a. "Introduction/Introduzione." In *The Value of the Norm/Il valore delle norme*, edited by Renata Ago, 6–33. Rome: Biblink.

———, ed. 2002b. *The Value of the Norm/Il valore delle norme.* Rome: Biblink.

Ago, Renata, Alessandra Camerano, Marina D'Amelia, and Emanuela Parisi. 1998. "I Trenta Notai Capitolini. Schedatura dei protocolli del 1645." In *Popolazione e società a Roma dal medioevo all'età contemporanea*, edited by Eugenio Sonnino, 373–97. Rome: Il Calamo.

Ajello, Raffaele. 1979. "La rivolta contro il formalismo." In *Stato e pubblica amministrazione nell'ancien régime*, edited by Aurelio Musi, 529–77. Naples: Guida.

Alessi Palazzolo, Giorgia. 1979. *Prova legale e pena. La crisi del sistema tra evo medio e moderno.* Naples: Jovene Editore.

Aliani, Antonio. 1995. *Il notariato a Parma. La 'matricula Collegii notarjorum [sic] Parmae' (1406–1805)*. Milan: Giuffrè.

Alidosi, Giovanni Niccolo Pasquali. 1616. *Li Proconsoli e correttori de' notari della città di Bologna dal loro principio sino all'anno 1616*. Bologna.

Andretta, Stefano. 1982–. "Clemente XI." *Dizionario biografico degli italiani*. Rome: Istituto della Enciclopedia Italiana.

———. 2000. "Clemente XI." *Enciclopedia dei Papi*, vol. 3. Rome: Istituto della Enciclopedia Italiana.

Andrieux, Maurice. 1968. *Daily Life in Papal Rome in the Eighteenth Century*. Translated by Mary Fitton. London: George Allen and Unwin.

Antonucci, Laura. 1989. "La scrittura giudicata: Perizie grafiche in processi romani del primo Seicento." *Scrittura e Civiltà* 13: 489–534.

———. 1992. "Tecniche dello scrivere e cultura grafica di un perito romano nel '600." *Scrittura e Civiltà* 16: 265–303.

Arcangeli, Massimo. 1994, 1995. "Due inventari inediti in romanesco del secolo XV. Con un saggio sul lessico di inventari di notari romani tra '400 e '500." *Contributi di filologia dell'Italia mediana* 8: 93–123, 9: 83–116.

Archivio di Stato di Roma. 1986. Vol. 3 of *Guida Generale degli Archivi di Stato Italiani*. Rome: Ministero per i Beni Culturali e Ambientali.

Archivio Urbani Erectio. 1629. Rome.

Ars notariatus. [1495–1500]. Rome.

Ascheri, Mario. 1989. *Tribunali, giuristi, istituzioni*. Bologna: Il Mulino.

———. 1990. "Le fonti statutarie: Problemi e prospettive da un'esperienza Toscana." In *Legislazione e società nell'Italia medievale*, 55–70. Bordighera: Museo Bicknell.

———. 1999. "Il processo civile tra diritto comune e diritto locale: Da questioni preliminari al caso della giustizia estense." *Quaderni storici* 101: 355–87.

Ascheri, Mario, Ingrid Baumgarten, and Julius Kirshner, eds. 1999. *Legal Consulting in the Civil Law Tradition*. Berkeley: Robbins Collection.

Baker, J. H., ed. 1989a. *Judicial Records, Law Reports and the Growth of Case Law*. Berlin: Duncker and Humblot.

———. 1989b. "Records, Reports and the Origins of Case-Law in England." In *Judicial Records, Law Reports and the Growth of Case Law*, edited by J. H. Baker, 15–46. Berlin: Duncker and Humblot.

Baldus de Ubaldis. 1546. "Tractatus de tabellionibus." In *Summa totius artis notariae Rolandini Rodulphini Bononiensis*. 2 vols. Venice. Reprint, Bologna: Arnaldo Forni Editore, 1977.

———. 1586. *Commentaria*. 8 vols. Venice.

———. 1599. *Commentaria*. 8 vols. Venice.

Balestracci, Duccio. 1989. *The Renaissance in the Fields*. Translated by Paolo Squatriti and Betsy Merideth. University Park: Pennsylvania State University Press.

Banti, Ottavio. 1899. "Il notaio e l'amminstrazione del Comune a Pisa (secc. XII–XIV)." In *Civiltà comunale: Libro, scrittura, documento*, 129–55. Genoa: Società Ligure di Storia Patria.

Barbalarga, Donatella, Paolo Cherubini, Giovanna Curcio, Anna Esposito, Anna Modigliani, and Micaela Procaccia. 1986. "Il rione Parione durante il pontificato Sistino: Analisi di un'area campione." In *Un pontificato ed una città. Sisto IV (1471–1484)*, edited by Massimo Miglio, 643–744. Vatican City: Associazione Roma nel Rinascimento.

Barraclough, Geoffrey. 1934. *Public Notaries and the Papal Curia: A Calendar and a Study of a Formularium Notariorum Curie from the Early Years of the Fourteenth Century*. London: Macmillan.

Bartoli Langeli, Attilio. 1977. "A proposito di storia del notariato italiano: Appunti sull'istituto, il ceto, l'ideologia notarile." *Il pensiero politico* 10: 98–113.

——. 1992. "Documentazione e notariato." *Origini. Età ducale*. Edited by Lellia Cracco Ruggini, 847–64. Vol. 1 of *Storia di Venezia*. Rome: Istituto della Enciclopedia Italiana.

——. 2000. *La scrittura dell'italiano*. Bologna: Il Mulino.

——. 2006. *Notai: Scrivere documenti nell'Italia medievale*. Rome: Viella.

Bauer, Clemens. 1927. "Die Epochen der Papstfinanz." In *Gesammelte Aufsätze zur Wirtschafts- und Sozialgeschichte*, 112–47. Vienna: Herder, 1965.

Bellingeri, Luca. 1989. "Editoria e mercato: la produzione giuridica." In *Il libro italiano del Cinquecento: produzione e commercio*, 155–85. Rome: Istituto Poligrafico e Zecca dello Stato.

Bellomo, Manlio. 1995. *The Common Legal Past of Europe, 1000–1800*. Translated by Lydia G. Cochrane. Washington, D.C.: Catholic University of America Press.

Benton, Lauren. 2002. *Law and Colonial Cultures: Legal Regimes in World History, 1400–1900*. Cambridge: Cambridge University Press.

Berengo, Marino. 1965. *Nobili e mercanti nella Lucca del Cinquecento*. Turin: Giulio Einaudi Editore.

——. 1976–77. "Lo studio degli atti notarili dal XIV al XVI secolo." In *Fonti medievali e problematica storiografica*, 1:149–72. Rome: Istituto Storico Italiano per il Medio Evo.

——. 1981. "Africo Clementi, agronomo padovano del Cinquecento." *Miscellanea Augusto Campana*, 27–69. Padua: Editrice Antenore.

Berengo, Marino, and Furio Diaz. 1975. "Noblesse et administration dans l'Italie de la Renaissance. La formation de la bureaucratie moderne." In *XIII International Congress of Historical Sciences*, 1: 151–63. Warsaw: Editions de l'Université de Varsovie.

Berges, Louis. 1991. "A propos du notariat genois en Corse de 1570 à 1770: Une expérience informatique au service de la recherche historique." In *Problèmes et méthodes d'analyse historique de l'activité notariale (XVe–XIXe siècles)*, edited by Jean L. Laffont, 65–74. Toulouse: Presses Universitaires du Mirail.

Besta, Enrico. 1923–25. *Fonti: Legislazione e scienza giuridica dalla caduta dell'impero romano al secolo decimo-quinto*. Vol. 1 of *Storia del diritto italiano*, edited by Pasquale del Giudice. Milan: U. Hoepli. Reprint, Florence: Libreria Gozzini, 1969.

Betri, Maria Luisa, and Alessandro Pastore, eds. 1997. *Avvocati, medici, ingegneri: Alle origini delle professioni moderni (secoli XVI–XIX)*. Bologna: CLUEB.

Bibliografia delle edizioni giuridiche antiche in lingua italiana. 1978. Vol. 1. Florence: Olschki Editore.

Bisazza, Giancarlo. 1993. "Notai tristi e notai sufficienti. Il ceto notarile di Vicenza tra Cinque e Seicento." *Società e storia*, no. 59: 3–33.

Bitossi, Carlo. 1995. "*La Repubblica è vecchia*": Patriziato e governo a Genova nel secondo Settecento. Rome: Istituto Storico per l'Età Moderna e Contemporanea.

Blouin, Francis, ed. 1998. *Vatican Archives: An Inventory and Guide to Historical Documents of the Holy See*. New York: Oxford University Press.

Bolzoni, Lina. 2001. *The Gallery of Memory: Literary and Iconographic Models in the Age of the Printing Press*. Toronto: University of Toronto Press.

Bonaventure, Saint. 1941. "Legenda maior. Miracula." *Analecta Franciscana* 10, no. 5: 557–652.

Booton, Harold W. 1989. "John and Andrew Cadiou: Aberdeen Notaries of the Fifteenth and Early Sixteenth Centuries." *Northern Scotland* 9: 17–20.

Bortolotti, Luca. 2001–. "Benedetto Giustiniano." *Dizionario biografico degli italiani*. Rome: Istituto della Enciclopedia Italiana.

Bowman, Jeffrey. 2004. *Shifting Landmarks: Property, Proof, and Dispute in Catalonia around the Year 1000*. Ithaca: Cornell University Press.

Brambilla, Elena. 1982. "Il sistema 'letterario' di Milano: professioni nobili e professioni borghesi dall'età spagnola alle riforme teresiane." In *Economia, istituzioni, cultura in Lombardia nell'età di Maria Teresa*, edited by Aldo De Maddalena, Ettore Rotelli, and Gennaro Barbarisi, 3:79–160. Bologna: Il Mulino.

Brandileone, Francesco. 1928. "La stipulatio nell'età imperiale romana e durante il medioevo." *Rivista di storia del diritto italiano* 1: 7–73, 270–310.

Brentano, Robert. 1974. *Rome before Avignon: A Social History of Thirteenth-Century Rome*. New York: Basic Books.

Brezzi, Paolo, and Egmont Lee. 1984. *Sources of Social History: Private Acts of the Late Middle Ages*. Toronto: Pontifical Institute of Mediaeval Studies.

Brooks, C. W. 1986. *Pettyfoggers and Vipers of the Commonwealth: The 'Lower Branch' of the Legal Profession in Early Modern England*. Cambridge: Cambridge University Press.

Bryson, W. H. 1989. "Law Reporting and Legal Records in Virginia, 1607–1800." In *Judicial Records, Law Reports and the Growth of Case Law*, edited by J. H. Baker, 319–35. Berlin: Duncker and Humblot.

Bullarium diplomatum et privilegiorum sanctorum Romanorum pontificum. 1857–72. 25 vols. Turin.

Burke, Peter. 1987. "The Uses of Literacy in Early Modern Italy." In *The Historical Anthropology of Early Modern Italy*, 110–31. Cambridge: Cambridge University Press.

———. 2002. "Rome as a centre of information and communication." In *From Rome to Eternity: Catholicism and the Arts in Italy, ca. 1550–1650*, edited by Pamela M. Jones and Thomas Worcester, 253–69. Boston: Brill.

Burns, Kathryn. 2005. "Notaries, Truth and Consequences." *American Historical Review* 110: 350–79.

Burns, Robert I., S. J. 1985. *Society and Documentation in Crusader Valencia*. Princeton: Princeton University Press.

———. 1996. *Jews in the Notarial Culture: Latinate Wills in Mediterranean Spain, 1250–1350*. Chicago: University of Chicago Press.

Butel, Paul. 1979. "Archives notariales et histoire économique: L'exemple d'Amsterdam." In *Les actes notariés: Source de l'histoire sociale XVIe–XIXe siècles*, 123–40. Strasbourg: Librairie Istra.

Camargo, Martin. 1991. *Ars dictaminis, ars dictandi*. Turnhout: Brepols.

Camerano, Alessandra. 1997. "Senatore e Governatore. Due tribunali a confronto nella Roma del XVI secolo." *Roma moderna e contemporanea* 5: 41–66.

Cammisa, Francesco. 1989. *La certificazione patrimoniale. I contrasti per l'istituzione degli archivi pubblici nel Regno di Napoli*. Naples: Jovene Editori.

Campitelli, Adriana. 1981. *Attività processuale e documentazione giuridica. Aspetti e problemi del processo civile nel medio evo*. Bari: Laterza.

———. 1987. "Processo civile (diritto intermedio)." *Enciclopedia del diritto*, vol. 36. Milan: Giuffrè.

Canepari, Eleonora. 2003. "Mestiere e spazio urbano nella costruzione dei legami sociali degli immigrati a Roma in età moderna." In *L'Italia delle migrazione interne*, edited by Angelina Arru and Franco Ramella, 33–76. Rome: Donzelli.

———. 2006. "Stare in 'compagnia.' Strategie di inurbamento e forme associative nella Roma del Seicento." Tesi di dottorato di ricerca, University of Turin.

Caravale, Mario. 1982. "La legislazione del Regno di Sicilia sul notariato durante il Medio Evo." In *Per una storia del notariato meridionale*, 95–176. Rome: Consiglio nazionale del notariato.

Carbonetti, Cristina. 1979. "Tabellioni e scriniari a Roma tra IX e XI secolo." *Archivio della società romana di storia patria* 102: 77–156.

Cardella, Lorenzo. 1792–97. *Memorie storiche de' Cardinali della Santa Romana Chiesa*. Rome.

Carrino, Annastella. 1998. "L'identità mancata: Notai a Mesagne in antico regime." In *Gruppi ed identità sociali nell'Italia di età moderna*, edited by Biagio Salvemini, 199–274. Bari: Edipuglia.

Il Cartolare di Giovanni Scriba. 1935. Edited by Mario Chiaudano and Mattia Moresco. 2 vols. Rome: Istituto storico italiano.

Castiglione, Caroline. 2005. *Patrons and Adversaries: Nobles and Villagers in Italian Politics, 1640–1760*. Oxford: Oxford University Press.

Catoni, Giuliano, and Sonia Fineschi, eds. 1975. *Archivio di Stato di Siena: L'archivio notarile (1221–1862), Inventario*. Rome: Ministero per i Beni Culturali e Ambientali.

Cau, Ettore. 1989. "Il falso nel documento privato fra XII e XIII secolo." In *Civiltà comunale: Libro, scrittura, documento*, 215–77. Genoa: Società Ligure di Storia Patria.

Cavallar, Osvaldo. 1991. *Francesco Guicciardini giurista: I ricordi degli onorari*. Milan: Giuffrè.

Cavallo, Sandra. 2007. *Artisans of the Body in Early Modern Italy: Identities, Families and Masculinities*. Manchester: Manchester University Press.

Cencetti, Giorgio. 1943. "I precedenti dell'archivio notarile a Bologna." In *Scritti archivistici*, 3:300–312. Rome: Il centro di ricerca,1970.

Ceresa, Massimo. 2000. *Una stamperia nella Roma del primo Seicento: Annali tipografici di Guglielmo Facciotti ed eredi (1592–1640)*. Rome: Bulzoni.

Cesarini Sforza, Walter. 1914. "Sull'ufficio bolognese dei Memoriali." *L'Archiginnasio* 9: 379–92.

Chartier, Roger. 1987. *The Cultural Uses of Print in Early Modern France*. Translated by Lydia G. Cochrane. Princeton: Princeton University Press.

———. 1989. "The Practical Impact of Writing." In *The Passions of the Renaissance*, edited by Roger Chartier, 110–59. Vol. 3 of *A History of Private Life*. Translated by Arthur Goldhammer. Cambridge, MA: Harvard University Press.

——. 1994. *The Order of Books: Readers, Authors, and Libraries in Europe between the 14th and 18th Centuries.* Translated by Lydia G. Cochrane. Stanford: Stanford University Press.

——. 1995. *Forms and Meanings: Texts, Performances, and Audiences from Codex to Computer.* Philadelphia: University of Pennsylvania Press.

Chellini, Giovacchino. 1647. *Ragguaglio della sontuosa cavalcata fatta in Roma per il possesso di Senatore preso nel Campidoglio dall'Ill.mo Sig. Gio. Inghirami.* Rome.

Cheney, C. R. 1972. *Notaries Public in England in the Thirteenth and Fourteenth Centuries.* London: Oxford University Press.

Cherubini, Paolo. 2001. "Una fonte poco nota per la storia di Roma: I processi della Curia del Campidoglio (sec. XV)." In *Roma memoria e oblio,* 157–82. Rome: Tiellemedia Editore.

Christin, Anne-Marie. 2002. *A History of Writing.* Paris: Flammarion.

Ciuffoni, Simona. 1992. "Il tribunale criminale del Senatore di Roma durante il pontificato di Sisto V." *Studi romani* 40: 268–77.

Civiltà comunale: Libro, scrittura, documento. 1989. Genoa: Società Ligure di Storia Patria.

Clanchy, Michael T. 1993. *From Memory to Written Record: England, 1066–1307.* 2nd ed. Oxford: Blackwell.

Cohen, Elizabeth S. 1993. "Between Oral and Written Culture: The Social Meaning of an Illustrated Love Letter." In *Culture and Identity in Early Modern Europe (1500–1800),* edited by Barbara Diefendorf and Carla Hesse, 181–201. Ann Arbor: University of Michigan Press.

Cohen, Elizabeth S., and Thomas V. Cohen. 1989. "Camilla the Go-Between: The Politics of Gender in a Roman Household (1559)." *Continuity and Change* 4: 53–77.

Cohen, Thomas V. 2004. *Love and Death in Renaissance Italy.* Chicago: University of Chicago Press.

Cohn, Samuel K., Jr. 1998. "Marriage in the Mountains: The Florentine Territorial State, 1348–1500." In *Marriage in Italy, 1300–1650,* edited by Trevor Dean and K. J. P. Lowe, 174–96. Cambridge: Cambridge University Press.

Cola, Lucilla. 1990. "La visita pastorale del Cardinale Galeazzo Marescotti nella diocesi di Tivoli nel 1681." 3 vols. Tesi di laurea. Università degli Studi di Roma "La Sapienza."

Collegio Notarile di Verona. 1966. *Il notariato veronese attraverso i secoli.* Verona: Collegio Notarile di Verona.

Colli, Gaetano. 1994. *Per una bibliografia dei trattati giuridici pubblicati nel XVI secolo. Indici dei "Tractatus universi iuris."* Milan: Giuffrè.

Colli, Vincenzo. 1999. "Consilia dei giuristi medievali e produzione libraria." In *Legal Consulting in the Civil Law Tradition,* edited by Mario Ascheri, Ingrid Baumgarten, and Julius Kirshner, 173–225. Berkeley: Robbins Collection.

Collins, Amanda. 2002. *Greater than Emperor: Cola di Rienzo (ca. 1313–54) and the World of Fourteenth-Century Rome.* Ann Arbor: University of Michigan Press.

Colzi, Francesco. 1999. *Il debito pubblico del Campidoglio: Finanza comunale e circolazione dei titoli a Roma fra Cinque e Seicento.* Naples: Edizioni Scientifiche Italiane.

Comune di Roma. 1920–58. *Regesti di bandi editti notificazioni e provvedimenti diversi relativi all città di Roma ed allo Stato Pontificio.* 7 vols. Rome: Tipografia della Pace.

——. 1989. *Il comune antico e il suo archivio.* Rome: Fratelli Palombi Editori.

Confirmatio decretorum Cong. Reform. Tribunalium Urbis. 1689. Rome: Reverenda Camera Apostolica.

Consiglio Nazionale del Notariato. 1961. *Il Notariato nella civiltà italiana: Biografie notarili dall'VIII al XX secolo.* Milan: Giuffrè.

Constitutio quae varia decreta, ordinationes et provisiones pro recta in Curiis Urbis justitiae administratione complectitur atque etiam pro publicis tabulis, instrumentis, aliisque scripturis ad rem alienam pertinentibus. 1728. Rome: Reverenda Camera Apostolica.

Constitutio super sportulis Trib. et Iudicum Urbis. 1693. Rome: Reverenda Camera Apostolica.

Corbo, Anna Maria. 1973. "I contratti di lavoro e di apprendistato nel secolo XV a Roma." *Studi romani* 21: 469–89.

——. 1984. "Relazione descrittiva degli archivi notarili Romani dei secoli XIV–XV nell'Archivio di Stato e nell'Archivio Capitolino." In *Sources of Social History: Private Acts of the Late Middle Ages,* edited by Paolo Brezzi and Egmont Lee, 49–67. Toronto: Pontifical Institute of Mediaeval Studies.

——. 1990. *Fonti per la storia sociale romana al tempo di Nicolò V e Callisto III.* Rome: Istituto Nazionale di Studi Romani.

Corpus Iuris Civilis. 1954. Edited by Paulus Krüger. 3 vols. 11th abr. ed. Berlin: Weidmann. Reprint, Dublin: Weidmann, 1967.

Corpus Juris Civilis: The Civil Law. 1932. Translated by S. P. Scott. 17 vols. Cincinnati: Central Trust Company. Reprint, 7 vols. New York: AMS Press, 1973.

Costamagna, Giorgio. 1961. *La triplice redazione dell'instrumentum Genovese.* Genoa: Società Ligure di Storia Patria.

——. 1970. *Il notaio a Genova tra prestigio e potere.* Rome: Consiglio Nazionale del Notariato.

——. 1978. "Notaio (diritto romano)." *Enciclopedia del diritto,* vol. 28. Milan: Giuffrè.

——. 1989. "La 'litera communis' e la progressiva affermazione del suo valore probatorio." In *Civiltà comunale: Libro, scrittura, documento,* 201–13. Genoa: Società Ligure di Storia Patria.

——. 1990a. "La conservazione della documentazione notarile nella Repubblica di Genova." *Archivi per la storia* 3: 7–20.

——. 1990b. "Scribi comunali e notai di collegio ad Albenga nel sec. XIII." In *Legislazione e società nell'Italia medievale,* 503–15. Bordighera: Museo Bicknell.

Courtright, Nicola. 2003. *The Papacy and the Art of Reform in Sixteenth-Century Rome: Gregory XIII's Tower of the Winds in the Vatican.* Cambridge: Cambridge University Press.

D'Addario, Arnaldo. 1951. "La conservazione degli atti notarili negli ordinamenti della repubblica lucchese." *Archivio storico italiano* 109: 193–226.

——, ed. 1984. *Il notaio nella civiltà fiorentina, secoli XIII-XVI.* Florence: Vallecchi Editore.

D'Amelia, Marina. 2004. "Bolle e brevi falsi nella Roma del Seicento." *Dimensioni e problemi della ricerca storica,* no. 2: 231–65.

——. 2007. "La Dataria sotto inchiesta: Il processo al sotto-datario canonici detto Mascambruno nel 1652." In *Les procès politiques (XIVe–XVIIe siècle),* edited by Yves-Marie Bercé, 319–50. Rome: École française de Rome.

D'Amico, Stefano. 1994. *Le contrade e la città. Sistema produttiva e spazio urbano a Milano fra Cinque e Seicento.* Milano: Franco Angeli Editore.

———. 1997. "Famiglie mercanti e professione notarile a Milano fra Cinque e Seicento." In *Avvocati, medici, ingegneri: Alle origini delle professioni moderni (secoli XVI–XIX)*, edited by Maria Luisa Betri and Alessandro Pastore, 145–53. Bologna: CLUEB.

Darnton, Robert. 1983. "What is the History of Books?" In *Books and Society in History*, edited by Kenneth Carpenter, 3–26. New York: R. R. Bowker.

Dattero, Alessandra. 1997. "Il notariato di una comunità di valle dello Stato di Milano durante l'età moderna: aspetti istituzionali e sociali." In *Avvocati, medici, ingegneri: Alle origini delle professioni moderni (secoli XVI–XIX)*, edited by Maria Luisa Betri and Alessandro Pastore, 155–67. Bologna: CLUEB.

Davis, Natalie Zemon. 1987. *Fiction in the Archives: Pardon Tales and Their Tellers in Sixteenth-Century France*. Stanford: Stanford University Press.

De Boüard, Alain. 1911. "Les notaries de Rome au moyen âge." *Mélanges d'archéologie et d'histoire* 31: 291–307.

Decreta et provisiones Congregationis Reformationis Tribunalium. 1679. Rome: Reverenda Camera Apostolica.

Decreta et provisiones Congregationis super visitatione, ac reformatione officiorum, & archiviorum Notariorum Urbis. 1704. Rome: Reverenda Camera Apostolica.

De Gregori, Luigi. 1942. "Cariche da burla del comune di Roma." *Strenna dei romanisti* 3: 268–74.

Del Giudice, Pasquale. 1923. *Fonti: Legislazione e scienza giuridica dal secolo decimosesto ai nostri giorni.* Vol. 2 of *Storia del diritto italiano*, edited by Pasquale del Giudice. Milan: U. Hoepli. Reprint, Florence: Libreria Gozzini, 1969.

Del Re, Niccolò. 1954. *La curia capitolina*. Rome: Regionale Editore.

———. 1957. "La curia Savella." *Studi romani* 5: 390–400.

———. 1970. *La curia romana: Lineamenti storico-giuridici.* 3rd ed. Rome: Edizioni di Storia e Letteratura.

———. 1972. *Monsignor Governatore di Roma.* Rome: Istituto di Studi Romani.

———. 1975. "Prospero Farinacci giureconsulto romano (1544–1618)." *Archivio della società romana di storia patria* 98: 135–220.

———. 1986. "Luca Peto giureconsulto e magistrato capitolino (1512–1581)." In *Scritti in onore di Filippo Caraffa*, 309–37. Anagni: Istituto di Storia e di Arte del Lazio Meridionale.

———. 1993. *La curia capitolina e tre altri antichi organi giudiziari romani.* Rome: Fondazione Marco Besso.

De Luca, Giovanni Battista. 1673. *Il dottor volgare.* 10 vols. Rome.

Delumeau, Jean. 1957–59. *Vie économique et sociale de Rome dans la seconde moitié du XVIe siècle.* 2 vols. Paris: E. De Boccard.

———. 1961. "Le progrès de la centralization dans l'état pontificale au XVIe siècle." *Revue historique* 226: 399–410.

De Renzi, Silvia. 2001. "La natura in tribunale: Conoscenze e pratiche medico-legali a Roma nel XVII secolo." *Quaderni storici* 36: 799–822.

Dethan, Georges. 1968. *Mazarin et ses amis: étude sur la jeunesse du Cardinal.* Paris: Berger Levraut.

Dezza, Ettore. 1989. *Accusa e inquisizione. Dal diritto comune ai codici moderni.* Milan: Giuffrè.

Dievoet, Guido van. 1986. *Les coutumiers, les styles, les formulaires et les "artes notariae."* Turnhout: Brepols.

Di Fabio, Marcello. 1978. "Notaio (diritto vigente)." *Enciclopedia del diritto*, vol. 28. Milan: Giuffrè.

The Digest of Justinian. 1985. Latin text edited by Theodor Mommsen with the aid of Paul Krueger. English translation edited by Alan Watson. 4 vols. Philadelphia: University of Pennsylvania Press.

Dinarelli, Bernardino. 1621. *Uffici della Corte romana*. Bologna.

Di Sivo, Michele. 1995. "Il tribunale criminale Capitolino nei secoli XVI–XVII: note da un lavoro in corso." *Roma moderna et contemporanea* 3: 201–16.

———. 1997. "Roman Criminal Justice between State and City: The Reform of Paul V." In *Rome-Amsterdam: Two Growing Cities in Seventeenth-Century Europe*, edited by Peter van Kessel and Elisja Schulte, 279–88. Amsterdam: Amsterdam University Press.

———. 1998. "Il popolo e il suo giudice. Studi sui documenti del Tribunale criminale del Senatore di Roma (1593–1599)." In *Popolazione e società a Roma dal medioevo all'età contemporanea*, edited by Eugenio Sonnino, 615–40. Rome: Il Calamo.

———. 2001. "Per via di giustizia. Sul processo penale a Roma tra XVI e XIX secolo." *Rivista storica del Lazio* 9: 13–35.

Dolan, Claire. 1998. *Le notaire, la famille et la ville: Aix-en-Provence à la fin du seixième siècle.* Toulouse: Presses Universitaires du Mirail.

Dolezalek, G. 1989. "Reports of the 'Rota' (12th–19th centuries)." In *Judicial Records, Law Reports and the Growth of Case Law*, edited by J. H. Baker, 69–99. Berlin: Duncker and Humblot.

Donati, Claudio. 1994. " 'Ad radicitus submovendum:' materiali per una storia dei progetti di riforma giudiziaria durante il pontificato di Innocenzo XII." In *Riforme, religione e politica durante il pontificato di Innocenzo XII (1691–1700)*, edited by Bruno Pellegrino, 159–78. Galatina: Congedo Editore.

Durand, Guillaume. *Speculum judicale*. 1574. 2 vols. Basel. Reprint, Aalen: Scientia Verlag, 1975.

Durando, Edoardo. 1897. *Il tabellionato*. Turin.

Elliott, Dyan. 2004. *Proving Woman: Female Spirituality and Inquisitional Culture in the Later Middle Ages*. Princeton: Princeton University Press.

Enchiridion archivorum Ecclesiasticorum. Documenta potiora Sanctae Sedis de archivis ecclesiasticis a Concilio Tridentino usque ad nostros dies. 1966. Edited by Simeon Duca and Simeon a S. Familia. Vatican City: Archivio Segreto Vaticano.

Era, Antonio. 1934. "Di Rolandino Passeggeri e della 'Summa artis notariae.' " *Rivista di storia del diritto italiano* 7: 388–407.

Esch, Arnold. 2000. *Rome entre le Moyen Âge et la Renaissance*. Stuttgart: Thorbecke.

———. 2001. "Un notaio tedesco e la sua clientela nella Roma del Rinascimento." *Archivio della società romana di storia patria* 124: 175–209.

Esposito, Anna. 1981. "Famiglia, mercanzia e libri nel testamento di Andrea Santacroce (1471)." In *Aspetti della vita economica e culturale a Roma nel Quattrocento*, edited by Arnold Esch, Ivan Ait, Gabriella Severino Polica, 197–220. Rome: Istituto Nazionale di Studi Romani.

———. 1994. " 'Li nobili huomini di Roma.' Strategie familiari tra città, curia e municipio." In *Roma capitale (1447–1527)*, edited by Sergio Gensini, 373–88. Pisa: Pacini.

Esposito, Anna, and Manuel Vaquero Piñeiro. 2005. "Rome during the Sack: Chronicles and Testimonies from an Occupied City." In *The Pontificate of Clement VII*, edited by Kenneth Gouwens and Sheryl E. Reiss, 125–42. Aldershot: Ashgate.

Evangelisti, Claudia. 1997. "Gli 'operai delle liti': Funzioni e *status* sociale dei procuratori legali a Bologna nella prima età moderna." In *Avvocati, medici, ingegneri: Alle origini delle professioni moderni (secoli XVI–XIX)*, edited by Maria Luisa Betri and Alessandro Pastore, 131–44. Bologna: CLUEB.

Farinacci, Prospero. 1612. *De falsitate et simulatione*. Vol. 6 of *Operum criminalium*. 8 vols. Nuremberg, 1676–1728.

Fasoli, Gina. 1968. "Giuristi, giudici e notai nell'ordinamento comunale e nella vita cittadina." In *Atti del convegno internazionale di studi accursiani*, edited by Guido Rossi, 1:25–39. Milan: Giuffrè.

———. 1977. "Il notaio nella vita cittadina bolognese (sec. XII–XV)." In *Notariato medievale bolognese*, 2:125–40. Rome: Consiglio Nazionale del Notariato.

Feci, Simona. 1997. "Riformare in antico regime. La costituzione di Paolo V e i lavori preparatori (1608–1612)." *Roma moderna e contemporanea* 5: 117–40.

———. 1998. " 'Sed quia ipsa est mulier.' Le risorse dell'identità giuridica femminile a Roma in età moderna." *Quaderni storici* 33: 275–300.

———. 2004. *Pesci fuor d'acqua. Donne a Roma in età moderna, diritti e patrimoni*. Rome: Viella.

Fenzonio, Giovanni Battista. 1636. *Annotationes in statuta, sive Ius municipale Romanae Urbis*. Rome.

Ferorelli, Nicola. 1920. "L'ufficio degli statuti del Comune di Milano detto Panigarola." *Bollettino della Società Pavese di Storia Patria* 20, nos. 3–4: 151–93.

Ferraro, Richard. 1994. "The Nobility of Rome 1560–1700: A Study of Its Composition, Wealth, and Investment." 2 vols. Ph.D. diss., University of Wisconsin.

Ferrière, Claude J. de. 1684. *La science parfaite des notaires*. Paris.

Fissore, Gian Giacomo. 1978. "La diplomatica del documento comunale fra notariato e cancelleria." *Studi medievali* ser. 3, 19, no. 1: 211–44.

———. 1989. "Alle origini del documento comunale: I rapporti fra i notai e l'institucione." In *Civiltà comunale: Libro, scrittura, documento*, 99–128. Genoa: Società Ligure di Storia Patria.

Folin, Marco. 1990. "Procedure testamentarie e alfabetismo a Venezia nel Quattrocento." *Scrittura e Civiltà* 14: 243–70.

Fontaine, Laurence. 1993. "L'activité notarile." *Annales: économies, sociétés, civilisations* 48: 475–83.

Foote, David. 2000. "How the Past Becomes a Rumor: The Notarialization of Historical Consciousness in Medieval Orvieto." *Speculum* 75: 794–815.

Formularium instrumentorum. [1480]. Rome.

Formularium instrumentorum et variorum processuum. 1575. Rome.

Formularium instrumentorum et variorum processuum. 1589. Rome.

Formularium terminorum seu registrorum secundum stilum Rom. Cur. 1581. Rome.

Fortunati, Maura. 1996. *Scrittura e prova. I libri di commercio nel diritto medievale e moderno*. Rome: Fondazione Sergio Mochi Onory per la Storia del Diritto Italiano.

Fosi, Irene. 1989. "Il consolato fiorentino a Roma ed il progetto per la chiesa nazionale." *Studi romani* 37: 50–70.

——. 1993. "Justice and Its Image: Political Propaganda and Judicial Reality in the Pontificate of Sixtus V." *Sixteenth Century Journal* 24: 75–95.

——. 1997. "Sudditi, tribunali e giudici nella Roma barocca." *Roma moderna e contemporanea* 5: 19–40.

——. 2002a. " 'Beatissimo Padre . . .': Suppliche e memoriali nella Roma barocca." In *Suppliche e 'gravamina.' Politica, amministrazione, giustizia in Europa (secoli XIV–XVIII)*, edited by C. Nubola and A. Würgler, 343–65. Bologna: Il Mulino.

——. 2002b. "Il governo della giustizia." In *Storia di Roma dall'antichità a oggi: Roma moderna*, edited by Giorgio Ciucci, 115–42. Bari: Editori Laterza.

——, ed. 2006. "La peste a Roma (1656–57)." Special issue, *Roma moderna e contemporanea* 14, nos. 1–3.

——. 2007. *La giustizia del papa: Sudditi e tribunali nello Stato Pontificio in età moderna.* Bari: Editori Laterza.

Fraenkel, Béatrice. 1992. *La signature: Genèse d'un signe.* Paris: Editions Gallimard.

Franceschini, Franco. 1991. "Il linguaggio della memoria: Le deposizioni dei testimoni in un tribunale corporativo fiorentino fra XIV e XV secolo." In *La parola all'accusato*, ed. Jean-Claude Maire-Vigueur and Agostino Paravicini Bagliani, 213–32. Palermo: Sellerio Editore.

Franceschini, Michele. 1991. "Il municipio romano e Sisto V: Apparato di rappresentanza o struttura di governo locale?" In *Il Campidoglio e Sisto V*, edited by Luigi Spezzaferro and M. E. Tittoni, 33–36. Rome: Carte Segrete.

Francesco di Ruggiero. 1993. *Notar Francesco di Ruggiero prattica de' notari (1713)*, edited by Antonio De Feo. Reprint, Naples: ESI.

François, Achille. 1886. *Elenco di notari che rogarono atti in Roma dal secolo XIV all'anno 1886.* Rome.

Franklin, James. 2001. *The Science of Conjecture: Evidence and Probability before Pascal.* Baltimore: Johns Hopkins University Press.

Frenz, Thomas. 1989. *I documenti pontifici nel medioevo e in età moderna.* Translated by Sergio Pagano. Vatican City: Scuola Vaticana di Paleografia, Diplomatica e Archivistica.

Gaudioso, Francesco. 1991. *Un prete-notaio d'antico regime: I protocolli di Domenico Diego de Monte, notaro apostolico in Terra d'Otranto (1697–1732).* Galatina: Congedo Editore.

Genicot, Léopold. 1972. *Les actes publiques.* Turnhout: Brepols.

Gheza Fabbri, L. 1983. "Per lo studio delle corporazioni bolognesi tra il XVI e il XVIII secolo: I libri 'matricularum,'" *Economia e storia* 30: 1–15.

Giansante, Massimo. 1998. *Retorica e politica nel Duecento. I notai bolognesi e l'ideologia comunale.* Rome: Istituto Storico Italiano per il Medio Evo.

Gibiat, Samuel. 2004. "Les notaries royaux de Montluçon à l'époque moderne: L'institution, les offices, la pratique et les hommes." *Revue historique* 304: 81–120.

Gigli, Giacinto. 1994. *Diario di Roma.* Edited by Manlio Barberito. 2 vols. Rome: Editore Colombo.

Goldberg, Jonathan. 1990. *Writing Matter: From the Hands of the English Renaissance.* Stanford: Stanford University Press.

Grafton, Anthony. 1997. *Commerce with the Classics: Ancient Books and Renaissance Readers.* Ann Arbor: University of Michigan Press.

Grisar, Josef. 1964. "Notare und Notariatsarchive im Kirchenstaat des 16. Jahrhunderts." *Mélanges Eugène Tisserant,* 4:251–300. Vatican City: Biblioteca Apostolica Vaticana.

Groppi, Angela. 2000. "Fili notarili e trace corporative: La ricomposizione di un mosaico." *Mélanges de l'École française de Rome: Italie et Méditerranée* 112, pt. 1: 61–78.

Grossi, Paolo. 1995. *L'ordine giuridico medievale.* Bari: Laterza.

Gualazzini, Ugo. 1964. "Documento e documentazione." *Enciclopedia del diritto,* vol. 13. Milan: Giuffrè.

Guasco, Luigi. 1919a. *L'archivio storico del comune di Roma.* Rome: Tipografia Cuggiani.

———. 1919b. "I rogiti originali dell'Archivio Urbano del comune di Roma." *Gli archivi italiani* 6: 240–50.

———. 1946. *L'archivio storico capitolino.* Rome: Reale Istituto di Studi Romani.

Guicciardini, Francesco. 1970–81. *Opere di Francesco Guicciardini.* Edited by Emanuella Lugnani Scarano. 3 vols. Turin: Unione tipografico-editrice torinese.

Hanlon, Gregory. 2004. "Justice in the Age of Lordship: A Feudal Court in Tuscany during the Medici Era (1619–66)." *Sixteenth Century Journal* 35: 1005–33.

Hardwick, Julie. 1998. *The Practice of Patriarchy: Gender and the Politics of Household Authority in Early Modern France.* University Park: Pennsylvania State University Press.

Harris, Roy. 1986. *The Origin of Writing.* Lasalle, IL: Open Court.

Helmholz, R. H. 2001. *The* Ius Commune *in England: Four Studies.* Oxford: Oxford University Press.

Hoberg, Hermann. 1994. *Inventario dell'archivio della Sacra Romana Rota (sec. XIV–XIX).* Vatican City: Archivio Segreto Vaticano.

Hoffman, Philip T., Gilles Postel-Vinay, and Jean-Laurent Rosenthal. 1999. "Information and Economic History: How the Credit Market in Old Regime Paris Forces Us to Rethink the Transition to Capitalism." *American Historical Review* 104: 69–94.

———. 2000. *Priceless Markets: The Political Economy of Credit in Paris, 1660–1870.* Chicago: University of Chicago Press.

Honthemius, Nicolaus [Honthem, Nikolaus]. 1607. *De syntaxi et fide instrumentorum sive de arte notariatus ad. Rom. Curiae imperialis spirensis, celeberrimorumque iudiciorum mores.* Mainz.

Howell, Martha. 1998. *The Marriage Exchange.* Chicago: University of Chicago Press.

Irnerius. 1892. "Formularium tabellionum." In *Bibliotheca juridica medii aevi. Scripta anecdota glossatorum,* edited by G. B. Palmerio, 1:11–45. Bologna.

Johns, Adrian. 1998. *The Nature of the Book: Print and Knowledge in the Making.* Chicago: University of Chicago Press.

Kagan, Richard. 1981. *Lawsuits and Litigants in Castile, 1500–1700.* Chapel Hill: University of North Carolina Press.

Kedar, Benjamin Z. 1977. "The Genoese Notaries of 1382: The Anatomy of an Urban Occupational Group." In *The Medieval City,* edited by Harry Miskimin, David Herlihy, and Abraham Udovitch, 73–94. New Haven: Yale University Press.

Kirshner, Julius, ed. 1995. *The Origins of the State in Italy, 1300–1600.* Chicago: University of Chicago Press.

———. 1999. "*Consilia* as Authority in Late Medieval Italy: The Case of Florence." In *Legal Consulting in the Civil Law Tradition*, edited by Mario Ascheri, Ingrid Baumgarten, and Julius Kirshner, 107–40. Berkeley: Robbins Collection.

Knafle, Louis A. 2005. "The Geographical, Jurisdictional and Jurisprudential Boundaries of English Litigation in the Early Seventeenth Century." In *Boundaries of the Law*, edited by Anthony Musson, 130–48. Aldershot: Ashgate.

Kosto, Adam J. 2001. *Making Agreements in Medieval Catalonia: Power, Order and the Written Word, 1000–1200.* Cambridge : Cambridge University Press.

Kristeller, Paul Oskar. 1951. "Matteo de' Libri, Bolognese Notary of the Thirteenth Century and His 'Artes Dictaminis.' " In *Miscellanea Giovanni Galbiati*, 2:283–320. Milan: U. Hoepli.

Kuehn, Thomas. 1989. "Reading Microhistory: The Example of Giovanni and Lusanna." *Journal of Modern History* 61: 512–34.

———. 1999. "*Consilia* as Juristic Literature in Private Law." In *Legal Consulting in the Civil Law Tradition*, edited by Mario Ascheri, Ingrid Baumgarten, and Julius Kirshner, 229–53. Berkeley: Robbins Collection.

Laffont, Jean L., ed. 1991. *Problèmes et méthodes d'analyse historique de l'activité notariale (XVe–XIXe siècles).* Toulouse: Presses Universitaires du Mirail.

Lafitau, Pierre François. 1752. *La vie de Clément XI.* 2 vols. Padua.

Lanconelli, Angela. 1983. "Manoscritti statutari romani. Contributo per una bibliografia delle fonti statutarie dell'età medioevale." In *Scrittura, biblioteche e stampa a Roma nel Quattrocento*, edited by Massimo Miglio, 305–21. Vatican City: Scuola Vaticana di Paleografia, Diplomatica e Archivistica.

Larner, John. 1965. *The Lords of Romagna.* Ithaca: Cornell University Press.

Lauro, Agostino. 1991. *Il cardinale Giovan Battista de Luca: Diritto e riforme nello Stato della Chiesa (1676–1683).* Naples: Jovene Editore.

Lavarda, Sergio. 2002. *L'incivile, disonesta e sordida vita. Storia di un notaio del Seicento.* Verona: Cierio Edizioni.

L'Engle, Susan, and Robert Gibbs. 2001. *Illuminating the Law: Legal Manuscripts in Cambridge Collections.* London: Harvey Miller.

Lenzi, Elena, Francesca Casamassino, and Rosa Savoia. 1993. "Tipologia di atti notarili rogati a Brindisi tra XVI e XVIII secolo: Primi scandagli." In "I protocolli notarili tra medioevo ed età moderna," ed. Francesco Magistrale. Special issue, *Archivi per la storia* 6, nos. 1–2: 303–12.

Leone, Alfonso. 1979. *Il notaio nella società del Quattrocento meridionale.* Salerno: P. Laveglia.

Lesellier, J. 1933. "Notaires et archives de la Curie Romaine (1507–1625). Les notaires français à Rome." *Mélanges d'archéologie et d'histoire* 50: 250–75.

Letteratura italiana. 1982–91. Edited by Alberto Asor Rosa. 7 vols. Turin: Giulio Einaudi Editore.

Levati, Stefano. 2000. "Notai e società nello Stato di Milano alla fine dell'antico regime (1750–1850): Strategie familiari, reclutamento e ruolo sociale di un gruppo professionale." In *Le regole dei mestieri e delle professioni, secoli XV–XIX*, edited by Marco Meriggi and Alessandro Pastore, 120–51. Milan: Franco Angeli.

Levi, Giovanni. 1985. *L'Eredità immateriale: Carriera di un esorcista nel Piemonte del Seicento.* Turin: Giulio Einaudi Editore.

Lévy, Jean Philippe. 1965a. "L'évolution de la preuve des origins à nos jours." *Recueils de la société Jean Bodin* 17, pt. 2: 9–70.

——. 1965b. "Le problème de la preuve dans les droits savants." *Recueils de la société Jean Bodin* 17, pt. 2: 137–67.

The Life of Cola di Rienzo. 1975. Edited by John Wright. Toronto: Pontifical Institute of Mediaeval Studies.

Limon, Monique. 1992. *Les notaires du Châtelet de Paris sous le règne de Louis XIV: Étude institutionelle et sociale.* Toulouse: Presses Universitaires du Mirail.

Liva, Alberto. 1979. *Notariato e documento notarile a Milano. Dall'alto medioevo alla fine del '700.* Rome: Consiglio Nazionale del Notariato.

Lockhart, James. 1992. *The Nahuas after the Conquest.* Stanford: Stanford University Press.

Lodolini, Elio. 1976. "Formazione dell'Archivio di Stato di Roma." *Archivio della società romana di storia patria* 99: 237–332.

Loevinson, Ermanno. 1916. "La costituzione di papa Benedetto XIII sugli archivi ecclesiastici: Un papa archivista. Contributo all'archivistica dei secoli 16⁰–18⁰." *Gli archivi italiani* 3: 159–205.

Lori Sanfilippo, Isa, ed. 1986. *Il protocollo notarile di Lorenzo Staglia (1372).* Rome: Società Romana di Storia Patria.

——. 1987. "I protocolli notarili romani del Trecento." *Archivio della società romana di storia patria* 110: 99–150.

——, ed. 1989. *Il protocollo notarile di Pietro di Nicola Astalli (1368).* Rome: Società Romana di Storia Patria.

——. 1990. "Appunti sui notai medievali a Roma e sulla conservazione dei loro atti." *Archivi per la storia* 3: 21–39.

——. 1992. "Notai e protocolli." In *Alle origini della nuova Roma: Martino V (1417–31),* 413–53. Rome: Istituto Storico Italiano per il Medio Evo.

——. 2001a. "L'arte del cambio a Roma nel XIV secolo." In *Studi in onore di Girolamo Arnaldi,* 309–32. Rome: Istituto Storico Italiano per il Medio Evo.

——. 2001b. *La Roma dei Romani: Arti, mestieri e professioni nella Roma del Trecento.* Rome: Istituto Storico Italiano per il Medio Evo.

——. 2008. *Constitutiones et Reformationes del Collegio dei notai di Roma (1446): Contributi per una storia del notariato romano dal XIII al XV secolo.* Rome: Società Romana di Storia Patria.

Love, Harold. 1993. *Scribal Publication in Seventeenth-Century England.* Oxford: Oxford University Press.

Maclean, Ian. 1992. *Interpretation and Meaning in the Renaissance: The Case of Law.* Cambridge: Cambridge University Press.

Magistrale, Francesco, ed. 1993. "I protocolli notarili tra medioevo ed età moderna." Special issue, *Archivi per la storia* 6, nos. 1–2.

Maire-Vigueur, Jean-Claude. 1976. "Classes dominantes et classes dirigeantes à Rome à la fin du Moyen Âge." *Storia della città* 1: 4–26.

——. 2001. "Il comune romano." In *Roma medievale,* edited by André Vauchez, 117–57. Bari: Laterza.

Maire-Vigueur, Jean-Claude, and Agostino Paravicini Bagliani, eds. 1991. *La parola all'accusato.* Palermo: Sellerio Editore.

Malatesta, Maria, ed. 1995. *Society and the Professions in Italy, 1860–1914.* Cambridge: Cambridge University Press.

Malkiel, David. 1996. "Jews and Wills in Renaissance Italy: A Case Study in the Jewish-Christian Cultural Encounter." *Italia* 12: 7–69.

Marchesini, Daniele. 1992. *Il bisogno di scrivere. Usi della scrittura nell'Italia moderna.* Bari: Laterza.

Marquis, André-Jean. 1979. "Le collège des correcteurs et scripteurs d'archives. Contribution à l'étude des charges vénales de la Curie Romaine." In *Römische Kurie, Kirchliche Finanzen, Vatikanischen Archiv: Studien zu Ehren von Hermann Hoberg,* 459–71. Rome: Università Gregoriana Editrice.

Marta, Giacomo Antonio [Martae, Ioannes Antonius]. 1638. *Tractatus de clausulis.* Bracciano.

Martin, Henri-Jean. 1994. *The History and Power of Writing.* Translated by Lydia G. Cochrane. Chicago: University of Chicago Press.

Martines, Lauro. 1968. *Lawyers and Statecraft in Renaissance Florence.* Princeton: Princeton University Press.

———. 1980. *Power and Imagination: City-States in Renaissance Italy.* London: Allen Lane.

Martini, Antonio. 1965. *Arti mestieri e fede nella Roma dei papi.* Bologna: Cappelli Editore.

Mascardi, Giuseppe. 1608. *Conclusiones omnium probationum quae in utroque foro quotidie versantur.* 3 vols. Turin.

Maxwell, William Harold, and F. Leslie, eds. 1957. *Scottish Law to 1956 Together with a List of Roman Law Books in the English Language.* Vol. 5 of *A Legal Bibliography of the British Commonwealth of Nations.* London: Sweet & Maxwell.

Mazzacane, Aldo. 1995–. "Prospero Farinacci." *Dizionario biografico degli italiani.* Rome: Istituto della Enciclopedia Italiana.

———. 1989. "Giambattista de Luca e la compagnia d'ufficio." In *Fisco, religione, stato nell'età confessionale,* edited by Herman Kellenbenz and Paolo Prodi, 505–30. Bologna: Il Mulino.

McKenzie, D. F. 1986. *Bibliography and the Sociology of Texts.* London: British Library.

Meriggi, Marco. 1997. "Arte, mestiere, professione. Problemi di lessico tra età moderna e età contemporanea." In *Avvocati, medici, ingegneri: Alle origini delle professioni moderni (secoli XVI–XIX),* edited by Maria Luisa Betri and Alessandro Pastore, 61–68. Bologna: CLUEB.

Merwick, Donna. 1999. *Death of a Notary: Conquest and Change in Colonial New York.* Ithaca: Cornell University Press.

Messick, Brinkley. 1993. *The Calligraphic State: Textual Domination and History in a Muslim Society.* Berkeley: University of California Press.

Modigliani, Anna. 1994. " 'Li nobilhuomini di Roma.' Comportamenti economici e scelte professionali." In *Roma capitale (1447–1527),* edited by Sergio Gensini, 345–72. Pisa: Pacini.

———. 2001. "Cittadini romani e libri a stampa." In *Roma di fronte all'Europa al tempo di Alessandro VI,* edited by M. Chiabò, S. Maddalo, M. Miglio, and A. M. Oliva, 2:469–94. Rome: Ministero per i Beni e le Attività Culturali.

Montorzi, Mario. 1984. *Fides in rem publicam: Ambiguità e tecniche del diritto comune.* Naples: Jovene Editore.

Mosti, Renzo, ed. 1982. *I protocolli di Iohannes Nicolai Pauli un notaio romano del '300 (1348–1379).* Rome: École française de Rome.

——, ed. 1984. "Due quaderni superstiti dei protocolli del notaio romano Paulus Nicolai Pauli (1361–62)." *Mélanges de l'École française de Rome: Moyen âge-temps modernes* 96, pt. 2: 777–844.

——, ed. http://www.srsp.it/body—testinotai.asp (accessed 1 June 2008).

Muir, Edward. 1999. "The Sources of Civil Society in Italy." *Journal of Interdisciplinary History* 29: 379–406.

Musto, Ronald. 2003. *Apocalypse in Rome: Cola di Rienzo and the Politics of the New Age.* Berkeley: University of California Press.

Nardella, Maria. 1993. "La legislazione sul notariato del Regno di Napoli tra '500 e '600 e la piazza notarile di Lucera." *Archivi per la storia* 6: 273–91.

Neuschel, Kristen B. 2001. "From 'Written Record' to the Paper Chase? The Documentation of Noble Life in the Sixteenth Century." *Historical Reflections/Réflexions historiques* 27: 201–18.

Nicolaj Petronio, Giovanna. 1983. "Notariato aretino tra medioevo ed età moderna: Collegio, statuti e matricole." In *Studi in onore di Leopoldo Sandri*, 2:633–60. Rome: Ministero per i Beni Culturali e Ambientali.

Noble, Thomas F. X. 1984. *The Republic of St. Peter: The Birth of the Papal State.* Philadelphia: University of Pennsylvania Press.

"Nouvelles approaches de la documentation notariale et histoire urbaine. Le cas italien (XVIIe–XIXe siècle)." 2000. Special issue, *Mélanges de l'École française de Rome: Italie et Méditerranée* 112, pt. 1.

Nussdorfer, Laurie. 1992. *Civic Politics in the Rome of Urban VIII.* Princeton: Princeton University Press.

——. 1993. "Writing and the Power of Speech: Notaries and Artisans in Baroque Rome." In *Culture and Identity in Early Modern Europe, 1500–1800,* edited by Barbara Diefendorf and Carla Hesse, 103–18. Ann Arbor: University of Michigan Press.

——. 2003. "Lost Faith: A Roman Prosecutor Reflects on Notaries' Crimes." In *Beyond Florence: The Contours of Medieval and Early Modern Italy,* edited by Paula Findlen, Michelle Fontaine, and Duane Osheim, 101–14. Stanford: Stanford University Press.

——. 2008. "The Boys at the Banco: Notaries' Scribes in Baroque Rome." In *The Politics of Writing Relations: American Scholars in Italian Archives,* edited by Deanna Shemek and Michael Wyatt, 121–38. Florence: Leo S. Olschki Editore.

——. Forthcoming. "Notes on the Margins: Notaries and the Accademia di San Luca." *The Accademia di San Luca in Rome, c. 1590–1635,* edited by Peter Lukehart. Washington, D.C.: Center for Advanced Study in the Visual Arts, National Gallery of Art.

Orlandelli, Gianfranco. 1965. "Genesi dell' 'ars notariae' nel secolo XIII." In *Studi medievali,* 3rd ser., 6, no. 2: 329–66.

Pacini, Antonio. 1789. *Il notajo principiante istruito o sia breve trattato istruttivo sopra il civile officio del notajo.* 8 vols. 3rd ed. Rome.

Pagano, Sergio. 1980. "Le visite apostoliche a Roma nei secoli XVI–XIX, repertorio delle fonti." *Ricerche per la storia religiosa di Roma* 4: 317–464.

Panella, Antonio. 1934. "Le origini dell'archivio notarile di Firenze." In *Scritti archivistici,* 163–91. Rome: Ministero dell'Interno, 1955.

Papon, Jean. 1568–80. *Trois notaires.* 3 vols. Lyons.

Partner, Peter. 1990. *The Pope's Men: The Papal Civil Service in the Renaissance.* Oxford: Oxford University Press.

Passeri, Nicolò. 1615. *De scriptura privata tractatus novus plenissimus.* Venice.

Pastor, Ludwig von. 1928–41. *The History of the Popes.* Translated by Ernest Graf and Ralph Kerr. Vols. 15–33. London: Kegan Paul, Trench, Trubner.

Pastore, Alessandro. 1982. "Testamenti in tempo di peste: La pratica notarile a Bologna nel 1630." *Società e storia* 5: 263–97.

Pavan, Paola. 1991. "Cives origine vel privilegio." In *Il Campidoglio e Sisto V*, edited by Luigi Spezzaferro and M. E. Tittoni, 37–41. Rome: Carte Segrete.

———. 1996. "I fondamenti del potere: la legislazione statutaria del Comune di Roma dal XV secolo alla Restaurazione." *Roma moderna e contemporanea* 4: 317–35.

Pedani Fabris, Maria Pia. 1996. *"Veneta auctoritate notarius." Storia del notariato veneziano (1514–1797).* Milan: Giuffrè.

Pellegrini, Mario. 1994. "Corte di Roma e aristocrazie italiane in età moderna. Per una lettura storico-sociale della Curia romana." *Rivista di storia e letteratura religiosa* 30: 543–602.

Pellegrino, Bruno, ed. 1994. *Riforme, religione e politica durante il pontificato di Innocenzo XII (1691–1700).* Galatina: Congedo Editore.

Pennington, Kenneth. 2001. "Innocent until Proven Guilty: The Origins of a Legal Maxim." In *A Ennio Cortese*, 3:59–73. Rome: Il Cigno Galileo Galilei Edizioni.

Peto, Luca [Paetus, Lucas]. 1587. *De judiciaria formula Capitolini Fori ad S.P.Q.R.* Rev. ed. Rome.

Petrucci, Armando, ed. 1958. *Notarii: Documenti per la storia del notariato italiano.* Milan: Giuffrè.

———. 1978a. "Per la storia dell'alfabetismo e della cultura scritta: Metodi, materiali, quesiti." *Quaderni storici* 38: 451–65.

———. 1978b. "Scrittura, alfabetismo ed educazione grafica nella Roma del primo Cinquecento. Da un libretto di conti di Maddalena pizzicarola in Trastevere." *Scrittura e Civiltà* 2: 163–207.

———. 1979–. "Alfonso Ceccarelli." *Dizionario biografico degli italiani.* Rome: Istituto della Enciclopedia Italiana.

———. 1982. *Scrittura e popolo nella Roma barocca, 1585–1721.* Rome: Edizioni Quasar.

———. 1983. "Scrivere a Roma nel Seicento: chi, cosa, perché." In *Italia linguistica: Idee, storia, strutture*, edited by Federico Albano Leoni, 241–45. Bologna: Il Mulino.

———. 1984a. "I documenti privati come fonte per lo studio dell'alfabetismo e della cultura scritta." In *Sources of Social History: Private Acts of the Late Middle Ages*, edited by Paolo Brezzi and Egmont Lee, 251–66. Toronto: Pontifical Institute of Mediaeval Studies.

———. 1984b. "Minuta, autografo, libro d'autore." In *Il libro e il testo*, edited by Cesare Questa and Renato Raffaelli, 397–414. Urbino: Università degli studi.

———. 1988a. "Pouvoir de l'écriture, pouvoir sur l'écriture dans la Renaissance italienne." *Annales: économies, sociétés, civilisations* 43: 823–47.

———. 1988b. "Storia e geografia delle culture scritte (dal secolo XI al secolo XVIII)." In *Storia e geografia. L'età moderna*, 1195–1292. Vol. 7, pt. 2 of *Letteratura italiana*, edited by Alberto Asor Rosa. Turin: Giulio Einaudi Editore.

———. 1989. "Scrivere per gli altri." *Scrittura e Civiltà* 13: 475–87.

———. 1993a. "Introduzione alle pratiche di scrittura." *Annali della scuola normale superiore di Pisa*, ser. 3, 23: 549–62.

———. 1993b. *Public Lettering: Script, Power, and Culture*. Translated by Linda Lappin. Chicago: University of Chicago Press.

———. 1995. *Writers and Readers in Medieval Italy*. Edited and translated by Charles M. Radding. New Haven: Yale University Press.

Piccialuti, Maura. 1999. *L'immortalità dei beni. Fedecommessi e primogenitura a Roma nei secoli XVII e XVIII*. Rome: Viella.

Piergiovanni, Vito, ed. 1987. *The Courts and the Development of Commercial Law*. Berlin: Duncker and Humblot.

———, ed. 1994. *Tra Siviglia e Genova: Notaio, documento e commercio nell'età colombiana*. Milan: Giuffrè.

Pieri, Silvano. 1972. "Formule notarili aretine del primo Trecento." *Studi di filologia italiana* 30: 207–14.

Pietrangeli, Carlo, ed. 1980. *Guide rionali di Roma. Rione III (Colonna)*. Pt. 1. Rome: Fratelli Palombi.

Piola Caselli, Fausto. 1973. "Aspetti del debito pubblico nello Stato Pontificio: Gli uffici vacabili." *Annali della facoltà di scienze politiche dell'Università degli studi di Perugia*, n.s., 1: 99–170.

———. 1991. "Gerarchie curiali e compravendita degli uffici." *Archivio della società romana di storia patria* 114: 117–25.

Poisson, Jean-Paul. 1985–90. *Notaires et société: Travaux d'histoire et de sociologie notariales*. 2 vols. Paris: Economica.

———. 1996. *Études notariales*. Paris: Economica.

Polain, Louis. 1898. "Note sur deux impressions poitevines du XVIe siècle." *Revue des bibliothèques* 8: 65–68.

Pomata, Gianna. 1998. *Contracting a Cure: Patients, Healers, and the Law in Early Modern Bologna*. Translated by the author with the assistance of Rosemarie Foy and Anna Taraboletti-Segre. Baltimore: Johns Hopkins University Press.

Pometti, F. 1898, 1899, 1900. "Studi sul pontificato di Clemente XI (1700–21)." *Archivio della società romana di storia patria* 21: 279–457; 22: 109–79; 23: 239–76, 449–515.

Pompeo, Augusto. 1991. "I tribunali del Senatore e del Governatore a Roma durante il pontificato di Sisto V." In *Il Campidoglio e Sisto V*, edited by Luigi Spezzaferro and M. E. Tittoni, 46–49. Rome: Carte Segrete.

Pratesi, Alessandro. 1955. "I 'dicta' e il documento privato romano." *Bullettino dell'archivio paleografico italiano*, n.s., 1: 93–109.

———. 1983. "Appunti per una storia dell'evoluzione del notariato." In *Studi in onore di Leopoldo Sandri*, 3:759–72. Rome: Ministero per i Beni Culturali e Ambientali.

———. 1992. *Tra carte e notai: Saggi di diplomatica dal 1951 al 1991*. Rome: Società Romana di Storia Patria.

Prodi, Paolo. 1982. *Il sovrano pontefice: Un corpo e due anime, la monarchia papale nella prima età moderna*. Bologna: Il Mulino.

Raccolta esattissima di tutti i notari dell'alma città di Roma dall'anno 1507 a tutti il 1785. 1785. Rome.

Radding, Charles M. 1988. *The Origins of Medieval Jurisprudence: Pavia and Bologna, 850–1150.* New Haven: Yale University Press.

——. 1990. "Legal Science 1000–1200: The Invention of a Discipline." *Rivista di storia del diritto italiano* 63: 409–32.

Radding, Charles M., and Antonio Ciaralli. 2007. *The Corpus Iuris Civilis in the Middle Ages.* Leiden: Brill.

Re, Camillo, ed. 1880. *Statuti della città di Roma* [1363]. Rome.

Renazzi, Filippo Maria. 1803–6. *Storia dell'università di Roma.* 4 vols. Rome. Reprint, Bologna: Arnaldo Forni Editore, 1971.

Richards, Thomas. 1992. "Archive and Utopia." *Representations* 37: 104–35.

Rietbergen, Peter. 1983. *Pausen, Prelaten, Bureaucraten. Aspecten van de geschiedenis van het Pausschap en de Pauselijke Staat in de 17e Eeuw.* Proefschrift: Catholic University of Nijmegen.

Robinson, O. F., T. D. Fergus, and W. M. Gordon. 1985. *An Introduction to European Legal History.* Abingdon: Professional Books.

Rocciolo, Domenico. 1998. "L'archivio della Pia Casa dei catecumeni e neofiti di Roma. Inventario." *Ricerche per la storia religiosa di Roma* 10: 545–82.

Rodocanachi, Emmanuel. 1901. *Les institutions communales de Rome sous la papauté.* Paris: Alphonse Picard et fils, Editeurs.

Rogerius. 1892. "Summa codicis." In *Bibliotheca juridica medii aevi. Scripta anecdota glossatorum,* edited by G. B. Palmerio, 1:49–233. Bologna.

Rolandino dei Passeggeri [Rolandinus Rudolphinus Bononiensis]. 1489. *Flos testamentum.* Edited by Baptista Guarini. Venice.

——. 1546a. "Apparatus iudiciorum." In *Summa totius artis notariae Rolandini Rodulphini Bononiensis.* 2 vols. Venice. Reprint, Bologna: Arnaldo Forni Editore, 1977.

——. 1546b. "Summa artis Notariae." In *Summa totius artis notariae Rolandini Rodulphini Bononiensis.* 2 vols. Venice. Reprint, Bologna: Arnaldo Forni Editore, 1977.

——. 1546c. "Tractatus Notularum." In *Summa totius artis notariae Rolandini Rodulphini Bononiensis.* 2 vols. Venice. Reprint, Bologna: Arnaldo Forni Editore, 1977.

Romani, Valentino. 1983. "Vicende archivistiche romane del Settecento: Francesco Maria Magni e l'archivio della Pia Casa degli orfani." In *Studi in onore di Leopoldo Sandri,* 3:783–812. Rome: Ministero per i Beni Culturali e Ambientali.

Romano, Andrea. 1993. "Bastardelli, protocolli e regestri. La registrazione notarile degli atti in Sicilia fra medioevo ed età moderna." In "I protocolli notarili tra medioevo ed età moderna," ed. Francesco Magistrale. Special issue, *Archivi per la storia* 6, nos. 1–2: 61–77.

Ruggiero, Maria Grazia Pastura. 1993. "Breve storia dello smembramento degli archivi della Camera Apostolica." *Roma moderna e contemporanea* 1: 159–82.

Rurale, Flavio. 2000. "Pio IV." *Enciclopedia dei Papi,* vol. 3. Rome: Istituto della Enciclopedia Italiana.

Sacchetti, Franco. 1996. *Il Trecentonovelle.* Edited by Valerio Marucci. Rome: Salerno.

Salvagni, Isabella. Forthcoming. "L'università dei pittori e l'Accademia di San Luca: Dall'insediamento in San Luca sull'Esquilino alla ricostruzione di Santa Martina al Foro Romano." *The Accademia di San Luca in Rome, c. 1590–1635,* edited by Peter Lukehart. Washington, D.C.: Center for Advanced Study in the Visual Arts, National Gallery of Art.

Salvioli, Giuseppe. 1925–27. *Storia della procedura civile e criminale*. Vol. 3 of *Storia del diritto italiano*, edited by Pasquale del Giudice. Milan: U. Hoepli. Reprint, Florence: Libreria Gozzini, 1969.

San Martini Barrovecchio, M. L. 1983. "Il collegio degli scrittori della curia romana e il suo ufficio notarile (sec. XVI–XIX)." In *Studi in onore di Leopoldo Sandri*, 3:847–72. Rome: Ministero per i Beni Culturali e Ambientali.

——. 1992. "Sul notariato dello stato pontificio prima e dopo la riforma di Sisto V." In *Sisto V. I. Roma e il Lazio*, edited by Maurizio Fagiolo and Maria Luisa Madonna, 235–42. Rome: Istituto Poligrafico e Zecca dello Stato.

Santoncini, Gabriella. 1998. *Il Buon Governo: Organizzazione e legittimazione del rapporto fra sovrano e comunità nello stato pontificio secc. XVI–XVIII*. Milan: Giuffrè.

Santoro, Marco. 1995. "Officials and Professionals. Notaries, the State and the Market Principle." In *Society and the Professions in Italy, 1860–1914*, edited by Maria Malatesta and translated by Adrian Belton, 111–44. Cambridge: Cambridge University Press.

——. 1998. *Notai. Storia sociale di una professione in Italia (1861–1940)*. Bologna: Il Mulino.

Sarti, Nicoletta, ed. 1988. *Gli statuti della società dei notai di Bologna dell'anno 1336*. Milan: Giuffrè.

Savelli, Rodolfo. 1995. "Modèles juridiques et culture marchande entre 16e et 17e siècles." In *Cultures et formations négociantes dans l'Europe moderne*, edited by Franco Angiolini and Daniel Roche, 403–20. Paris: L'École des Hautes Études en Sciences Sociales.

——. 2001. "The Censoring of Law Books." In *Church Censorship and Culture in Early Modern Italy*, edited by Gigliola Fragnito and translated by Adrian Belton, 223–53. Cambridge: Cambridge University Press.

Sbriccoli, Mario. 1969. *L'interpretazione dello statuto. Contributo allo studio della funzione dei giuristi nell'età comunale*. Milan: Giuffrè.

——. 1986. "Storia del diritto e storia della società. Questioni di metodo e problemi di ricerca." In *Storia sociale e dimensione giuridica*, edited by Paolo Grossi, 127–48. Milan: Giuffrè.

——. 1988. "Fonti giudiziarie e fonti giuridiche. Riflessioni sulla fase attuale degli studi di storia del crimine e della giustizia criminale." *Studi storici* 29: 491–502.

Scano, Gaetana. 1962. "L'Archivio Capitolino ha quattrocento anni." *Strenna dei romanisti* 23: 302–5.

——. 1979. "Appunti sull'Archivio Capitolino." *L'urbe* 42, no. 2: 40–44.

——. 1988. "L'Archivio Capitolino." *Archivio della società romana di storia patria* 111: 381–446.

——. 1989. "I testamenti chiusi dell'Archivio Capitolino e una carta Altieri." *Archivio della società romana di storia patria* 112: 481–92.

Schwartz, Hillel. 1996. *The Culture of the Copy: Striking Likenesses, Unreasonable Facsimiles*. New York: Zone Books.

Scoccianti, Sandro. 1992. "La legislazione di Sisto V sugli archivi notarili: Struttura e validità." In *Sisto V. I. Roma e il Lazio*, edited by Maurizio Fagiolo and Maria Luisa Madonna, 185–209. Rome: Istituto Poligrafico e Zecca dello Stato.

Sella, Pietro. 1927. *Il procedimento civile nella legislazione statutaria italiana*. Milan: U. Hoepli.

Serianni, Luca. 1972. "Appunti linguistici sulle formule notarili aretine del primo Trecento." *Studi di filologia italiana* 30: 215–23.

Serjeantson, Richard W. 1999. "Testimony and Proof in Early Modern England." *Studies in the History and Philosophy of Science* 30: 195–236.

Serpi, Giuseppe. 1972. *Il notariato nella giurisprudenza*. Padua: CEDAM.

Seth, John E. 1999. "Notaries in the American Colonies." *John Marshall Law Review* 32 : 863–86.

Sinisi, Daniela. 1996. "I Notarii Magistrorum Stratarum nel '500: Nascita di un ufficio notarile privativo per le magistrature di acque e strade." *Roma moderna e contemporanea* 14: 363–78.

Sinisi, Lorenzo. 1997. *Formulari e cultura giuridica notarile nell'età moderna. L'esperienza genovese*. Milan: Giuffrè.

Smail, Daniel L. 2003. *The Consumption of Justice: Emotions, Publicity and Legal Culture in Marseille, 1264–1423*. Ithaca: Cornell University Press.

———. 1999. *Imaginary Cartographies: Possession and Identity in Late Medieval Marseille*. Ithaca: Cornell University Press.

La società dei notai di Bologna: Saggio storico e inventario. 1988. Edited by Giorgio Tamba. Rome: Ministero per i Beni Culturali e Ambientali.

Sonnino, Eugenio. 1994. "In the Male City: The 'Status animarum' of Rome in the Seventeenth Century." In *Socio-economic Consequences of Sex-Ratios in Historical Perspective, 1500–1900*, edited by Antoinette Fauve-Chamoux and Sølvi Sogner, 19–29. Milan: Università Bocconi.

———. 1997. "The Population in Baroque Rome." In *Rome-Amsterdam: Two Growing Cities in Seventeenth-Century Europe*, edited by Peter van Kessel and Elisja Schulte, 50–70. Amsterdam: Amsterdam University Press.

———, ed. 1998. *Popolazione e società a Roma dal medioevo all'età contemporanea*. Rome: Il Calamo.

Spagnoletti, Angelantonio. 1993. "I notai nella realtà meridionale di antico regime: Tra istituzioni e società." In "I protocolli notarili tra medioevo ed età moderna," ed. Francesco Magistrale. Special issue, *Archivi per la storia* 6, nos. 1–2: 95–109.

Spezzaferro, Luigi, and M. E. Tittoni, eds. 1991. *Il Campidoglio e Sisto V*. Rome: Carte Segrete.

Spotti Tantillo, Alda. 1975. "Inventari inediti di interesse librario tratti da protocolli notarili romani (1468–1523)." *Archivio della società romana di storia patria* 98: 77–94.

SPQR statuta et novae reformationes urbis Romae eiusdemq[ue] varia privilegia a diversis romanis pontificibus emanata in sex libros divisa novissime compilata. 1519–23. Rome.

Statuta almae urbis Romae. 1580. Rome.

Statuta venerabilis collegii DD. Notariorum Curiae Capitolii eorumque facultates et privilegia. N.d. [1711?]. Rome.

Statuta venerabilis collegii DD. Notariorum Curiae Capitolinae eorumque facultates et privilegia. 1831. Rome.

Statuta venerandi collegii Notariorum civitatis Cremonae. 1597. Cremona.

Stein, Peter. 1999. *Roman Law in European History*. Cambridge: Cambridge University Press.

Stern, Laura Ikins. 1994. *The Criminal Law System of Medieval and Renaissance Florence*. Baltimore: Johns Hopkins University Press.

Stevens, Kevin M. 2003. "Sibling Rivalry: Honor, Ambition and Identity in the Printing Trade in Early Modern Milan." *Mélanges de l'École française de Rome: Italie et Méditerranée* 115, pt. 1: 107–22.

Stow, Kenneth. 2001. *Theater of Acculturation: The Roman Ghetto in the 16th Century.* Seattle: University of Washington Press.

Stumpo, Enrico. 1985. *Il capitale finanziario a Roma fra Cinque e Seicento.* Milan: Giuffrè.

Suleiman, Ezra. 1987. *Private Power and Centralization in France: The Notaries and the State.* Princeton: Princeton University Press.

Summarium, Erectio Officij Notaratus [sic] Vicaris Urbis. 1700. Rome.

Supino Martini, Paola. 1995. "Alfabetismo e sottoscrizioni testimoniali al documento privato dell'Italia centrale (sec. VIII)." In *Escribir y leer en Occidente,* edited by Armando Petrucci and Francisco M. Gimeno Blay, 47–61. Valencia: Departamento de Historia de la Antigüedad y de la Cultura Escrita, Universitat de València.

Tabacchi, Stefano. 1997. "Le riforme giudiziarie nella Roma di fine Seicento." *Roma moderna e contemporanea* 5: 155–74.

Talamanca, Mario. 1987. "Processo civile (diritto romano)." *Enciclopedia del diritto,* vol. 36. Milan: Giuffrè.

Tiberi, Salustio. 1612. *Formularium cuiusuis generis instrumentorum ad stylum & communem usum Romanae Curiae, Urbis & Orbis.* Rome.

Tonelli, Giovanna. 2000. "Il 'notarile' come fonte per la storia del commercio e della finanza a Milano (1615–1650)." *Mélanges de l'École française de Rome: Italie et Méditerranée* 112, pt. 1: 79–104.

Tractatus universi iuris. 1584. 24 vols. Venice.

Trasselli, Carmelo. 1936a. "Ancora sugli atti del tribunale civile del Senatore di Roma nel secolo XV. Ultima nota." *Archivi,* ser. 2, 4: 24–25.

———. 1936b. "Note sugli atti del tribunale civile del Senatore di Roma nel secolo XV." *Archivi,* ser. 2, 3: 90–109.

———. 1937. "Un uffficio notarile per gli ebrei di Roma (secolo XVI e XVII). Notizia." *Archivio della società romana di storia patria* 60: 231–44.

Tucci, Ugo. 1989. "Il documento del mercante." In *Civiltà comunale: Libro, scrittura, documento,* 541–65. Genoa: Società Ligure di Storia Patria.

Tyan, Emile. 1959. *Le notariat et le régime de la preuve par écrit dans la pratique du droit musulman.* 2nd ed. Beirut: L'imprimerie Saint Paul.

Valesio, Francesco. 1977–79. *Diario di Roma (1700–1742).* Edited by Gaetana Scano. 6 vols. Milan: Longanesi.

Vallerani, Massimo. 2001. "I fatti nella logica del processo medievale. Note introduttive." *Quaderni storici* 36: 665–93.

Verdi, Orietta. 2005. " 'Hic est liber sive prothocollum.' I protocolli del collegio dei Trenta Notai Capitolini." *Roma moderna e contemporanea* 13: 427–73.

Vianello, Pietro. 1869. "Sull'archivio notarile di Treviso." *Atti del Istituto Veneto,* ser. 3, 14: 524–39.

Visceglia, Maria Antonietta. 1995. "Burocrazia, mobilità sociale e *patronage* alla Corte di Roma. Alcuni aspetti del recente dibattito storiografico e prospettive di ricerca." *Roma moderna e contemporanea* 3: 11–55.

———. 2004. "Etichetta cardinalizia in età barocca." In *Estetica barocca,* edited by Sebastian Schütze, 263–84. Rome: Accademia Nazionale dei Lincei, Bibliotheca Hertziana, Istituto Italiano per gli Studi Filosofici.

Wakin, Jeanette. 1972. *The Function of Documents in Islamic Law*. Albany: State University of New York Press.

Watson, Alan. 1981. *The Making of the Civil Law*. Cambridge MA: Harvard University Press.

———. 1985. *The Evolution of Law*. Baltimore: Johns Hopkins University Press.

Wray, Shona Kelly. 2001. "Speculum et exemplar: The Notaries of Bologna during the Black Death." *Quellen und Forschungen aus Italienischen Archiven und Bibliotheken* 81: 200–227.

Zabbia, Marino. 1999. *I notai e la cronachistica cittadina italiana nel Trecento*. Rome: Istituto Storico Italiano per il Medioevo.